Stars

IN THE
RING

JEWISH CHAMPIONS
IN THE GOLDEN AGE
OF BOXING

Also by Mike Silver

The Arc of Boxing: The Rise and Decline of the Sweet Science

Stars
IN THE
RING

JEWISH CHAMPIONS IN THE GOLDEN AGE OF BOXING

A PHOTOGRAPHIC HISTORY

MIKE SILVER

LP

Guilford, Connecticut

An imprint of Rowman & Littlefield

Distributed by NATIONAL BOOK NETWORK

Copyright © 2016 Mike Silver

All photos are in the public domain unless otherwise credited

British Library Cataloguing-in-Publication Information Available

Library of Congress Cataloging-in-Publication Data Available

ISBN 978-1-63076-139-4 (hardcover)
ISBN 978-1-63076-140-0 (e-book)

♾™ The paper used in this publication meets the minimum requirements of American National Standard for Information Sciences—Permanence of Paper for Printed Library Materials, ANSI/NISO Z39.48-1992.

Many persons outside of the ring were important contributors
to the Golden Age of the Jewish boxer,
but they are not the central characters in this epic saga.

That distinction belongs to the boxers without whom there would be no sport.

This book is dedicated to them.

CONTENTS

ACKNOWLEDGMENTS

My appreciation and gratitude go to my hard-working independent editor and agent Bonny V. Fetterman. Bonny never wavered in her belief and confidence in my project. Her professionalism, perseverance, and understanding of the publishing industry were instrumental in bringing this book to fruition. Kudos to our mutual friend, Rabbi Manes Kogan, spiritual leader of the Hillcrest Jewish Center, who upon hearing that I was writing another book suggested I contact Bonny.

I also want to thank Christen Karniski, sports editor at Rowman & Littlefield Publishers, for her enthusiasm for my project and for referring it to Rick Rinehart, editor-at-large for Globe Pequot, who believed in my book and took it on.

As will quickly become apparent to anyone who peruses the pages of this book, an enormous amount of research was required to compile the history, statistics, and photographs contained herein. Information came from many sources, and I wish to express my gratitude to the following people and institutions:

Excerpts from my previous book, *The Arc of Boxing: The Rise and Decline of the Sweet Science*, are reprinted by permission of McFarland & Company, Inc., Box 611, Jefferson NC 28640, www.mcfarlandpub.com.

A vast amount of information and statistical data was provided by BoxRec.com, the best record-keeping boxing resource in existence. BoxRec has documented nearly every professional boxing match from the beginning of the Queensberry Rules in the 1890s up to the present time. It is an invaluable resource for authors, historians, and fans. As an added bonus, since 2012 the site has also hosted Barry Hugman's "History of World Championship Boxing."

The International Boxing Research Organization (IBRO) and its dedicated director, Dan Cuoco, provided essential material on many old-time boxers. IBRO's mission to accurately chronicle the history of the sport is very commendable. The Golden Age still lives within the pages of its quarterly journal. Two other exceptional resources were the American Jewish Historical Society's digital archive record of Jewish athletes—JewsInSports.org—and the Hank Kaplan Boxing Archive at the Brooklyn College Library. The library's staff was very helpful with my requests for information on specific boxers. Thank you Jon, Marianne, and Isabella.

Under circumstances that can only be described as serendipitous, at the beginning of writing this book five years ago I met the noted artist Sol Korby, who, astonishingly, had just started work on a large painting depicting the panorama of Jewish boxing history. Our shared interest and mutual support for each other's projects led to the start of a beautiful friendship. Sol is a member of "The Greatest Generation," having served as a medic during World War II. As I told him on many occasions, he would finish his masterpiece when I finished my book—and that is exactly how it worked out!

I am indebted to the following boxing experts, past and present, who shared their profound insights and knowledge of the sweet science with the author: Ray Arcel, Tony Arnold and Erik Arnold, Teddy Atlas, Mike Capriano Jr., Bob Carson, Bobby Franklin, Bill Goodman, Willie Grunes, Rollie Hackmer, Henry Hascup, Chuck Hasson, Mike Hunnicut, J. J. Johnston, Hank Kaplan, Yossi Katz, Jack Kincaid, Ted Lidsky, Ted Lowry, Bill Schutte, Bob Shepard, Bob Sherrick, Kevin Smith, Rolando Vitale, Mike Wolf, and Vic Zimet. "From all those who taught me I gained understanding" (Psalm 119:99).

Tony Gee and Hazel Gee were instrumental in helping to ensure my chapter on the pre–Queensberry era of boxing was accurate. Tony is the world's foremost authority on the English bare-knuckle scene and especially noted for his work, "Up To Scratch." His input is greatly appreciated. In addition, the writings of two very gifted boxing journalists, Mike Casey and Springs Toledo, were a source of inspiration and insight.

Over the years I was privileged to meet and get to know several Golden Age Jewish boxers, all of whom have since passed on: Sammy Farber, Harry Haft, Danny Kapilow, Herbie Kronowitz, Artie Levine, Phil Pollack, and Morris Reif all added to my knowledge and appreciation for the particular era in which they fought.

I am also grateful to the following people who provided photos from their collections: Stephanie Arcel, Dave Bergin (Pugilistica.com), Douglas Century, Toby Weston Cone, John DiSanto (PhillyBoxingHistory.com), John Gay, Steve Lott (Boxing Hall of Fame Las Vegas), Lou Manfra (heavyweightcollectibles.com), Jerry Fitch, Jim Houlihan, Don Cogswell, Doug Cavanaugh, Sonny Rosenberg, Thomas Scharf, and Professors Terry and Jan Todd of the University of Texas at Austin. Thanks also to computer whiz Howard Solomon, of Creative Business Technologies, for his extraordinary technical expertise and advice.

I want to thank my sister, Penni, and my sister-in-law Gail for their support and encouragement. Last, but not least, I want to thank my brother, Bennett, who is always in my corner.

KEY TO ABBREVIATIONS

KO: Shorthand for a knockout victory. Occurs when a fighter, after having been knocked down, cannot arise before the referee's count of 10.

TKO: A technical knockout. Occurs when a bout is stopped to save the fighter from absorbing further punishment, or when the fighter has incurred an injury (most often a facial cut) that is severe enough to end the bout before the final bell. The bout can be stopped either by the referee, the corner man, the ringside physician, or the fighter himself.

ND: "No decision." In certain jurisdictions, unless a fight ended by way of a foul or a knockout, no official decision was rendered at the conclusion. In other words, there was no winner and no loser. Bouts which lasted the full scheduled number of rounds went into the record books with an "ND" (No-decision) citation. The law existed in a number of states from about 1910 to 1925, and was created to pacify anti-gambling factions and other reformers opposed to the legalization of professional boxing. The theory was that if a fighter could not win on points, the bribing of judges and referees would be eliminated and gambling on fights discouraged. Ringside reporters usually named a winner in the next day's newspaper anyway, and these unofficial verdicts were often used to settle bets. Because of this, "ND" also meant "Newspaper Decision."

NC: "No contest." On rare occasions, at the discretion of the referee, a fight could be stopped if both fighters were putting forth minimal effort, or were exhibiting suspicious behavior that indicated an obvious fixed fight was in progress.

Draw: A "tie" decision. In the judges' opinion the contest was too close to declare a winner or loser.

DQ: Stands for "disqualification." A fighter committing a foul (usually a punch that landed below the beltline) was subject to disqualification by the referee. In records that appear in the appendix, a win by disqualification is listed as either W DQ (won by disqualification) or WF (won by foul).

WEIGHT DIVISIONS

From the early 1900s to the 1950s professional boxing had eight weight divisions. Two new divisions—junior lightweight and junior welterweight—were added to the original eight in the 1920s. The poundage listed below indicates the maximum limit for each division:

Flyweight: 112 pounds

Bantamweight: 118 pounds

Featherweight: 126 pounds

Junior Lightweight: 130 pounds (1924–1939)

Lightweight: 135 pounds

Junior Welterweight: 140 pounds (1925–1942)

Welterweight: 147 pounds

Middleweight: 160 pounds

Light heavyweight: 175 pounds

Heavyweight: Unlimited

INTRODUCTION

A psalm of David: Blessed be the Lord, my Rock, Who teaches my hands to battle and my fingers to fight.

—PSALM 144

In my scheme of things, Slapsie Maxie was a more miraculous Jewish phenomenon by far than Dr. Albert Einstein.

—PHILIP ROTH, *THE FACTS: A NOVELIST'S AUTOBIOGRAPHY*

In the 1920s the most famous Jew in America was not a scientist, entertainer, author, or Supreme Court justice. The most famous Jewish person in America during "The Roaring Twenties" was a world champion boxer named Benny Leonard.[1]

Not only was Benny Leonard one of the greatest boxers who ever lived, but he was also the first Jewish sports superstar of the mass media age, and the first Jewish-American pop culture icon. He was written about and photographed more than any other Jewish entertainer or artist of his day. But ask a person today if he or she has ever heard of Benny Leonard, and more than likely you will be met with a blank stare.

In the first half of the twentieth century, boxing was an integral part of American culture, rivaling baseball in popularity. Champions and contenders, most of whom came from ethnic minorities, were elevated to hero status in poor urban communities. They were a source of inspiration, pride, and hope to a population struggling to break free of the cycle of poverty and enter the social and economic mainstream. The first four decades of the last century were a Golden Age for the sport of boxing in terms of status, the quantity and quality of talent, media coverage, and attendance figures. It was no less a Golden Age for Jewish boxers.

Over 100 years ago an unprecedented confluence of social and historic events converged to create one of the most unique and colorful chapters of the Jewish immigrant experience in America. Yet, except for a few names, the elite athletes who made it possible are all but forgotten today. This book is intended to remedy that by shining a spotlight on 166 outstanding Jewish boxers of the Golden Age. Who were they? What did they accomplish? What happened to them after they hung up their gloves?

Embedded in each mini-biography is a historical nugget that, when dusted off and polished, reveals a story of ethnic pride, resilience,

Benny Leonard, lightweight champion of the world, 1917–1925.

tragedy, and triumph. When viewed collectively, it is the story of an immigrant people striving to overcome adversity.

No other sport lends itself so perfectly to metaphor. Getting knocked down and picking yourself up to continue the battle can be seen as a metaphor for life's ups and downs. Despite the hardships they encountered, the tough Jewish boxers of the Golden Age were individuals who kept on punching, never quit, and refused to be counted out.

For nearly half a century many working-class Americans admired qualities they perceived as inherent in the makeup of the professional boxer. A sport that required courage, physical strength, and athletic prowess was seen as a proving ground of sorts, as a test of one's character. At a time when boxing mattered to society far more than it does today, when it was the most popular sport in America, Jewish people were earning the attention and respect of their fellow citizens in the prize ring. They didn't need to be doctors, lawyers, accountants, or Nobel Prize winners. Back then being a boxer was more than enough.

In those days there weren't many choices for a young man seeking fame and fortune as a professional athlete. There were only three major professional sports of any note in America: baseball, boxing, and horse racing. While basketball was a very popular inner-city sport (in which Jewish players excelled), there was no money to be made shooting hoops for a living. Even the best professional players had to supplement their basketball incomes with full-time jobs. There was money in

baseball, but it was limited to only 400 major league players (16 teams comprised of 25 players each). From 1900 to 1940, only 52 Jewish athletes played major league baseball.[2] Less than half that number played professional football.

The limited participation by Jewish athletes in baseball and football was influenced by the fact that neither was an inner-city sport. They required an outdoor field to practice and money to spend on uniforms and equipment. Both were in short supply in Jewish immigrant neighborhoods. While some city high schools had football teams and a field to practice on, Jewish boys often dropped out of high school to look for work.

On the other hand, boxing gyms required little space and a limited amount of equipment. They could be found in every inner-city neighborhood. Professional boxing was open to anyone who could pass a rudimentary physical examination—and sometimes even that was unnecessary. The opportunity to make quick money drew thousands of young men to the prize ring. As a result, boxing was the first professional sport in which many Jewish Americans participated.

Between 1901 and 1939 there were 29 Jewish world-champion boxers—about 16 percent of the total number of champions. During those years fighters of Irish, Jewish, and Italian descent were the dominant groups within the sport. Irish Americans dominated the sport in the latter half of the 19th century. In the 1890s, 50 percent of the champions and most of the leading contenders were Irish. But over the next two decades a flood of new immigrants inundated the sport, and the number of Irish champions shrank back to 25 percent. The decline was due to both competition from other ethnic groups and improving opportunities for Irish youth. As noted by historian Steven A. Riess, "The ethnic succession in the ring reflected the changing racial and ethnic complexion of the inner city as older ethnic groups who were doing better economically moved out and were replaced by the new urban poor."[3]

In the 1920s, 14 of the 66 world champions were Jewish, placing them second behind Italians, who had 19 world champions, but ahead of the Irish, who had 11.[4] Back then, winning a title was a rare and venerated accomplishment. Until the rise of numerous quasi-official "sanctioning organizations" in the 1970s, there were never more than 10 weight divisions, and generally only one champion per division. Today there are over 100 world champions spread across 17 weight divisions.

By 1928 Jewish boxers comprised the single largest ethnic group among title contenders in the 10 weight divisions. The majority were ranked in the six lighter-weight classes, from flyweight (112-pound limit) to junior welterweight (140-pound limit). This was no small achievement in an era when competition was brutal and only a fraction of the thousands of professional boxers made it to contender status. To be a contender a fighter had to be ranked among the top 10 challengers in his particular weight division.

Jewish boxers were most numerous from the first decade of the twentieth century until the

end of the Great Depression, with the largest percentage active during the 1920s. By the time I became interested in the sport as a child in 1959, they had all but disappeared. But where had they gone? Most of the boxers I saw on the Wednesday and Friday night televised broadcasts had names like Ortiz, Jones, Fernandez, or Griffith. Not a Goldstein, Schwartz, Kaplan, or Cohen among them.

The answer is that social and economic success put an end to the Golden Age of the Jewish boxer. When Jewish people could afford to leave Delancey Street for "Main Street," they didn't look back. The sons and grandsons of Jewish boxers became accountants and entrepreneurs, doctors, lawyers, teachers, and dentists—anything but boxers. That is called progress. But if they had been born just 50 years earlier, many of them would have been nursing a broken nose and cauliflower ear after battling through a tough preliminary bout.

Upwards of 3,000 Jewish professional boxers were active during the Golden Age, or about 7 to 10 percent of the total number of professionals. Many times that number fought as amateurs but never entered the "punch for pay" professional ranks. Some historians consider the numbers to be much higher, but record-keeping prior to the 1920s was inconsistent, and exact figures are difficult to ascertain. Not counted are many boxers who never went beyond the four- or six-round preliminary stage, or quit after a few pro bouts. Their names seldom made it into the record books.

Program for the July 23, 1923, title bout between Benny Leonard and Lew Tendler. Over 60,000 fans paid to see the contest in the brand new Yankee Stadium.

Currently there are fewer than two dozen Jewish professional boxers (who compete in at least one bout per year) throughout the world.[5] Compare that to 1930, when 16 men named Cohen had one or more professional fights in American rings![6] Is it any wonder that boxing has produced more world-class Jewish athletes than any other professional sport?

Another startling fact: From 1900 to 1950 New York's Madison Square Garden (the sport's premier arena) presented 866 boxing shows. Two hundred and forty (28 percent) of those shows featured a Jewish boxer in the main event. (See complete list in appendix.) What made this possible was the large number of outstanding Jewish boxers (especially in New York City) and their popularity with Jewish fans who paid to see them fight.

While many individual Jews excelled in science, education, merchandising, public service, the judiciary, and in literature, it was in show business and sports that accomplishments were most visible to the general public. Jewish success in any field of endeavor was cause for celebration, but nowhere was the surge of pride expressed more tangibly—and loudly—than in the arenas and stadiums where the sight of a victorious Hebrew gladiator wearing the six-pointed Star of David on his boxing trunks elicited the cheers of thousands.

In America the "Golden Age" of boxing existed in tandem with the Golden Ages of Hollywood, vaudeville, radio, musical theater, music publishing, comic books, and the garment industry. All were linked by a common thread, in that first- and second-generation American Jews were instrumental in their birth, development, and growth. There was virtually no anti-Semitism in any of these industries because Jews made up the majority of owners and employees. The collective creative genius that built these industries flourished because America was one of the few places that allowed Jewish people the unencumbered freedom and opportunity to open new doors when others were closed to them.

Those with entrepreneurial talent used their skills to take boxing to unprecedented levels of popularity. Outside the ring Jewish promoters, managers, trainers, corner men, gym owners, equipment manufacturers, and magazine publishers quickly ascended to leadership roles within the sport. Jews were involved in every aspect of boxing and were largely responsible for turning it into a profitable and respectable multi-million-dollar business. At the same time, Jewish athletes were showing the world how successful they could be as competitors in the toughest of all sports.

For many immigrant parents the idea of their sons earning a living in a boxing ring was unacceptable, and cause for great distress. But young Jews who came of age in the tough inner-city neighborhoods of New York, Philadelphia, Chicago, Pittsburgh, Baltimore, Boston, Cleveland, and Detroit were different in thought and behavior than their ancestors, the poor and oppressed Eastern European *shtetl* Jews victimized by the Russian Czar's anti-Semitic policies and the drunken Christian peasants who added to their misery in that pogrom-scarred land. This is not to say that Jewish boxers in early-twentieth-century America were not profoundly connected to their Jewish origins. Many were, but they also proudly embraced their newfound American identities.

Although the need to economically improve their lot through hard work and education was of paramount importance to Jewish immigrants and their children, this new environment demanded something extra from them, and perhaps, at the time, even more important. As Teddy Atlas, the renowned trainer and ringside analyst for ESPN Sports, commented in a recent interview:

> The Jewish fighters did not just box for themselves. They were representing a race of people and the reputation of that race. . . . Jewish immigrants and their children lived in a rough and tumble environment. Within this domain it was very important for some Jews to be able to go into the ring and be as tough as the next guy, or even tougher to a greater extent, because of where they were coming from and the way they were perceived . . . and some of the bullying that would go along with that.
>
> Yes, the Jew could be smart, yes, the Jew could find a way out and be prosperous, but at a time when boxing was the biggest sport in this country the Jew also had to prove that he could be as tough as anybody and could also be as proud as anybody.[7]

As representatives of their people, Jewish boxers, whether they realized it or not, carried a heavy burden. The result of their efforts not only changed the way other Americans perceived the Jewish people, but it also changed the way Jewish people viewed themselves. Journalist Pete Hamill, the son of Irish immigrants, recalls that as a teenager he used the word "kike" to describe Jews at the family dinner table; his father promptly admonished him: "Benny Leonard is a Jew."

As a young man growing up in Brownsville, Brooklyn, author Ron Ross remembers the esteem accorded to boxers who lived in his neighborhood. When Morris Reif, the last of Brownsville's Golden Age Jewish boxers, passed away at the age of 90 in 2013, Ross eulogized him with words that are descriptive of an entire generation of Jewish boxers:

> He was the last of a breed that at one time was both commonplace and conversely, unique; feared by some, admired by others but never underrated or ignored. Fighting was their business and they were a rough-and-tumble lot, respected and acknowledged among the rulers of their domain, and all who knew them. . . . Maybe it was because they were the children of a generation of passive resistors, the sons of stoic, but non-combative fathers, tough, thick-skinned peddlers, farmers and merchants who tolerated their indignities with an almost incomprehensible resoluteness and strength of

purpose that made fighting the natural evolution of their species. . . . Chins jutting, fists flying, they came to fight. It was their business, it was their lives. They were a new breed and they shocked a world that couldn't conceive of Jewish battlers.[8]

Many persons outside of the ring were important contributors to the Golden Age of the Jewish boxer, but they are not the central characters in this epic saga. That distinction belongs to the boxers without whom there would be no sport. This book is divided into six chapters, each representing a significant era in the sport's evolution. Within each chapter dozens of notable Jewish boxers are identified. My regret is that space limitations prevented me from adding the names and bios of hundreds of additional Jewish contenders, journeymen, and main-event club fighters, all of whom contributed their own special luster to boxing's rich, historic tapestry. They too deserve to be remembered. It is the intention of this book to be a fitting tribute to all of them.

I now invite the reader to enter the arena with me and take a seat as I climb the steps into the ring of history and introduce you to these extraordinary athletes and the legacy they have left for all of us.

"Ding, ding, ding! Ladies and gentlemen, in this corner . . ."

CHAPTER 1

BARE-KNUCKLE BRUISERS

The name of Mendoza has been resounded from one part of the kingdom to the other; and the fame of this once-celebrated pugilist was the theme of universal panegyric.

—PIERCE EGAN, *BOXIANA: OR, SKETCHES OF ANCIENT AND MODERN PUGILISM*

Boxing is a very ancient sport with a history dating back thousands of years. The first mention of boxing in literature appears in Homer's *Iliad* written in the eighth century BCE. The sport was a staple of Greek and Roman culture, but disappeared as an organized form of entertainment after the fall of the Western Roman Empire in the fifth century CE.

After a 1,000-year hiatus, boxing reemerged in 17th-century England after the death of Oliver Cromwell. Freed from Puritan restraint, the populace began to enjoy a wide variety of old and new sporting diversions in the restored monarchy of Charles II (1660–1685). London, with its roiling urban suburbs and large population of poor people, became the perfect spawning ground for the beginning of a new generation of fistic exponents, although the sport did not properly take off until the following century.

Both the rich (including members of the aristocracy) and poorer elements of English society enjoyed betting on the outcome of prizefights, as these competitions came to be known. (The original prizefighters were weapons exponents who fought with swords, quarterstaff, or cudgels. Their contests were termed "trials of skill," while the early regular fistic battles that gradually superseded them were usually called "trials of manhood.")

The rules for the sport were quite different than today. The combatants fought bare-fisted in what can best be described as a hybrid sport—sort of a variation of today's mixed martial arts contests. In addition to allowing punches, the contestants were also permitted to use wrestling maneuvers to throw an opponent to the ground, provided he was grabbed above the waist. Unprotected hands were particularly vulnerable to injury, especially when bare fists collided with the hard skull of an opponent. Wrestling and punches to softer targets, such as the liver, kidneys, and midsection, provided a respite for bruised knuckles.

In 1885 this 2000 year old bronze statue of a boxer (believed to be of Greek origin) was discovered intact during an excavation for an apartment building in Rome, Italy. (Photograph by Sol Korby)

Daniel Mendoza proved that brains could triumph over brawn in the bare-knuckle arena.

A round ended when a fighter was either punched, thrown, or wrestled to the ground, whereupon the contestants were given 30 seconds to rest before having to return to the "scratch mark" (originally their side of a three-foot-square drawn in the center of the ring). If one of them was unable, or unwilling, to "come up to scratch" or "toe the mark" within the allotted time, he forfeited the match. The loser was considered "knocked out of time."

Under the rudimentary Broughton's Rules of 1743, a fighter could be ruled out for hitting his opponent when down or seizing him below the waist. This was considerably expanded in the "New Rules" of 1838 to also include falling down without being hit, head-butting, kicking, gouging, biting, and hitting below the waist. Another amendment gave the fighters eight additional seconds after their half-minute break to reach the scratch mark in the center of the ring unaided.

Bare-knuckle fights ran the gamut from insufferably boring (much wrestling and stalling) to extremely savage, bloody, and sometimes fatal. Strength, endurance, aggressive rushing, and brute force were emphasized. For many years there were no formalized weight divisions, with classifications, such as there were, appearing to be fluid. Significant weight differences between combatants were not particularly unusual. Despite the fact that pugilism for most of the bare-knuckle era was considered illegal (usually as a breach of the peace), the authorities did not by any means always interfere.

DANIEL MENDOZA, FIRST HEBREW HERO OF THE PRIZE RING

One of the greatest fighters to emerge during the English bare-knuckle period was a Sephardic Jew named Daniel Mendoza. He was born in 1765 and grew up in the Aldgate area of London, home to some of that city's poorest Jews.*

Mendoza stood five feet, seven inches tall and weighed about 160 pounds. Contemporary prints show a muscular young man with a powerful upper torso. Many of his early bouts were against bigger and stronger opponents who significantly outweighed him.

Realizing his career would be short-lived unless he could figure out some way to even the playing field when faced with a much heavier opponent, Mendoza devised strategies that relied on his natural speed and agility. He became adept at utilizing his dexterity, particularly in stopping his opponents' punches in superior style and countering with quick and frequent blows.

At first Mendoza's perceived defensive methods were derided. Spectators were used to seeing crude brawlers throwing each other to the ground, or engaged in vicious toe-to-toe exchanges until the stronger man prevailed. The young Mendoza answered his critics with one decisive victory after another, often defeating opponents who considerably outweighed him. Eventually his critics realized they were witnessing a new and revolutionary style of fighting. Derision soon turned to

---

* In his memoirs, Mendoza states his birth year as 1764; it was changed later to match synagogue records of his circumcision. Most historians agree that 1765 is the correct date of birth.

acclaim as they began to appreciate his technical skill and physical courage.

Mendoza achieved something like superstar status in the early 1790s after defeating two of England's top fighters, Richard Humphries and Bill Ward (later erroneously called Warr). His three epic grudge battles with Humphries, a former mentor with whom he had a bitter falling-out, captured the imagination of the entire country and inspired poems and songs, as well as memorabilia such as ceramics, medals, and a number of prints.

With his services in great demand, Mendoza toured throughout the British Isles, lecturing and giving sparring exhibitions. He also appeared on the theatrical stage, was the author of one of the sport's first instruction books, and opened an academy in London for the tuition of gentlemen. According to Mendoza, he was even granted an audience with King George III (the same King George of the American Revolution) at Windsor Castle, thus purportedly becoming the first Jew to have an audience with a reigning British monarch.

Other English Jews were inspired to follow Mendoza into the ring. Among the most famous were Dutch Sam (Samuel Elias) and Barney Aaron, known as "The Star of the East." Aaron's son, Young Barney Aaron, a lightweight pugilist, emigrated to America in the 1850s, where he became the first Jewish bare-knuckle prizefighter to win an American title.

Mendoza retired after losing to "Gentleman" John Jackson in 1795 (although he did return to the ring twice as a veteran). In the time-honored tradition of former boxers he became a publican,

the owner of a public house, or saloon. With a wife and large family to support, Mendoza periodically suffered financial problems that resulted in occasional stays in debtors' prison, but his friends usually bailed him out.

The man who did more to popularize scientific fighting than any other pugilist of his generation died in poverty at the age of 71. An obituary in the September 11, 1836, issue of *Bell's Life in London, and Sporting Chronicle*, summed up the colorful fighter's legacy: "Dan, though not 'The Jew that Shakespeare drew,' was yet an extraordinary character in his way and may be said to have been the first 'great master' of pugilistic science in this country."

To this day Mendoza's name still carries weight in England. Many people have proudly claimed to be descendants of the legendary (and prolific) pugilist, including the actor and comedian Peter Sellers.

Daniel Mendoza was an important contributor to England's Golden Age of bare-knuckle prizefighting, an era that spanned the 1780s to the 1820s. As one of the founding fathers of the scientific school of pugilism, he is unquestionably a seminal figure in the history of the sport.

THE QUEENSBERRY RULES

In the decades following the high point of bare-knuckle prizefighting, society's changing attitudes—as a result of betting scandals, fixed fights, and widely reported fatalities in the ring—fueled a growing reform movement in England that sought to abolish the sport. Furthermore, crowd control was virtually nonexistent at prizefights,

Mendoza (left) vs. Humphries in their final encounter on September 29, 1790. The three fight trilogy (1788–1790) captivated all England.

allowing pickpockets and ruffians to roam freely among the spectators. Disgruntled gamblers and supporters of the fighters would sometimes rush the ring if they were not satisfied with the way a bout was going. As a result, the aristocracy became disillusioned and withdrew their patronage. It was obvious that if pugilism was to survive in the public realm, it needed to reinvent itself.

In the late 1860s a new code of conduct was devised by John Graham Chambers, a well-known amateur sportsman and administrator. Originally created for amateur boxing, the new rules gradually replaced those that had previously governed bare-knuckle contests. Chambers's friend, John Sholto Douglas, the eighth (now considered the ninth) Marquess of Queensberry, was a wealthy and influential sportsman who endorsed the regulations (any degree of input being a matter of debate) and lent the prestige of his name to the new rules. By the early 1890s virtually all professional fights were being conducted under Marquess of Queensberry Rules.

Queensberry boxing limited a round to three minutes, followed by one minute of rest. Throwing or wrestling an opponent to the ground was outlawed. If a boxer was knocked down by a punch, he was given 10 seconds to stand up under his own power or be counted out by the referee. These basic rules are still in force today.

But the most revolutionary aspect of Queensberry boxing was its mandated use of padded leather gloves (usually weighing between two to five ounces) for all contests. Padded gloves gave the impression boxing was now less dangerous than the bare-knuckle version.* Taken together, the new rules provided the veneer of civility the sport needed if it was to gain acceptance with the general public.

The new rules also changed the physical location of boxing contests. Initially bare-knuckle prizefights had been staged in the same indoor amphitheaters originally built for fencing contests, but the unruly behavior of the crowds at these amphitheaters created problems for the local populace. Although boxing was never outlawed in London, eventually a law was passed that made it a breach of the peace to hold any form of entertainment in an amphitheater. From the mid-18th century on, most bare-knuckle fights were generally staged at random outdoor locations and increasingly on bare turf (the latter was actually stipulated in the revised rules of 1838). The Queensberry rules banned turf fights and moved the sport indoors, with the ring set upon an elevated stage or platform. As Elliot Gorn notes: "By facilitating bouts on the indoor stage rather than turf, the Queensbury [sic] rules allowed promoter-entrepreneurs to [always] charge admission, thereby opening the way for crowd control by police and private security officers."[1] (The last bare-knuckle heavyweight championship held in an outdoor location on turf took place in 1889 between John L. Sullivan and Jake Kilrain. The first Queensberry heavyweight title fight, indoors with gloves, was in 1892.)

---

* Of course, it can be argued that with gloves offering greater protection to their hands, boxers could now direct a greater volume of powerful blows to their opponents' heads, but the intention at the time was undoubtedly to cushion the blows for benefit of both hands and head.

Pugilists making the transition from bare-knuckle to Queensberry rules had to incorporate radical changes in style and strategy. The elimination of wrestling served to focus attention on perfecting boxing technique. Fighting on bare turf had required shoes with spikes (which could not exceed three-eighths of an inch). A canvas-covered wooden platform was better suited to leather soled athletic shoes, thereby enhancing the speed and mobility of footwork.

Another significant change was the acceptance of internationally recognized weight classes. In 1909 the National Sporting Club in London decided to standardize weights (eight specified divisions), and thereafter began to reach agreement with other international bodies.

England, the cradle of modern pugilism, continued to be a boxing stronghold for many decades. It was also home to hundreds of outstanding Jewish professional boxers, including several who rank among the greatest of all time. But in the waning years of the 19th century, England's dominance over the sport was about to be challenged—and a new and astonishing epoch was about to begin on American shores.

THE GREAT SULLIVAN-KILRAIN FIGHT.

AT RICHBURG, MISS, ON MONDAY, JULY 8th, 1889.

SECONDS TO KILRAIN: CHAS. MITCHELL & MIKE DONOVAN.   REFEREE: JNO. FITZPATRICK.   SECONDS TO SULLIVAN: WM. MULDOON & MIKE CLEARY.

Richburg, Mississippi, July 8, 1889. Rare photograph shows Sullivan (left) closing with Jake Kilrain in the 15th round of the last bare-knuckle heavyweight championship match. (Library of Congress)

CHAPTER 2

THE MELTING POT SPORT

In a world where men felt increasingly powerless, a tough guy who battled to the top could become an instant hero to those still trapped below.
—EDWARD G. BURROWS AND MIKE WALLACE, *GOTHAM: A HISTORY OF NEW YORK CITY TO 1890*

Between 1881 and 1924, approximately 24 million immigrants came to America, including nearly two million Jews, mostly from Eastern Europe. The vast majority of immigrants, often penniless and uneducated, crossed the Atlantic in steerage.[1] They sailed into New York harbor past the Statue of Liberty and disembarked at Castle Garden, located at the tip of Manhattan. After 1892 all immigrants entering New York Harbor came through Ellis Island, where almost one million people were processed annually until the government severely restricted immigration in 1924.

By 1914 at least half the populations of major cities in the United States lived in poverty. The urban poor, not surprisingly, were disproportionately new immigrants.[2] Most of the Jewish immigrants lived in the tenement neighborhoods of New York's Lower East Side, downtown Philadelphia, the West Side of Chicago, or Boston's North End—enclaves that ranked among America's worst slums. These and other inner-city neighborhoods provided most of the fighters and the spectators for boxing.

Although America may not have been *di goldene medina* ("the golden land") the immigrants had envisioned, it was still preferable to life in the Russian Pale of Settlement, where many Jews had lived on the edge of starvation and under the thumb of state-sponsored anti-Semitism.

Of immediate concern to city dwellers was the need to find work to pay for food and shelter. But having a job was no guarantee of financial security. Most immigrant workers labored long hours for pitiful wages, and about four of every 10 did not earn enough to support a family.[3] Still, there were a few alternatives to the pushcart or sweatshop. If a person could play an instrument, or had a talent for singing, comedy, acting, or dancing, he or she might venture off into the world of vaudeville, live theater, or moving pictures. Show business, especially the flourishing vaudeville circuit, employed thousands of people, many of whom were Jewish.

Another thriving industry with close ties to show business was professional boxing. By the early 1900s there was already a large contingent

of Jewish boxers involved in the sport. Indeed, there were so many Jewish people in show business and boxing that anti-Semitism was not a significant problem in either industry. Undoubtedly many fighters would have preferred a career in show business, but their talent was for boxing.

What drove so many impoverished young men to enter the ring was the common knowledge that successful boxers were the highest-paid athletes in the world. It was not unusual for champion boxers to be paid thousands of dollars for just one bout. In 1892 heavyweight champion John L. Sullivan fought James J. Corbett in New Orleans for a "winner-take-all" purse of $25,000, and a side bet of $10,000 apiece, for a total of $45,000 to the winner. The previous evening George Dixon—the first black world boxing champion—was paid $7,500 for successfully defending his featherweight title.[4] These were astounding figures when one considers the average annual income for most American workers was less than $1,000.

New York City's Lower East Side 1910. Crowded tenement streets were a fertile breeding ground for a generation of prizefighters. (Library of Congress)

In the 1920s superstar boxers Mickey Walker, Benny Leonard, and Harry Greb were each taking in well over $100,000 in annual income—the equivalent of several million dollars in today's currency. The $80,000 salary paid to baseball great Babe Ruth in 1927 paled in comparison to the one million dollars heavyweight champion Gene Tunney received for his title bout with Jack Dempsey that same year.

While it is true that only a few top-tier fighters were paid such extravagant sums of money, one did not have to be a world champion or top contender to earn a better-than-average wage. In the same way a mediocre actor or singer might not make it to the Broadway stage but could still find gainful employment in smaller or less-prestigious theaters, the average boxer, despite his limitations, could make a decent living by fighting in the many small arenas (also known as "fight clubs") that dotted the landscape of every city in America.

In the 1910s and '20s, even a preliminary boxer could earn more money in one four-round bout than a sweatshop laborer earned in an entire week. Of course, trading punches in a boxing ring was a far riskier activity than bending over a sewing machine for 12 to 14 hours a day, but many young men were willing to accept the risks in exchange for the quick monetary rewards boxing provided.

Venues that featured boxing shows were as ubiquitous as vaudeville theaters. In the New York metropolitan area—the epicenter of the sport for more than half a century—over two dozen arenas operated on a weekly basis within a 10-mile radius of Times Square. A number of National Guard armories also opened their doors to boxing in order to showcase local talent and encourage enlistments. Other cities, large and small, were also hotbeds of activity at both the amateur and professional levels. The supply of available boxers easily matched the demand for their services.

Another reason so many poor boys gravitated toward boxing was the sport's easy accessibility. Boxing gyms could be found in every urban neighborhood. Free instruction was readily available in settlement houses, boys clubs, community centers, church basements, and public schools. The sport did not require uniforms, expensive equipment, or a field to practice. All that was needed was a room with enough space to spar, exercise, and hit a punching bag. The various weight divisions also made it possible for smaller boys to compete regardless of size.

THE FANS

Boxing attracted a diverse audience from every social stratum, and Jewish fans were among the most enthusiastic. Virtually all were either born in America or arrived as infants or youngsters. It was the same for baseball. There were very few baseball or boxing fans among adult immigrants who came to America in the early years of the last century.

In New York City Jewish boxing fans accounted for about one-quarter to one-third of the audience. The financial success of every major promotion in the city was dependent on the presence of Jewish fans.[5] As in all sports, rooting for the home team (in this case, Jewish boxers) motivated participation as spectators. As author David Margolick points out: "For the Jewish boxers themselves, fighting may have been a strictly economic proposition, a brutal but lucrative alternative to the sweatshops. But for their fans, its appeal was more tribal, and primeval. It was a way to assert their status as bona fide Americans, to express ethnic pride, settle ethnic scores, refute ethnic stereotypes; after all, no one ever cast the Irish and Italians as victims and bookworms, cowards and runts. Every Jewish kid ever set upon by street toughs lived vicariously through his Jewish ring heroes, and the heroes encouraged this, often wearing Stars of David on their trunks."[6]

Nevertheless, it would be a mistake to believe fan interest was solely based on rooting for "the home team." Any attractive boxing match, irrespective of the ethnic makeup of the fighters, drew the fans. In addition, just the simple pleasure of a night's entertainment could provide enough motivation. Margolick: "What drew fans to boxing was more than chauvinism . . . Perhaps it was also part of relishing America after their cloistered lives in Europe, or the Jewish love of going out, whether to vaudeville or to Broadway or to the Yiddish theater on Second Avenue."[7]

Boxing promoters sought to exploit ethnic rivalries in order to increase ticket sales by mixing and matching Irish, Jewish, and Italian boxers. Advertising posters often stoked partisan passions with words that would be considered unacceptable today. A 1929 Chicago bout between Jewish Ray Miller and Italian Mike Dundee was advertised as "The Battle of the Hebe and Wop." The fight was a benefit for the poor of Chicago, and other Jewish fighters were included on the card. "Nobody took offense [to the racial slurs], short and sweet," says Chicago historian and former boxer J. J. Johnston. "Neighborhood and ethnic rivalries were common and were considered to be just part of the sport."[8]

Inter-ethnic bouts kept the turnstiles humming, but any intriguing match, as noted above, was capable of attracting throngs of fans. In 1923, at Yankee Stadium, an all-Jewish title bout matching lightweight champion Benny Leonard of New York against Lew Tendler of Philadelphia drew a record 63,000 fans and earned nearly half a million dollars.

"MY SON, THE BOX-FIGHTER"

Jewish boxers proved they were brave and tough, but they did fear one personage above all others—their mothers. Despite its popularity, boxing was anathema to immigrant parents who considered the sport to be a violation of the values and traditions of Judaism, not to mention the potential for serious injury. Most Jewish parents became apoplectic when confronted with the knowledge that their son had become a "box-fighter." They considered the activity a waste of time—*goyishe naches* ("gentile pleasures")—and not far removed from a life of crime.

But their children did not see it that way. How could it be otherwise? These young men were growing up as Americans. They belonged much more to the culture of the streets than to that of their families. As historian David Nasaw writes in *Children of the City*, "The early twentieth-century city was a city of strangers. Most of its inhabitants had been born or raised elsewhere. Only the children were native to the city—with no memory, no longing, no historic commitment to another land, another way of life. . . . Work, money, and the fun that money bought were located on the streets of the city."[9]

In order to avoid familial conflict many Jewish fighters attempted to hide their profession from disapproving parents by fighting under anglicized versions of their surnames, as did future ring greats Benny Leonard (Benjamin Leiner), Jackie Fields (Jacob Finkelstein), and Barney Ross (Beryl Rosofsky). Some fighters took Irish names for this purpose as well.

The angst produced when parents found out that a son had become a professional fighter was mitigated somewhat by the financial assistance the boxers provided to the family. Benny Leonard described an experience shared by many other

Jewish pugilists. During his first year as a pro, Benny came home from a fight with a black eye. He could no longer hide the fact that he had been fighting. "My mother," Benny recalled, "looked at my black eye and wept." Benny was guilt-ridden and at a loss for words. He turned to his father, a tailor who worked long hours in a sweatshop. Not knowing what else to do, Benny reached into his pocket and took out the $20 he had earned in the ring that night and handed it over to his father. "My father, who had to work all week for $20, said, 'All right, Benny, keep on fighting. It's worth getting a black eye for $20; I am getting *verschwartzt* ("blackened") for $20 a week.' "[10]

HEBREW HIBERNIANS

On July 10, 1917, lightweight boxers "Irish" Frankie Callahan squared off against "Irish" Jimmy Hanlon in the Boston Armory. A Bean-town battle between two Celtic warriors was sure to please the fans, and the arena was packed for their 12-round bout. But what most fans in attendance did not know was that neither fighter was Irish. Callahan was a Jew from New York City whose real name was Sam Holtzman. Jimmy Hanlon was no more Irish than Holtzman. He was an Italian out of Denver, Colorado, whose real name was Louis Quarantino.

Frankie Callahan (né Holtzman) was not alone in adopting an Irish surname. Dozens of Jewish boxers assumed Irish surnames for the duration of their careers, especially if they lived in cities with large non-Jewish populations. For Jewish boxers the name change served a dual purpose: It not only kept parents from finding out (at least initially) about a son's boxing activities, but it also enhanced his marketability, since Irish boxers were perceived as both tough and crowd pleasers.

Two Jewish fighters with Irish surnames became world champions: Al McCoy (Albert Rudolph), middleweight champion from 1914 to 1917, and Mushy Callahan (Morris Scheer), junior welterweight champion from 1926 to 1930. ("Mushy" was a derivation of Morris's Hebrew name, Moishe.)

Adopting an anglicized version of a name or an Irish *nom de box* was even more prevalent among boxers of Italian heritage who wished to downplay their own ethnicity at a time when prejudicial attitudes toward Italian immigrants were at a high-water mark. Boxing historian Chuck Hasson has documented over 300 Italian-American professional boxers who fought using Irish names, including four world champions.

The story is told of a manager answering the phone in Stillman's gym. When the promoter on the other end asked to speak with "Kelly," the manager responded with "Do you want the Jewish Kelly or the Italian Kelly?"[11]

By the mid-1920s Jewish boxers had become so popular and numerous that taking an Irish name was no longer necessary. In fact, several gentile fighters changed their names to Jewish-sounding ones to enhance their careers. The best known was Italian American Sammy Mandell (lightweight champion, 1927–1930), whose actual surname was Mandella.

"Oakland" Jimmy Duffy, a 1920s lightweight contender, with his wife and child. Duffy's real name was Hyman Gold. Scores of Jewish boxers took Irish names to hide their boxing activity from parents and to enhance their marketability.

Other notable Italian fighters who changed their names included Boston's Frankie Ross (Frank Toscano), who named himself after the great Jewish champion, Barney Ross. There was also Joey Ross (Joe Nisivoccia) and Pee Wee Ross (Fred Rossi), Mickey Diamond (Michael Porecca), Al Diamond (Al Pescatore), Tony Fisher (Anthony Fesce), Henry "Kid" Wolfe (Harry Graio), Nick Bass (Nick Basciano), Sammy Fuller (Sabino Ferullo), and George Levy (Mike Paglione).

One of the oddest name changes involved a 1920s Italian preliminary fighter named Lou Centonella, who boxed out of Utica, New York. Jewish fans had difficulty pronouncing his name, so they simply referred to him as "The Luxsh" (Yiddish for "noodle," as in spaghetti). Lou decided that it would be easier for his Jewish fans to remember his name—and pronounce it—if he renamed himself "Kid Lux."

At a time when many American Jews found it prudent "for professional reasons" to not call attention to their ethnicity in a sometimes hostile and discriminating environment, their counterparts in boxing were doing just the opposite by proudly emphasizing their heritage—and some of them weren't even Jewish!

KEY PLAYERS OUTSIDE THE RING

The boxing industry employed thousands of people who worked in various capacities outside of the ring. As they had in show business and the garment trade, Jewish people were involved in every aspect of the professional boxing scene. No other ethnic group, before or since, has so dominated a major spectator sport. They were promoters, managers, trainers, corner men, gym owners, equipment manufacturers, and publishers. All had a significant and positive impact on the sport. Their presence enriched boxing in many ways, and helped to make it respectable, as the following examples illustrate:

In 1935 Michael Strauss Jacobs, a former associate and financial backer of the legendary 1920s promoter, Tex Rickard, signed an African-American heavyweight contender named Joe Louis to an exclusive promotional contract. Jacobs maneuvered the exciting young prospect onto the world stage while other less resourceful and far-sighted power brokers would have preferred to keep him at the back of the bus, so to speak.

"Uncle Mike," as reporters liked to call him, made it possible for Joe Louis to get a shot at the heavyweight championship in 1937. The great fighter remained champion for the next 12 years, defending his title a record 25 times. Louis's popularity cut across racial lines. He became an American icon and one of the country's key black figures of the twentieth century. "The Brown Bomber's" brilliant record as champion, his service with the army during World War II, and the dignified manner in which he wore the crown paved the way for Jackie Robinson, in 1947, to become the first African American to integrate major league baseball.

Joe Louis was always generous in his praise of Jacobs, whom he considered more than just a business acquaintance. "If it wasn't for Mike Jacobs I would never have got to be champion,"

The great Joe Louis, with promoter Mike Jacobs, in October 1945. Louis is signing a contract to defend his heavyweight title against Billy Conn in 1946. Jacobs promoted most of Joe's 27 title bouts. (AP Photo/John Rooney)

said Louis. "He fixed it for me to get a crack at the title, and he never once asked me to do anything wrong or phony in the ring. . . . He made a lot of money through me, but he figured to lose, too."[12]

In 1937 Jacobs formed a partnership with Madison Square Garden and became the director of its boxing department. Over the next 10 years

his Twentieth Century Sporting Club staged 320 boxing cards, including 61 world-title bouts.

Jacobs maintained his headquarters in the Brill Building, which was located halfway down the block from his theater ticket agency. Both were located on 49th Street between Broadway and Eighth Avenue. The sidewalk in front of both establishments, especially on days when a

Nat Fleischer, editor and publisher of *The Ring* magazine, about 1957, holding a copy of *The Ring Record Book and Boxing Encyclopedia*. (*The Ring*)

big fight was coming up, was always crowded with fighters, managers, and promoters from out of town who were seeking favors from Jacobs. Damon Runyon dubbed the area "Jacobs Beach." For the fight crowd this was the place to be seen, the place to make contacts.

The boxing industry thrived and prospered under Mike Jacobs's watch. Although a hard-nosed businessman, he was fair and honest in his business dealings with the boxers he promoted. He never abused his position to the detriment of the sport. The fans always knew they would get their money's worth when attending a Mike Jacobs promotion.

Jacobs's most famous promotion was the historic Joe Louis vs. Max Schmeling heavyweight championship bout in 1938. His highest-grossing fight was the second Louis vs. Billy Conn title bout in 1946, which drew a live gate of almost two million dollars, second only to the Dempsey-Tunney "long count" bout of 1927. In the late 1940s ill health forced Jacobs to relinquish his position with the Garden. He passed away in 1953 at age 73.

THE BIBLE OF BOXING

One cannot imagine boxing's Golden Age without the presence of *The Ring* magazine and its irreplaceable publisher, Nat Fleischer. In 1922 Fleischer, a 33-year-old sports editor for several New York dailies, launched *The Ring* magazine with promoter Tex Rickard serving as a silent partner. Fleischer acquired sole ownership in 1929. *The Ring* quickly became boxing's most important and authoritative publication. Every month for 50 years Fleischer produced the magazine that came to be known throughout the world as "The Bible of Boxing."

In 1924 Fleischer initiated a rating system for boxers. He also wrote numerous books related to the sport, and published the annual *Ring Record Book and Boxing Encyclopedia*, an indispensable source of data for matchmakers,[13] managers, and fans. In the 1930s he began presenting title belts to every new world champion. *The Ring* established boxing's first hall of fame in 1954.

Using the editorial pulpit of his magazine, Fleischer often spoke out against corruption within the sport, and advocated for standardized physical exams and rules. In a 1936 editorial he urged support for an American boycott of the Berlin Olympics to protest the Nazi government's treatment of Jews. The boycott did not happen, but the effort was typical of the man. Under his stewardship *The Ring* was not only the sport's most influential publication, but also its moral compass, as well. Issues of the magazine from the 1920s to the 1950s are considered collectors' items today, and are still sought after and read avidly by historians and fans.

Fleischer loved boxing and devoted his life to it. He traveled extensively as an informal ambassador for the sport, and was welcomed by royalty and foreign dignitaries. If anyone deserved the title of "Mr. Boxing," it was Nat Fleischer.

Sadly, after Fleischer's death in 1972, *The Ring* began to deteriorate along with the sport. The magazine remained in operation under relatives of Fleischer, but a devastating blow occurred in 1978 when it was discovered that a key employee had altered the magazine's monthly ratings to favor fighters connected to a Don King–produced televised boxing tournament. King's promotion was discovered to be riddled with corruption involving payoffs, extortion, and phony ratings. The resulting scandal ruined *The Ring*'s once-stellar reputation—a reputation Nat Fleischer had spent most of his adult life building. In later years the magazine attempted, under several different owners, to reclaim its former status.

The late Harry Shaffer, a boxing historian and archivist, provided a very accurate assessment of Fleischer's legacy: "When Nat Fleischer died, that was the end of boxing as an organized sport. Fleischer is what held it together. . . . They talk of having a commissioner for boxing. That's really what he was. He was the one they all went to. He was an honest broker, a situation which boxing has never had again."[14]

EVERLAST

Who is not familiar with the name "Everlast"? The company started by Russian-Jewish immigrants in 1910 became the largest manufacturer of boxing equipment in the world, and a trademark synonymous with the sport ever since.

The manufacture of boxing apparel was an offshoot of the Jewish-dominated garment industry. Before Everlast made its first pair of boxing trunks, the company name was used to identify its line of swimsuits. Today Everlast is a publicly traded corporation. In addition to boxing equipment (now less than 5 percent of its total sales), Everlast also licenses its logo to companies selling men's and women's athletic apparel, sports nutrition products, and footwear. Other major suppliers of boxing gloves, trunks, and equipment from the 1920s to the 1960s included Levinson, G & S, Tuf-Wear, and Ben Lee, all owned by Jewish entrepreneurs.

STILLMAN'S GYM

In 1920 a former Jewish policeman named Louis Ingber was managing a gym on 125th Street and Eighth Avenue in Manhattan for disaffected youth. The gym was operated by the Marshall Stillman Movement. Marshall Stillman was a millionaire and philanthropist who built gyms for underprivileged children to get them off the streets and into a healthful environment.

At that time many of the city's top professional boxers, including the famous lightweight champion Benny Leonard, worked out at Grupp's gymnasium, an established professional boxing gym located nine blocks south on 116th Street. Unfortunately, the owner of that gym had a drinking problem, and when plastered started blaming the Jews for World War I, which certainly wasn't good for business, since the majority of the gym members were Jewish. Fed up with his anti-Semitic tirades, Benny Leonard led a mass exodus of all the Jewish fighters to the gym operated by Marshall Stillman. Leonard asked Lou Ingber if they could use his gym in the evenings to work out (the kids used the gym in the

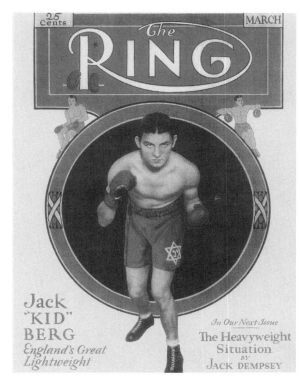

Jackie "Kid" Berg on the cover of *The Ring*, March 1930. Between 1922 and 1940 42 issues of *The Ring* featured a Jewish boxer on the cover. (*The Ring*)

Entrance to Stillman's Gym, 1954. (Courtesy of the Stanley Weston Collection)

afternoons). Ingber was thrilled to have the great champion and the other boxers use the gym.

When word got out that Leonard was now training at a new gym, scores of other fighters and trainers joined him. Within a very short time Stillman's became the top boxing gym in the city and a magnet not just for the city's professional boxers, but for hundreds of fans who came to the gym every week to watch them train. The spectators were more than willing to pay the 15-cent entrance fee (raised to 25 cents in the 1940s, and then 50 cents in the 1950s). Posted on a sign outside the gym were the names of famous boxers who were training that day.

Everybody called Lou Ingber "Mr. Stillman," thinking that was his name. He decided it was easier just to be known as "Lou Stillman," and that was the name he answered to for the next 40 years.

In 1931 Stillman purchased the gym outright from the owners and moved it to much larger quarters on Eighth Avenue, between 54th and 55th Streets, just four blocks north of Madison Square Garden. The new gym occupied the second and third floors of a three-story loft building. Two full-size rings for sparring occupied the second floor, with 10 rows of wooden chairs for spectators. The third floor contained another ring, but also had plenty of space for shadow boxing, floor exercises, jumping rope, and hitting the various punching bags. (The third ring was removed in the 1950s.) The place even had a small lunch counter on the second floor where the aroma of hot dogs and coffee mingled with

the pungent odor of leather, sweat, cigar smoke, and liniment.

For little more than the price of a cup of coffee, fans got to see Jack Dempsey, Benny Leonard, Johnny Dundee, Joe Louis, Henry Armstrong, Tony Canzoneri, Primo Carnera, and hundreds of other world-famous boxers work out.

Lou Stillman was a colorful and irascible Damon Runyonesque character right out of central casting. The former beat cop always wore a .38 pistol in a shoulder holster underneath his suit jacket. He ran the gym like a dictator, and the fighters, managers, and trainers took his abuse because he had the key that opened the door to the most famous training site in the world.

Lou would sit on his perch near one of the rings and announce in his raspy voice which fighters were about to spar. At times the spectators taking in the scene not only saw the leading fighters of the day, but also movie stars, Broadway performers, and such famous Mob tough guys as Legs Diamond, Dutch Schultz, and Owney Madden. For decades Stillman's was a place where rival elements of the underworld could meet under a flag of truce. During boxing's heyday an afternoon at Stillman's gym provided one of the greatest shows in town. Many visitors to the city considered Stillman's as important a New York City landmark as the Empire State Building, Statue of Liberty, or Radio City Music Hall.

The gym made an appearance in two classic Hollywood movies: *Somebody Up There Likes Me* (1956), which depicted the life story of former

Interior of Stillman's Gym, 1946. (Getty Images/The LIFE Images Collection/ Leonard McComb)

The irascible Lou Stillman in 1954. (Courtesy of the Stanley Weston Collection)

middleweight champion Rocky Graziano, and *The Naked City* (1948), a film shot entirely on the streets of New York. Character actor Matt Crowley played the role of Lou Stillman in the Graziano biography.

Gene Tunney once put a knock on the gym, claiming the windows were kept closed and never washed. He considered the facility unsanitary and refused to train there. But Rocky Graziano spoke for most members when, after a few days at an outdoor mountain training camp, he rebelled and returned to his favorite gym, saying "that fresh air would poison a guy."[15]

During its 40-year run, from 1921 to 1961, it is estimated that more than 30,000 boxers passed through Stillman's grimy but hallowed environs.

THE JEWISH PRESS AND BOXING

In the 1920s New York's four major Yiddish dailies had a combined circulation in excess of 400,000. Despite boxing's popularity, the negative attitude of immigrant parents toward the

"In the World of Sports" reads the *Jewish Daily Forward* headline in a 1929 edition. Boxing column appears on the left. (Forward Association)

sport was apparently shared by the learned editors and publishers of the Jewish press. *The Jewish Daily Forward*—the most widely read Yiddish newspaper, with a circulation of 275,000—rarely reported any news related to the sport. But not all sports were dismissed out of hand; *The Forward* did print the results of European soccer matches, since many older immigrants had followed the sport in Europe.[16]

The Forward began publication in 1897 under the able leadership of Abraham Cahan. The newspaper became known as "the conscience of the ghetto" for its advocacy of Jewish causes, American democracy, and its defense of the rights of working men and women. In addition to general news, it also featured articles on literature, art, drama, and politics.

Aside from educating its readers in the American way of life, *The Forward* was also a strong advocate for social reform, and was heavily supportive of labor unions and the fight for a just society. The editors probably viewed the gambler-infested world of professional boxing as a further exploitation of the working-class poor, and an unworthy profession for Jewish boys. But in its ambivalence toward the sport, *The Forward* ignored a significant aspect of life in the city.

The Forward's first mention of boxing did not appear until July 22, 1923, the day before lightweight champion Benny Leonard fought his great rival, Lew Tendler, at Yankee Stadium. The event was just too big to ignore. Two days later a headline announcing Leonard's victory appeared on the front page. Boxing was not mentioned again for another five years.[17]

Finally, in 1928, at the apex of Jewish involvement in the sport, *The Forward* inaugurated a weekly boxing column that appeared next to the European soccer scores. The column lasted about a year, after which boxing was reported only sporadically.

END OF AN ERA

By the 1950s there was no need to report on the activities of Jewish boxers because they had essentially disappeared, along with the grinding poverty, pushcarts, and sweatshops of the ghetto neighborhoods. American Jews had become fully integrated into the economic and social mainstream of society. Their children were encouraged to attend college and pursue professional careers. The Jewish boxer was a rapidly vanishing species.

The sons and grandsons of Irish and Italian immigrants were slower to leave the sport, but their numbers were also greatly reduced. In the decades following World War II, African-American and Latino boxers would take their place and inexorably rise to the forefront of the boxing pantheon.

CHAPTER 3

PIONEERS OF PUGILISM: THE EARLY QUEENSBERRY ERA, 1892–1919

Benny Leonard moved with the grace of a ballet dancer and wore an air of arrogance that belonged to royalty.

—DAN PARKER, NEW YORK SPORTSWRITER[1]

Perhaps the most famous date in boxing history is September 7, 1892. In the first heavyweight championship fight conducted under Marquess of Queensberry rules, James J. "Gentleman Jim" Corbett knocked out defending champion John L. Sullivan ("The Boston Strongboy") in the 21st round of a fight to the finish. The historic event took place in New Orleans in front of 20,000 spectators. Both fighters wore five-ounce leather gloves.

Sullivan, the son of Irish immigrants, was the nation's first sports superstar. He won the bareknuckle heavyweight championship in 1882 and held the title for 10 years. The powerfully built champion stood five feet, ten inches tall and weighed about 200 pounds in his prime. A man with a prodigious appetite for food and liquor, and the ego to match, Sullivan was famous for entering saloons and bellowing, "I can beat any sonofabitch in the house." America loved him.

"Gentleman Jim" Corbett, a 26-year-old former bank clerk, stood a shade over six feet and tipped the scales at 180 pounds. A superb athlete and former amateur boxing star, he was the quintessential "Fancy Dan"–type boxer, relying heavily on speed, timing, accurate jabs, evasive footwork, and skillful counterpunching to wear down opponents.

Sullivan, 34 years old, had not defended his title in three years. Nevertheless, the hugely popular champion was still considered invincible. Corbett's great victory over the legendary champion was a shocking upset that signaled the beginning of a new era for the sport. From that moment on virtually all boxing matches would be conducted using Marquess of Queensberry

John L. Sullivan in 1885. The legendary "Boston Strongboy," the son of Irish immigrants, was America's first sports superstar and the last bare-knuckle heavyweight champion. (Courtesy of the Jim Houlihan Collection)

"Gentleman Jim" Corbett defeated Sullivan for the title in 1892 and later became a major star of vaudeville. (Courtesy of Steve Lott/Boxing Hall of Fame Las Vegas)

rules. The bare-knuckle era of prizefighting had officially come to an end.

Unlike the brash, boisterous, and hard-drinking Sullivan, Corbett was an elegant and refined individual who helped to transform boxing into a respectable sport. With his matinee-idol looks Corbett parlayed the championship into a successful career in vaudeville, eventually becoming one of the highest-paid stage actors of his day.[2]

Corbett's clever style of boxing influenced other fighters to adopt a more-cerebral approach to the game, and it is not inaccurate to label him the father of modern scientific boxing. But old traditions die hard. Many boxers continued to advance and retreat in a straight line while attempting to land hard singular punches. Another holdover from the bare-knuckle era was the "finish fight" that allowed a bout to continue indefinitely until one of the contestants was either knocked out or disqualified. Finish fights remained in vogue until the early 1900s. They were eventually phased out, but taking their place for a time were marathon contests scheduled for 25 or 45 rounds.

Boxers preparing for a marathon contest trained and fought with the distance in mind. Pacing was extremely important. There was always the danger of expending too much energy too soon. Marathon bouts followed a familiar pattern. After a few moments of sparring an attempt was made to land one or two quick punches, after which the fighters fell into a clinch and continued close-quarter infighting interspersed with a great deal of pushing, pulling, and tugging on the arms. At the referee's discretion the boxers were separated and the process would begin again. The purpose of this strategy was to gradually wear down an opponent over the long haul. A fighter showing signs of fatigue would be the signal for his adversary to pick up the pace and try for a knockout.[3]

After 1910 boxing contests scheduled for more than 20 rounds were rare. For a while some cities and states went to the opposite extreme by limiting all professional bouts to not more than four or six rounds, as was the case in Philadelphia and California. As a result, the tempo of fights speeded up and boxing styles became more fluid and rhythmic. Mobile footwork took on added significance as fighters realized that constant movement was not only a good defensive strategy, but also presented more opportunities to set up a variety of combination punches. With the elimination of marathon bouts it was no longer necessary to "coast" for several rounds in order to conserve energy, as was the case in fights exceeding 20 rounds.

From an economic standpoint the shorter contests also made it easier for boxers to compete more often and earn additional paydays. Even die-hard bare-knuckle fans had to admit that boxing had become a faster, more interesting, and more enjoyable sport to watch.

SETTING THE BAR

As with any new art form—and make no mistake, Queensberry boxing had transformed the sport into a new art form—there is always a small group of pioneers who exhibit a singular genius for their craft and set the standard for later generations. Some of the greatest boxers who ever lived reached their primes during the first two decades of the twentieth century. "Sweet scientists"—boxers with especially skillful techniques—such as Joe Gans, Abe Attell, Sam Langford, Joe Walcott, Jack Johnson, Jack Blackburn, Owen Moran, Freddie Welsh, Jem Driscoll, Packey McFarland, Mike Gibbons, and Benny Leonard—were among a small group of brilliant innovators who would have stood out at any time. The few existing films of these early pioneers bear witness to their extraordinary boxing skills.

THE "NO-DECISION" ERA

Boxing's growing popularity in America during the early years of the last century did not deter government authorities and social reformers from attempting to outlaw the sport, primarily because of its association with gambling, and the view that public displays of violence were immoral.

Nevertheless, a total ban was difficult to enforce. Enterprising promoters skirted laws that banned boxing in their states or municipalities by staging sparring "exhibitions" for private club members. The price of admission made the purchaser a member of the club, albeit for one night only. The majority of these bouts were authentic boxing contests with each competitor doing his best to win.

Yet even in places where professional boxing was both legal and popular, the sport was never more than a scandal or two away from being banned. A compromise of sorts was reached with the creation of the so-called "no-decision" rule. The rule mandated that unless a bout ended in a knockout there would be no winner or loser declared. No-decision bouts were intended to discourage gambling and rid the sport of crooked referees, judges, and fixed fights.

At least a dozen states adhered to the no-decision rule from about 1910 to 1925. The policy was frustrating to both boxers and fans. A champion could be dominated by a worthy challenger yet still retain his title as long as he stayed on his feet to the final bell. Any fighter who realized he was overmatched or just didn't feel like extending himself could stall, clinch, and backpedal to the final bell. By avoiding a knockout an official loss would not be posted to his record.

No-decision bouts (indicated by the letters "ND" in the record books) failed to curtail gambling. In order to satisfy bets gamblers agreed to abide by the opinions of a consensus of sportswriters as reported in the next day's newspapers. Therefore the letters "ND" came to also stand for "newspaper decision."

Over the past 20 years dedicated researchers affiliated with the International Boxing Research Organization (IBRO) have spent countless hours tracking down these newspaper reports in an effort to try and determine the actual winner of thousands of no-decision bouts that did not end in a knockout. The results are posted on the Boxrec.com Internet site. (Even though newspaper decisions cannot be considered "official," and the opinions of the sportswriters not always reliable or accurate, I have decided to include the newspaper verdicts, when available, in the records of the boxers who appear in this book.)

TITLE CLAIMANTS

Prior to 1921 a boxer's contender status, or his designation as a world champion, was not dependent on a sanctioning organization. Rather, it was determined by his record against quality opponents with established reputations. In either case it was acceptance by the press *and* public that was key to a fighter's recognition factor. Of course, imperfections existed. There was the problem of no-decision bouts and of some deserving fighters being denied the opportunity to challenge for a title despite their excellent records. The latter injustice applied especially to several great black boxers, most notably Sam Langford.

Yet, despite its flaws, the system worked to the extent that a boxer could not enter the golden circle of top contenders without first establishing legitimate credentials by defeating other quality boxers. Any claim to a title by a fighter whose accomplishments in the ring did not measure up to that standard would be ignored.

When boxing reached unprecedented levels of popularity in the 1920s, a more-formalized structure was called for. In 1921 the powerful New York State Athletic Commission and the newly formed National Boxing Association (a loose confederation of 23 state boxing commissions, soon to expand to 43) gave their imprimatur to boxers who they felt deserved the title of "world champion."

Boxing has always been a difficult sport to regulate. Even during the best of times there were disparate claims and counterclaims of men purporting to be world champions. Nevertheless, from the 1890s to the 1960s the boxing establishment was able to maintain a semblance of order when it came to anointing legitimate world champions. Before boxing's traditional organizational structure fell apart in the late 1970s—and became hopelessly Balkanized by a gaggle of competing quasi-official boxing authorities doling out scores of title belts—there was much less confusion as to who deserved the title of "world champion." Prior to the 1970s a fighter who won a title recognized by either the National Boxing Association, New York State Athletic Commission, or the European Boxing Union, was considered a legitimate champion. More often than not, all of these organizations recognized the same world champion.

ADDING TO BOXING'S MOSAIC

Beginning in 1914 large numbers of Southern blacks began to migrate north to escape racial violence and to seek greater opportunities for employment and a higher standard of living. The exodus continued into the 1920s and '30s.

Eventually some two million (over 20 percent of the South's black population) moved from the rural South to the industrial North. In Chicago the black population more than tripled in a decade.[4] Like the first- and second-generation European immigrants, some chose to make their living as boxers to escape the ghetto and perhaps get rich. By the 1930s there were nearly 2,000 black professional boxers in the United States.[5]

Despite their hopes for a better way of life, most blacks in Northern cities continued to live at or below the poverty level. Buying a ticket to see a boxing show was a luxury few could afford. Without the support of a substantial fan base, African-American fighters had no economic leverage when attempting to obtain a title bout, since white audiences made up the majority of spectators. With the exception of a few crossover stars, there was no economic benefit for a promoter to risk a popular white champion's title against a black fighter who, if he won, would not bring in the crowds.

Between 1890 and 1936 only 12 black fighters won a world title as compared to more than 100 white/Anglo fighters of several different nationalities.[6] While it is true there were many more white prizefighters at the time, several highly ranked black contenders were denied the opportunity to fight for a championship, or, when granted the opportunity, were often the victims of wrongful decisions favoring a white opponent. Sometimes black fighters of the era had to agree in advance to take a dive or "carry" a good local boxer in order to get a payday or secure future bouts.

Heavyweight contenders had an especially tough time in the aftermath of the controversial reign of Jack Johnson, the first African-American heavyweight champion (1908–1915). Johnson, the son of ex-slaves, was the most famous black person of his day, and also the most controversial. He lived by his own rules and wanted nothing more than to be treated as an equal to any white man. But he antagonized much of white America by not only winning the world's most prestigious sports title, but also by blatantly defying the Jim Crow conventions of his era. He was married twice to white women, lived extravagantly, was outspoken, and enjoyed taunting white challengers in the ring (all of whom could not lay a glove on him). During his tenure as heavyweight champion he famously hired a white chauffeur to drive him around.

Ironically, after winning the championship Johnson refused to risk it against two other great black boxers, Sam Langford and Joe Jeanette. Although he defeated both men prior to winning the championship, they were still considered his toughest challengers. Instead, Johnson preferred to defend his title—and earn more money—by facing a series of less-talented white challengers.

Johnson could not be defeated in the ring, but the courts were another matter. In 1912 the government accused him of violating the Mann Act (bringing a woman across state lines "for immoral purposes"). An all-white jury convicted Johnson on the trumped-up charges and he was sentenced to a year in prison. While out on bail pending an appeal, Johnson fled to Canada, and then to Europe. In 1915, while still in exile, he lost the title to "White Hope" Jess Willard in Havana, Cuba. More than two decades would pass before another black man would have

Jack Johnson, heavyweight champion 1908–1915. The most famous black person of his day and the most controversial. (Copyright Bettman/Corbis/AP Images)

the opportunity to fight for the heavyweight championship.

Johnson returned to the United States in 1920 and served out a one-year sentence in a federal prison.

In 2013, for the third time in less than a decade, a bipartisan group of US lawmakers sent a resolution to the president's desk, urging him to grant Jack Johnson a posthumous pardon. If granted, the pardon would rectify a historical wrong and clear Johnson's name for a criminal conviction that was obviously based on racism.

Even though it was impossible to completely bypass the blatant racism and elitist attitudes of the era, no other professional sport was more receptive to black athletes. Prior to 1947, when baseball finally allowed the great Jackie Robinson to integrate the major leagues, boxing was the only major professional sport that was open to African-American athletes, and was one of the few professions that gave black people access to the type of wealth and fame that would have been unthinkable a generation earlier. That fact in no way diminishes the humiliations and privations they suffered as second-class citizens. It should also be noted that not all white champions or top contenders avoided meeting highly rated black boxers. Jewish champions Benny Leonard and Maxie Rosenbloom were among those who unhesitatingly faced the finest black contenders both before and during their title reigns. It is a matter of record that Rosenbloom fought more black boxers (70) than any other white fighter of the 1930s.

THE INTER-ALLIED GAMES OF 1919

During America's participation in World War I (1917–1918), boxing was used to entertain and condition American soldiers and sailors. Famous boxers such as Benny Leonard, Johnny Kilbane, Freddie Welsh, Johnny Coulon, and Mike and Tommy Gibbons led mass exercise drills and participated in exhibition bouts on military bases.

The "War to End All Wars" came to an end on November 11, 1918, but it would be months before millions of Allied soldiers stationed in France could be sent home. An American Expeditionary Force (AEF) boxing tournament proved to be very popular with the doughboys and military brass. The army's director of athletics suggested an even bigger Olympic-style sports tournament that would involve all the nations that had fought on the Allied side. The idea was to keep the doughboys and other Allied soldiers entertained, "to avoid the peace-time threat to the moral standards and conduct of idle troops waiting to be discharged." Soldiers of the 29 nations who fought on the Allied side were invited to compete. Eighteen nations accepted the invitation. The tournament was open to both amateur and professional athletes.[7]

The French government welcomed the idea and authorized the building of a stadium in Paris with a seating capacity of 25,000. The structure was built by the US military in cooperation with the YMCA and was named Pershing Stadium, after the renowned general who led the American Expeditionary Force.[8]

Of the 14 Olympic events in the "Inter-Allied Games," none was more popular than boxing.

The huge number of preliminary bouts over the five months leading up to the finals drew thousands of competitors into the ring. Three of the seven weight-division championships were won by Americans.

The results of the boxing tournament were reported daily in the American press and proved to be a public relations bonanza for the sport. The success of the tournament was instrumental in helping to legalize boxing throughout the United States. As Jeffrey T. Sammons notes in *Beyond the Ring: The Role of Boxing in American Society*, the tournament "legitimated the martial arts and fused boxing with patriotism. . . . After the horrors of mustard gas, bombs, mortars and machine guns, boxing represented a more simple and noble past, with men in control of their destiny. Indeed, the barbarism of real war made boxing seem dignified, if not dainty."[9]

TOUGH GUYS

Most of the boxers who appear in this chapter fought at weights ranging from 118 to 160 pounds. This is not surprising, since prior to 1920, most men, on average, weighed below 160 pounds. Although there was no shortage of heavyweights (over 175 pounds), there were far more boxers competing in the lighter-weight divisions.

Also evident are a high number of losses in many of the records. Those losses must be evaluated in the context of the era in which these men fought. Boxing was a full-time occupation. One could not depend on the occasional big payday to pay the bills, so it was desirable to fight as often as possible. Fights were spaced weeks or sometimes days apart. It was not uncommon for boxers to average 12 to 20 fights a year. (Today the average is about four fights a year.)

Out of necessity the old-timers often competed with bruised knuckles and facial cuts or contusions that had not fully healed. One could not be expected to perform at his very best each and every time under these circumstances. Sometimes the goal was just to fight cautiously and go the distance without getting too banged up. It would not make sense for a fighter to wear himself out or risk injury against a tough but mediocre opponent if he was committed to fight a more-important bout two or three weeks later. Another factor to keep in mind is that the best boxers often faced each other. A loss now and then was to be expected.

The intense level of activity looks almost unbelievable today. For some of these fighters the end result had dire physical and mental repercussions in later years, most often if they fought too long beyond their prime. The damage caused by repetitive head trauma often led to various stages of dementia in later life. Others were more fortunate; they were able to get on with their lives without the consequences of too much damage.

The fighters profiled in this chapter began their professional careers prior to 1915. Among them are some whose careers bridged the 1910s and '20s. If a fighter's prime extended into the second half of the 1920s, he is included in the next chapter.

Debates still rage as to how these early pioneers of gloved boxing compared to the best boxers in the decades that followed. But one conclusion is incontestable: The contenders and champions who fought from the 1890s to the late 1910s were as tough and determined a bunch of pugs as ever laced on a pair of boxing gloves—maybe the toughest.

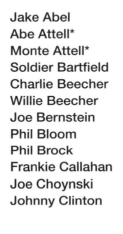

Jake Abel	Leach Cross	Battling Levinsky*	Yankee Schwartz
Abe Attell*	Joe Fox	Gussie Lewis	Jewey Smith
Monte Attell*	Abe Friedman	Harry Lewis*	Sammy Smith
Soldier Bartfield	Charley Goldman	Ted "Kid" Lewis*	Sid Smith*
Charlie Beecher	Abe "Kid" Goodman	Louisiana	Harry Stone
Willie Beecher	Harry Harris*	Alf Mansfield	Izzy Strauss
Joe Bernstein	Kid Herman	Blink McCloskey	Joe Tiplitz
Phil Bloom	Freddie Jacks	Al McCoy	Matt Wells*
Phil Brock	Willie Jackson	Eddie O'Keefe	Charley White
Frankie Callahan	Young Joseph	Young Otto	Jackie "Kid" Wolfe
Joe Choynski	Benny Kaufman	Johnny Ray	
Johnny Clinton	Benny Leonard*	Johnny Rosner	* world champion

JAKE ABEL

(Jacob Abelson)
Born: January 1, 1893
Died January 10, 1963 (Age: 70)
Hometown: Atlanta, Georgia
Weight: 135–145 lbs.
Professional Career: 1911–1922

Total Bouts	Won	Lost	Draw	ND
95 (812 rounds)	45 (21 by KO)	18 (2 by KO)	18	8-2-4

Russian-born **Jake Abel** lived most of his life in Atlanta, Georgia. He fought often in Georgia, Tennessee, and Florida, with an occasional foray into Cuba. Only three of his 95 documented bouts took place north of the Mason-Dixon Line.

During World War I Jake interrupted his career to enlist in the United States Army. Because of his boxing background the army assigned him to be a bayonet instructor. After the war Jake took part in the American Expeditionary Force boxing tournament (a precursor to the Inter-Allied Tournament) and won the lightweight championship. The finals were staged at the Cirque de Paris on April 26, 1919. General Pershing and other high-ranking officers were among a capacity crowd of 14,000. Abel was awarded a medal for sportsmanship by the Prince of Wales.

Jake was a highly skilled and durable ring technician who eagerly took on all comers, including such renowned fighters as Benny Leonard, Jack Britton, Ted "Kid" Lewis, Charley White, Knockout Brown, Eddie Hanlon, Joe Mandot, and Yankee Schwartz.

The $1,000 purse he received in 1919 for a 10-round no-decision bout (non-title) in Atlanta with the great lightweight champion Benny Leonard represented the largest purse of his career. The Associated Press reported that Leonard "gave an exhibition of speed and cleverness that outdid what Abel had to offer."

Jake retired in 1922 at the age of 29. It was a smart move by a smart fighter. He was just past his prime, and continuing with his career would have made him a stepping-stone for younger fighters on the way up.

After hanging up his gloves Jake went into the hotel business, and for many years managed the Jefferson Hotel in downtown Atlanta. He was active in civic affairs throughout his life, and eventually became president of the Atlanta Hotel Association.

ABE ATTELL
"The Little Hebrew"
Featherweight Champion: 1903–1912
Born: February 22, 1883
Died: February 6, 1970 (Age: 86)
Hometown: San Francisco, California
Height: 5' 4" Weight: 122–133 lbs.
Professional Career: 1900–1917

Total Bouts	Won	Lost	Draw	ND	NC
154 (1,477 rounds)	72 (39 by KO)	10 (5 by KO)	17	41-6-6	2

Abe Attell was the 13th of 16 children born to Russian immigrant parents. He grew up in an Irish neighborhood of San Francisco, so knowing how to fight became a matter of survival. Young Abe quickly established a reputation as a tough and tenacious street fighter. The young brawler turned pro at the age of 17, and within two years was competitive with the best featherweight boxers in the world.

In 1903 Abe won universal acclaim as featherweight champion, and over the next nine years successfully defended his title a record 23 times. While champion he also engaged in over 100 non-title bouts. Attell credited early ring scientists James J. Corbett and George Dixon for influencing his style of fighting. He rarely weighed more than 130 pounds, yet took on and defeated opponents outweighing him by 15 to 20 pounds.

Attell loved to gamble, and often bet on his own fights. In one famous incident he wagered his entire $5,000 purse that he would knock out challenger Harry Forbes inside five rounds. He won the bet. Another favorite gambit was to hold back his full arsenal against a hometown favorite to make it appear that he was having a rough time, but do just enough to win. The idea was to generate fan interest and anticipation for a return bout. The betting odds for the rematch would reflect the closeness of the first fight. After placing a hefty wager on himself, Attell would then proceed to take apart his surprised opponent. (He was not the only fighter to occasionally engage in this type of subterfuge.) Famous sports

journalist Red Smith accurately described Attell as "a master boxer, dedicated gambler, and tireless schemer."

Abe lost the featherweight title in 1912 when he was outpointed by Johnny Kilbane in a 20-round bout. His disappointment was somewhat assuaged by the $15,500 he received as his share of the gate—the largest purse of his career. Only two weeks after losing to Kilbane, Attell fought a bloody 20-round draw with lightweight contender "Harlem" Tommy Murphy.

Abe was 29 years old and a veteran of close to 200 fights. He fought for another year and then announced his retirement. Two years later there was the inevitable comeback, but after a few fights it was obvious to his fans that the old magic was gone.

After his ring career ended Abe dabbled in vaudeville and, in the time-honored tradition, opened a saloon. For the next few years not much was heard of Abe until his name suddenly appeared on the front page of every newspaper in America: Abe Attell had been linked to the infamous Black Sox baseball scandal of 1919.

The audacious plan to fix the 1919 World Series was rumored to have been hatched, or, at the very least, abetted by Attell's close friend, the notorious gambler and racketeer Arnold Rothstein. Abe was alleged to have been the bagman for Rothstein, delivering the $10,000 payoffs to the eight Chicago White Sox players who agreed to throw the Series with Cincinnati. But before he could be subpoenaed, Attell fled to Canada. The self-imposed exile lasted a year. When he returned to face prosecution, a jury found him not guilty because of insufficient evidence.

In 1939 Abe married the former Mae O'Brien. (His first marriage had ended in divorce.) Together they managed a tavern on the East Side of Manhattan. He often attended the fights at Madison Square Garden. Even into his eighties he seemed not to suffer from the debilitating effects of his long career in the ring, unlike so many of his brothers-in-arms.

MONTE ATTELL

Bantamweight Champion 1909–1911
Born: July 28, 1885
Died: November 11, 1960 (Age: 75)
Hometown: San Francisco, California
Height: 5' 4½" Weight: 118–125 lbs.
Professional Career: 1902–1916

Total Bouts	Won	Lost	Draw	ND	NC
112 (1,047 rounds)	44 (22 by KO)	23 (7 by KO)	16	10-14-4	1

Monte Attell (on left) posing with big brother Abe.

Monte Attell followed his older brothers Caesar and Abe into the prize ring. By the time Monte turned pro in 1902, big brother Abe had already claimed the world featherweight title. Monte's rise was not nearly as meteoric as Abe's. It took at least four years before he established his own credentials as a top bantamweight contender. During his prime (1906 to 1909), Monte lost only two of 34 documented fights.

On June 19, 1909, he knocked out Frankie Neil in the 18th round to win the world bantamweight title. It was a historic moment in that Monte and Abe became the first brothers to hold world titles.

After four successful defenses Monte lost the title to Frankie Conley (Francesco Conte) in the 42nd round of a 45-round marathon bout. Just 57 days later he was back in the ring for a 10-round no-decision with Joe Wagner.

In 1912 brother Abe lost his featherweight title to Johnny Kilbane. Ten months later Monte sought revenge and took on the new champion in a non-title bout. Monte was stopped in the eighth round.

Three years after his bout with Kilbane, Monte incurred an eye injury that became infected. The other eye had already been permanently damaged several years earlier in a 20-round bout with the great British boxer, Owen Moran. By 1920 Monte was legally blind.

The Great Depression and a failed business enterprise wiped out his savings. Blind and broke, the former champion took a job selling peanuts at the weekly fights in the Bay City. He was led around the arena by a little boy who would yell out, "World champion peanuts!" Thankfully, when former heavyweight champion Jack Dempsey heard about Monte's plight, he came to the rescue and financed a cigar stand in San Francisco that provided the old champ with a decent living for many years.

SOLDIER BARTFIELD
(Jacob Bartfeldt)
Born: March 15, 1892
Died: October 2, 1970 (Age: 78)
Hometown: New York, New York
Height: 5' 7½" Weight: 142–152 lbs.
Professional Career: 1911–1925, 1932

Total Bouts	Won	Lost	Draw	ND	NC
221 (1,956 rounds)	52 (34 by KO)	29 (5 by KO)	8	67-46-18	1

Austrian-born **Jacob "Soldier" Bartfield** came to America at the age of 16. Jake acquired his nickname after service with the US Army's 11th Infantry. His division was assigned to the Mexican border in the days of the Pancho Villa raids. "We had a good outfit," he told boxing journalist Lester Bromberg in 1967, "and those bandits knew it. Soon as we turned up, they ran like hell."

The converted southpaw's boxing record reads like a Hall of Fame roster. Opponents included world champions Benny Leonard, Jack Britton, Ted "Kid" Lewis, Harry Greb, Mickey Walker, Mike Gibbons, Billy Papke, Jock Malone, Mike O'Dowd, Jimmy Slattery, Johnny Wilson, and Bryan Downey.

Of all the great boxers that he fought, Soldier said that Harry Greb gave him the toughest fight of his career. He fought Greb six times, and is one of only a handful of boxers to win a newspaper decision over the great "Pittsburgh Windmill." Two of the bouts (ten and 15 rounds) occurred just nine days apart.

In 14 years this iron man fought over 1,900 rounds, encompassing 221 recorded fights (although it is believed the actual number of fights is closer to 300). He faced scores of

THE EDUCATIONAL ALLIANCE

In 1889 several leading Jewish philanthropists raised funds for the construction of a neighborhood settlement house on New York's Lower East Side. Most of the money was donated by educated Jews who came to America from Germany in the 1840s and '50s in the first wave of Jewish immigration. Several had become wealthy in merchandising (mostly manufacturing and distribution of clothing) or in investment banking firms they founded. They took it upon themselves to establish social agencies for the large number of mostly uneducated and poverty-stricken East European Jews coming to America.

At the beginning this was not always a comfortable arrangement, as they regarded their East European "coreligionists" as socially and culturally inferior. As pointed out by Arthur Hertzberg, in their view these new arrivals "were underscoring the foreignness of Jews in America. Their very first concern was thus to try to limit immigration, but, if not, at least to 'Americanize' the new immigrants as quickly as possible. On the surface this meant to teach them English and Western manners, but much more than that was soon attempted." Their concern was not entirely self-serving. Genuine compassion for their poor East European cousins (most of whom came from Russia and Poland) motivated their actions as well.[10]

The Educational Alliance Settlement House officially opened in 1891. Its purpose was to help growing numbers of poor East European Jewish immigrants, who were arriving in downtown New York by the thousands every month, to adapt to American society. The staff conducted English classes, gave lectures on how to be a good American

Educational Alliance Building, 1930. (From the Archives of the Yivo Institute for Jewish Research, New York)

citizen, provided free legal aid, and operated a summer camp for children, which was located in upstate New York. It also housed an art school and a theater. In 1895 banker and philanthropist Jacob Schiff purchased another building on the Lower East Side to house the Henry Street Settlement, a social and health service agency. Eight years later the Hebrew Institute of Chicago was established. Like the Educational Alliance, it played a key role in the Americanization of Chicago's Eastern European immigrant population.

For Jewish boys the icing on the cake of these wonderful institutions was their first-class athletic facilities. Both had fully equipped gymnasiums that included basketball and handball courts, exercise apparatus, a regulation boxing ring, and punching bags. Danny Goodman, one of Chicago's first Jewish boxing stars, was an instructor at the Hebrew Institute.

In New York City thousands of Jewish boys received their first exposure to boxing in the Educational Alliance's gymnasium. Famous alumni include Leach Cross, Willie Jackson, Charley Beecher, Sid Terris, Ruby Goldstein, Sammy Dorfman, Lew Kirsch, and world champions Dave Rosenberg, Abe Goldstein, Ben Jeby, and Bob Olin.

By 1910 over 100 settlement houses and community centers, catering to a mostly Jewish clientele, had opened in virtually every major urban center of the United States.[11] The boxing programs were not intended to prepare future professional boxers. Their goal was to promote fitness and self-confidence. Nevertheless, knowing how to box was a useful skill that could come in handy, especially for Jewish boys living in poor immigrant neighborhoods.

Today, the Educational Alliance is still housed in its seven-story flagship building at 197 East Broadway. In addition, there are several other sites affiliated with the Alliance that offer a variety of services, including residential and outpatient drug treatment centers, counseling, after-school programs in New York City Public Schools, senior citizen residential facilities, and other programs serving the community.

top-rated contenders, and traded punches with 13 world champions, 45 times. In 1918 he boxed the great Ted "Kid" Lewis six times, with three of the bouts occurring within 32 days of each other. Nearing the end of his career he took on future champion Mickey Walker three times in six weeks, the last one a 12-rounder.

Bartfield was most proud of his 1915 no-decision bout against the famed "St. Paul Phantom," Mike Gibbons, at Brooklyn's Ebbets Field. He entered the ring a 10–1 underdog. But Gibbons, one of the finest scientific boxers of his era, could not cope with the Soldier's special brand of pressure and incessant body punching. (Bartfield broke three of Gibbons's ribs.) All four newspapers covering the bout scored it for Bartfield. He received $25,000 for the bout—the largest purse of his career.

Soldier retired in 1925 (although there was a brief two-bout comeback in 1932). He worked for 18 years in the Brooklyn Navy Yard as a ship fitter. In retirement he split his time between a 50-acre farm he owned near Hunter, New York, and a home in Canarsie, Brooklyn.

CHARLIE BEECHER

Born: July 30, 1898
Died: February 1976 (Age: 77)
Hometown: New York, New York
Weight: 125 lbs.
Professional Career: 1918–1923

Total Bouts	Won	Lost	Draw	ND
56 (501 rounds)	23 (5 by KO)	6 (2 by KO)	2	19-6

Charlie Beecher was 16 years old when he took his first boxing lesson at the famous Educational Alliance Settlement House in New York's Lower East Side. Three years later he won the New York State amateur bantamweight championship. For most of his brief but successful professional career (1918–1923), Charlie was rated among the top featherweight contenders. He proved his mettle against the likes of Red Chapman, Jackie "Kid" Wolfe, Andy Chaney, Freddie Jacks, Benny Gould, Johnny Brown, Frankie Garcia, Dick Loadman, and Frankie Burns.

In the late 1920s Charlie opened "Beecher's Gym" in the back of a pool hall he owned in Brownsville, Brooklyn. The gym became a popular training site and an active part of the New York boxing scene for the next quarter of a century.

WILLIE BEECHER

Born: January 1, 1893
Died: April 1, 1957 (Age: 64)
Hometown: New York, New York
Height: 5' 6½" Weight: 135–140 lbs.
Professional Career: 1908–1921

Total Bouts	Won	Lost	Draw	ND	NC
163 (1,436 rounds)	19 (17 by KO)	12 (3 by KO)	4	62-48-17	1

Willie Beecher is the older brother of featherweight contender Charlie Beecher. During his 13-year career Willie met virtually every outstanding lightweight contender and recorded memorable no-decision bouts against world champions Abe Attell, Ted "Kid" Lewis, and Jack Britton. The rugged 140-pounder was stopped only three times in 163 fights, with all three losses occurring either early or late in his career.

In 1914 Beecher lost a 20-round decision to lightweight contender Mexican Joe Rivers. Just three weeks later he fought a 20-round draw with future featherweight champion Johnny Dundee. His next bout was a non-title 10-rounder against lightweight champion Freddie Welsh at Madison Square Garden. According to newspaper accounts the brilliant Welshman easily outpointed Beecher.

From 1917 to 1919 Willie served in the United States Marine Corps. He launched a brief comeback in 1920, but retired the following year.

JOE BERNSTEIN

"The Pride of the Bowery"
Born: November 7, 1877
Died: January 21, 1930 (Age: 53)
Hometown: New York, New York
Height: 5' 6" Weight: 125–135 lbs.
Professional Career: 1895–1906

Total Bouts	Won	Lost	Draw	ND	NC
83 (1,055 rounds)	24 (6 by KO)	21 (9 by KO)	27	1-6-2	2

(Courtesy of Albert Davis Collection The Stark Center/University of Texas at Austin)

The first Jewish boxer from New York City to achieve a measure of notoriety at the turn of the last century was Dolly Lyons. Not much is known about Lyons. Only about a dozen contests have been documented, although it is assumed he fought many clandestine bouts at a time when the sport was illegal in New York. After losing a 20-round decision to Joe Bernstein in 1899, Lyons faded from the scene.

Within months of defeating Lyons, **Joe Bernstein**'s name was known to every boxing fan in America when he lost a close 25-round decision to the top-ranked bantamweight contender, Terry McGovern. Just one month later, in another 25-round bout, he challenged the great featherweight champion, George Dixon. Dixon, a Canadian, was the first black world champion in any weight class. Joe put up stubborn resistance but lost the decision. Ten weeks after his defeat by Dixon, Bernstein knocked out former champion Solly Smith in the 13th round.

"The Pride of the Bowery" failed in two subsequent attempts to capture the featherweight title, losing to both McGovern and Young Corbett II. On the plus side he scored important victories over Tommy White, Eddie Santry, and Young Griffo. Three 25-round draws with the formidable Dave Sullivan solidified Bernstein's status as one of the world's top featherweight contenders.

Joe's pro career lasted 12 fruitful years. He retired in 1908 after a fourth round TKO loss to Leach Cross.

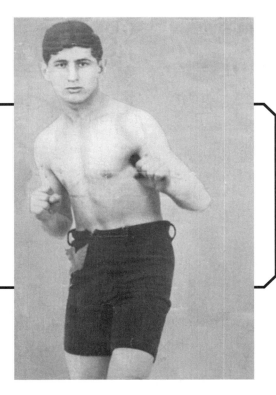

PHIL BLOOM

Born: October 24, 1894
Died: February 8, 1979 (Age: 84)
Hometown: New York, New York
Height: 5' 7" Weight: 125–148 lbs.
Professional Career: 1911–1923

Total Bouts	Won	Lost	Draw	ND
200 (1,926 rounds)	40 (19 by KO)	22 (4 by KO)	9	54-57-18

Phil Bloom was born in the Whitechapel district of London's East End, home to most of England's great Jewish boxers. In 1911 Bloom's father, a tailor, took his wife and eight children to America. The family settled in Williamsburg, Brooklyn. Phil had boxed as an amateur in England and decided to turn pro that same year. The high points of his 201-bout career were eight encounters with the great lightweight champion, Benny Leonard. Bloom was KO'd twice by Leonard but finished on his feet the other times.

In addition to Leonard, Bloom fought five other world champions—Jack Britton, Ted "Kid" Lewis, Johnny Dundee, Rocky Kansas, and Dave Rosenberg.

Even in an era of iron men, Bloom stood out as a remarkably durable fighter. On December 2, 1916, he boxed 20 rounds with perennial contender Irish Patsy Cline in Brooklyn. Four days later he was in Detroit where he went 10 rounds with tough veteran Stanley Yoakum. After one day's

rest Bloom hustled back to New Haven, Connecticut, where he dropped a 15-round decision to top lightweight contender Joe Welling. Seventeen days after losing to Welling he was back in Brooklyn for a 10-rounder against Chuck Simler.

In 1920 Bloom returned to London and won a 20-round decision over former welterweight champion Matt Wells. Eight days later he fought another 20-rounder, outpointing Danny Arthurs. Bloom finally hung up his well-worn boxing gloves in 1923. He moved to Los Angeles in the late 1920s, where he became an extra and bit player in many Hollywood movies.

(Courtesy of Jerry Fitch)

PHIL BROCK
(Phil Slomovitz)
Born: June 25, 1889
Died: Unknown
Height: 5' 3½" Weight: 135 lbs.
Hometown: Cleveland, Ohio
Professional Career: 1904–1916

Total Bouts	Won	Lost	Draw	ND	NC
102 (916 rounds)	35 (22)	17 (7)	10	13-9-8	10

Phil Brock and his younger brother Matt were Cleveland, Ohio's, first Jewish boxing stars. Both were lightweights. Matt was the harder puncher, but Phil was considered the better boxer.

Phil turned pro in 1904, and within six years was competitive with the world's finest lightweight boxers. Among his victims were Philadelphia Pal Moore, Fighting Dick Hyland, Jack

Redmond, and Matty Baldwin. He also had draw decisions with Harlem Tommy Murphy, former featherweight champion Young Corbett II, and future lightweight champion Willie Ritchie. Losses to Owen Moran, Packey McFarland, and Freddie Welsh did not tarnish Phil's reputation, as they were rated among the greatest fighters of their era.

FRANKIE CALLAHAN

(Samuel Holtzman)
Hometown: Brooklyn, New York
Born: February 10, 1895
Died: September 5, 1927 (Age: 32)
Height: 5' 4½" Weight: 135 lbs.
Professional Career: 1910–1922

Total Bouts	Won	Lost	Draw	ND
174 (1,480 rounds)	29 (24 by KO)	10 (4 by KO)	3	77-34-21

Brooklyn's Sam Holtzman adopted the very Irish name "**Frankie Callahan**" to keep his parents from finding out he was a boxer.* Before hanging up his gloves in 1922, he fought 175 documented professional bouts. His opponents included five world champions and most of the top lightweights of his era, including Pete Hartley, Charley White, George KO Chaney, Willie Jackson, Phil Bloom, Pal Moore, and future champion Rocky Kansas.

The highlight of his career occurred in 1917 when two of three newspapers awarded Callahan the unofficial victory in a 10-round no-decision bout with a near-prime Benny Leonard. Three months later Leonard won the lightweight title. Previous to his bout with Leonard, Callahan had won a newspaper verdict over future featherweight champion Johnny Dundee.

Nineteen days after his bout with Leonard, Callahan fought another no-decision bout against Dundee. Two newspapers favored Callahan and two others called it a draw. Five weeks later the 22-year-old faux Irishman knocked out lightweight contender Jimmy Hanlon in the 19th round.

The one fighter that Callahan could not solve was Lew Tendler. He lost three newspaper decisions to Tendler and, nearing the end of his career, was stopped twice by the great Philadelphia southpaw.

An obituary in the *New York Times* reported that Callahan passed away after contracting pneumonia. He was 32 years old.

---

* Not to be confused with non-Jewish boxer Frankie Callahan, who fought out of Columbus, Ohio.

JOE CHOYNSKI

Born: November 8, 1868
Died: January 24, 1943 (Age: 74)
Hometown: San Francisco, California
Height: 5' 11" **Weight:** 165–178 lbs.
Professional Career: 1887–1903

Total Bouts	Won	Lost	Draw	ND	NC
83 (478 rounds)	55 (37 by KO)	15 (11 by KO)	5	1-3-1	3

San Francisco's **Joe Choynski** (pronounced Co-IN-sky) was the first Jewish athlete to achieve international prominence. Joe had an interesting pedigree. He was one of the few professional boxers not born into poverty. His father, Isadore, the son of a rabbi, had attended Yale College, where he earned a teaching degree. After moving to San Francisco Isadore became a dealer in rare books, and was the West Coast correspondent for *The American Israelite* newspaper for 20 years. The elder Choynski also published his own periodical called *Public Opinion*, which he used as a vehicle for exposing municipal corruption and anti-Semitism.[12]

While his father traveled in intellectual circles (he counted Mark Twain among his friends), Joe danced to a different drummer. Although he was highly intelligent and articulate, formal education did not interest him. After dropping out of high school he found work as a blacksmith and then as a candy puller in San Francisco's notorious

Barbary Coast. Both of these physically rigorous jobs proved to be excellent preparation for boxing.

Choynski was five-foot-11 and weighed around 170 pounds. Before 1903 there was no light-heavyweight division for fighters who weighed between 160 and 175 pounds. As a result, over the course of his 83-bout career, Joe often took on opponents who outweighed him by 20 to 60 pounds. Fortunately for Joe, he was not only a superb boxer, but also one of the sport's deadliest punchers.

On May 30, 1889, 19 months after his pro debut, Choynski was matched with San Francisco rival and future heavyweight champion James J. Corbett. Their fight was halted by the police after the fourth round (professional boxing was outlawed in San Francisco), and a rematch was scheduled one week later. In order to avoid police interference, the fight took place on a barge anchored in San Francisco Bay, near the town of Benicia.

Several hundred people crowded onto the barge to witness one of boxing's legendary fights. In a brutal seesaw battle that saw both men come back from the brink of defeat, Corbett knocked out Choynski in the 27th round. The bout, fought under Queensberry rules (three-minute rounds separated by one minute of rest), had lasted just under two hours.

During his illustrious 16-year career Joe Choynski took on three past or future heavyweight champions. Outweighed by 40 pounds, he fought a 20-round draw with James J. Jeffries, was stopped in five by Bob Fitzsimmons, and knocked out Jack Johnson in three rounds. Other legendary opponents included Tom Sharkey, Philadelphia Jack O'Brien, Kid McCoy, and Barbados Joe Walcott.

Choynski always considered his 1901 knockout of future heavyweight champion Jack Johnson the most significant victory of his career. (Seven years after their fight, Johnson would become the first black heavyweight champion.) At 32 years of age Joe was 10 years older and 25 pounds lighter than Johnson. Most people expected the veteran to lose. The fight took place in Johnson's hometown of Galveston, Texas.

In the third round Choynski landed a tremendous left hook that knocked Johnson cold. As soon as the referee completed the 10-count, five Texas Rangers stormed into the ring and arrested both fighters for violating a local ordinance against professional boxing contests.

Johnson and Choynski shared the same prison cell for two weeks but were treated more like celebrities than outlaws. They were even allowed to leave the prison in the evenings—Choynski to his hotel, and Johnson to his home—but had to return the following morning. Both fighters staged sparring exhibitions for the warden and his staff while state politicians used the jail sentence to score points as protectors of public decency.

During their confinement Johnson asked his cellmate to teach him the tricks of an old pro. In his autobiography Johnson credited Choynski with helping to refine his boxing style. "Every day we would box in the jail yard, surrounded by police officers and guests," wrote Johnson. "Joe had great affection for me, and to prove it, he gave me lessons, showing me the best punches anyone has ever seen in a jail yard. I learned more in those two weeks than I had learned in my entire existence up to that point."[13] Jack Johnson is still rated by many experts to be among the top five heavyweights of all time.

Choynski continued to box for three more years, finally retiring in 1904, at the age of 36, after having fought 83 professional fights. He had a brief fling as an actor, costarring in a touring stage production of *Uncle Tom's Cabin* with the great Australian heavyweight, Peter Jackson (the first prominent black fighter of the gloved era). The show's climax was a sparring session between the stars. After the sparring session an announcement was made offering $500 to anyone in the audience who could last three minutes with either fighter. It is not known if anyone took up the challenge.

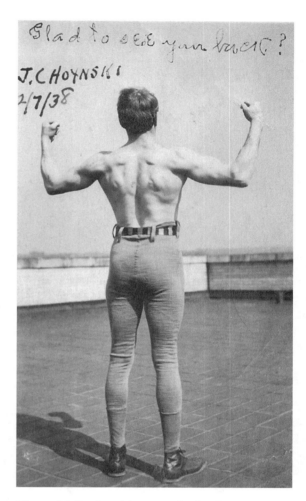

Choynski displays his muscular back, circa 1900. (Courtesy of Christopher J. LaForce)

Choynski and Johnson in Galveston County Jail, 1901. Posing for the camera are (L to R) deputy sherriff Walter Burns, Choynski, Johnson, sheriff Henry Thomas, jailer Frank Schreiber.

Joe eventually moved to Chicago and entered the insurance business. In 1942, shortly before he passed away at the age of 74, he was hired as technical consultant for the movie *Gentleman Jim*, starring Errol Flynn as Corbett. The legendary 1889 barge fight was re-created for the film.

A bit of poetic license was taken, as the Hollywood version shows Corbett getting knocked off the barge and splashing into San Francisco Bay and then climbing back to resume the battle. (The Raoul Walsh–directed film is a classic, and the author's personal favorite.)

JOHNNY CLINTON

(Morris Elstein)
Born: November 20, 1897
Died: August 1971 (Age: 73)
Hometown: Boston, Massachusetts
Height: 5' 6" Weight: 135–140 lbs.
Professional Career: 1915–1927

Total Bouts	Won	Lost	Draw	ND	NC
109 (937 rounds)	52 (15 by KO)	19 (2 by KO)	9	15-9-3	2

The Boston Irish would have been proud to call **Johnny Clinton** one of their own. He always put forth a 100 percent effort, gave no quarter, and asked for none in return. But he was Irish in name only. Johnny Clinton was a Jew from Boston's West End whose real name was Morris Elstein.

This faux Irishman had already fought some of the best lightweight boxers in the world before his 21st birthday, including multiple bouts with Mel Coogan, Frankie Conifrey, Joe Welling, Lou Bogash, Frankie Schoell, and Johnny Shugrue. But his proudest moments in the ring were his two no-decision bouts with the incomparable lightweight champion Benny Leonard. They met twice—the first time in 1919, and in a rematch two and a half years later. Both fights went the full 10 rounds. There was no doubt about Leonard's superiority, but Clinton was no pushover, and the champion had to perform at his best each time.

Even at the tail end of his busy career, Clinton was still meeting top contenders. In 1923 he lost a 10-rounder to Sailor Friedman, but rebounded less than three months later with a 12-round nod over England's Harry Mason. As his career wound down Clinton lost decisions to Pete August, Young Harry Wills, and future middleweight champion Joe Dundee. Shortly after his thirtieth birthday Clinton announced his retirement. Potential opponents, both Irish and Jewish, breathed a sigh of relief.

LEACH CROSS

(Louis Wallach)
"The Fighting Dentist"
Born: February 12, 1886
Died: September 7, 1957 (Age: 71)
Hometown: New York, New York
Height: 5' 7" Weight: 133–139 lbs.
Professional Career: 1905–1916, 1921

Total Bouts	Won	Lost	Draw	ND
146 (1,107 rounds)	35 (22 by KO)	10 (4 by KO)	4	55-28-14

Until the rise of Benny Leonard a decade later, **Leach Cross** was the most popular fighter to ever come out of New York's Lower East Side neighborhood. The son of Austrian immigrants, Leach's actual birth name was Louis Charles Wallach. The name change was an attempt to hide his fistic activities from his father. "Leach" was a derivation of his childhood nickname, "Lachey." Three of his younger brothers, Phil, Dave, and Marty, also became pro boxers, with varying degrees of success.

Before he embarked on his busy pro career, Leach Cross began studying dentistry at New York University. He graduated in 1907 and went to work at the office of a dentist friend. Leach practiced dentistry by day while boxing at night—hence, his nickname, "The Fighting Dentist."

By 1908 Leach was earning $15 a week as a dentist. That same year his first main event paid him $35. Leach temporarily suspended his dental

practice to devote full-time to his more lucrative pugilistic endeavors.

Two years into his pro career, the dentist/fighter became a ghetto sensation when he stopped the much-admired Joe Bernstein in four rounds. By then he had earned enough money to open his own dental practice on the East Side. The establishment soon had enough patients to keep two assistants busy, but Leach's main source of income still came from boxing. His earnings in the ring were estimated at from $1,500 to $3,000 a month.[14]

From 1909 to 1916, "Leachie," as he was called by friends, had 89 bouts. Among his opponents were boxing legends Freddie Welsh, Jack Britton, Johnny Dundee, Jem Driscoll, Packey McFarland, Charley White, Matt Wells, and Ad Wolgast.

"The Fighting Dentist" knew all the tricks of the trade. He fought out of a low crouch, which made him difficult to hit. His right uppercut and right cross were his most effective weapons. One of his favorite maneuvers was to feign grogginess in order to draw an opponent into making a careless mistake. When his opponent lunged forward, Leach timed the punch, slipped it, and countered. Opponents eventually caught on to the trick, but they never knew for sure if Leach was really hurt or just faking. Neither did the fans, who came out in droves to watch the colorful and exciting fighter in action.

The most memorable fight of his career was a 1909 encounter with Fighting Dick Hyland in Colma, California. The bout was a marathon contest scheduled for 45 rounds. After more than two hours of fighting Leach was knocked out in the 41st round. Bad weather had kept attendance down. He was paid only $350 for the toughest and most punishing fight of his career.

During the day Leach attended to his dental practice, while at night he could often be found topping a card at one of New York City's many fight clubs. In his last bout of 1911, Leach was matched against the dangerous lightweight contender Knockout Brown. The bout took place in Manhattan's Empire Athletic Club. Both fighters were seasoned campaigners with more than 80 bouts apiece. Knockout Brown, whose real first name was Valentine, packed the heavier wallop. Over a dozen of his opponents had not made it past the first round.

On the day of the fight a standing-room-only crowd was on hand to see the highly anticipated match. The 10-round bout was a closely contested, action-packed battle. Brown kept boring into Leach, pressuring him throughout the fight, but it was Leach who was more accurate with his punches and who did most of the scoring.

During the fight Brown had a couple of his teeth loosened. The following day his manager took him to a dentist's office to have them checked. Brown was dumbfounded when he saw who the dentist was. Standing in front of him, dressed in a white medical smock, was none other than Dr. Louis C. Wallach, alias Leach Cross.[15]

Leach finally hung up his gloves in 1916. His good friend, the singer Al Jolson, suggested he move to California. With his nest egg of $46,000 Leach built a house in Hollywood, and later opened up a gymnasium that became very popular with movie stars and businessmen. He counted Rudolph Valentino, Douglas Fairbanks, Mary Pickford, and Charlie Chaplin among his close friends.

Eventually bad investments and a costly divorce wiped out his savings, driving him into bankruptcy. Leach decided to leave California and return to New York City, where he reopened his dental practice in Union Square.

In his early sixties, Leach began to suffer the effects of his lengthy boxing career. Failing eyesight and increasing dementia forced him to close his office. He passed away in 1957 at the age of 71.

BOXING TRADING CARDS

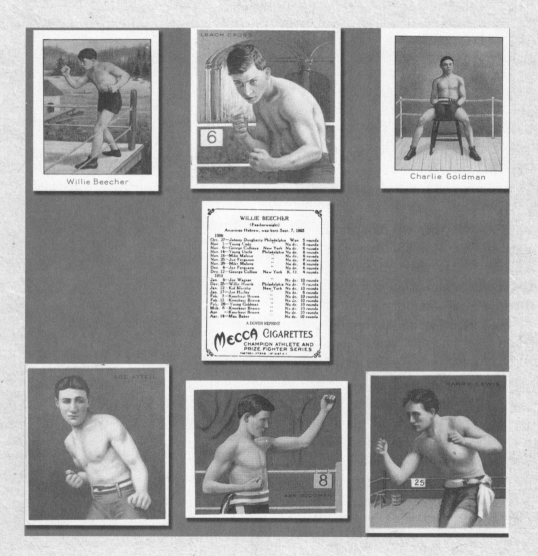

The popularity of the charismatic heavyweight champion John L. Sullivan led to an active market for boxing collectibles, most notably trading cards. In the 1880s American tobacco companies began to insert pictures of Sullivan and other famous boxers into cigarette packs as a way to promote their products. (A pack of 10 cigarettes usually sold for five cents.) Other inserts might include pictures of baseball players, actresses, Indian chiefs, frontier heroes, kings, police chiefs, billiard players, birds, and ships.

In 1910 the American cigarette industry introduced several Turkish brands named Hasson, Mecca, Fatima, and Turkish Whiffs. Each included a series of colorful boxing inserts. A full set (usually numbering around 50) is considered a valuable collector's item today.

England, with its rich boxing history, was also a major producer of boxing trading cards. The two most popular

The series of boxing cards issued by the Mecca cigarette company, c. 1909-10, are a valued collector's item today. Cards featuring Jewish boxers are illustrated here. Top row (L to R) Willie Beecher, Leach Cross, Charley Goldman. Bottom row (L to R) Abe Attell, Abe Goodman, Harry Lewis. Middle row: Back of Willie Beecher card displays a recent record of the boxer.

sets of cards were those produced in the 1930s and '40s by the W. A. & A. C. Churchman Cigarette Company of London and Knock-Out Razor Blades of Sheffield.

Beginning in 1921 the Exhibit Supply Company of Chicago began selling postcard-size photos of contemporary boxing stars from vending machines for a penny each. The boxer's record appeared on the opposite side of the card. A new series of cards was printed in 1928, but did not include the fighter's record. The Exhibit Supply cards featured champions and contenders from the past and present.

The first post–World War II set of boxing cards was issued by two major chewing gum companies, Topps and Leaf, although their brilliantly colored cards did not meet the standards of workmanship displayed in the cigarette-pack inserts of a generation earlier.

A final set of Exhibit Supply cards was issued in the early 1960s. They were sold in amusement parks and penny arcades for five cents each. Today, depending on the fighter pictured, collectors pay between $20 and $150 per card

Cards issued by the Churchman Cigarette Co., London, in the 1930s featured both American and English boxing stars. Shown here are noted Anglo Jewish boxers (L to R) Ted "Kid" Lewis, Harry Mizler, and Jack "Kid" Berg. (Photo by Studio Lisa Ross).

JOE FOX

Born: February 8, 1894
Died: April 2, 1965 (Age: 71)
Hometown: Leeds, England
Weight: 118–125 lbs.
Professional Career: 1909–1925

Total Bouts	Won	Lost	Draw	ND	NC
151 (1,688 rounds)	70 (27 by KO)	29 (4 by KO)	18	16-13-3	2

(Courtesy of Albert Davis Collection The Stark Center/University of Texas at Austin)

Joe Fox fought in the classic stand-up style popular with British boxers. For most of his 16-year professional career, he ranked among the world's best bantamweights and featherweights. Fox was awarded the prestigious Lonsdale Belt after winning British titles in both divisions. (The Lonsdale Belt, named after the first president of London's National Sporting Club, is awarded to all British champions). He made two trips to America, in 1913 and 1919, where he crossed gloves with such outstanding ring men as Joe Tiplitz, Babe Herman, Al Shubert, Benny Valgar, and future champions Joe Lynch, Sammy Mandell, and Eugène Criqui. In 1919 he lost a six-round newspaper decision (non-title) to world featherweight champion Johnny Kilbane.

One year after he retired, Fox married and settled down. He opened a candy shop where he proudly displayed his Lonsdale Belt in a framed cabinet above the counter.

ABE FRIEDMAN

Born: 1894
Died: August 11, 1926 (Age: 32)
Hometown: Boston, Massachusetts
Weight: 118–126 lbs.
Professional Career: 1915–1925

Total Bouts	Won	Lost	Draw	ND
122 (1,186 rounds)	39 (6 by KO)	33	1	36-10-3

Abe Friedman was never knocked out in 122 professional fights, despite facing virtually every top bantamweight and featherweight in the 1910s and early 1920s. That was no small accomplishment considering the extraordinary depth of talent in those divisions. His opponents included the likes of Pete Herman, Kid Williams, Pancho Villa, Joe Lynch, Young Montreal, Danny Kramer, Joe Burman, Johnny Ertle, and Roy Moore. He also fought two no-decision bouts with Charley Goldman, who later gained fame as the trainer of heavyweight champion Rocky Marciano.

Friedman served in the US Army during World War I. He resumed his career in 1919, fighting mostly in the Boston area. In the last few years of his career he was plagued by failing vision. On May 4, 1925, Friedman lost an eight-round decision to Rosey Stoy and announced his retirement. Tragically, three months later, while crossing a street near his home, Friedman was hit by a truck and killed.

CHARLEY GOLDMAN

Born: December 22, 1887
Died: December 11, 1968 (Age: 81)
Hometown: Brooklyn, New York
Height: 5' 1" Weight: 112–118 lbs.
Professional Career: 1904–1918

Total Bouts	Won	Lost	Draw	ND
129 (956 rounds)	28 (19 by KO)	6 (2 by KO)	2	31-25-37

Before **Charley Goldman** gained recognition as one of boxing's all-time great trainers, he was a serious contender for the bantamweight championship of the world.

Growing up in Brooklyn's tough Red Hook section at the turn of the last century, young Charley idolized his neighbor, the great featherweight champion "Terrible" Terry McGovern.

He was thrilled when the champ gave him the honor of carrying his gym bag to workouts. In imitation of his hero Goldman began parting his hair in the middle, and for his entire life always wore a derby, just like McGovern.

Charley claimed to have had over 400 bouts, but only 129 have been documented. His earliest recorded pro fight was a 42-round draw with

Young Gardner in 1904. Since boxing was illegal in New York, the bout took place in the back of a saloon in Manhattan's Bowery neighborhood.

The highlight of Charley's career was a 1912 non-title fight against the great bantamweight champion Johnny Coulon. Two newspapers scored the 10-round no-decision bout for Coulon, while two others scored it a draw.

In 1913 Charley began training middleweight contender Al McCoy (Albert Rudolph). After McCoy won the title Goldman decided to devote himself full-time to training fighters. In 1924 he formed a partnership with manager Al Weill that continued for the next 32 years. Goldman trained scores of boxers for Weill and was also outsourced to train fighters for other managers. Charley trained four world champions for Weill: Lou Ambers (lightweight), Joey Archibald (featherweight), Marty Servo (welterweight), and his most famous pupil, Rocky Marciano, the only heavyweight champion to retire undefeated.

ABE "KID" GOODMAN
Born: August 19, 1885
Died: Unknown
Hometown: Boston, Massachusetts
Weight: 130–135 lbs.
Professional Career: 1899–1916

Total Bouts	Won	Lost	Draw	ND	NC
189 (1,567 rounds)	68 (44 by KO)	34 (5 by KO)	40	16-20-7	4

Abe "Kid" Goodman was the first Jewish boxing star from Boston. He turned pro in 1899, and over the next four years lost only seven of 95 fights. Highlights of Goodman's career include decisions over top lightweight contender Aurelio Herrera, future welterweight champion Harry Lewis, and draw decisions with featherweight champion Abe Attell (non-title) and former champion Young Corbett II.

Other notable opponents were Benny Yanger, Matty Baldwin, Harlem Tommy Murphy, Packey McFarland, Dick Hyland, and Cyclone Johnny Thompson.

By 1910 it was obvious Goodman had passed his peak, but he continued to fight for another six years, losing to fighters he could have easily beaten in his prime. After he retired Goodman became a deputy sheriff in Boston.

HARRY HARRIS

Bantamweight Champion: 1901
Born: October 18, 1880
Died: June 5, 1959 (Age: 78)
Hometown: Chicago, Illinois
Height: 5' 7½" Weight: 115–130 lbs.
Professional Career: 1896–1902, 1905–1907

Total Bouts	Won	Lost	Draw	ND
52 (338 rounds)	38 (14 by KO)	2	7	3-1-1

Harry Harris was the first Jewish world champion of the twentieth century. At five-foot-eight and 115 pounds, he was one of the tallest bantamweight champions in the history of the division. He was also one of the most accomplished boxers of his era. As a teenager he was mentored by the famous Kid McCoy, who taught him the tricks of the trade, including his signature "corkscrew punch."

In 1901 Harry won the bantamweight championship of the world by outpointing England's Pedlar Palmer in 15 rounds. He fought only three more times before announcing his retirement.

The decision to retire while still in his prime was prompted by a fortuitous meeting with theatrical impresario E. A. Erlanger. Impressed by Harry's intelligence and engaging personality, Erlanger offered him a job managing the New Amsterdam Theatre in New York City. While working at his new profession Harry met his future wife, the actress Desiree Lazard, while she was costarring at the New Amsterdam with George M. Cohan in his hit musical, *45 Minutes from Broadway.*

Harry liked the theater world and enjoyed his work, but he missed being center stage as the star of his own show. In 1905, three years after his last fight, Harry launched a brief comeback and engaged in six contests before returning to his job as a theater manager.

A man of many interests and talents, Harry became fascinated by the world of finance. In 1919, at the age of 39, he purchased a seat on the New York Curb (forerunner of the American Stock Exchange). He remained a Wall Street broker for the next 30 years, specializing in international securities.

BOXING SUFFRAGETTES

In America, prior to the 1920s, boxing had been off limits to women spectators. It was not considered "proper behavior" for a woman to attend a prizefight, and although no official ban existed, they were usually barred from entering an arena. That attitude began to change with the arrival of Tex Rickard, the great visionary promoter of the early 1900s. Not that Tex was a champion of egalitarianism; his motives had more to do with expanding his bottom line than expanding women's rights. Tex believed the sport's low-class image would improve if he could attract significant numbers of women to attend his boxing shows.

Rickard's first attempt to integrate the all-male enclave occurred in 1906, the year he promoted his first "fight of the century"—an interracial title bout featuring the great African-American lightweight champion Joe Gans defending his title against Oscar "Battling" Nelson (aka, "The Durable Dane") in the gold-mining boomtown of Goldfield, Nevada. Rickard announced to the press that he would allow women to attend the event. In an article published 11 days before the bout, Tex told a reporter he expected 250 to 300 women to witness the contest. He further explained that special preparations were being made to accommodate the female spectators.

"The arena will be filled by specially sworn-in officers who will see that nothing offensive is said or done," said Tex. "No one under the influence of liquor will be allowed within the gates, and the officers will be instructed to eject any man who in any way transgresses the rules laid down by the club for the protection and comfort of the women."[16]

Tex's pronouncement was condemned by the local clergy. The pastor of the First Presbyterian Church of Goldfield, Reverend James Byers, warned his female congregants: "I will expel any woman who attends any prize fight from my flock."[17] Rickard could care less what the keepers of public decency had to say. He reveled in the pre-fight publicity the controversy aroused.

The Gans vs. Nelson title bout lived up to expectations. The grueling contest between "The Old Master" and "The Durable Dane" lasted an incredible 42 rounds under the broiling Nevada sun, until an exhausted "Battling" Nelson was disqualified for landing a deliberate low blow. How many women attended the bout was difficult to determine, as they disappeared into the crowd of more than 18,000 fans. But no matter the actual number, Rickard had irrevocably shattered a boxing taboo.

A decade and a half later, in the midst of the freewheeling Roaring Twenties, the presence of women at prizefights, especially for important contests, was by then a common occurrence.

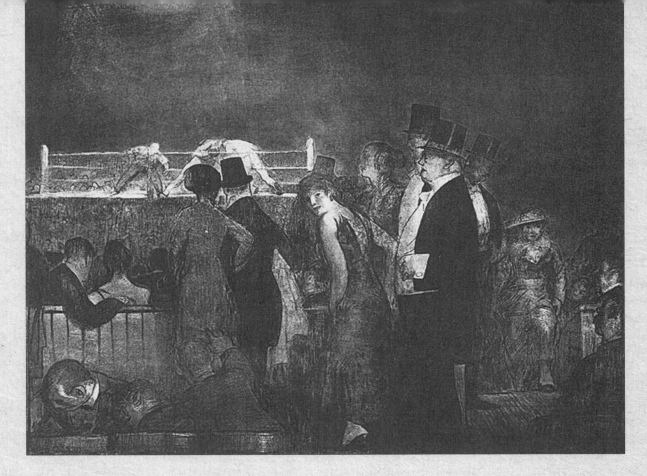

Men in tuxedos and women in evening gowns attend a boxing match in this 1916 George Bellows print titled "Preliminaries."

Tex Rickard, now ensconced in New York City, kept to his strategy of providing an atmosphere conducive to attracting the fairer sex. Under Rickard's management, major boxing matches had become glamorous and exciting happenings. When the new Madison Square Garden opened in 1925, more than 17,000 thousand fans filled the arena for its first title fight, including a large segment of showbiz royalty and New York high society. They were all there to see and be seen. They filled the ringside section dressed in their evening clothes, the women among them "conspicuous in attendance and draped in elegant attire and wearing fine jewelry."[18]

While it's doubtful the presence of women at prizefights in the early years of the twentieth century contributed significantly to the women's suffrage movement and the 19th Amendment, ratified in 1920, I wouldn't dismiss the idea entirely. Sometimes it's the accumulation of many small and seemingly insignificant advances that contribute to the larger victory. I like to think that Tex and those gutsy women who first entered the all-male world of the boxing arena did their part.

KID HERMAN

(Herman Landfield)
Born: September 23, 1883
Died: June 11, 1934 (Age: 50)
Hometown: Chicago, Illinois
Height: 5' 3" Weight: 133 lbs.
Professional Career: 1899–1907

Total Bouts	Won	Lost	Draw	ND	NC
69 (521 rounds)	35 (18 by KO)	9 (2 by KO)	18	3-2-1	1

Kid Herman was born in Montreal, Canada, but moved to Chicago at an early age (not to be confused with another "Kid Herman," who fought out of New York several years later). In his prime, Chicago's Kid Herman fought draw decisions against the likes of Abe Attell, Aurelio Herrera, and Harry Lewis.

In 1907 Herman won a 10-round decision over highly rated lightweight contender Benny Yanger. That victory earned him a title bout with the brilliant lightweight champion Joe Gans, nicknamed "The Old Master" because of his artistic boxing skills. (Gans was the first black American to win a world boxing title, and is still considered one of the greatest boxers of all time.)

Herman made a good showing for seven rounds but was in over his head. Gans bided his time and knocked him out with a picture-perfect right cross in the eighth round. (A film of the fight exists and is available for viewing on YouTube.) Eleven months later he was badly beaten by Packey McFarland and retired. Kid Herman was killed in an auto accident in 1934.

FREDDIE JACKS

"The Aldgate Ironman"
Born: February 12, 1893
Died: August 3, 1961 (Age: 69)
Hometown: London, England
Weight: 125–135 lbs.
Professional Career: 1910–1928

Total Bouts	Won	Lost	Draw	ND
187 (2,127 rounds)	75 (25 by KO)	77 (6 by KO)	14	6-12-1

The boxing world used to stand on the shoulders of such men as England's **Freddie Jacks**. A "have gloves, will travel" type, Jacks was a tough and seasoned journeyman who would fight anyone, anywhere. His services were always in demand because win or lose, he always put up stiff resistance and was rarely stopped. In his heyday Jacks was known as "The Aldgate Ironman."

Jacks fought under several different names early in his career. His official record lists 175 fights, but the actual number is believed to exceed 200. Top opponents included world champions Johnny Kilbane, Rocky Kansas, Louis "Kid" Kaplan, Joe Dundee, and Jimmy Goodrich. Toward the end of 1922, Freddie traveled to Australia and had five 20-rounders in four months. He was also very popular in America, where he stayed for five years while participating in over 80 contests.

On June 25, 1923, in his only shot at a world title, Freddie was stopped in the fifth round by the great junior lightweight champion, Jack Bernstein.

WILLIE JACKSON

(Oscar Tobin)
Born: July 11, 1897
Died: November 13, 1961 (Age: 64)
Hometown: Bronx, New York
Height: 5' 6" Weight: 135 lbs.
Professional Career: 1913–1922, 1924

Total Bouts	Won	Lost	Draw	ND	NC
148 (1,186 rounds)	28 (20 by KO)	11 (4 by KO)	10	58-30-7	4

There was no mistaking **Willie Jackson**'s profession: his flattened nose and heavily scarred eyebrows provided mute testimony to the countless punches he absorbed in 144 professional fights. Famed boxing journalist Dan Parker wrote that Jackson "was possibly the best club fighter of this or any other century."*

Willie Jackson began his career as a "stick and move" speedster, scoring only six knockouts in his first 39 bouts. But on January 15, 1917, he shocked the boxing world (and himself) with a first-round knockout of the number-one featherweight contender, Johnny Dundee.

One of Dundee's signature moves was to rebound off the ropes to gain extra momentum in his punches. But this time the great fighter miscalculated. As he caromed off the ropes his chin ran smack into Jackson's right cross and he was counted out. (Not until 14 years later was another fighter able to stop the great Dundee, well past his peak and in his 328th professional bout.) Jackson and Dundee fought nine more times (a total of 105 rounds). All of their bouts were competitive, but Jackson was unable to duplicate his KO victory.

Jackson's sensational upset of Dundee skyrocketed him to national prominence overnight. Convinced that he possessed knockout power in his right fist, Jackson abruptly altered his style, transforming himself into an aggressive pressure fighter who was willing to take a punch to land one. But the speed of his impressive windmill attack rarely allowed him time to set down on his punches, which accounted for his low KO percentage. Nevertheless, it was a style that was pleasing to the fans and earned him lucrative purses.

* A "club fighter" was a boxer active in the many "fight clubs," or smaller boxing arenas, that were common at the time. A good club fighter was not quite good enough to beat the best, but always gave a performance that pleased the fans.

Other formidable opponents include Lew Tendler, Frankie Callahan, Leo Johnson, Pete Hartley, Jimmy Hanlon, Frankie Britt, Matt Brock, and future champion Rocky Kansas.

Jackson was past his prime when he suffered a brutal beating by lightweight contender Charley White while losing a 15-round decision at Madison Square Garden in 1922. Less than a year later Joe Shugrue stopped him in the 10th round. It was only the third stoppage he'd suffered in 147 pro bouts.

Jackson retired in 1924 and became a paper and twine salesman in New York City. But his long and punishing career as a boxer eventually took its toll. He was forced to retire in his late fifties, no longer able to work due to progressive dementia caused by the countless punches he'd absorbed in the ring.

YOUNG JOSEPH

(Harry "Aschel" Joseph)
Born: January 1, 1885
Died: October 23, 1952 (Age: 67)
Hometown: London, England
Height: 5' 5" Weight: 115–147 lbs.
Professional Career: 1903–1914

Total Bouts	Won	Lost	Draw
110 (1,006 rounds)	71 (9 by KO)	23 (6 by KO)	16

Young Joseph was one of England's first Jewish boxing stars of the twentieth century and a role model to such boxers as Ted "Kid" Lewis and Jackie "Kid" Berg. He first attracted attention in 1903 after a series of victories at the legendary Wonderland Arena, a 2,000-seat emporium located on Whitechapel Road in London's East End. The popular 18-year-old boxer did not pack much of a punch, instead relying on speed and cleverness to defeat his opponents. It was a style appreciated by knowledgeable English boxing fans. Joseph weighed about 120 pounds at the beginning of his career. The young boxer would eventually grow into a 145-pound welterweight.

In 1907 Joseph advanced his career by winning two 20-round decisions (two-minute rounds) over former British lightweight champion Jack Goldswain. Over the next three years he acquired both the British and European welterweight titles. Joseph traded punches with the likes of Johnny Summers, Young Otto, Rudy Unholz, Owen Moran, and future lightweight champion Freddie Welsh.

After his victory over Otto in 1909 Joseph claimed the world welterweight title. The claim was generally ignored by most boxing fans and authorities. The following year Joseph challenged the recognized welterweight champion of the world, Harry Lewis, and was stopped in the seventh round. In 1911 he lost his European welterweight title to France's future light-heavyweight king Georges Carpentier via a 10th-round knockout. After hanging up his gloves Joseph stayed active in boxing as a manager and promoter.

(Courtesy of PhillyBoxingHistory.com)

BENNY KAUFMAN

(Jacob Flinkman)
Born: September 8, 1888
Died: December 1972 (Age: 84)
Height 5' 4" Weight: 135 lbs.
Hometown: Philadelphia, Pennsylvania
Professional Career: 1906–1922

Total Bouts	Won	Lost	Draw	ND	NC
186 (1,226 rounds)	22 (16 by KO)	11 (5 by KO)	5	73-43-30	2

Russian-born Jacob Flinkman came to Philadelphia with his parents as a young boy in 1895. He began boxing in local amateur clubs at age 16. Two years later he turned professional as "Battling Flink," but soon settled on the ring name of **Benny Kaufman**.

Kaufman was a five-foot-four, 135-pound block of granite. He plowed through 102 opponents in his first five years as a pro. Among his best performances was a 12-round draw with the great Charley White, along with newspaper verdicts over lightweight contenders Patsy Brannigan and Frankie Conley. In officially scored contests he lost decisions to highly rated lightweights Dutch Brandt and Al Shubert.

Other great opponents included Johnny Kilbane, Willie Jackson, Lew Tendler, George KO Chaney, Frankie Burns, former bantamweight champion Kid Williams, and a host of other long-forgotten featherweight and lightweight contenders. No-decision matches accounted for 136 of his 183 career bouts.

BENNY LEONARD

(Benjamin Leiner)
Lightweight Champion 1917–1925
Born: April 7, 1896
Died: April 18, 1947 (Age: 51)
Hometown: New York, New York
Height: 5" 5" Weight: 130–153 lbs.
Professional Career: 1911–1925, 1931–1932

Total Bouts	Won	Lost	Draw	ND	NC
219 (1,581 rounds)	89 (70 by KO)	6 (5 by KO)	1	96-16-7	4

No decade produced more Jewish boxers than the 1920s—and the person most responsible for inspiring the flood of Jewish talent was **Benny Leonard**, who ruled the lightweight division from 1917 until his retirement as undefeated champion eight years later, in 1925. The greatest compliment any Jewish boxer could receive was to be called "the next Benny Leonard."

It is not surprising that a fighter who considered his brain the most important weapon in his formidable arsenal would view boxing as a physical game of chess. And like a master chessman, Benny Leonard set subtle traps and ambushes without ever "telegraphing" his intentions. His goal as a boxer was to quickly determine an opponent's habits, his strengths and his weaknesses, disrupt his game plan, and then do what was necessary to win. He developed his superb jab and defensive maneuvers during his early teen years when he was a slightly built 115-pound

bantamweight who could not afford to mix it up with stronger opponents. As his frame filled out and he grew stronger and heavier, Leonard added a powerful right-hand punch to his repertoire.

In his prime Leonard was far superior to most of his opponents, but he never sought to humiliate them. "I don't want to hurt the other guy," said Leonard. "I want to stop him. But that does not mean I am eager to cut him up and murder his self-respect. The credo of the professional ring is to win with speed and your best means of execution. As for that 'killer instinct,' I never had it as a kid when bringing home the pay was very important, and I never had it as champion."[19]

Oftentimes Leonard would be content just to outbox an opponent and sharpen his reflexes while getting a good workout. But every now and then he would decide to deviate from the plan. "Many a night I would be in there just looking for a workout with no idea of knocking my man out," Leonard said after his retirement. "But there'd always be a loudmouth who'd start yelling, 'Leonard, you're a freaking bum,' or worse. He'd keep it up and I'd get sore and quite a few guys got flattened that wouldn't have been hurt otherwise, just because some dope in the crowd wouldn't keep his mouth shut."[20]

In his all-consuming desire to understand and master the *art* of boxing, Leonard set about to deconstruct and analyze every aspect of the sport. Leonard was a brilliant boxer, but he also had the heart of a warrior, and was not averse—when the situation called for it—to throw caution to the wind and mix it up. But always that nimble brain would be working overtime as he sought openings for his devastating right-hand counterpunch. He did not start out as a puncher, but after several years developed knockout power by perfecting the right combination of timing, distance, leverage, and speed, and began to score knockouts over some of the toughest lightweights who ever lived. Leonard had taken the science of pugilism to a level not seen before. Historians consistently rank him among the 10 greatest fighters, pound for pound, of all time.

Who was this man who brought a ballet-like grace to the sport? He didn't even look like a fighter. His face was unmarked, and his body, not particularly muscular. He was really a nice Jewish boy with an extraordinary talent and a driving ambition to be the best at his craft. If you didn't know his true profession you'd think he was an accountant, perhaps a teacher or businessman—the type you could bring home to dinner and introduce to your sister.

Leonard was well-spoken (he once challenged the noted philosopher Bertrand Russell to a debate as to the merits of boxing). He took his responsibility as a representative of the Jewish people seriously, often donating his services to both Jewish and Catholic charitable causes. As noted by author Franklin Foer, Leonard's conduct, in and out of the ring, and his impeccable public image "stood as the refutation of the immigrants' anxiety that boxing would suck their children into a criminal underworld or somehow undermine the very rationale for fleeing to the Golden Land. Benny Leonard legitimized boxing as an acceptable Jewish pursuit—and even more than that, he helped make sports a perfectly kosher fixation."[21]

Like all great artists Leonard constantly strove for perfection but was never satisfied. When asked by legendary trainer Ray Arcel why he studied four-round preliminary fighters sparring in the gym, Leonard replied, "You can never tell when one of those kids might do something by accident that I can use."[22]

When it was time for his own workout to begin, every fighter in the gym stopped to watch this "professor of pugilism" shadowbox or spar. To sharpen his alertness he would sometimes spar with two boxers at the same time. The day after a fight he'd be back in the gym, talking over tactical mistakes.

"The coordination of mind and muscle was just outstanding," recalled Arcel. "Leonard would feint you into knots. If you were a rough tough fellow he would back you up. If you were a very clever fellow and laid back waiting to counterpunch, he would draw you in, make you lead, and then have you fall short with your punches and counter. Leonard was a student of the human body. He was a place puncher who knew just where to hit you. A left hook to the liver was his favorite punch. He moved with terrific speed, in and out, in and out, side to side, and if you weren't in perfect condition you'd be pretty tired after that first round and he would be just starting in."

Benjamin Leiner was born on April 7, 1896, in a tenement on New York's Lower East Side. His parents, Minnie and Gershon Leiner, were recent immigrants from Russia. Gershon struggled to support a wife and eight children by working 12- to 14-hour days in a garment-trade sweatshop for $20 a week. It was a hardscrabble life.

Benny began his professional boxing career in 1911 at the age of 15. Six years and 116 fights later he won the lightweight championship of the world via a ninth-round TKO of Freddie Welsh. It was the only time Welsh was ever stopped in 168 fights.

Less than two months after defeating Welsh, Leonard knocked out the great featherweight champion, Johnny Kilbane, in the third round. It was only the second KO loss in 122 bouts for Kilbane, who would continue to rule the featherweight division for another six years.

Leonard boasted that no fighter could muss his hair in a fight. (It helped that he plastered down his "patent-leather locks" with an industrial-strength gel that would have held up in a wind tunnel.) When Leo Johnson, the country's outstanding black lightweight contender, attempted to unnerve him by mussing up his hair during a clinch, Leonard responded by knocking Leo out in less than two minutes of the first round. (It was only the second time in some 150 bouts that Leo Johnson was stopped; his other knockout loss had occurred six years earlier against the great Abe Attell.)

During Leonard's tenure as champion his toughest challenger was the great Philadelphia southpaw, Lew Tendler. Their first bout took place in Jersey City. Over 50,000 fans were on hand to witness an intense and dramatic 12-round seesaw battle.

In the eighth round Tendler connected with a right to the body and left hook to the head that caused the champion's knees to sag. Although hurt, Leonard's hair-trigger brain came to the rescue. As Tendler closed in for the kill Leonard spoke to him. It has come down the pike as either "Keep your punches up, Lew," or the same words (or some variation) addressed to Lew in Yiddish. Whatever was said, in whatever language, it was enough to cause Tendler to hesitate for the few seconds Leonard needed to clear his head and recover his equilibrium. The 12-round bout was "no-decision," so there was no official winner or loser. A majority of newspapers covering the match had Leonard winning a close 12-round decision. Several others either named Tendler the winner or scored it a draw.

Benny Leonard and number one challenger Lew Tendler pose for the camera moments before their 1923 title fight in Yankee Stadium. Left to right: "Scootles" Reinfeld (Tendler's trainer), Joe Tiplitz (cornerman), Tendler, Joe Humphries (announcer), Andy Griffin (referee) and Leonard.

Benny Leonard and mother the day after he announced his retirement as undefeated lightweight champion of the world.

The highly anticipated rematch took place on July 22, 1923, in Yankee Stadium, one year after their first meeting. Sixty-three thousand fans witnessed the two great Jewish boxers fight it out for the lightweight championship of the world.

Leonard's exquisite performance that hot July evening was nothing short of astonishing. In their first fight Tendler's awkward southpaw style had disrupted Leonard's rhythm. That was no longer a problem. No matter what the challenger tried—and to his credit, he tried incessantly—he could not land a solid punch on the elusive champion, who seemed to anticipate Tendler's every move. In the last few rounds he absorbed a tremendous pounding but would not go down.

Leonard won a unanimous 15-round decision.

Eighteen months later, on January 15, 1925, Leonard announced his retirement as undefeated champion. He was only 28 years old, but had been a pro for 13 years. Despite having engaged in almost 200 professional fights, his intellect was intact, and he was financially set for life.

True to his public image Leonard told the press that his mother had wanted him to retire, and it was concern for her health that had prompted him to hang up his gloves. A headline in the *New York Times* the following day read, "Leonard Quits Ring on Mother's Plea." Leonard is quoted as saying: "I am retiring from boxing for the love of my mother, who has begged me not to fight again." Photos of Leonard and his mother appeared in newspapers across America with the caption, "Benny Leonard's Ma announces his retirement."

A few days after the announcement, Arthur Brisbane, a nationally syndicated columnist for the Hearst newspaper chain (the largest newspaper chain in the country), wrote a column stating that Benny's reputation as champion and his numerous charitable contributions "did more to conquer anti-Semitism than 1,000 textbooks . . . and has done more to evoke the respect of the non-Jew for the Jew than all the brilliant Jewish writers combined."[23] Whether one agrees with those words or not, they accurately reflect the importance of boxing to the popular culture at that time.

After he retired Leonard kept busy with vaudeville engagements, appearing in plays or acts that combined elements of dancing, sparring exhibitions, and comedy. He also starred in a silent-film serial. Leonard invested some of his ring earnings in commercial enterprises, such as a dry-cleaning business, real estate properties, and a professional hockey team. In the late 1920s he was partner in a summer camp in New York's Catskill Mountains named Camp Hakoah (in Hebrew, "strength") that taught young Jewish boys self-defense.

But everything went sour in 1929 with the collapse of the financial markets and the beginning of the Great Depression. Millions of people lost their life savings, including Leonard, whose personal fortune, heavily invested in stocks and estimated at close to a million dollars, was wiped out.

The former ring great was in dire financial straits. Boxing offered the best opportunity for him to recoup some of his losses. So two years after the market crash, the greatest Jewish boxer who ever lived was back in the ring at the age of 35, sporting an uncharacteristic paunch and a receding hairline. He'd been out of boxing for almost seven years.

From 1931 to 1932 Leonard won 19 fights against handpicked opponents unlikely to derail his comeback. His speed, timing, and coordination began to improve to the point where he would, on occasion, show flashes of his old form. What he was hoping for was one big payday against a name opponent.

The opportunity materialized on October 7, 1932, at Madison Square Garden, almost a year

Benny Leonard
Makes First Appearance In Omaha

Every boxing enthusiast in Omaha has long harbored a desire to see Benny Leonard, who has reigned supreme in the lightweight division for so many years.

There is not a fistic fan in the city but whom admires this clever exponent of the Marquis of Queensbury sport, and it is a marked triumph for the Omaha Orpheum theatre that it has the distinction of being the first to present Leonard—the master of science, the Apollo of the Ring—in Omaha.

Leonard is not only a master boxer, he is a master showman. In his act he has combined such elements of dancing, ring exhibition and comedy as make for continuous entertainment. His traversety prize-fight with Herman Timberg is one of the funniest burlesques in vaudeville.

He will give some helpful hints on reducing for the benefit of women patrons following each matinee.

Orpheum
ORPHEUM CIRCUIT
The only Theatre i Omaha Presenting "The Best in vaudeville"
AT. 9911

WEEK STARTING SUNDAY, DEC. 2

BENNY LEONARD
World's Lightweight Champion

Flyer for one of Benny Leonard's many Vaudeville appearances.

to the day from the start of Leonard's comeback. His opponent was a tartar—the number-one welterweight contender, Jimmy McLarnin, one of the deadliest punchers in the division.

Leonard vs. McLarnin generated tremendous excitement, because Irish Jimmy had already knocked out half a dozen outstanding Jewish fighters. If Leonard could defeat McLarnin he would accomplish the dual goals of payback and payday. A few newspapermen and many fans—thinking more with their hearts than their heads—were of the opinion that the aging ex-champion stood a good chance to outbox McLarnin. Of course, this was wishful thinking. McLarnin was a great fighter in his prime, and only seven months later he would win the welterweight championship of the world with a first-round knockout.

The Garden was packed to the rafters with 19,000 fans, many of them Jewish, who were hoping and praying for a miracle.

Less than two minutes into the fight Leonard's right hand struck "like a serpent's tongue" and made contact with McLarnin's chin. The punch and its setup was vintage Leonard. Stunned momentarily by the punch, McLarnin's knees brushed the canvas. The crowd was in a frenzy. McLarnin was hurt and forced to retreat and clinch. But Leonard at age 36 was too slow to follow up his brief advantage. McLarnin quickly recovered, and by the end of the round had taken charge. He dropped Leonard in the second round and from then on retained the initiative. Only Leonard's superb defensive skills kept him in the fight for the next three rounds.

In the sixth round a series of damaging punches dazed Leonard and had him hanging on. In an act of mercy that no one in the arena objected to, referee Arthur Donovan halted the fight to save Leonard from further punishment. The old champ protested, saying he had not been floored, but Donovan had made the right call.

The $15,000 Leonard received for the McLarnin fight helped to ease his financial problems. The following year he married his longtime secretary, Jacqueline Stern, and settled into married life. In his post-retirement years Benny, an entertaining storyteller, was in great demand as a lecturer and after-dinner speaker. In the mid-1930s he was briefly employed by the City College of New York, where he taught boxing in their physical education department. When the United States entered World War II he enlisted in the Maritime Service and was placed in charge of the physical training of nearly 100,000 men. (He had served in a similar capacity in the army during World War I.) Before his three years of service ended, he rose to the rank of lieutenant commander.

Benny always stayed close to his beloved sport. He was a licensed referee and often officiated in New York and Philadelphia. On April 18, 1947, he was assigned by the New York State Athletic Commission to referee an entire fight card at the St. Nicholas Arena in New York City. During the first round of the last fight of the night, he suddenly collapsed in the ring. The ringside physician, Dr. Vincent Nardiello, attempted to revive him, but to no avail. Benny Leonard had suffered a fatal massive heart attack. He was 51 years old.

For as long as the sport of boxing survives, Benny Leonard will always remain the Gold Standard to which all other Jewish boxers are compared.

NEWSIES

At the turn of the last century most people in America read a daily newspaper if they wanted to know what was going on in the world. Every major city had at least five or more dailies for sale. Newsboys, some as young as five or six, could earn change by hawking the papers on street corners. Old movies often featured a realistic scene of a newsboy shouting "Extra, extra, read all about it!" Most of the "newsies," as they were called, were school truants, and all were born into poverty. Times were tough, but so were the street urchins who sold their employer's newspapers. Bullies looking to take over a smaller boy's "territory" were a constant threat. Knowing how to fight was a useful survival tool. Thousands of future professional boxers first put up their dukes in defense of their prized street corners. No wonder many of them sported the nickname "Newsboy."

Competition among newspapers in the same city was intense. Owners were known to hire "sluggers" (aka, "head breakers") armed with blackjacks to take over the most lucrative corners from the competition. Older boys banded together and stood their ground against the sluggers, fighting back with fists, bricks, and whatever else was at hand.

Around 1905 someone got the idea to stage an amateur boxing tournament featuring the best of the newsboy fighters. The newsboy tournaments became an annual event in several cities, and lasted into the 1920s. In Philadelphia the bouts were usually the opening act at burlesque houses and were very popular with audiences. The newsies were paid just pennies for their efforts.

The first New York City tournament culminated in the crowning of an "American Newsboy Champion." Future Jewish lightweight contenders Harry Stone and Lew Tendler were among the first tournament winners.[24]

4 p.m. Group of Newsies ready for work are photographed in front of South Station, Boston, January 1917. (Library of Congress/Photograph by Lewis Wickes Hine)

(Courtesy of Corey Lavinsky)

BATTLING LEVINSKY

(Barney Lebrowitz)
Born: June 10, 1891
Died: February 12, 1949 (Age: 57)
Hometown: Philadelphia, Pennsylvania
Height: 5' 11" Weight: 165–180 lbs.
Professional Career: 1906–1922, 1926–1930

Total Bouts	Won	Lost	Draw	ND
289 (2,558 rounds)	71 (31 by KO)	19 (4 by KO)	14	126-34-25

Barney Lebrowitz's all-consuming desire to become a professional fighter was tempered by the knowledge that his Russian-born immigrant parents would be greatly distressed if they knew of his career choice. So when Barney turned pro in 1906, at the age of 15, he adopted the name "Barney Williams."

Barney knew that if he came home with a black eye or broken nose his parents might suspect the worst, so he made it his business to perfect his defense. He spent countless hours in Philadelphia gyms studying the defensive maneuvers of master boxers Jack Blackburn, Harry Lewis, and Philadelphia Jack O'Brien.

With these great fighters as his mentors, Barney learned how to use his footwork for both offense and defense. He also learned how to smother an opponent's punches by maneuvering inside or to blunt an assault with a vise-like clinch. The young fighter became adept at "riding" with punches to lessen their full effect. Barney eventually mastered the finer points of his art as few have, and developed into a very clever but unexciting boxer.

Seven years into his career Barney acquired a new manager, the very capable "Dumb" Dan Morgan. The dapper manager was anything but dumb. In fact, he was one of the shrewdest managers in the business. Aside from his sharp negotiating skills, Morgan was a master publicist. The ink was barely dry on their contract when he insisted that his new meal ticket change his fighting name to the more colorful "**Battling Levinsky.**" Morgan then sent out press releases to hundreds of newspapers challenging every Irish contender east of the Mississippi to step into the ring with his Jewish tiger.

The strategy worked. Offers began flooding Morgan's office. Within a very short time Levinsky became one of the world's busiest fighters.

His official record lists a total of 288 fights, but a more-accurate number would fall somewhere between 300 and 400 contests.

One story in particular captures the unique quality of Levinsky's over-the-top ring activity. On a rare night off, the Battler decided to attend a Broadway show with a date. Just as the curtain was about to go up, his manager appeared and told him he was needed over at St. Nick's arena, a few blocks from the theater, to sub for another fighter who failed to show. After telling the young lady he would be right back and not to worry, he dashed over to St. Nick's, changed into his ring togs, and proceeded to flatten his opponent in the second round. The second act of the show was still in progress when he arrived back at the theater to take his seat.[25]

Although he was a light heavyweight who rarely tipped the scales over 180 pounds, he often crossed gloves with the top heavyweight contenders. He more than held his own with Gunboat Smith (six times), Bill Brennan (four times), Fireman Jim Flynn, and Billy Miske. Levinsky's superlative defensive skills made him almost impossible to knock out.

The highlight of his long career occurred in Boston on October 24, 1916, when the 25-year-old boxer won the light-heavyweight championship of the world by outpointing Jack Dillon over 12 rounds. Levinsky was already quite familiar with Dillon's style—it was their 10th meeting!

Levinsky remained champion for the next four years. The shrewd Morgan would only have him risk his title in no-decision fights, so the only way he could be dethroned was by knockout. His toughest bouts were six no-decision encounters with the famed "Pittsburgh Windmill" Harry Greb.

In November 1918 Levinsky was knocked out in the third round by future heavyweight champion Jack Dempsey. It was the first knockout defeat suffered by Levinsky in over 250 fights. Three weeks later the Battler was back in the ring, outpointing middleweight contender Leo Houck in a six-round bout.

Levinsky lost the light-heavyweight title in 1920 to France's Georges Carpentier via a fourth-round KO. The quick ending was so unexpected that many people thought the fight had to have been fixed, but the allegations were never substantiated.

The Battler's last major fight was a 12-round decision loss to future heavyweight champion Gene Tunney in 1922. The 31-year-old Levinsky could not match the speed and accuracy of his much younger opponent. The loss convinced him it was time to retire.

Several business reversals forced Levinsky back to the ring four years after his loss to Tunney. He had 40 additional fights, mostly against second-rate opposition. Unfortunately, most of his savings and investments were wiped out in the 1929 stock market crash. Too old to make another comeback, he struggled to support his wife and two young children by working as a real estate agent and as the owner of a boxing gym. During World War II he was a steelworker in a Philadelphia shipyard.

Have gloves, will travel. Battling Levinsky (right) with manager "Dumb Dan Morgan," circa 1914.

In January 1945 the old Battler received a blow that he never recovered from: His 22-year-old son, Stanley, a private in the United States Army, was killed in the Battle of the Bulge.

Barney Lebrowitz, aka, Battling Levinsky, passed away four years later after contracting pneumonia. He was 57 years old.

(Courtesy of PhillyBoxingHistory.com)

GUSSIE LEWIS

(Gus Besterman)
Birth and death dates unknown
Hometown: Philadelphia, Pennsylvania
Weight: 125 lbs.
Professional Career: 1914–1923

Total Bouts	Won	Lost	Draw	ND
85 (535 rounds)	8 (4 by KO)	6 (3 by KO)	1	48-12-10

Gussie Lewis is the younger brother of the great welterweight champion Harry Lewis. He was an outstanding bantamweight contender during the second decade of the twentieth century. Most of his bouts took place in Philadelphia at a time when local law required all prizefights not to exceed six rounds. Only 11 of Lewis's 85 documented bouts were scheduled beyond six rounds. Over the short route he outhustled the likes of Benny Valgar, Dutch Brandt, Joe Tiplitz, Benny Kaufman, and future champion Steve "Kid" Sullivan. Although not a heavy puncher, Gussie was extremely fast and difficult to hit. He retired after a knockout loss to Benny Valgar in 1919, but returned four years later for one more bout.

HARRY LEWIS

(Harry Besterman)
Welterweight Champion: 1908
Born: September 16, 1886
Died: February 22, 1956 (Age: 69)
Hometown: Philadelphia, Pennsylvania
Height: 5' 7" Weight: 147–156 lbs.
Professional Career: 1903–1912

Total Bouts	Won	Lost	Draw	ND	NC
171 (1,167 rounds)	59 (46 by KO)	17 (2 by KO)	6	48-21-18	2

At age 21, **Harry Lewis** was already a veteran of 100 professional fights. He claimed the welterweight title in 1908 after knocking out Frank Mantell in three rounds. Three months later he solidified his claim with a fourth-round knockout of former champion Honey Mellody.

During his drive to the title Harry encountered the best fighters of his era, including future lightweight champion Joe Gans and top contenders Jack Blackburn, Aurelio Herrera, Young Erne, Jimmy Gardner, and Benny Yanger. Unfortunately, one of his earlier fights ended in tragedy when his opponent, Mike Ward, died of a brain injury after being knocked out in the ninth round.

In 1910 Harry traveled to Paris for a fight with New York's welterweight contender Willie Lewis (no relation). Both contests ended in 25-round draws. The Parisians loved the elegant boxing style of the handsome American redhead. In all,

Harry fought 13 times in Paris. He also crossed the English Channel a dozen times to display his talent for British boxing fans. Harry's first fight in London was against another Jewish fighter, the very popular English welterweight champion "Young" Joseph. Harry won by a seventh-round knockout. In his last fight in Paris, Harry was outpointed by future light-heavyweight champion Georges Carpentier.

Harry gave up the welterweight title in 1911 when he could no longer make the 147-pound weight limit. For the next two years he campaigned as a middleweight.

Six months before facing Philadelphia middleweight contender Joe Borrell, Harry was badly injured in an automobile accident. Perhaps his collapse in the ring before the start of the sixth round of his bout with Borrell was related to the accident, and compounded by his opponent's punches.

Harry was rushed to a hospital where doctors diagnosed a blood clot on his brain. He regained consciousness but remained partially paralyzed on his left side. Eventually he recovered enough to obtain a job as a security guard for Gimbels department store in New York City.

Although he is one of the lesser-known Jewish world champions, Harry Lewis was held in very high esteem by his contemporaries. In 1958 boxing historian Nat Fleischer, founder and publisher of *The Ring* magazine, rated him the sixth-greatest welterweight.

TED "KID" LEWIS
(Gershon Mendeloff)
"The Aldgate Sphinx"
Welterweight Champion 1915–1916, 1917–1919
Born: October 28, 1893
Died: October 20, 1970 (Age: 76)
Hometown: London, England
Height: 5' 8½" Weight: 116–166 lbs.
Professional Career: 1909–1929

Total Bouts	Won	Lost	Draw	ND
302 (2,644 rounds)	192 (79 by KO)	32 (6 by KO)	14	40-13-11

Ted "Kid" Lewis established one of the most remarkable records in the annals of the prize ring. Even in an era when many boxers fought two or three times a month, Lewis's schedule of activity was off the charts. He belongs to that small group of iron men who fought over 300 professional bouts. Lewis also holds another distinction: In 1913 he became the first professional fighter to wear a dentist-designed rubber mouthguard (or gumshield). Lewis's action encouraged the acceptance of the mouthguard for all boxing matches throughout the world.

Born Gershon Mendeloff in the Aldgate section of London's East End, the future ring great was one of eight children of an immigrant cabinetmaker. He began his boxing career as a member of the Judean Athletic Club. Inspired by the success of American Jewish welterweight champion Harry Lewis (who appeared over a dozen times in London rings), Gershon decided that Ted "Kid" Lewis would be a better *nom de box* than Gershon "Kid" Mendeloff.

Lewis entered the punch for pay ranks in 1909 at the age of 14, weighing all of 116 pounds. That year he won 16 of 23 fights. The following year he increased his output to 58 professional fights. Over the next two years 72 fights were added to his résumé, for a grand total of 153 fights in just four years! This incredible pace would continue for the balance of his career.

His nickname, "The Aldgate Sphinx," referred to his tough London neighborhood and, in the words of boxing historian Mike Casey, "the quite terrifyingly impassive expression he carried into battle. Like the eyes of the shark, those menacing peepers of Ted's were emotionally dead yet vibrantly alive in their scope and intelligence."

Five years after turning pro Lewis traveled to America, where he began taking on the best fighters in both the lightweight and welterweight divisions. He was a tireless, extremely aggressive perpetual punching machine whose exciting style and engaging personality endeared him to American boxing fans. The British papers called him "The Smashing, Dashing, Crashing Kid"—which pretty much sums up the way he fought.

On August 31, 1915, in Boston, Lewis became the first British boxer to win a world title in America when he outpointed the great Jack Britton in 12 rounds to capture the welterweight championship. Lewis was two months shy of his twentieth birthday but was already a veteran of 150 professional fights.

His first tenure as champion lasted just four months. In a rematch at the same Boston venue Britton outpointed Lewis over 20 rounds and won back the title. Over the next two years they fought over a dozen times. All of the bouts were no-decision. On June 25, 1917, in Dayton, Ohio, Lewis regained the title with a 20-round decision. (Ohio did not adhere to the no-decision rule.) It was their fourth meeting in five weeks. Promoters across the country were now advertising the series as English/Jewish (Lewis) vs. Irish/Catholic (Britton). The rivalry was accentuated when Britton labeled Lewis a dirty fighter and refused to shake his hand before the opening bell.

Jack Britton and Ted "Kid" Lewis are forever paired in boxing lore. The two great champions met a total of 20 times over six years. They fought so many times the Englishman's corner could no longer yell out advice in Yiddish, since Britton had learned all the phrases![26]

Every one of their bouts was a crowd-pleaser. Britton was a classic stand-up boxer. His educated left jab and superb defensive maneuvers earned him a reputation as one of the finest boxers of his era. Oddly enough it was a style that was more English than American. Ted, on the other hand, fought in a style that was more American than English, as he emphasized an aggressive nonstop offense that endeared him to stateside fans.

The Britton vs. Lewis series reached its climax on March 17, 1919. In the only one of their fights to end in a knockout, Britton stopped Lewis in the ninth round and regained the title. The result puzzled many aficionados. Britton was a light puncher, and it was Lewis who had scored the only knockdowns in their previous bouts. It was later revealed that Lewis was still recovering from a flu-type illness and was in a weakened

Three legends get together in 1967. Left to right, Ted "Kid" Lewis, Richard Burton and Jackie "Kid" Berg.

state when he fought Britton. The final tally had Britton winning four, Lewis three, with 12 no-decisions and one draw.

Aside from his world welterweight title Lewis won nine British and European championships from featherweight to light heavyweight. At one point he held the British welterweight, middleweight, and light-heavyweight titles simultaneously despite rarely weighing more than 145 pounds. He thought nothing of conceding 20 or more pounds or venturing into an opponent's home turf. In addition to Jack Britton, his top opponents included Benny Leonard, Willie Ritchie, Mike O'Dowd, Soldier Bartfield, Brian Downey, Mike Gibbons, Joe Mandot, Italian Joe Gans, Tommy Robson, Georges Carpentier, and "Slapsie Maxie" Rosenbloom.

The indefatigable boxer was well past his prime when he finally decided to retire in 1929 at the age of 35. But he ended his career on a winning note by knocking out old rival Johnny Basham in the third round. The win was just icing on the cake. Lewis had long since earned a reputation as one of the greatest fighters of all time, and in the opinion of many experts, he is the best fighter the British Isles have ever produced.

MARATHON MEN

Of the tens of thousands of professional boxers from 1892 to the present, only 120 of them fought more than 200 times.[27] This remarkable group of athletes includes 11 Jewish boxers, eight of whom turned pro prior to 1920. Harry Stone (222 bouts) and Benny Valgar (215 bouts) are the only two boxers in the history of the sport with more than 200 bouts to have never been knocked out or stopped.

Only 16 fighters have ever fought an astounding 300 or more documented professional fights. England's Ted "Kid" Lewis is the one Jewish fighter in that exclusive club, with "Slapsie Maxie" Rosenbloom just missing, with 297 fights. (The names of Jewish fighters with more than 200 bouts appear in the appendix.)

LOUISIANA
(Joseph Biderberg)
Born: November 18, 1891
Died: August 1965 (age 73)
Hometown: Philadelphia, Pennsylvania
Height: 5' 5" Weight: 116–128 lbs.
Professional Career: 1907–1921

Total Bouts	Won	Lost	Draw	ND	NC
124 (918 rounds)	11 (5 by KO)	10 (2 by KO)	6	45-28-23	1

Why a Jewish fighter who was born and bred in Philadelphia would take as his fighting name the state of Louisiana remains a mystery. But aside from his odd but colorful *nom de box*, Joseph Biderberg, aka, **"Louisiana,"** was a legitimate world-class boxer. Within three years of turning pro he was competing on even terms with future bantamweight champions Kid Williams, Joe Lynch, Pete Herman, and Monte Attell. Louisiana was fast, clever, and extremely durable. He was stopped just twice in 124 professional bouts. Over the next 11 years, until his retirement in 1921, he added 95 additional fights to his résumé, and was never knocked out. He constantly took on the toughest featherweight and lightweight fighters of his era, and in his prime crossed gloves with such outstanding ring men as Lew Tendler, Willie Jackson, Eddie O'Keefe, Dutch Brandt, Frankie Burns, Eddie Campi, and Sid Smith. Louisiana appeared in the state for which he was named just three times. In one of those fights he lost a 20-round decision to New Orleans's favorite son, Pete Herman, considered by experts to be one of the greatest bantamweight champions of all time.

ALF MANSFIELD

Birth and death dates unknown
Hometown: London, England
Weight: 118 lbs.
Professional Career: 1910–1920

Total Bouts	Won	Lost	Draw	ND	NC
135 (1,159 rounds)	47 (9 by KO)	52 (14 by KO)	22	5-3-4	2

Bantamweight **Alf Mansfield** crammed 135 bouts into a 10-year boxing career. During his prime he fought competitively against some of the best flyweights and bantamweights in England and America. He lasted the 15-round limit in two bouts with the great flyweight champion Jimmy Wilde, considered by most historians to be the hardest puncher the division has ever known.

In 1916 Alf traveled to America where he crossed gloves with ace featherweight contenders Abe Friedman, Johnny Ertle, Gussie Lewis, Young Diggins, and bantamweight champion Kid Williams (non-title). One year before he retired Alf met flyweight champion Jimmy Wilde for the third time (non-title), and was stopped by "The Mighty Atom" in the 13th round.

Mansfield was forced to hang up his gloves due to failing vision. The condition worsened and he eventually went blind. After he retired Mansfield earned a living by selling embrocation (ointments and salves) to arthritis sufferers.

BLINK MCCLOSKEY

(Louis Silverman)
Birth and death dates unknown
Hometown: Philadelphia, Pennsylvania
Weight: 145–170 lbs.
Professional Career: 1902–1921

Total Bouts	Won	Lost	Draw	ND	NC
132 (1,146 rounds)	32 (9 by KO)	41 (18 by KO)	20	11-13-13	2

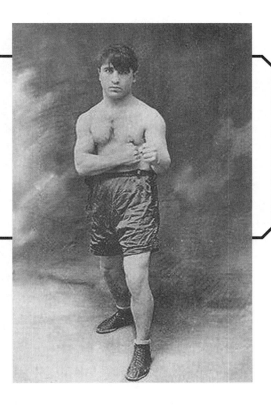

Blink McCloskey's career is one of the strangest in the annals of boxing history. It would not have been possible in an era of more-stringent medical exams, but was not unusual during a period of lax oversight by whatever boxing authorities (or lack thereof) existed at the time. At some point McCloskey lost the sight in one of his eyes. He refused to retire, instead opting for a cosmetic procedure that removed the damaged orb and replaced it with a prosthetic eye made of glass. Of course he could not fight with a glass eye, so before the bell rang to begin every bout, he carefully removed the eye and handed it over to his corner man for safekeeping—ergo, his nickname, "Blink."

Blink was not alone in his desire to continue fighting despite this severe handicap. Many other fighters have continued to box despite eye injuries sustained in the ring. The most famous examples are Sam Langford and Harry Greb. Both of these great fighters lost sight in an eye, yet fought for many years thereafter. (Nearing the end of his 24-year boxing career, Langford, one of the greatest fighters who ever lived, had only partial vision in one eye and was totally blind in the other. He only quit when it became obvious he could no longer see his opponents.) It is a sad fact that brain damage and blindness are the two most common occupational hazards for the professional boxer.

Louis Silverman (Blink's real name) began his pro career in 1902. He had about 80 fights in American rings before becoming a world traveler. Between 1909 and 1921 Blink fought overseas some 50 times, most often in England and France, with occasional appearances in Antwerp, Milan, Rotterdam, Tunis, Algiers, and Alexandria. He once traveled to Madrid to fight exiled heavyweight champion Jack Johnson. (After six rounds, McCloskey did not come out for the seventh, claiming an injury to his right hand.) Other top fighters he traded punches with included Jack Blackburn, Harry Lewis, The Dixie Kid, Willie

Fitzgerald, George "Elbows" McFadden, Joe Borrell, and Georges Carpentier.

In 1912 McCloskey fought a scheduled 15-round bout in Paris against American light-heavyweight Bob Scanlon and was knocked out in the eighth round. The *New York Times* reported that he was unconscious for half an hour. Blink took four months off before entering the ring again for a six-round no-decision bout with Jack McCarron. Two months after that he fought a 10-round no-decision bout with hard-punching middleweight contender, Willie "KO" Brennan. His weight could vary by as much as 20 pounds, but in or out of shape, Blink was always ready for another payday.

McCloskey finally hung up his gloves in 1921 after a 19-year career that encompassed at least 132 professional bouts. His name reappeared in the news two years later when the *New York Times* reported that he was training an Egyptian prince for a fight with heavyweight champion Jack Dempsey. The prince offered to bet $100,000 that Dempsey could not knock him out. According to the article the boxer had been training secretly for two months under Blink's direction in the prince's luxurious apartment on the Champs-Élysées in Paris. McCloskey told the reporter, "The Prince has developed a right-hand blow which he calls the 'pyramid punch.' This blow lands with the force of a falling pyramid and knocks a rival stiffer than a sphinx." Of course the bout never took place, and no one knows what became of the prince.

AL MCCOY
(Alexander Rudolph)
Middleweight Champion 1914–1917
Born: October 23, 1894
Died: August 22, 1966 (Age: 71)
Hometown: Brooklyn, New York
Height: 5' 8" Weight: 145–162 lbs.
Professional Record: 1910–1920, 1923–1924

Total Bouts	Won	Lost	Draw	ND
155 (1,182 rounds)	31 (27 by KO)	12 (4 by KO)	6	41-38-27

Al McCoy (left) with his trainer Charley Goldman.

Alex Rudolph turned pro in 1908 at the tender age of 14. The youngster changed his last name to **McCoy** to keep his parents from learning about his new avocation. The secret didn't last long. When his father, a kosher butcher, found out, he forbade his son from ever boxing again. Al's response was to run away from home. Over the next four years he had 90 professional bouts.

On April 6, 1914, McCoy, a 4–1 underdog, knocked out George Chip in the first round to win the middleweight championship of the world. Not only was the 19-year-old the youngest middleweight champion, he was also the first southpaw to hold a world title.

The new champion put his title on the line many times against top contenders, but always in jurisdictions that only allowed no-decision bouts, so the only way he could lose the title was by a knockout. In at least half a dozen of these fights his opponents were judged to have outpointed him according to newspaper reports. As a result sportswriters began referring to McCoy as a "cheese champion." In one of those fights the great Harry Greb gave him an awful pasting while trying desperately to win by a knockout. Greb couldn't do it, and Al retained his title.

McCoy possessed a world-class chin. He had over 100 fights before anyone was able to knock him out. Although his boxing skills were often denigrated, he was good enough to earn draw decisions with future light-heavyweight champion Jack Dillon and welterweight contender Soldier Bartfield. He also outpointed quality middleweights Willie Lewis, Italian Joe Gans, and Joe Borrell.

But the wear and tear of so many fights against top competition in such a short span of time took its toll on the young fighter, and was a factor in his loss of the title to Mike O'Dowd in 1917. O'Dowd dropped McCoy five times before finally putting him out for the full count in the sixth round. It was McCoy's third knockout loss in 147 fights.

Al McCoy did not deserve the label of "cheese champ." He stood up to the toughest fighters of his era and gave his all every time.

(Courtesy of PhillyBoxingHistory.com)

EDDIE O'KEEFE

(Morris Edward Paley)
Born: January 23, 1891
Died: September 26, 1963 (Age: 72)
Hometown: Philadelphia, Pennsylvania
Weight: 125–133 lbs.
Professional Career: 1908–1920, 1921

Total Bouts	Won	Lost	Draw	ND
127 (871 rounds)	17 (14 by KO)	14 (9 by KO)	1	63-19-13

Eddie O'Keefe (né Morris Edward Paley) was one of several outstanding Philadelphia Jewish boxers who adopted Irish names. Brother Ben also fought professionally using the Irish pseudonym "Barney Ford."

In 1911 Eddie fought a 10-round draw with the great bantamweight champion Johnny Coulon. That fight established his credentials as a serious contender. Showing that he was no flash in the pan, Eddie fought two subsequent non-title bouts with undisputed featherweight kingpin Johnny Kilbane. Both bouts—ten and 12 rounds—went the distance. In the rubber match a year later Kilbane won by a first-round knockout.

Other notable bouts for O'Keefe included newspaper decisions over contenders Harry Forbes, Lew Tendler, Dutch Brandt, Jackie "Kid" Wolfe, and former bantamweight champion Kid Williams. In the final bout of his career he was stopped by future featherweight champion Benny Bass.

After retiring Eddie took a job as a physical training instructor at Philadelphia's Locust Club. He then served as a boxing coach at the fashionable Tome School at Port Deposit, Maryland. After several years Eddie left Maryland and returned to Philadelphia, where he opened a tavern.

YOUNG OTTO

(Arthur Susskind)
Born: October 12, 1886
Died: March 10, 1967 (Age: 80)
Hometown: New York, New York
Height: 5' 6" Weight: 135 lbs.
Professional Career: 1903–1919, 1922–1924

Total Bouts	Won	Lost	Draw	ND
156 (872 rounds)	71 (51 by KO)	13 (5 by KO)	3	40-19-10

At the opening bell **Young Otto** would storm out of his corner intent on flattening his opponent before the first round ended. He was quite successful in this regard. In 171 career bouts Otto knocked out 42 opponents in the first round. But this amazing record is misleading. Most of his KO victims were obscure nonentities who were never heard from again. In 1908 Otto stepped up the level of his competition, which resulted in only three knockouts in 11 fights.

On January 21, 1909, a standing-room-only crowd of over 3,000 excited fans crammed into the Bronx's Fairmont Athletic Club to watch the young KO artist take on top-ranked lightweight contender Leach Cross.

Otto entered the ring with a record of 48 knockouts (28 in the first round) in 85 bouts. Leach had 50 fights and only eight knockouts, but his level of competition was far superior to Otto's.

Showing respect for his more-experienced opponent, Otto did not go for the quick kill. He boxed cautiously and kept the action at long range while looking for an opening to land his haymaker. In the fifth round Leach turned up the heat and dropped Otto with a right cross to the jaw. He staggered to his feet at the count of eight, but was dropped again by two more rights and took the full count.

Three months later Otto traveled to London where he lost a 20-round decision to Young Joseph, one of England's top Jewish lightweights. Other quality boxers Otto faced were Leo Houck, Unk Russell, Westside Jimmy Duffy, Joe Fox, and future middleweight champion Al McCoy.

In the 1930s Otto was appointed head coach for New York's Inter-City Golden Gloves squads. He was also a licensed referee and boxing judge in New York for over 20 years.

JEWISH OLYMPIANS

In 1904 Sam Berger became the first heavyweight champion of the modern Olympic Games.

The modern Olympic Games were revived in 1896 after a 1,500-year-hiatus. Boxing, a staple of the ancient games, made its modern debut in 1904 as part of the St. Louis World's Fair. Except for 1912, the sport has been featured in every Olympic Games since then. Sam Berger, a 6' 3", 200-pound amateur from San Francisco, won the gold medal in 1904, thus becoming the first heavyweight champion of the modern Games, and the first of seven Jewish boxers to win an Olympic gold medal. Sixteen-year-old Jackie Fields (Jacob Finkelstein), the 1924 champion, was the youngest boxer to ever win a gold medal, and is the only Jewish Olympic champion to later win a professional title.

The Olympic Games were not held during the war years of 1916, 1940, and 1944. Since 1948, the Games have been staged in different countries every four years.

Between 1960 and 1980, three Jewish gold medal winners hailed from Soviet Bloc countries. It is believed there may have been other Jewish medalists from the Soviet Union who purposely kept their religious background hidden because of the anti-Semitic policies of the Soviet government. (The names of thirteen Jewish boxers who won an Olympic medal appear in the appendix.)

JOHNNY RAY

(Harold Pitler)
Born: September 14, 1896
Died: July 16, 1961 (Age: 64)
Hometown: Pittsburgh, Pennsylvania
Height: 5' 7" Weight: 125–138 lbs.
Professional Career: 1913–1924

Total Bouts	Won	Lost	Draw	ND	NC
138 (983 rounds)	16 (14 by KO)	3	4	63-31-19	2

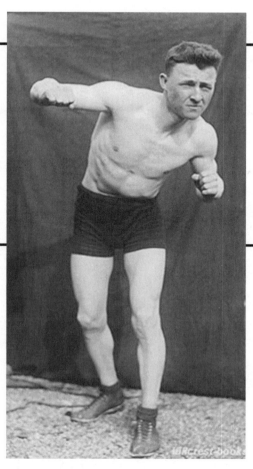

(Courtesy of Douglas Cavanaugh)

Before he turned pro in 1913, Harry Pitler's manager, Red Mason, suggested he could improve his box-office appeal by adopting an Irish name. So young Harry decided to combine the names of a popular vaudeville team he enjoyed, Johnny and Emma Ray. He retained the name **"Johnny Ray"** for the rest of his life.

In the years following his service with the US Navy in World War I, Johnny Ray established a reputation as an outstanding contender and one of the best lightweight boxers to ever come out of Pittsburgh. He was a stablemate of the great middleweight champion Harry Greb ("The Pittsburgh Windmill"), and often fought on the same cards with Greb.

Ray had 138 documented bouts and was never knocked out. At five-foot-seven, he was taller than most of his opponents, and made good use of his height and reach advantages.

After he retired in 1924 Ray became a successful manager and trainer. His most famous pupil was the great light-heavyweight champion Billy Conn, who ruled the division from 1939 to 1941. Conn came very close to upsetting heavyweight champion Joe Louis before taking the count in the 13th round. Ahead on points after 12 rounds, Conn made the fatal mistake of trying to knock out Louis after hurting him in the previous round. Instead of playing it safe against the always-dangerous Louis and settling for a decision victory, he went on the offensive and was caught by a series of devastating punches, thus ending one of the greatest heavyweight championship contests of all time. In his dressing room after the fight Conn explained his audacious behavior: "What's the use of being Irish if you can't be thick?" His trainer's quote: "If Billy had a Jewish head instead of an Irish one, he'd be the champ."[28]

In the 1950s Ray became matchmaker at Detroit's Motor Square Arena. His brother, Jake Pitler, was a former professional baseball player and a longtime member of the Brooklyn Dodgers' coaching staff.

JOHNNY ROSNER

Born: June 18, 1895
Died: Unknown
Hometown: New York
Height: 5' 0" **Weight:** 109 lbs.
Professional Career: 1909–1923

Total Bouts	Won	Lost	Draw	ND	NC
102 (864 rounds)	14 (10 by KO)	11 (3 by KO)	1	12-20-6	38

On April 24, 1916, **Johnny Rosner** became the first American to challenge for the world's flyweight title when he traveled to Liverpool, England, for a 20-round bout with the great Jimmy Wilde. Nicknamed "The Mighty Atom" because of his explosive power (he scored 98 knockouts), Wilde is still considered by many experts to be the greatest flyweight champion of all time.

In a torrid seesaw battle Rosner suffered a cut to his eyelid in the 11th round. If the cut worsened he risked permanent damage to his sight. Eugene Corri, the most respected referee in Europe, correctly stopped the action and awarded the bout to Wilde. Although bitterly disappointed, Rosner was gracious in defeat. The British fans cheered his sportsmanship and gave him a rousing ovation. Rosner's end of the purse came to $2,800, the largest of his career.

Following his return to America Rosner won a 12-round decision over Young Montreal (Morris Billingkoff). Six days later he appeared in Philadelphia for a six-round no-decision bout with Al Murray. The very next day Rosner faced Young Zulu Kid (Giuseppe Di Melfi) for the American flyweight title. It was the seventh meeting between these two miniature maulers. While all of their previous encounters had gone the distance, this time Rosner won by a seventh-round TKO.

In addition to Wilde, Rosner boxed the greatest flyweight and bantamweight boxers of his era, including Johnny Buff, Pete Herman, Young Montreal, Abe "Kid" Goodman, Young Zulu Kid, Frankie Mason, Battling Murray, and future flyweight champion Frankie Genaro. He retired in 1923 after losing a 10-round decision to Genaro.

YANKEE SCHWARTZ

(Julius Schwartz)
Born: 1889
Died: 1957 (Age: 68)
Hometown: Philadelphia, Pennsylvania
Weight: 125–135 lbs.
Professional Career: 1905–1914

Total Bouts	Won	Lost	Draw	ND
154 (1,000 rounds)	20 (4 by KO)	10 (2 by KO)	10	69-23-22

Julius "Yankee" Schwartz was born in Russia and emigrated to the United States with his family in the early 1890s. In 1905 he accompanied his father, a jewelry merchant, on a trip to South Africa's diamond market. Julius stayed in South Africa for almost three years. At some point he began boxing in Cape Town, where he fought at least eight preliminary bouts. Locals dubbed him "Yankee," and the nickname stuck.

In 1907 Yankee returned to Philadelphia and continued with his boxing career. He was mentored by future ring great Jack Britton, so it is not surprising that newspaper reports of his fights describe graceful footwork, clever feints, and an educated left jab—all hallmarks of the Britton style of boxing.

In only his 31st pro bout Yankee fought a six-round no-decision scrap with the great bantamweight champion Johnny Coulon. One of two newspapers covering the bout gave the decision to Schwartz. Yankee also won unofficial newspaper verdicts over Patsy Brannigan, Willie Houck, and future lightweight champion Freddie Welsh. He came away with mixed results in a series of bouts against Pal Moore, Joe Mandot, and Jake Abel—all top-rated boxers.

By 1912 Yankee had outgrown the 125-pound division and was now fighting as a lightweight. But his chance to fight for the 135-pound title was thwarted when future champion Willie Ritchie knocked him out in the second round. It was only Yankee's second knockout loss in 153 professional bouts. He retired two years later.

JEWEY SMITH
(Joseph Smith)
Heavyweight
Born: January 7, 1884
Died: Unknown
Height: 5' 8½" Weight: 185 lbs.
Hometown: London, England
Professional Career: 1908–1913

Total Bouts	Won	Lost	Draw	ND	NC
58 (458 rounds)	28 (9 by KO)	21 (11 by KO)	3	3-2	1

Jewey Smith, a former sailor in the Royal Navy, was the first Jewish boxer of the Queensberry era to challenge for the heavyweight championship. That historic distinction earns him a place in this compendium. On April 4, 1908, in London, Smith challenged heavyweight champion Tommy Burns and was knocked out in the fifth round.

Many of Smith's early fights have not been documented. What is available shows that he did not have a winning record against the top fighters of his era (he was knocked out by Sam McVea, Joe Jeanette, and Willie Lewis), but performed credibly against second-tier competition. His best performance was a 20-round decision over England's Iron Hague, after which he claimed the British heavyweight title. He subsequently lost to Hague in two return bouts. In 1911 Smith traveled to America and engaged in a series of bouts before returning to England, where he finished out his career.

SAMMY SMITH

(Sam Rosetzky)
Birth and death dates unknown
Hometown: Philadelphia, Pennsylvania
Weight: 135–145 lbs.
Professional Career: 1899–1919

Total Bouts	Won	Lost	Draw	ND	NC
157 (898 rounds)	18 (10 by KO)	9 (5 by KO)	2	62-38-27	3

Over the course of his 20-year career Philadelphia's **Sammy Smith** swapped punches with world champions Joe Gans, Harry Lewis, Young Corbett II, and Dave Rosenberg. He fought in both the lightweight and welterweight divisions. Joe Gans, one of the greatest lightweight fighters who ever lived, was one of only two fighters able to stop Smith during his prime. Other notable opponents included Joe Bernstein, Leach Cross, Harlem Tommy Murphy, Patsy Haley, and Young Otto.

Sammy is the older brother of "Young Sammy Smith" (Isaac Rosetzky), a popular welterweight contender who was active between 1908 and 1913. The Smith brothers were among Philadelphia's first Jewish boxing stars.

(Courtesy of PhillyBoxingHistory.com)

SID SMITH

World Flyweight Champion 1913
Born: February 2, 1889
Died: April 2 1948 (Age: 59)
Hometown: London, England
Height: 5' 4" Weight: 112 lbs.
Professional Career: 1907–1919

Total Bouts	Won	Lost	Draw	ND
108 (1,026 rounds)	84 (11 by KO)	16 (8 by KO)	7	0-1

In 1911, only two years after turning pro, **Sid Smith** won the British Empire flyweight title and successfully defended it twice. Two years later he won a 20-round decision over France's Eugène Criqui to win the world flyweight championship (weight limit, 112 pounds) as recognized by Great Britain and the International Boxing Union. (At the time there was no flyweight division in the United States.) Less than seven weeks after defeating Criqui, Smith lost the title to Bill Ladbury via an 11th-round TKO.

Smith's nemesis was the great "Mighty Atom," Jimmy Wilde. Smith was stopped three times by the dynamic little Welshman. Their last fight occurred nine months before Wilde won the flyweight championship.

After he retired from boxing, Smith was plagued by health problems. For work he would go around guessing people's weight for money.

HARRY STONE

(Henry Siegstein)
Born: March 4, 1889
Died: December 13, 1950 (Age: 61)
Hometown: New York, New York
Height: 5' 7½" Weight: 135–145 lbs.
Professional Career: 1906–1929

Total Bouts	Won	Lost	Draw	ND	NC
219 (3,022 rounds)	81 (17)	47 (0 KOs)	18	38-19-12	4

Harry Stone belongs to a very exclusive club. He is one of only two boxers (the other is Benny Valgar) known to have fought over 200 documented bouts without ever being stopped. Stone is officially credited with 219 bouts, although the actual number is probably much higher. He can also lay claim to another first: Harry was the first boxer to wear a *tallis* (prayer shawl) into a boxing ring.

In 1909, barely three years into his pro career, Harry fought a competitive 10-round no-decision bout (non-title) with the great featherweight champion Abe Attell. Two months later he came up even after 15 rounds with top contender Leach Cross. But his most impressive victory occurred in Australia, where he won a 20-round decision over future welterweight champion Matt Wells.

Harry was tremedously popular with Aussie fans. According to British boxing historian Barry Hugman, Stone was a claimant to the Welterweight Championship of the World between 1914 and 1916. The claim was dismissed on March 1, 1916, after Stone dropped a 20-round decision to the widely recognized welterweight champion Ted "Kid" Lewis in New Orleans. Harry was an experienced boxer and almost impossible to hurt, but he was out of his league against the great Lewis.

After he failed in his bid to win the welterweight championship, Harry returned to Australia.

He remained Down Under for the next 10 years, and had over 100 fights, most of 20 rounds' duration. Harry was a true iron man of the ring. His record shows that he once fought three 20-rounders in one week. In the last two months of his hectic career, at age 40, he fought two 15-round battles just five weeks apart.

After he retired in 1929, Harry decided to make his home in Australia. He married a local girl and remained there for the rest of his life. For many years he owned and operated a garage in Sydney.

IZZY STRAUSS
(Isadore Strauss)
Born: 1872
Died: Unknown
Hometown: Philadelphia, Pennsylvania
Weight: 150–160 lbs.
Professional Career: 1893–1905

Total Bouts	Won	Lost	Draw	ND	NC
64 (331)	13 (8 by KO)	14 (5 by KO)	3	11-11-9	3

Izzy Strauss was Philadelphia's first Jewish boxing star. He turned pro in the early 1890s, and is officially credited with 64 bouts. Izzy fought in both the welterweight and middleweight divisions. He crossed gloves with four future world champions: Philadelphia Jack O'Brien (four times), Joe Gans, Rube Ferns, and Matty Mathews (twice).

Other top opponents included Kid Carter, Owen Ziegler, and Jack Bennett.

Except for an occasional out-of-town appearance, virtually all of Izzy's fights took place in Philadelphia, where he remained a popular attraction until his retirement in 1905.

(Courtesy of PhillyBoxingHistory.com)

JOE TIPLITZ

Born: October 3, 1899
Died: July 21, 1962 (Age: 62)
Hometown: Philadelphia, Pennsylvania
Height: 5' 6" Weight: 133–145 lbs.
Professional Career: 1915–1927

Total Bouts	Won	Lost	Draw	ND	NC
176 (1,272 rounds)	44 (24 by KO)	23 (5 by KO)	4	56-37-10	2

In the vernacular of the boxing trade, Philadelphia's **Joe Tiplitz** "fought 'em all." Numbered among his 177 opponents were world champions Johnny Dundee, Willie Ritchie, Rocky Kansas, Joe Dundee, and top contenders Lew Tendler, Benny Valgar, George KO Chaney, Packy Hommey, and Ritchie Mitchell.

The Russian-born Tiplitz averaged over 15 bouts a year, and went through his first 161 bouts without ever being stopped. But like so many fighters he overstayed his welcome and paid the price for fighting well beyond his prime. In the last few months of his busy career, Tiplitz suffered five knockout losses, the last four in a row.

MATT WELLS

Welterweight Champion 1914–1915
Born: December 14, 1886
Died: July 8, 1953 (Age: 66)
Hometown: London, England
Height: 5' 4" Weight: 133–147 lbs.
Professional Record: 1909–1922

Total Bouts	Won	Lost	Draw	ND	NC
88 (1,045 rounds)	31 (8 by KO)	18 (2 by KO)	3	18-12-1	5

Before **Matt Wells** turned pro he was one of England's finest amateur boxers, winning three consecutive British lightweight titles. He also represented his country in the 1908 Olympic Games, losing a close decision in the lightweight class to the eventual gold medal winner, fellow Englishman Fred Grace.

Wells won 32 of his first 34 pro fights, including 20-round decisions over Owen Moran and Freddie Welsh, two of England's greatest fighters. By defeating Welsh he won both the British and European lightweight title and became the first Jewish fighter to win the prestigious Lonsdale Belt.

Wells made frequent trips to New York where he faced, among others, Leach Cross, Knockout Brown, Packey McFarland, Pal Moore, Charley White, Johnny Dundee, Ted "Kid" Lewis, Johnny Basham, and Phil Bloom. In 1911 he fought the great featherweight champion Abe Attell in a 10-round no decision bout. The following day most newspapers reported Wells the clear winner.

During a tour of Australia in 1914, Wells outpointed welterweight champion Tom McCormick in 20 rounds, thus becoming the second English-born Jewish fighter to win a world title in the twentieth century. (The first was Sid Smith.) 15 months later Wells lost the title on a 12-round decision to Mike Glover in the challenger's hometown of Boston.

Ted "Kid" Lewis and Charley White were the only opponents able to stop him. Both fights occurred near the end of Matt's career. His low knockout ratio (eight KOs in 88 fights) is misleading. It says less about his punching power than it does about the quality of opponents he faced. Matt Wells consistently fought men who were rarely knocked out by anyone.

CHARLEY WHITE
(Charles Anchowitz)
Born: March 25, 1891
Died: July 24, 1959 (Age: 68)
Hometown: Chicago, Illinois
Height: 5' 6" Weight: 133–138 lbs.
Professional Career: 1907–1923, 1930

Total Bouts	Won	Lost	Draw	ND	NC
171 (1,386 rounds)	86 (57 by KO)	16 (4 by KO)	5	34-19-9	2

If anyone deserves the title of "uncrowned champion," it is **Charley White**. In 1914 White dominated lightweight champion Willie Ritchie in a 10-round no-decision bout. Two years later he clearly outpointed Ritchie's successor, Freddie Welsh, in a 20-round bout. Charley's misfortune was to have fought both men in states that adhered to the no-decision rule requiring a knockout to dethrone a world champion.

Charles Anchowitz was born in Liverpool, England, and came to the Jewish ghetto on Chicago's West Side at an early age. In 1906 the 15-year-old changed his last name to White and began a professional boxing career. His brothers, Jack White and Billy Wagner, were also professional fighters.

White's trademark punch, a devastating left hook, knocked out 58 opponents. After sampling his portside wallop, lightweight champion Benny Leonard was nearly blasted out of the ring in the fifth round of their 1920 title bout. But Leonard recovered and flattened White in the ninth round.

The record books reveal that White fought 13 world champions a total of 22 times. Among his 174 opponents were legendary fighters Abe Attell, Freddie Welsh, Johnny Kilbane, Johnny Dundee, Owen Moran, Jack Britton, Ad Wolgast, Ted "Kid" Lewis, Leach Cross, and Benny Leonard—a breathtaking array of all-time greats.

White retired in 1923, but seven years later, at the age of 39, made an ill-advised comeback and was stopped in the second round by Chicago rival Herman Perlick.

After hanging up his gloves White operated a successful gym in Chicago's Loop district, which catered to wealthy women. He subsequently relocated to Los Angeles, where he trained movie stars. In his sixties, the countless punches of 171 professional fights caught up with him. White was diagnosed with dementia pugilistica and committed to a sanitarium.

In 1958 Nat Fleischer, publisher of *The Ring*, ranked Charley White the 10th-greatest lightweight of all time.

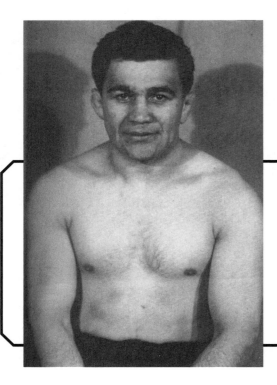

JACKIE "KID" WOLFE

Born: June 11, 1895
Died: April 22, 1976 (Age: 80)
Hometown: Cleveland, Ohio
Height: 5' 2" Weight: 118–125 lbs.
Professional Career: 1911–1925, 1931

Total Bouts	Won	Lost	Draw	ND	NC
111 (1,070 rounds)	25 (5 by KO)	13 (3 by KO)	8	35-13-12	5

The problem for **Jackie "Kid" Wolfe**—as with so many other small boxers of his era—was the huge number of similarly talented bantamweights and featherweights. Jackie fought during a time of fierce competition in the lighter weight divisions. Nevertheless, he was good enough to defeat the likes of Frankie Jerome, Young Montreal, and former bantamweight champion Kid Williams. He is also credited with newspaper decisions over Johnny Ertle, Joe Burman, and bantamweight champion Pete Herman (non-title).

In 1922 Jackie fought former bantamweight champion Joe Lynch for the fourth time. Three previous encounters were closely contested no-decisions bouts. Newspaper verdicts had Wolfe leading the series, two to one. Their final bout was a 15-rounder in New York's Madison Square Garden. This time the contest would be officially scored. The promoter tried to generate interest by advertising the fight as a competition for the "junior featherweight championship of the world"—a new weight division with a limit of 122 pounds.

Jackie won a hard-fought 15-round decision over one of the best bantamweight boxers of the decade, but his title was not recognized by the New York boxing commission, or any other governing body, for that matter. Most fans did not consider the new weight division as legitimate or necessary, since it was only four pounds below featherweight (126 pounds) and four pounds above bantamweight (118 pounds). The "junior featherweight" championship never took off and was soon discarded. But with or without a title, Jackie "Kid" Wolfe's impressive record proved beyond a doubt that he was a championship-caliber boxer.*

---

* Some 50 years later, the "junior featherweight" title would be revived (along with five other unnecessary weight divisions) by a group of corrupt quasi-official boxing organizations in order to extort "sanctioning fees" from boxers competing for the newly manufactured titles.

Heavyweight champion Jack Dempsey was box office gold in the 1920s.

CHAPTER 4

GOLDEN AGE GLADIATORS: 1920–1940

The United States today is the greatest fistic nation in the world, and a close examination of its 4,000 or more fighters shows that the cream of its talent is Jewish.

—BOXING ANNOUNCER JOE HUMPHREYS, 1930

The year 1921 was a watershed year for the sport of boxing, thanks to the efforts of the great promoter, George Lewis "Tex" Rickard, and a superstar heavyweight champion named Jack Dempsey. On July 2, 1921, Rickard staged a heavyweight title bout between Dempsey and challenger Georges Carpentier of France. Carpentier, the light-heavyweight champion of the world, was a debonair Frenchman and World War I hero with movie-star looks.

Jack Dempsey, a steel-hard ex-hobo and mining-camp brawler, was one of the most destructive forces ever seen in a prize ring. He stood a shade over six feet and weighed 187 pounds. "The Manassa Mauler"—named for his birthplace in Manassa, Colorado—was an electrifying presence in or out of the ring. No other athlete of his time so embodied the unsettled nervous energy of the Roaring Twenties.

In his 1960 biography, Dempsey, of Scotch-Irish parentage, claimed a Jewish connection: "I am basically Irish, with Cherokee blood from both parents, plus a Jewish strain from my father's great-grandmother, Rachel Solomon."[1]

If Tex Rickard had known of Dempsey's remote Jewish ancestry, the PR-savvy promoter might have advertised the rugged slugger as a former yeshiva student turned heavyweight boxer. But it wasn't necessary. Dempsey's charisma would carry the day. Rickard added to the excitement by using the press and movie newsreels to fan the flame of public interest into a roaring fire.

On the day of the fight over 90,000 fans—the largest crowd to ever attend a sporting event up until that time—paid their way into a huge monolithic wooden stadium (a structure built especially for the occasion) located on the New Jersey side of the Hudson River.

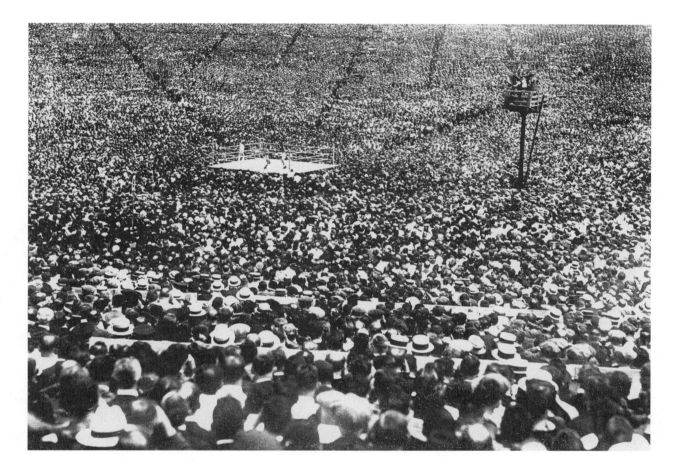

Part of the vast crowd of 90,000 people who witnessed the Dempsey vs. Carpentier heavyweight title fight on July 2, 1921. (Courtesy of Steve Lott/ Boxing Hall of Fame Las Vegas)

Ringside seats went for $50 apiece (the cheapest seats cost $5.50). Telegraph operators seated in the press section transmitted a round-by-round summary of the fight around the world, and for the first time the new medium of radio was used to broadcast a blow-by-blow account of a championship-boxing match. Stars of stage and screen, giants of commerce, mayors, governors, and senators were sprinkled throughout the ringside spectators.

The result of the Dempsey-Carpentier extravaganza (Dempsey flattened the overmatched Frenchman in four rounds) was less important than the significance of the event. For the first time in history a sporting event had drawn over one million dollars in paid admissions ($1,785,000, to be exact). Jack Dempsey was paid $300,000 for less than 12 minutes of work.

Before the decade was over, four more million-dollar gates featuring Dempsey and

Tex Rickard, the world's greatest boxing promoter. (Courtesy of Albert Davis Collection The Stark Center/University of Texas at Austin)

promoted by Rickard would enthrall the entire nation. In two of those fights the live attendance figures exceeded 100,000 persons.

During the 1920s boxing reached unprecedented levels of popularity with the general populace, even eclipsing baseball in terms of live attendance figures and newspaper coverage. Heavyweight title fights became the most lavish and anticipated spectacle in sports. The social, artistic, and cultural dynamism of the Roaring Twenties, in concert with the media's focus on celebrities (especially sports heroes and movie stars), glamorized boxing and made Jack Dempsey the first boxing superstar of the twentieth century. But due credit must be given to the promotional genius of Tex Rickard. Under his watch boxing gained a respectability it had never known before, and was transformed into popular entertainment for a mass audience. The business of sports entertainment would never be the same.

The record-breaking gate receipts of the Dempsey-Carpentier fight convinced other states to reconsider their anti-boxing laws. The realization that substantial tax revenues and other ancillary income could be generated by professional boxing pushed them into the fold. Whereas in 1917 only 23 states had officially legalized the sport, by 1925 the number was up to 43.

Boxing gyms and arenas seemed to pop up everywhere. Much like traveling vaudevillians, professional boxers utilized America's extensive rail system to go from city to city. Most kept to a busy schedule by fighting every two or three

weeks. The constant activity kept them sharp and in fighting trim. There were so many boxing venues, especially in major population centers, that even a lowly bucket carrier could earn a modest living working corners up to six nights a week.

New York City quickly regained its position as the boxing capital of the world. The energy, ambition, and creativity of the world's greatest city found its way into every aspect of the sport. New York had more fighters, trainers, managers, gyms, and arenas than any other metropolis, and it was home to boxing's holiest shrine—Madison Square Garden.

THE WALKER LAW

In 1920, after a three-year moratorium, professional boxing returned to New York State with the passage of the "Walker Law." Under the new law a reorganized State Athletic Commission would be responsible for collecting taxes and issuing licenses to boxers, managers, promoters, matchmakers, corner men, referees, judges, and medical personnel. It also attempted, with mixed results, to curtail gambling and criminal infestation.

Boxers and fans rejoiced when the first edict of the commission was to rescind the state's "no-decision" rule. The new law mandated that the outcome of any bout that did not end in a knockout was to be decided by the scorecards of a referee and two judges. A boxer's ability to outpoint his opponent would now be officially rewarded. Other states followed New York's lead, and by the early 1920s, the no-decision era was history.

The boxing industry also realized the need to create a more-formal system for recognizing world champions. The aforementioned New York State Athletic Commission, the 23 member states of the newly formed National Boxing Association (NBA), and the European Boxing Union were the sport's three main governing bodies. New York, the epicenter of the boxing universe, did not join the NBA, preferring to maintain its independence. California, the second-busiest boxing state, also had a powerful and prestigious boxing commission, and on a few occasions recognized its own world champions.

Although there were occasional disputes, these organizations, more often than not, recognized the same world champions, especially when it came to the sport's most important title—the heavyweight championship.

The champions featured in this section were recognized by at least one or more of these respected organizations, but it should also be noted that possessing a title did not necessarily mean a particular fighter was the best in his weight class. In the various all-time ratings at the back of this book, some boxers who never won a title are placed ahead of some who did. Not every championship-caliber boxer actually won a championship.

A ROBUST SPORT

The 1920s represented the pinnacle of boxing activity in the United States.

New York City's active fight scene reflected the robust health of the sport throughout the rest of the country. As boxing grew in popularity, so did the number of boxers. In 1927 the New York State Athletic Commission issued licenses to 2,000 professional boxers who resided in the Empire State (up from 1,654 in 1925). California issued an equal number of licenses to their resident pro boxers. The two busiest boxing states—New York and California— supervised a combined total of 1,800 boxing promotions. (In 2012 the total number of professional boxers in the United States was less than 3,500, and annual promotions, under 1,000.)[2] By 1932 there were approximately 8,000 licensed professional boxers throughout the world.[3]

THE RATINGS ARRIVE

The first rating system for boxers was started in 1921 by the National Boxing Association. In 1925 *The Ring* magazine began an annual rating of the top 10 fighters for each of nine weight divisions (later expanded to 10 weight divisions). Three years later the magazine switched to a monthly ratings format.

From the 1920s to the 1960s, both *The Ring* and the NBA published separate top-10 contender lists for each weight division. No rating system is perfect, or completely unbiased, but in this time frame the listings of both organizations were considered to be reliable and trustworthy. They were also consistently similar, thereby giving the ratings a semblance of order and legitimacy that is sorely missing today.

IMPACT OF THE GREAT DEPRESSION: 1929–1940

In the 1930s boxing in America suffered economically along with the rest of the country during the Great Depression. Revenues and attendance figures declined. Promoters were forced to drop ticket prices as they struggled to stay in business. At one point Madison Square Garden was charging only 40 cents for balcony seats. Journeymen boxers, often fighting for a percentage of the gate, were barely able to cover travel expenses.

By 1933, 50 percent of Americans between the ages of 15 and 19 were unemployed. Young men with few job prospects entered the prize ring to earn a few dollars and hopefully avoid the relief rolls. In the United States more pro boxers were licensed annually during the 1930s than in any previous decade, but only the champions and leading contenders could make a decent living.

Yet despite the economic hardships the anticipation of a great fight could still draw a huge audience, even in Depression-era America. In the mid-1930s the Barney Ross vs. Jimmy McLarnin welterweight title trilogy drew over 100,000 fans. In 1935 a non-championship heavyweight match between Max Baer and Joe Louis drew 83,000 fans to Yankee Stadium and generated one million dollars in revenue.

While the economy was in decline, boxing's deep well of talent was not. The 1930s produced dozens of all-time great fighters, in addition to hundreds of outstanding contenders. A partial roll call of the decade's finest reveals an astonishing array of super athletes: Joe Louis, Henry Armstrong, Barney Ross, Tony Canzoneri, Jimmy McLarnin, "Slapsie Maxie" Rosenbloom, Charley Burley, Lou Ambers, Billy Conn, Fritzie Zivic, Kid Chocolate, Holman Williams, Jackie "Kid" Berg, John Henry Lewis, Freddie Miller, Tony Zale, Benny Lynch, Freddie Steele, and Panama Al Brown, just to name a few.

GAMBLERS AND GANGSTERS

The professional boxing industry has always been fertile territory for exploitation by professional gamblers because of the ease with which a fight could be fixed by either influencing one of the contestants or bribing a referee or judge. During the Prohibition Era (1920–1933) mobsters were usually too busy making tons of money from illegal booze to become overly involved with boxing. Managing a fighter, like owning a racehorse, was a glamorous and lucrative sideline activity. Fixing the occasional boxing match or horse race came with the territory.

With the repeal of Prohibition in 1933, Mob interest in big-time boxing accelerated as new sources of income were sought. The syndicate's greatest coup was their taking control of the giant Italian heavyweight, Primo Carnera. Most boxing historians believe Carnera won the heavyweight championship in a fixed fight against Jack Sharkey in 1933. Nonetheless, fixed fights, although not uncommon, were the exception rather than the rule. Most of the thousands of professional bouts that took place every year were fought on the level.

It is no coincidence that the Golden Age of the Jewish boxer in America coincided with the Golden Age of the Jewish gangster. Both came from the same gritty rough-and-tumble city streets, and their worlds often intersected. In 1921 Jews represented 14 percent of New York State's prison inmate population. By 1940, the figure had dropped to 7 percent. Jewish juvenile delinquency rates paralleled these trends, declining from 21 percent of all juveniles arraigned in 1922 to 8 percent in 1940. Women were also not immune to the consequences of poverty. In 1910, Jewish women accounted for 20 percent of all female prisoners in New York State. Thirty years later the number was down to 4 percent.[4]

The declining rates of criminality among the Jewish populations of New York, Chicago, Philadelphia, and other major urban centers indicated steadily improving social and economic trends. But as long as boxing remained lucrative, criminal infiltration would remain a part of the industry's subculture, no matter what ethnic groups were involved. Jewish mobsters such as Waxey Gordon, Arnold Rothstein, Dutch Schultz, and Max "Boo Boo" Hoff operated as undercover managers, since their criminal records disqualified them from obtaining a legitimate manager's license. Their connections could help a promising boxer by securing important bouts that would advance his career—but they could also order the boxer under their control to throw a fight. Little was done to thwart underworld influence. Ineffective state boxing commissions, mostly staffed by political hacks and bureaucratic ciphers, rarely made any attempt to clean up the sport.

While the tough ghetto neighborhoods were breeding grounds for both Jewish boxers and Jewish criminals seeking ways to earn quick money, it did not mean they were one and the same. They were not. While only a small proportion of the total number of poverty-stricken inner-city Jewish youth became professional boxers, an even tinier fraction turned to a life of crime. It was no different for Irish-, Italian-, Greek-, Polish-, and African-American boxers. The vast majority of professional boxers of every race and ethnicity were law-abiding citizens, and they remained that way even after coming in contact with the unsavory characters that inhabited their world.

FIGHTING NAZISM IN THE ARENA

On June 8, 1933, over 60,000 fans attended an important boxing match at New York's Yankee Stadium between the colorful American heavyweight contender Max Baer and Germany's Max Schmeling, a former heavyweight champion of the world. Five months earlier the Nazis had taken control of Germany, and almost immediately began a policy of state-sponsored anti-Semitism. At the time Max Baer was generally assumed to be Jewish, but in fact he was the son of a half-Jewish father and a Protestant mother of Scotch-Irish descent. He was not raised in the religion, and it is not clear that he ever considered himself Jewish. Nevertheless, fighting Nazi Germany's best boxer in a city with the largest Jewish population made it important for Baer

June 8, 1933. Max Baer, wearing the Star of David, has hand raised after stopping German champion Max Schmeling in the 10th round. (Copyright Bettman/Corbis/AP Images)

disappointed. The end came suddenly in the 10th round when Baer, a murderous puncher, dropped Schmeling with a thunderous right hand to the jaw. Upon arising at the count of nine Schmeling was subjected to a series of brutal punches before the referee stopped the fight. With his victory Baer became an instant hero to Jews throughout the world. The following year he would win the heavyweight championship of the world.

Whether Max Baer was Jewish or not, at that moment in time—facing a German opponent who was seen as a representative of the Nazi regime—he chose to identify himself with the Jewish people. His army of Jewish fans was forever grateful for the stand he took, both in and out of the ring.

The victory of Max Baer over Germany's Max Schmeling in June 1933 occurred at a time when the Third Reich, despite its insidious internal racial policies, was still in its infancy, and not yet perceived by the United States as a potential threat. But by mid-1938 that view had drastically changed. Not only did Nazi Germany possess one of the most powerful armies in the world, but its aggressive expansionist policies were threatening world peace. At the same time, Max Schmeling, mirroring Germany's ascendancy, had staged a dramatic comeback after his loss to Baer, which included a tremendous upset victory over the seemingly invincible Joe Louis in 1936. Louis had been undefeated in 27 fights, including 23 by knockout. Sixteen of his victims had never made it past the fourth round. Louis was an 8–1 favorite to defeat Schmeling.

to emphasize his Hebrew heritage. At the suggestion of his Jewish manager, Ancil Hoffman, for the first time he entered the ring wearing the Star of David on his trunks—something that he would do for the rest of his career. Baer left no doubt about his intentions when he told reporters, "Every punch in the eye I give Schmeling is one for Adolf Hitler."[5]

Jewish fans flocked to the stadium in hopes of seeing just that, even though the betting odds heavily favored Schmeling. They were not

In a sensational upset Schmeling punished Louis severely before knocking him out in the 12th round. Schmeling instantly became a huge national hero in Germany, and the Nazi propaganda machine used his victory as proof of Aryan racial superiority.

The return bout between Joe Louis and Max Schmeling for the heavyweight championship of the world took place in Yankee Stadium on June 22, 1938. On the eve of World War II, the highly anticipated contest took on a heavy symbolism. Louis represented democracy and the civilized world, while Schmeling was vilified in the American press as a representative of Hitler. (Despite his status in Germany, Max Schmeling never joined the Nazi party. Nevertheless, as international tensions worsened, Schmeling was seen as an extension of the evil Nazi regime. From the moment Hitler came to power in 1933, comments writer David Margolick, Schmeling "had walked a tightrope, seeking simultaneously to please the Nazis while maintaining his relations in New York, the world capital of boxing."[6])

The fight turned into a transcendent event. No other sporting contest had ever aroused more passion or worldwide interest. Over 70,000 fans were on hand to witness it in person, while another 100 million listened, transfixed to their radios. It is believed to be the largest audience for a single radio broadcast up until this point. Randy Roberts writes: "No event had ever attracted an audience that large—not a sporting event, a political speech, or an entertainment show."[7]

Seeking revenge for his humiliating defeat two years earlier, Louis relentlessly attacked Schmeling. The savage beating took only 124 seconds of the first round before the referee stopped the one-sided fight—the second-shortest title fight in heavyweight history. On that night Joe Louis became an American icon and the entire nation, black and white, celebrated his great victory. African Americans were euphoric, as were Jews throughout the world, who rejoiced over "The Brown Bomber's" utter destruction of a representative of "the master race."

The politically charged return bout between heavyweight champion Joe Louis and Max Schmeling had international ramifications. Seeking to avenge his knockout defeat two years earlier, Louis annihilated Max Schmeling in 124 seconds. (AP Photo)

THE INTERNATIONAL SCENE

In the years between the two world wars, Jewish sporting clubs sprang up throughout Europe—in Poland, Germany, Austria, Italy, Hungary, Czechoslovakia, Greece, Holland, and France. Jewish athletes from these countries excelled in many sports, winning titles in soccer, boxing, fencing, gymnastics, weightlifting, and table tennis. Hungarian Jewish athletes were especially adept at fencing. From 1896 to 1936 they won 14 gold medals in Olympic competition. The majority of Jewish boxers on the European continent remained amateurs, although several dozen achieved success as professionals, either as world champions or leading contenders, most notably Victor "Young" Perez (Tunisian-born French champion who won the world flyweight title in 1931), Leone Efrati (Italian featherweight who challenged for a world title in 1938), Kid Francis (Italian-born French bantamweight champion who challenged for a world title in 1932), and Erich Seelig (German middleweight and light heavyweight champion, 1931–1933).

During the inter-war years soccer remained the number-one sport in Europe. In the 1920s the famous Hakoah soccer team of Vienna attracted the best Jewish players in Central Europe. The team won the Austrian National Championship in 1925. The following year it toured the United States and drew over 26,000 fans to a match at the Polo Grounds in New York City.

The International Maccabee movement was the most popular of the many Jewish athletic clubs in Europe. It had been organized in 1903, and by the early 1930s numbered 200,000 Jewish athletes in 27 countries.[8] Talented amateur boxers representing the Maccabee and various other Jewish sports organizations won national boxing titles in Poland, France, Italy, Germany, England, and Greece.

Poland had the second-largest Jewish population in the world next to the United States, so it is not surprising that it also had more Jewish athletes than any other European nation. By 1936 there were 150 Maccabee athletic clubs in Poland, with some 40,000 members.[9] The idea of a "muscular Judaism"—the phrase coined by Max Nordhau at the second Zionist Congress in 1898—was especially strong in the Polish Maccabee clubs that were home to many distinguished amateur athletes.

In July 1933, six months after the Nazis came to power in Germany, the Maccabee organization relocated its world headquarters from Berlin to London, noting that "there was no longer any place for Maccabi under the bestial Hitler activities."[10] But for many of the athletes who remained in Europe during the gathering storm, both professionals and amateurs, there was no escape. Several of Germany's top Jewish boxers fled the country in 1933. Harry Stein emigrated to Prague and then to Moscow. That same year Erich Seelig fled to France, and eventually to the United States via Cuba in 1935. Leone Efrati, Victor Perez, and Kid Francis were murdered in the Holocaust.

The German army's invasion of Poland on September 1, 1939, ignited World War II. Over the next six years the Nazi occupiers and their collaborators carried out the systematic murder of six million Jews, including 90 percent of Poland's prewar Jewish population of three million.

A few Jewish boxers were able to survive the death camps by fighting for the amusement of Nazi guards, as did Salamo Arouch and Jacko Razon, former Greek amateur champions. Literally fighting for their lives, they were given an extra ration of food after each victory. The loser was invariably shot or gassed. Another survivor was Amsterdam's Ben Bril, that country's outstanding amateur boxer, who competed in the 1928 Olympics and won a gold medal in the flyweight division at the 1935 Maccabiah Games. He won the Dutch national amateur championship eight times, but was barred from the 1932 Summer Olympics because the head of his country's Olympic committee was a member of the Dutch Nazi party. Four years later Bril boycotted the 1936 Games in Berlin.

During the German occupation of the Netherlands Bril was deported and imprisoned at the Bergen-Belsen concentration camp in Germany. He and a younger brother survived to the end of the war, but his other five siblings (all but one were married with children) died in the camps.

After the war Ben Bril returned to the Netherlands and stayed active in boxing as a referee, officiating important fights throughout Europe. Bril is a boxing legend in the Netherlands, and was the subject of a book and movie based on his life. After his passing in 2003, the annual Ben Bril Memorial Boxing Gala was inaugurated to honor his memory. The event features a series of boxing matches held every October in Amsterdam.

BATTLING BRITS

The country with the most Jewish boxers outside of the United States was England. From 1881 to 1914 over 150,000 Jewish immigrants from Eastern Europe settled in London, increasing that country's Jewish population to 250,000 (about one-eighth of the population that resided in America).

Most lived in the East London areas of Whitechapel, Shoreditch, Aldgate, Stepney, Bethnal Green, and Hackney.[11] At the turn of the last century the poorest sections of these enclaves matched New York City's Lower East Side for their poverty and squalor. So it is not surprising that thousands of London's Jewish youths took up boxing in an effort to quickly improve their economic circumstances. Boxing held enormous significance for the country's Jews, especially among the working class. Once the country's national sport, boxing has a rich and storied history in England, and Jewish boxers, beginning with Daniel Mendoza in the late 18th century, were a significant part of it. As in America, the boxing experience in England facilitated the ongoing integration and upward social mobility of the Anglo-Jewish population, while at the same time countering negative anti-Semitic stereotypes.

Outside the ring Jewish entrepreneurs in London were instrumental in sustaining a thriving

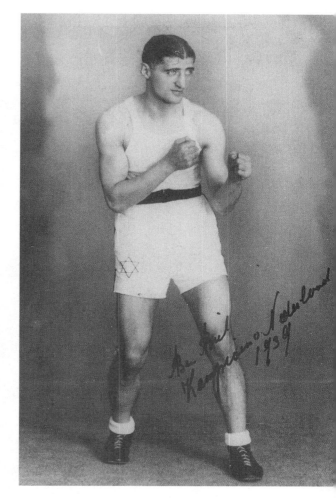

Ben Bril, former Olympian and eight time Dutch national amateur champion.

boxing industry. From 1894 through the 1930s they opened at least five popular boxing halls in the East End Jewish community.[12] The most popular among them were the Judean Club and Premierland Arena. Most Jewish boxers got their start at these two legendary arenas.

The amateur boxing network in Britain that nurtured and developed future professional stars was extensive. The largest Jewish amateur boxing clubs were located in London and Manchester. They performed with amazing success. Between 1921 and 1939 the boxing teams, known collectively as the Jewish Lads' Brigades (JLB), won the Prince of Wales Shield (the preeminent tournament for all British youth clubs) 12 times. In six of these tournaments the final was contested between the London and Manchester JLBs.[13]

Professional boxing activity and participation were greatest during the Great Depression. In the 1930s Great Britain averaged an incredible 3,500 shows per year.[14] (Since 1961 the annual numbers rarely exceed 200 shows.)

Between 1908 and 1935 Anglo-Jewish professional boxers won 13 British titles and four world championships. Ted "Kid" Lewis (Welterweight Champion 1915–1916, 1917–1919), a Jewish boxer from East London, is considered by many historians to be the greatest British boxer of all time. A partial list of the best Anglo-Jewish professional boxers of the Golden Age includes Sid Smith (flyweight champion), Young Joseph, Matt Wells (welterweight champion), Harry Mizler, Jackie "Kid" Berg (junior lightweight champion), Jack Goldswain, Harry Mason,

Harry Reeve, Jack Hyams, Phil Lolosky, Jimmy Lester, Johnny Brown, Young Johnny Brown, Joe Fox, Jack Bloomfield, Benny Sharkey, Solly Schwartz, Benny Caplan, Phil Richards, Al Phillips, Harry Lazar, and Lew Lazar. The fabulous history of Anglo-Jewish boxers deserves an entire book of its own.

LEARNING THE OLD-FASHIONED WAY

Over the past quarter-century professional boxers have averaged between 15 and 30 bouts and less than 150 rounds before winning a title. From the 1920s to the 1950s the averages were 71 bouts and 479 rounds. In both eras it took about four to five years of activity to accumulate those numbers.[15]

Economic necessity was the main reason the old-timers fought so often. The bouts provided steady income. The goal was to accumulate a decent-size nest egg before retirement. Fighting often had other benefits. It was not just the number of fights and rounds that helped to season and sharpen the skills of the Golden Age pros—it was also the competitive quality of those rounds. By the time a boxer achieved contender status he'd already gained enough experience to improvise and adjust his strategy when faced with a variety of different styles. If staggered or hurt by a punch, he knew how to clinch, stall, run, slip, bend, roll, and weave his way out of trouble. Such fighters were very difficult to stop.

An undefeated record is not that difficult to establish if a fighter consistently meets inferior opposition. Years ago it wasn't that important to remain undefeated. Managers expected their fighters to win, but were not always sure they would. At some point the fighter had to be tested, and if the outcome was a loss, it was seen as a learning experience, providing the fighter was not seriously overmatched and damaged. Losses were considered an accepted part of the learning process.

"One of the biggest differences between then and now was that the manager wasn't burdened with navigating to protect the fighter from losing," explained ESPN boxing analyst Teddy Atlas. "There wasn't the pressure that there is today to remain undefeated. You could let the fighters get the fights that were going to let them develop—win or lose. It was just a matter of fighting and getting better . . . fighting and moving up . . . and trying to get to Madison Square Garden. That's all that mattered."[16] Boxing historian Kevin Smith agrees: "It wasn't a big deal to lose back then as it is now," says Smith. "Losses were considered a lot more like baseball in that you lose a game and you go on and try to win the next series."[17]

As was the case in the previous generation of boxers, even the best had trouble maintaining undefeated records because the top men often fought each other. The low knockout percentages of the old-timers did not mean they were not hard punchers. It was rather an indication of the type of competition they faced month after month, and the fine defensive skills they had mastered. An undefeated prospect with a long winning streak and a high percentage of knockout victories aroused suspicion among the cognoscenti because it was so unusual.

Even journeymen boxers with mediocre records were capable, on a good night, of pulling an upset and defeating a top-ranked contender, or even a world champion. As Kevin Smith notes: "If you look at any of the 1920s fighters, even an ordinary main event fighter from some obscure tank town, you are going to recognize names on his record. These guys fought each other. There was not as much avoiding competitive fights as there is today. They went where the money was and it didn't really matter a lot of times who it was they were fighting. Every fight was experience. Most fighters of that era had 100 or more fights."[18]

One of the many ways boxing has veered off course in recent years is the importance placed on win-loss records by the media and fans. Boxing, unlike baseball or basketball, is not a sport of statistics. One cannot determine the quality of a fighter by simply counting up the wins and losses on his record. The classic example is Fritzie Zivic, whose record showed over 30 losses in 129 fights when he upset the great Henry Armstrong to win the welterweight championship in 1940.

There are champions and contenders profiled in this section whose win-loss records are inferior to lesser boxers who would not stand a chance against them. When evaluating the quality of a Golden Age gladiator, one must go beyond mere statistics. The main question is how well, and for how long, did the fighter perform against top competition? Also strongly influencing my selections was the length of time a fighter's name appeared in *The Ring*'s listing of top 10 contenders for his weight class. Extra consideration was given to those fighters who maintained a rating for at least several months or longer. In a few instances a fighter who otherwise might not have made it into the book is mentioned because his story is compelling from a historical or human-interest perspective. All of the boxers reached their prime between 1920 and 1940.

Georgie Abrams
Nat Arno
Milt Aron
Abie Bain
Benny Bass*
Sylvan Bass
Archie Bell
Joe Benjamin
Jackie "Kid" Berg*
Maxie Berger
Jack Bernstein*
Harry Blitman
Harry "Kid" Brown
Johnny Brown
Natie Brown
Newsboy Brown*
Joe Burman
Mushy Callahan*
Red Chapman
Mickey Cohen
Al "Bummy" Davis
Jackie Davis
Davey Day
Sammy Dorfman
Leone Efrati
Irving Eldridge
Murray Elkins
Armand Emanuel

Lew Farber
Abe Feldman
Lew Feldman
Jackie Fields*
Al Foreman
Kid Francis
Bernie Friedkin
Sailor Friedman
Danny Frush
Joe Glick
Marty Gold
Benny Goldberg
Abe Goldstein*
Ruby Goldstein
Charley Gomer
Joey Goodman
Al Gordon
Jack Gross
Izzy Grove
Willie Harmon
Gustave Humery
Abie Israel
Ben Jeby*
Andre Jessurun
Louis "Kid" Kaplan*
Mike Kaplan
"KO" Phil Kaplan
Herbie Katz

Lew Kirsch
Danny Kramer
Solly Krieger*
Art Lasky
Roy Lazer
Georgie Levine
King Levinsky
Nat Litfin
Sammy Luftspring
Georgie Marks
Harry Mason
Joey Medill
Benny Miller
Ray Miller
Harry Mizler
Young Montreal
Yale Okun
Bob Olin*
Victor "Young" Perez*
Bill Poland
Jack Portney
Augie Ratner
Al Reid
Charley Phil
    Rosenberg*
Dave Rosenberg*
"Slapsie Maxie"
    Rosenbloom*

Barney Ross*
Al Roth
Ted Sandwina
Joey Sangor
Morrie Schlaifer
Benny Schwartz
Corporal Izzy
    Schwartz*
Erich Seelig
Solly Seeman
Benny Sharkey
Pinky Silverberg*
Pal Silvers
Abe Simon
Al Singer*
Lew Tendler
Sid Terris
Phil Tobias
Benny Valgar
Sammy Vogel
Eddie "Kid" Wagner
Archie Walker
Eddie "Kid" Wolfe
Norman "Baby" Yack

* world champion

GEORGIE ABRAMS

Born: November 11, 1918
Died: June 30, 1994 (Age: 75)
Hometown: Washington, DC
Height: 5' 9" Weight: 160 pounds
Professional Career: 1937–1942, 1946–1948

Total Bouts	Won	Lost	Draw
61 (474 rounds)	48 (9 by KO)	10 (3 by KO)	3

There is a strong case to be made for **Georgie Abrams** as the best Jewish middleweight of all time. But fate did not decree that he would win a title.

The son of a shoemaker, Georgie Abrams was born in Roanoke, Virginia, and raised in Washington, DC. He was a gifted athlete and an "A" student in high school, but the need to find employment during the Great Depression trumped any plans for higher education, even though two colleges offered him athletic scholarships in swimming and boxing. Georgie had been an outstanding amateur boxer, compiling a 62-3 record that included AAU (Amateur Athletic Union) and Golden Gloves titles.

Georgie's parents gave him the middle name "Freedom" in honor of his being born on Armistice Day 1918. Twenty-three years later, on November 28, 1941, at Madison Square Garden, Georgie Abrams was hoping for a belated birthday present—the middleweight championship of the world. But first he would have to earn it by defeating one of the toughest fighters who ever lived, Gary, Indiana's, "Man of Steel," Tony Zale.

Abrams appeared to be on his way to a quick victory after dropping Zale for a nine-count in the very first round. But in the next round an errant thumb from Zale's glove poked into Abrams's left eye, causing severe pain and blurred vision. Making matters worse, in the third round an accidental head butt opened a cut over his other eye. With his left eye swollen shut from the fourth round on, Georgie fought the rest of the bout half blind.

Despite these handicaps, Abrams, using every ounce of his extraordinary boxing skill and courage, fought a sensational battle for 15 exciting rounds. The bout was very close, but in the opinion of the two judges and the referee, Zale's incessant body attack in the late rounds had swayed the fight in his favor.

Georgie was confident that with two good eyes he could defeat Zale in a rematch. But it was not to be. On December 7, 1941, the Japanese bombed Pearl Harbor, and everything changed.

Abrams, like millions of other patriotic Americans, heard the call to duty and volunteered for service. In the navy he was involved with physical training of recruits. He also boxed in over 200 exhibitions in the Pacific and on ships. When he was discharged in 1946, Abrams was 27 years old, still young enough to resume his career.

After four tune-up fights, including a 10-round decision over highly ranked middleweight contender Steve Belloise, Abrams appeared to be near his old form. In his next fight he lost a disputed decision to the great French middleweight Marcel Cerdan. The 17,000 fans attending the fight in Madison Square Garden would have been satisfied had the bout ended in a draw.

Georgie was anxious for another shot at his old foe, Tony Zale, also a navy veteran. Zale's title had been frozen during his service. But before Abrams could challenge Zale, he had a tall order to fill: He had to get past the great Sugar Ray Robinson.

Robinson, the welterweight champion of the world, was then at the peak of his extraordinary powers. The "Harlem Dandy" was seeking to add the middleweight title to his already-impressive résumé. He'd already beaten a slew of tough middleweight contenders, including four victories over the only man to defeat him in 165 amateur and professional fights—the Bronx Bull, Jake La Motta. It didn't matter to Robinson that he would be giving away 12 or more pounds to a heavier opponent. He figured to handle Abrams without much trouble.

But the overconfident Robinson was about to be surprised. Abrams was a master boxer and superb infighter. He was able to maneuver inside Sugar Ray's longer reach, keeping most of the action at close quarters. During one exchange he even managed to open a cut over Robinson's right eye.

Although hampered by blood running into his eye, Ray kept up a vicious body attack, but was still unable to land a knockout blow. At the end of 10 furious rounds, one judge scored for Abrams but was outvoted by the other judge and referee, both of whom gave the fight to Robinson by a narrow margin. The Madison Square Garden crowd immediately voiced their displeasure with a prolonged chorus of boos when the decision was announced.

Abrams's impressive showing against Robinson and Cerdan is not the only evidence of his magnificent ring artistry. Before the war he challenged middleweight champion Billy Soose and won an easy 10-round decision. But since both fighters weighed over the middleweight limit of 160 pounds, the title was not at stake. The win was no fluke. Before he became champion, Soose (considered one of the best middleweight boxers of the 1930s) had already lost to Abrams twice. After his non-title win over Soose, an independent Midwest sanctioning organization called the "American Federation of Boxing" recognized Abrams as world middleweight champion, but the organization carried no clout and soon disappeared.

Leading up to his series of fights with Soose, Abrams outpointed Izzy Jannazzo and defeated former middleweight champions Lou Brouillard and Teddy Yaroz. The victories highlighted Abrams's ability to adjust to any style. He could outmaneuver a rough infighter like Brouillard, and was equally effective at long range against master boxers Jannazzo and Yaroz.

As if these accomplishments were not enough to enshrine Abrams in every boxing hall of fame, he then took on the legendary Charley Burley, one of the most feared black fighters of the twentieth century. In his prime Burley was scrupulously avoided by champions in both the welterweight and middleweight divisions. On July 29, 1940, Abrams held Burley to a 10-round draw in the latter's hometown of Pittsburgh. Two weeks later Abrams won a split 10-round decision over Cocoa Kid, another highly rated black contender.

Two months after his stirring effort against Sugar Ray Robinson, Georgie was back in Madison Square Garden to face the always-dangerous Steve Belloise. A year earlier Abrams had outpointed Belloise. This time Belloise, a vicious puncher with 45 knockout victories in 84 bouts, stopped him in the fifth round.

After a four-month layoff, Abrams faced another navy vet, former middleweight champion Fred Apostoli. The fight took place in Apostoli's hometown of San Francisco. At the end of 10 grueling rounds, the local boxer won a split decision that could have easily gone the other way.

In Abrams's last fight, on April 21, 1948, he was mauled by power-punching Anton Raadik,

Georgie Abrams (left) and the great Sugar Ray Robinson fought a sizzling 10 rounder in 1947.

an opponent he'd easily outpointed a year earlier. The fight was stopped in the 10th round after Abrams had been decked twice. Chris Dundee, Georgie's very capable manager, advised his fighter it was time to retire, and the obedient boxer agreed.

In his post-boxing life Abrams, a talented illustrator, tried to make a career for himself as an artist, but it did not pan out. Over the next 30 years he held a variety of jobs that included stints as an auto dealer, liquor salesman, and tavern owner. He lived in Florida for a while before settling in Las Vegas, where he worked as a security guard at the Tropicana Hotel. Twice divorced, he

MADISON SQUARE GARDEN

When Tex Rickard took control of Madison Square Garden in 1920, his goal was to establish the arena as the world's foremost boxing showplace. So successful was Tex that in 1925, a new and much larger Madison Square Garden was built to accommodate twenty thousand persons. (The seating capacity of the old arena was about 12,000.)

"The house that Tex built" was the third and most famous incarnation of the legendary arena. The edifice occupied an entire block on the west side of New York's Eighth Avenue, between 49th and 50th Streets. It stood as a monument to the sport from 1925 to 1968, when it was torn down and replaced by a new arena constructed atop the old Pennsylvania train station, at 33rd Street and Seventh Avenue.

The honor of performing in the world's most famous arena was every boxer's dream, even if it was only in a four-round preliminary. But to be featured in a Madison Square Garden main event was the equivalent of landing the lead role in a Broadway theatrical production! The prestige of topping the card at "The Garden" was second only to winning a world title. In the Roaring Twenties, at the height of Jewish activity within the sport, nearly half of the arena's 288 shows featured a Jewish boxer in the main event. The fact that so many quality Jewish fighters had huge followings in New York City guaranteed that they would often appear in the featured bout of the evening. Overall, from 1900 to 1950, Jewish boxers appeared in 240 of 866 Garden main events. In twelve of those bouts, Jewish boxers squared off against each other. (See appendix for a complete list of Madison Square Garden main events featuring Jewish boxers.)

During boxing's heyday a typical season at the 50th Street arena averaged 25 to 35 shows per year. The main event was usually preceded by six or seven preliminary bouts. In the summer months the fights were staged in outdoor arenas and stadiums. There was also a six-week hiatus in the spring while the Ringling Bros. and Barnum & Bailey Circus took over the Garden.

Madison Square Garden, 1940.

married his third wife, Vicki Lee, a former singer for Tommy Dorsey, in 1984. Abrams was already exhibiting signs of the progressive dementia that afflicts so many ex-fighters. But he never expressed regrets about his career, other than his frustration at not winning the middleweight championship.

Georgie Abrams's record is immensely impressive. Very few fighters can boast of victories over Soose, Brouillard, Yaroz, and Cocoa Kid, or fighting on even terms with the likes of Burley, Cerdan, and Robinson. That says it all. They did not come much better than Georgie Abrams.

(Newark Public Library)

NAT ARNO
(Sidney Nathaniel Abramowitz)
Born: April 10, 1910
Died: August 8, 1973 (Age: 63)
Hometown: Newark, New Jersey
Weight: 130–135 lbs.
Professional Career: 1925–1932

Total Bouts	Won	Lost	Draw	ND
129 (902 rounds)	87 (22 by KO)	17 (1 by KO)	15	3-5-2

Nat Arno had his first boxing match on his 15th birthday. He had five more bouts before his father found out and forbade the youngster from continuing. Unable to fight in New Jersey without his parents' permission, Arno hitchhiked alone to Florida in January 1926. Over the next 13 months, he lost only one of 49 fights. He returned home and reconciled with his father. All of his subsequent fights took place in New Jersey.

Arno established solid credentials in the junior lightweight division by holding his own against the likes of Pete Nebo, Vic Burrone, Young Zazzarino, Lope Tenorio, and Benny Cross. An aggressive and durable brawler, Arno was very proud of the fact that none of the 129 opponents he faced was able to stop him. The lone TKO loss on his record happened when the ringside physician ordered the bout stopped because of a cut above Arno's right eye.

During Prohibition several of Newark's boxers, including Arno, were employed by Longy Zwillman, the powerful New Jersey Jewish Mob boss, to transport and protect his bootleg shipments. Although Zwillman never became a boxer himself, he was a supporter of Newark's Jewish boxers, and had sponsored several promotions.

Nat Arno (center) and his "Minutemen" picket a Bund rally in Newark, September 26, 1938. (Newark Public Library)

In the mid-1930s Zwillman recruited and organized Jewish boxers from Newark's Third Ward into a group called "The Minutemen." The group's purpose was to use their muscle to break up pro-Nazi meetings and propaganda activities in Newark. The Minutemen included boxers Benny Levine, Lou Halper, Abie Bain, Al Fisher, Puddy Hinkes, and Moe Fischer. It was active right up to the beginning of World War II, when America joined the fight against Nazi Germany.[19]

In 1941 Arno was drafted into the army. He saw action with the 29th Infantry Division, and was wounded during the Normandy invasion. After returning to civilian life he married and relocated to California, where he worked in the furniture industry. Arno's "Minutemen" activities were renewed in the early 1960s when he heard that the American Nazi Party was staging a rally in downtown Los Angeles. He gathered a group of veterans to protest. During an anti-Semitic tirade by one of the speakers, Arno rushed the stage and threw him to the ground. He was arrested but released without being charged. Chalk up another victory for this feisty former pro boxer and veteran.

MILT ARON
(Milton Aronson)
Born: June 2, 1917
Died: March 6, 1942 (Age: 24)
Hometown: Chicago, Illinois
Height: 5' 8½" Weight: 147–155 lbs.
Professional Career: 1936–1941

Total Bouts	Won	Lost	Draw	NC
86 (568 rounds)	65 (34 by KO)	13 (2 by KO)	7	1

Ill-fated **Milt Aron**, the son of a rabbi, was one of Chicago's most popular boxers. He was an aggressive pressure fighter with an exciting style and knockout power in his right fist.

Aron's enthusiastic fan base extended well beyond his loyal Jewish following.

From 1934 to 1939, Aron lost only seven of 69 fights. Knockouts over Pete Nebo and Lou

Halper, plus a decision over Chicago rival Harry Dublinsky, earned him a top-10 rating in the welterweight division. But it was his sensational knockout of Fritzie Zivic that moved him into the number-one-contender slot. Zivic had floored Aron three times before the Chicago slugger connected with a dynamite right cross in the eighth round that flattened the future welterweight champion for the full count. It was only the second time in 115 fights that Zivic had been knocked out.

Eight months after his victory over Zivic, Milt's plans for a title shot against welterweight champion Henry Armstrong were disrupted when he dropped two decisions to contenders Mike Kaplan and Steve Mamakos.

Those losses moved Aron back a few notches, but he quickly rebounded with three consecutive knockout victories. He then agreed to a rematch with Zivic. This time the wily veteran turned the tables and stopped him in the fifth round.

In a tragic turn of events Aron came down with blood poisoning shortly after his second bout with Zivic. He battled the infection for five months before succumbing on March 6, 1942.

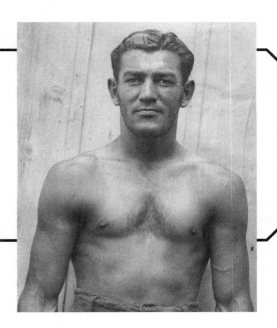

ABIE BAIN
Born: August 10, 1906
Died: April 9, 1993 (Age: 86)
Hometown: Newark, New Jersey
Weight: 160–173 lbs.
Professional Career: 1923–1936

Total Bouts	Won	Lost	Draw	ND
108 (732 rounds)	48 (24 by KO)	26 (11 by KO)	5	16-10-3

According to **Abie Bain**'s daughter, Riselle, the distinctive hoarse voice that Anthony Quinn used in his portrayal of "Mountain Rivera," the washed-up fighter in the 1962 movie *Requiem for a Heavyweight*, was based on her father. Quinn and Bain had been friends for many years. Bain's voice was actually the result of damage to his vocal cords caused by a botched surgery, and not his boxing career.

Abie Bain turned pro in 1923. Four years later he was mixing it up with the likes of Jack McVey, KO Phil Kaplan, Vince Forgione, Phil

Krug, Rene DeVos, George Courtney, and Vince Dundee. All were highly ranked middleweight contenders.

In 1930 Abie moved up a division and challenged the great light-heavyweight champion "Slapsie Maxie" Rosenbloom. Maxie stopped him in the 11th round when a severe laceration over Bain's left eye caused the referee to halt the bout. Less than a year later he was matched with "Two Ton" Tony Galento, who outweighed him by over 50 pounds. Galento scored a fourth-round TKO. Like the fictional "Mountain Rivera," Bain continued to fight past his prime. Thirteen of his 26 losses came in the last four years of his career.

BENNY BASS

Featherweight Champion 1927–1928
Junior Lightweight Champion 1929
Born: December 15, 1904
Died: June 25, 1975 (Age: 70)
Hometown: Philadelphia, Pennsylvania
Height: 5' 2" Weight: 118–135 lbs.
Professional Career: 1921–1937, 1939–1940

Total Bouts	Won	Lost	Draw	ND	NC
242 (1,691 rounds)	156 (71 by KO)	28 (2 by KO)	6	34-13-3	2

Benny Bass, a five-foot-two, pocket-size Hercules, stood out in an era that churned out great featherweight and lightweight boxers in assembly-line fashion. This tireless warrior fought an amazing 242 professional fights over 17 years, and won titles in two weight divisions. It would not be a stretch to place him among the all-time top-10 featherweight champions.

Bass was born in Kiev, Russia, on December 15, 1904, and came to America with his family in 1907. At the age of 10 he was selling newspapers on a busy Philadelphia street corner. The diminutive but scrappy youngster discovered his talent for fighting while defending his prized corner against bullies and competitors who sought to take over his territory.

From the ages of 12 to 16, Benny won 95 of 100 amateur bouts. In 1920 he qualified for the Olympic trials in the flyweight class, where he lost a close decision to the eventual gold medal winner and future professional champion, Frankie Genaro. Bass turned pro the following year under the management of Phil Glassman, handler of the great Lew Tendler and many other outstanding Philadelphia boxers.

Five years later, with victories over Joe Glick, Chuck Suggs, Dominic Petrone, and Johnny Farr, Bass was rated the number-one featherweight contender. His 39 knockout triumphs in 115 bouts stamped him as one of the hardest punchers in the division. In 1927 he met Boston's Red Chapman (Morris Kaplan) for the featherweight championship left vacant by Louis "Kid" Kaplan. Chapman, the number-two contender, had an impressive 64-13-1 (won-lost-draw) record, including 19 wins by knockout.

Over 30,000 fans paid their way into Philadelphia's Municipal Stadium to witness a great fight between two evenly matched fighters at the top of their game.

In the third round, an accidental head butt opened a cut over Bass's right eye. Calling upon all his ring savvy and experience, Bass fought the next four rounds at long range and managed to foil Chapman's attempt to target the injury and inflict further damage. In the seventh round Bass opened a bloody gash over Chapman's eye.

With both fighters fearing a TKO loss, they decided to throw caution to the wind and go for a knockout. In the ninth round, in the midst of a savage exchange, Bass and Chapman landed simultaneous right-hand bombs to the jaw, resulting in that rarest of boxing spectacles—the double knockdown! The startled referee began counting over both fighters. Bass wobbled up at the count of seven while the referee continued to

Photograph taken moments after the simultaneous knockdown in the 9th round. Bass (right) managed to get to his feet a few seconds before Chapman.

count over Chapman, who just managed to beat the count and last out the round. The 10th and final round had the exhausted and bloodied gladiators fighting on pure instinct. Bass was awarded a unanimous decision.

In the first defense of his title he faced the great Tony Canzoneri, who was recognized as world featherweight champ by the New York State Athletic Commission. Bass held the National Boxing Association version of the title. The bout was intended to unify the title.

After 15 furious rounds Tony was awarded a split decision for the undisputed championship. It was revealed afterwards that Bass had suffered a broken collarbone in the third round (some sources say 10th round), but despite the handicap had fought on, even rallying in the last few rounds to make the fight very close.

Following a four-month layoff (the longest of his career) to allow his broken collarbone to heal, Bass returned to action, scoring impressive victories over top contenders Harry Blitman, Gaston Charles, Davey Abad, and Harry Forbes.

In 1929 Bass fought Tod Morgan for the junior welterweight title. Knocked down in the first round, Bass came back to stop Morgan in the second round. It was only Morgan's second KO loss in over 100 fights.

After two successful title defenses Bass took another crack at Canzoneri in August 1930. They both weighed over the 130-pound junior lightweight limit, so Bass's title was not at risk if he lost. That was his sole consolation as he dropped another close decision to Canzoneri.

Benny won 11 of his next 13 fights. All seemed to be going well until he met Cuban sensation Kid Chocolate on July 15, 1931. In the first defense of his junior lightweight crown Bass suffered a deep cut over his left eye that caused the bout to be stopped in the seventh round.

For the remainder of his career Bass was competitive with the world's top lightweights, but never received another title shot. Even past his prime he continued to average one to three fights a month.

In 1937 the great triple champion Henry Armstrong, then at the peak of his extraordinary powers, stopped the 32-year-old ex-champ in the fourth round. It was the only time Bass was ever counted out.

Bass retired after the Armstrong fight, but money problems forced a comeback in August 1939. Over the next nine months he won four of seven bouts, including one draw. In his last two bouts the aging veteran dropped 10-round decisions to Philly neighbors Jimmy Tyghe and Tommy Spiegal. The losses finally convinced him to hang up his gloves.

Bass was offered a job as a salesman for Penn Beer Distributors, and the popular ex-champ did quite well selling suds to the local barkeeps, restaurants, and supermarkets.

Although he was a grade-school dropout, those who knew Benny recall an individual of above-average intelligence who was reputed to be fluent in five languages—English, Ukrainian, Russian, Polish, and Yiddish. He eventually moved from selling beer to a job in civil service, and for many years worked for the city of Philadelphia as a clerk in their traffic court system.

Benny Bass may have been small in stature, but he was a giant in the ring. If he were boxing today he'd be worth his weight in gold.

SYLVAN BASS

Born: August 15, 1909
Died: November 30, 1984 (Age: 75)
Hometown: Baltimore, Maryland
Weight: 142–155 lbs.
Professional Career: 1924–1936

Total Bouts	Won	Lost	Draw	ND
125 (868 rounds)	82 (28 by KO)	28 (5 by KO)	9	3-1-2

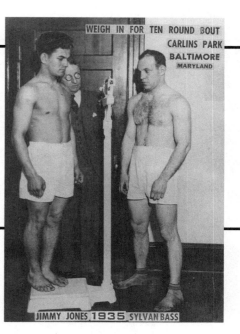

Baltimore's **Sylvan Bass** began his career in 1924 as a 118-pound welterweight and ended it 12 years later as a 152-pound middleweight. He was very popular in his hometown of Baltimore when that city was one of the country's hottest boxing venues.

A converted southpaw, Bass combined a powerful left hook with an aggressive infighting style. Top opponents included Jack Portney, Andy Divodi, Sergeant Sammy Baker, Georgie Levine, Young Terry, Cuddy DeMarco, and former welterweight champion Tommy Freeman. In 1933 he scored his greatest victory by winning an upset eight-round decision over future middleweight champion Ken Overlin. After Bass retired he served as matchmaker for the Century Athletic Club in Baltimore for 12 years.

Sylvan Bass (right) weighs in for his 120th professional fight on March 25, 1935. (Courtesy of Thomas Scharf)

ARCHIE BELL

(Archie Sapon)
Born: November 12, 1904
Died: April 15, 1988 (Age: 84)
Hometown: Brooklyn, New York
Weight: 118 lbs.
Professional Career: 1923–1932

Total Bouts	Won	Lost	Draw	ND	NC
99 (740 rounds)	50 (6 by KO)	20 (2 by KO)	13	7-4-1	4

Archie Bell turned pro on December 10, 1923. Over the next 12 months he averaged a fight every two weeks. That type of activity, unthinkable today, was not unusual for a boxer of his era. Neither was the fact that 15 of his first 23 opponents were Jewish.

Archie fought in one of the most competitive eras in the history of the bantamweight division, and was good enough to be rated among the top 10 contenders for over four years. He beat many good fighters, but also had a habit of losing the big ones. Archie chalked up victories over contenders Dominick Petrone, Johnny Vacca, Young Nationalista, Eugene Huat, and Ignacio Fernandez, but lost to Nel Tarleton, Kid Francis, Teddy Baldock, and former champion Bushy Graham. In all, Bell fought nine fighters who at one time or another claimed a world title.

On December 2, 1932, in Los Angeles, Archie lost a 10-round decision to Mexican fireplug Alberto "Baby" Arizmendi for the California version of the world featherweight title. Thirty-five days later Arizmendi repeated his victory in San Francisco. Shortly after this fight Bell decided to hang up his gloves.

In a career spanning nine years and 99 fights, Archie Bell was stopped only twice, the first time very early in his career. The second stoppage was a TKO (cut over the eye) to future champion Tony Canzoneri.

JOE BENJAMIN
"The Sheik of San Joaquin"
Born: September 8, 1898
Died: July 5, 1983 (Age: 84)
Hometown: San Francisco, California
Weight: 135 lbs.
Professional Career: 1915–1925

Total Bouts	Won	Lost	Draw	ND	NC
101 (563 rounds)	46 (19 by KO)	21 (2 by KO)	2	24-4-1	3

Few fighters have entered the pro ranks with more natural talent than handsome, fun-loving **Joe Benjamin**. A flashy and clever lightweight boxer, Joe was a solid performer but lacked consistency. On a good night he was capable of outpointing the likes of Joe Welling, Benny Valgar, and Pete Hartley. On not-so-good nights he lost to Ritchie Mitchell, Johnny Dundee, and Joe Tiplitz. All were top-rated lightweights. (Mitchell was one of only two fighters to knock him out.)

In 1925 Benjamin was among 50 top lightweight boxers who took part in an international tournament to crown a successor to the retired lightweight champion Benny Leonard. In Joe's first bout, in San Francisco, he outpointed Jack Silver in front of 20,000 fans. He then made the mistake of picking up an extra payday by taking an interim non-tournament bout against the formidable Ace Hudkins. After losing an upset decision to Hudkins, Benjamin was dropped from the tournament. Although only 26 years old, and still in his prime, Joe decided to hang up his gloves. He used his ring earnings to open a liquor store in Los Angeles.

Joe had been a stablemate of heavyweight champion Jack Dempsey. They maintained a lifelong friendship. In fact, Benjamin was Dempsey's best man when the heavyweight champion married actress Estelle Taylor in 1925. It was Dempsey who introduced Joe to the Hollywood crowd. The charming and friendly former contender became personal trainer to Charlie Chaplin and Douglas Fairbanks, connections that helped him land several movie cameo roles.

During World War II Benjamin enlisted in the US Marine Corps and served as a hand-to-hand-combat instructor. After the war he worked for many years as a salesman and West Coast public relations representative for Schenley Industries.

JACKIE "KID" BERG

(Judah Bergman)
"The Whitechapel Windmill"
Junior Welterweight Champion 1930–1931
Born: June 28, 1909
Died: April 22, 1991 (Age: 81)
Hometown: London, England
Height: 5' 9" Weight: 134–148 lbs.
Professional Career: 1924–1945

Total Bouts	Won	Lost	Draw
192 (1,701 rounds)	157 (61 by KO)	26 (9 by KO)	9

Judah Bergman donned boxing gloves at a very young age and quickly established himself as an exceptionally talented amateur boxer. But amateur trophies would not put food on the table. Judah's father, a Yiddish-speaking Polish immigrant, worked as a tailor and was barely able to support his wife and seven children with his meager earnings. So in 1924 Judah Bergman joined the ranks of England's professional prizefighters. He was three weeks shy of his 15th birthday.

Jackie "Kid" Berg always seemed to be in a hurry, as if he feared slowing down might cause him to sputter and stall. His nervous energy was even more pronounced in a boxing ring. The kid had the lungs and stamina of a marathon runner. He was one of those rare individuals who could move at top speed for 15 rounds and never seem to tire.

With his arms pumping like pistons the Kid set a relentless pace. His nickname, "The Whitechapel Windmill," only hinted at what it must have been like to fight him. This is not to imply that he was just a "swarmer" with inordinate stamina. Jackie was well schooled in the basics. He possessed a fine left jab and could box effectively at long range.

Within five months of turning pro Jackie was fighting ten- and 15-round main events. From June 1924 to February 1928 he had 62 bouts, losing only three. Included among his victories was a 15-round decision over future featherweight champion Andre Routis.

In 1929 Jackie made his Madison Square Garden debut against lightweight contender Bruce Flowers, one of the finest African-American fighters of his era. Flowers, a slight betting favorite, had height and reach advantages over Berg, but none of that mattered.

Nineteen-year-old Jackie set a tremendous pace. Flowers was so busy defending himself against the frenzied, nonstop onslaught of punches that he was unable to launch an effective counterattack. He appeared, as one sportswriter put it, "like a scarecrow caught in a windstorm." The Garden crowd, numbering close to 20,000, had not seen anything like it since the halcyon days of the legendary "Pittsburgh Windmill," Harry Greb. Some reporters were even calling Berg "the English Harry Greb."

Berg had something else in common with Greb. He was an inveterate womanizer. Berg's trainers often had to stand guard outside his bedroom to make sure he avoided female companionship on the night before a fight. Once, in a New York hotel lobby, Berg was chatting up an attractive brunette. He invited her to join him for dinner the following evening. Big mistake. The woman was the girlfriend of mobster Legs Diamond. Word got out that Legs was enraged and that his torpedoes were out gunning for Berg. Ray Arcel and Whitey Bimstein, Berg's trainers, used all their charm and salesmanship to convince Diamond that it was all a misunderstanding. The duo quickly hustled Berg to an upstate training camp.

"The Whitechapel Windmill" became an overnight sensation in New York after his impressive showing against Bruce Flowers. Fight fans couldn't wait to see him in action again. Only 13 days after their first encounter Jackie and Bruce Flowers were back in Madison Square Garden for a second go-round. Flowers told reporters that he'd been taken off guard by Berg's unusual style, but would outbox him this time.

Like many other Jewish fighters, Jackie wore the Star of David on his boxing trunks. But on this occasion he decided to take the display of his heritage one step further by wearing his *tallis* and *tefillin* into the ring! The somewhat surreal scene was described in *The Ring* magazine:

> Berg entered the ring wrapped in a tallis, the prayer shawl worn in synagogues. Around his right arm and on his head he wore tefillin, the small leather box containing sacred scripture, trailed by leather straps, which are put on by observant Jews for early morning prayers. Berg proceeded to go through an elaborate ritual of slowly unwinding the leather straps from around his body, tenderly kissing them, and placing the materials in a gold-embossed velvet bag, which he then carefully handed to his chief second, Ray Arcel. Berg's trunks, as always, were adorned with the Star of David.[20]

The majority of his fellow Jews among the 20,000 fans in the sold-out arena were exhilarated by the display. But some skeptics questioned what they called a gimmick to pull in the crowds. Berg's trainer, Ray Arcel, disagreed. "To understand why Berg always wore symbols of his religion into the ring, you had to know the man," said Arcel. "True, he wasn't what you call a religious Jew, but he was superstitious beyond reason. When I put the question to him one day, he seemed embarrassed. 'It's comforting to have God on your side no matter what you are doing,' he said soberly."[21]

In the return bout Berg got off to a slow start before taking charge in the third round, whereupon the action followed the same pattern as their previous encounter. Berg won another 10-round unanimous decision by "gluing his head to the Negro's chin and slamming away at his middle."[22]

"The Whitechapel Windmill" was box-office gold, and was kept busy for the rest of the year. Promoters all over the country wanted him to appear in their arenas. He won 13 additional fights in 1929. Among his victims were lightweight contenders Mushy Callahan, Phil McGraw, and, for the third time, the persistent Bruce Flowers.

In 1930 Jackie met the great Tony Canzoneri. Two years earlier Canzoneri had won and lost the featherweight championship. Now competing as a lightweight, Tony set his sights on adding another title to his impressive list of accomplishments.

The Canzoneri vs. Berg fight took place in Madison Square Garden before another sellout crowd. The 6–5 odds favored Canzoneri because he had beaten more quality opponents and was the harder puncher. But even as great a fighter as Canzoneri was, he could not cope with Berg's maniacal but controlled fury. Canzoneri was given the full Berg treatment. The overwhelming speed and volume of Berg's punches prevented him from mounting an effective counterattack. He did manage to land several haymakers, but the "Whitechapel Windmill" just kept plowing forward. During the course of the battle Canzoneri was cut over both eyes and bled from his nose and mouth. At the end of ten rounds of fierce fighting, Berg's arm was raised in victory.

A month and a day after his spectacular upset of Canzoneri, the 20-year-old whiz kid was back in London to fight Mushy Callahan for the junior lightweight title (weight limit 140 pounds). By the 10th round, with his left eye swollen shut and bleeding from assorted cuts, Mushy's corner signaled surrender by throwing a towel into the ring. Jackie was now a world champion, but he would not be satisfied until he won the more-prestigious lightweight crown.

On April 4, 1930, just six weeks after defeating Callahan, the new champion was back in Madison Square Garden, where he outpointed perennial contender Joe Glick in the first defense of his new title. Just three days later, in a non-title fight, he outpointed Jackie Phillips in Toronto, Canada. The following month, at Dreamland Park, in Newark, New Jersey, Berg defended his title for the second time by stopping Al Delmont in the fourth round. In June and July he outpointed the Perlick twins, Herman and Henry. The dizzying schedule reached a climax on August 7, 1930, when he faced the great Cuban boxing star, Kid Chocolate.

In an era loaded with talent, Kid Chocolate stood out among his peers as something very special. He fought as if performing a rumba interspersed with a dazzling array of combination punches. Up to that time no boxer, not even the great Benny Leonard, had fought with more balletic grace than this beautifully built, ebony-hued superathlete.

Kid Chocolate (real name, Eligio Sardinias Montalvo) had come to the United States from Cuba in 1928. He rocketed to the top of the featherweight division with a sensational string of victories, including a close decision (non-title) over lightweight champion Al Singer.

Not only was Kid Chocolate a master boxer, but he also possessed the speed to match Berg's whirlwind style. Since turning pro 32 months earlier, "The Cuban Bon Bon" had gone through 56 opponents without a loss.

Although the Great Depression had begun a year earlier, the dream match between Kid Chocolate and Jackie "Kid" Berg attracted over 40,000 paying customers to New York's Polo Grounds. The fight was rated "even money" by oddsmakers.

In the first three rounds Kid Chocolate utilized his great speed, shifty footwork, and quick counterpunches to keep Berg from getting inside. It usually took Berg a few rounds to warm to the task and switch into high gear.

Making good use of his almost-nine-pound weight advantage, Berg charged out of his corner in the fourth round and bulled the Cuban fighter into the ropes. Chocolate tried to fight back and get a rally going, but he could not sustain the assault for more than a few moments, nor could he match Berg's excessive volume of punches. The only way he could slow down the assault was by clinching, a tactic that drew boos from the fans. There were no boos when Berg was awarded the 10-round decision.

Following his victory over Chocolate, Berg defended his title against Buster Brown, and then won a second decision over Joe Glick (non-title). In his final bout of 1930 Jackie exacted sweet revenge against former conqueror Billy Petrolle by winning a unanimous 10-round decision over the "The Fargo Express" at Madison Square Garden. In less than a year Berg defeated 11 quality opponents, counting among his victims the likes of Tony Canzoneri, Mushy Callahan, Joe Glick (twice), Kid Chocolate, and Billy Petrolle—an amazing record of accomplishment matched by very few fighters of any era.

Berg continued his relentless schedule in 1931. He defended his junior welterweight title twice within seven days. Ten weeks later he outpointed Billy Wallace in yet another successful defense of his title. It was Berg's 95th victory against only five losses.

On April 24, 1931, only two weeks after defeating Wallace, Berg challenged Tony Canzoneri for the lightweight championship of the world. Since losing to Berg 15 months earlier, Canzoneri had won the lightweight title with a first-round knockout of Al Singer. Tony's record showed only nine losses in 93 fights.

From the opening bell it was apparent that Canzoneri had no intention of letting the fight go to a decision. He was looking to land a haymaker, and that is exactly what happened in the third round, when he landed a perfectly timed right cross to the point of Berg's jaw. Berg was caught coming into the punch (thereby exacerbating its effect) and was counted out for the first time in 106 fights.

Canzoneri agreed to a rematch on September 9, 1931, at New York's Polo Grounds. Each man knew he would have to be at his best to win. In round eight it was still anyone's fight when Canzoneri hit Berg below the beltline with a punch that sent Jackie to the canvas, writhing in pain. The New York Commission's rules stated that a fight could not be won on a foul since every fighter was required to wear a foul cup under his boxing shorts as protection against errant punches below the belt. Berg struggled to his feet and continued fighting but never regained his momentum. He staged a furious rally in the 15th and final round, but it was not enough to make up for the rounds he had lost. The unanimous decision went to Canzoneri. If the fight had been staged in England—its originally intended venue—the championship would have changed hands when Berg was fouled in the eighth round.

By the mid-1930s the marvelous fighting machine had finally begun to slow down. But even past his prime, "The Whitechapel Windmill" could still surprise with an outstanding performance. He appeared to be finished after lightweight contender Pedro Montanez stopped him in five rounds at New York's Hippodrome in 1939. Yet three months later he upset the odds by outpointing master boxer Tippy Larkin. Previous to his meeting with Berg, Larkin had lost only four of 69 fights. Jackie returned to England to finish out the balance of his career.

During World War II Jackie enlisted in the Royal Air Force. While in the service he married for the second time (his first marriage had ended in divorce). In 1946, with a wife and infant daughter to support, he decided to open a restaurant in London's Soho district. After selling the restaurant he worked for many years as a stuntman and stunt coordinator for films produced in England. To the end of his life he remained an active and beloved member of the English boxing fraternity, and his presence was often requested at major prizefights.

One could say that the lineage of England's great Jewish prizefighters that began with Daniel Mendoza 150 years earlier had come to an end with the retirement of the one and only Jackie "Kid" Berg.

MAXIE BERGER
Born: February 23, 1917
Died: August 2000 (Age: 83)
Hometown: Montreal, Canada
Height: 5' 8" Weight: 126–152 lbs.
Professional Career: 1935–1946

Total Bouts	Won	Lost	Draw	NC
131 (961 rounds)	98 (25 by KO)	23 (6 by KO)	9	1

Maxie Berger was one of the greatest boxers to ever come out of Canada. He first laced on the gloves in 1931 at the Montreal Young Men's Hebrew Association (YMHA). Three years later he capped off a sterling amateur career with a silver medal at the British Empire Games. Maxie turned pro in 1935 and breezed through his first 10 opponents before moving to New York City.

The following year he outpointed Dave Castilloux for the Canadian lightweight championship. Less than a month later he successfully defended the title with a 10-round decision over Orville Drouillard. In 1938, after defeating veteran contender Wesley Ramey (gaining revenge for two previous losses to Ramey), the Montreal Athletic Commission recognized Berger as the junior welterweight champion of the world. But

ART IMITATES LIFE

One of the best of the silent-era boxing films is a 1925 melodrama titled *His People*. The film tells the story of a Jewish family on the Lower East Side of Manhattan. Two brothers, Sammy and Morris Cominsky (played by George Lewis and Arthur Lubin), are the sons of poor immigrant parents. Good son Sammy decides to become a professional boxer to help pay for his older brother's law school education and ease his family's financial burden. (Papa Cominsky barely ekes out a living as a pushcart peddler.)

Sammy cannot let his family know that he is a boxer, so he fights using the name "Battling Rooney." When a nosy neighbor spills the beans about Sammy's boxing activities, his religiously observant father (Rudolph Schildkraut) is horrified and orders Sammy out of their home. "G-d of Israel! That a son of mine should sink so low."

Meanwhile, Sammy's older brother Morris, the lawyer, is revealed to be a self-absorbed and unscrupulous social climber. He becomes romantically involved with the daughter of a wealthy senior partner in a prestigious law firm. But Morris is so embarrassed by his family's poverty and Old World ways, he tells his fiancée that he is an orphan. The plot thickens when Papa Cominsky is taken ill and is told by a doctor he must move to a warmer climate. With no funds to pay for the move, Sammy agrees to a lucrative but dangerous fight against an experienced opponent. Needless to say, all dilemmas are eventually resolved. Sammy wins the big fight, Papa recovers, and Morris comes to his senses and asks forgiveness from his family for his boorish behavior.

The film, directed by Edward Sloman, still holds up. In his book, *Hollywood's Image of the Jew*, author Lester B. Friedman wrote, "Sloman's compelling vision of the painful depths and joyous heights of immigrant life endow the film with an exuberant vitality that captivates modern filmgoers and enlightens film historians."[23]

Scene from 1925 silent film *His People*. (L to R: Blanche Mehaffy, Rosa Rosanova, George J. Lewis, Virginia Brown Faire.)

no one beyond the city's borders gave any credence to the title.

They loved Maxie in Montreal, but the big money was in New York City, Philadelphia, and Chicago. Only 32 of his 131 fights took place in Canada.

In order to smooth the way for Maxie in New York City his managers had to cut in a character named Jimmy Doyle. Only later did Maxie find out that Doyle's real name was Jimmy Plumeri, a garment-center racketeer who managed fighters on the side.

Maxie impressed the New York fans with sensational victories over contenders Wesley Ramey, Leonard Del Genio, Enrico Venturi, Billy Beauhuld, and Bobby McIntire, but he is best remembered for a fight he lost. On February 2, 1942, he met 20-year-old phenomenon Sugar Ray Robinson in Madison Square Garden. A crowd of 12,000 excited fans saw Robinson win by a TKO in the second round. Berger had been dropped twice before the referee intervened to stop the bout—some thought prematurely. It was the first time in 97 professional fights that Maxie was stopped, and only his 13th loss up to that time. His share of the gate was $2,200.

Maxie continued to meet highly rated opponents throughout his career, even after he'd passed his prime. In his final two years as a pro he was outpointed by Beau Jack and stopped by Ike Williams. He finally retired in 1946 after a KO loss to George Costner.

A few weeks into his retirement Maxie was approached by professional gamblers with a proposition for one more bout. In 1972 he related the story to *Montreal Gazette* journalist Marvin Moss: "They offered me $10,000 to fight Johnny Greco. There was one catch: I had to lay down. I told them 'No way.' I wasn't going to go against something I believed all my life. So there never was any fight. And that was the end of it."[24]

Maxie used part of his boxing nest egg to open a store in Montreal that sold custom-made shirts. But the punches he took over the course of his 131-bout career eventually took a toll on his health. He was 83 when he passed away, but the last 10 years of his life were marked by increasingly severe dementia.

JACK BERNSTEIN
(John Dodick)
Junior Lightweight Champion 1923
Born: November 5, 1899
Died: December 26, 1945 (Age: 46)
Hometown: Yonkers, New York
Height: 5' 4" Weight: 130–134 lbs.
Professional Career: 1914–1931

Total Bouts	Won	Lost	Draw	ND
88 (872 rounds)	54 (10 by KO)	22 (1 by KO)	7	3-2

Perhaps the most underrated of all the Jewish champions is **Jack Bernstein**. Noted boxing historian Hank Kaplan ranked Bernstein the third-greatest Jewish lightweight after Benny Leonard and Lew Tendler.[25]

Indeed, very few lightweights could boast of having beaten the likes of Johnny Dundee, Solly Seeman, Babe Herman, Ray Miller, Jimmy Goodrich, Rocky Kansas, Eddie "Kid" Wagner, and Luis Vicentini. Throw in a 15-round draw with a prime Sammy Mandell and an unpopular loss to top contender Sid Terris, and it becomes obvious that Jack Bernstein, in his prime, was a fighter for the ages.

The boy who dropped out of grade school to help his father peddle fruit from a pushcart started fighting for money at the age of 14 in his hometown of Yonkers, New York. Since there weren't many Jewish boxing fans in Yonkers, young John Dodick (Bernstein's real name) began his boxing career as Kid Murphy.

From 1914 to 1920, Kid Murphy paid his dues the old-fashioned way—by fighting often and meeting fighters of every conceivable style. The muscular lad displayed an aggressive two-fisted attack combined with an effective left jab and airtight defense.

In 1920 Kid Murphy acquired a new manager who told him that since he did most of his fighting in New York City, he'd attract an even larger following with a Jewish name. To honor his hero, turn-of-the-century Jewish boxing star Joe Bernstein, Kid Murphy renamed himself Jack Bernstein. The change seemed to have a rejuvenating influence on his career.

Jack Bernstein became a force to be reckoned with in the lightweight division. In 1922 he lost only one of 17 fights. He reversed the loss to tough Archie Walker and then went on to decision Solly Seeman, Babe Herman, and Eddie "Kid" Wagner—three of the world's best lightweight contenders.

In 1923 Bernstein fought the great featherweight champion Johnny Dundee for the revived junior lightweight title at Brooklyn's Coney Island Velodrome. Dundee, in his 14th year as a pro, had already fought over 300 professional fights and was past his prime. Even so, Dundee was considered such a great fighter, he was a four to one favorite to defeat Bernstein.

Fifteen thousand fans saw Bernstein defeat the odds and win a unanimous decision over Dundee in a scorching 15-round battle.

Seven months later Bernstein lost the title back to Dundee at Madison Square Garden. Rumors of a fix were rampant after the two judges voted for the challenger (the referee had scored it for Bernstein). The Garden audience was in an uproar at the injustice, as Bernstein appeared to have won ten of the 15 rounds. Not one of more than a dozen sportswriters covering the fight thought Dundee deserved the win.

Bernstein returned to Madison Square Garden three weeks later where he fought a 15-round draw with future lightweight champ Sammy Mandell. Nine months later he fought the rubber match with Dundee (now an ex-champ, having lost the title two months earlier). He easily outpointed the fading ring great.

From 1924 to 1927 Bernstein remained a viable title threat, with victories over Tommy O'Brien, Cuddy DeMarco, Ray Miller, and former champion Jimmy Goodrich. His return match with Sid Terris in 1925, at New York's Polo Grounds, was yet another travesty of boxing justice. The decision for Terris shocked the audience. For the first time "The Ghetto Ghost" was booed as his hand was raised in victory. But fan disapproval could not change the result.

In 1927 Jack began to notice that he was losing stamina in the late rounds. This had never happened before. Something was wrong, but he could not figure out the cause. After losing twice to Yonkers neighbor Bruce Flowers, and then dropping a 10-round decision to Joe Glick in the new Madison Square Garden, Jack decided a long rest was in order.

He returned to the ring in mid-1928 and lost to a run-of-the-mill club fighter. In Bernstein's next fight he was knocked out for the first and only time in his career by Bruce Flowers. There was no shame in losing to a fighter of Flowers's caliber, but a Jack Bernstein in his prime would not have been stopped by Flowers, or any other lightweight, for that matter.

In 1931 Jack Bernstein wisely decided it was time to hang up his gloves. Although it cannot be said with certainty, the heart condition that eventually took his life 14 years later, when he was only 46 years old, may have played a factor in the stamina problems Jack was experiencing late in his career.

HARRY BLITMAN

Born: March 14, 1910
Died: May 1972 (Age: 62)
Hometown: Philadelphia, Pennsylvania
Height: 5' 7" Weight: 122–138 lbs.
Professional Career: 1926–1934

Total Bouts	Won	Lost	Draw	ND
77 (520 rounds)	53 (25 by KO)	11 (6 by KO)	4	9-0

(Courtesy of PhillyBoxingHistory.com)

If **Harry Blitman**, the Russian-born son of a tailor, had done nothing exceptional beyond his 10-round decision over featherweight champion Tony Canzoneri in 1928, that victory alone would have given him bragging rights for the rest of his life. In a startling upset the 18-year-old phenom gave Canzoneri one of the worst beatings of his career. Unfortunately the fight was a non-title affair, since both fighters weighed over the 125-pound limit. Harry walked off with the decision but not the title. When the rangy five-foot-seven southpaw was on his game, he was capable of defeating any featherweight in the world.

As an amateur, 16-year-old Harry had won the Junior National AAU flyweight championship in 1926. He entered the pro ranks with an outstanding 93-2 amateur record, and was undefeated in his first 35 professional bouts. Among his victims were Dave Adelman, Dominick Petrone, Johnny Farr, and Seminole Indian Pete Nebo. (Harry rated Nebo as his toughest opponent.)

Ten weeks after stomping Canzoneri, Harry challenged hometown rival Benny Bass in Philadelphia's Shibe Park. Canzoneri had outpointed Bass to win the featherweight championship less than a year earlier

The five-foot-two Bass was one of the strongest boxers to ever hold the featherweight title, and far more experienced than Harry. In a savagely fought battle Bass maneuvered inside his taller opponent's guard and punished him severely about the body. A left hook to the jaw put Blitman down and out in the sixth round. The bout had been advertised as for both the Pennsylvania and Jewish featherweight championships. A crowd of 35,000 fans witnessed the fight, with gate receipts topping $100,000. Blitman's end came to $25,000—the largest purse of his career.

After the loss Blitman rebounded with decisions over highly rated contenders Babe Herman, Lew Massey, and Pete Nebo, but then lost to Nebo and Massey in return bouts. By 1932

Harry was losing to fighters he could have easily defeated in his prime. It was obvious that his management had rushed the young fighter too quickly. Too many tough fights against formidable opposition had finally taken a toll. At age 24 his days as a top contender were over. After winning only one of four fights in 1934, Harry called it a career.

After hanging up his gloves Harry worked as a stevedore at the Ford Motor Company's riverfront plant in Chester, Pennsylvania. He also wrote a series of articles on old-time fighters for the *Camden Courier Post*. When the United States entered World War II, Blitman became a physical training instructor in the navy, but received a medical discharge after one year.

Harry returned to the newspaper business and was a columnist for the *Philadelphia Record* and the *Philadelphia Daily News*. He was a vocal advocate for stricter medical examinations for fighters, which he wrote about in an article in the *Saturday Evening Post*.

(Courtesy of PhillyBoxingHistory.com)

HARRY "KID" BROWN

Born: March 10, 1901
Died: March 28, 1985 (Age: 84)
Hometown: Philadelphia, Pennsylvania
Weight: 132–143 lbs.
Professional Career: 1915–1932

Total Bouts	Won	Lost	Draw	ND	NC
183 (1,469 rounds)	61 (19 by KO)	26 (3 by KO)	10	56-16-12	2

From 1900 to 1930 Philadelphia produced a veritable cornucopia of world-class Jewish ring talent. One of the best of the Philadelphia elite was lightweight contender **Harry "Kid" Brown**. In his prime he scored impressive victories over top-rated Baby Joe Gans and Young Harry Wills, and drew with Cuddy DeMarco, Manuel Quintero, and Johnny Indrisano (newspaper decision). There was no shame in losing to the likes of Sid Terris and future champions Sammy Mandell, Jackie Fields, and Young Jack Thompson.

In his post-boxing career Harry operated the popular Olympia Gym (also known as Harry "Kid" Brown's gym) and managed a bar and grill, located on Marshall Street in Philadelphia. Harry is the brother of the famous sculptor, Joe Brown, who taught at Princeton University for many years and whose work often depicted boxing scenes.

JOHNNY BROWN

(Philip Hickman)
Born: July 18, 1902
Died July 1, 1976 (Age: 73)
Hometown: London, England
Weight: 122–128 lbs.
Professional Career: 1919–1928

Total Bouts	Won	Lost	Draw	ND
93 (820 rounds)	52 (29 by KO)	25 (9 by KO)	4	8-3-1

After establishing his reputation in London rings, **Johnny Brown** traveled to America in 1921 to engage in 18 bouts against the world's top bantamweights. During the mid-1920s he was consistently rated among the top 10 bantamweights in the world. He split his boxing activity between America and England, with occasional forays into Canada.

On November 26, 1923, in London, Brown won the European, British, and Commonwealth (Empire) bantamweight titles via a 20-round decision over Bugler Harry Lake. He defended successfully against Harry Corbett and Mick Hill. In the last fight of his career Brown lost his British titles to former bantamweight champion Teddy Baldock.

Johnny is the older brother of "Young" Johnny Brown, a fine featherweight contender who also fought in both America and England.

(Hank Kaplan Boxing Archive, Brooklyn College Archives and Special Collections)

NATIE BROWN

Born: March 2, 1910
Died: June 24, 1991 (Age: 81)
Hometown: Washington, DC
Height: 6' 1" Weight: 183–233 lbs.
Professional Career: 1928–1940, 1943–1949

Total Bouts	Won	Lost	Draw	NC
83 (623 rounds)	41 (13 by KO)	30 (8 by KO)	10	1

Natie Brown's claim to fame was surviving ten rounds with Joe Louis. They fought on March 29, 1935, in Joe's hometown of Detroit, Michigan. The future heavyweight champion was only nine months into his professional career but had already knocked out 13 of 16 opponents.

Brown had been a pro since 1928. He was a tough and seasoned journeyman, with 53 bouts under his belt. Although there were 17 losses on his record, most were to good fighters such as Max Baer, Fred Lenhart, Joe Knight, Tony Galento, and Maxie Rosenbloom.

In 1935 Brown was rated among the top 10 heavyweight challengers after victories over Johnny Risko and Tony Galento, and draws with Walter Neusel and former middleweight champion Mickey Walker.

The veteran heavyweight's experience enabled him to survive the first round against Louis after getting knocked down. Brown realized it would be suicide to risk swapping punches with Joe, so he went into survival mode and managed to last the full 10 rounds. Even though he lost, going the distance with Louis was a kind of victory in itself.

In a return bout with Louis two years later, Brown was KO'd in the fourth round. He fought just 19 times over the next 12 years before retiring in 1949. A few months later Brown returned to the ring, but not as a boxer. The former heavyweight contender traded in his boxing trunks for wrestling tights and became a professional wrestler, joining his old foe "Two Ton" Tony Galento on the grunt-and-groan circuit.

NEWSBOY BROWN

(Dave Montrose)
Flyweight Champion 1928
Born: August 8, 1917
Died: February 1977 (Age: 71)
Hometown: Los Angeles, California
Height: 5' 1" Weight: 112–120 lbs.
Professional Career: 1922–1933

Total Bouts	Won	Lost	Draw	ND
91 (818 rounds)	56 (11 by KO)	13 (1 by KO)	5	12-0-5

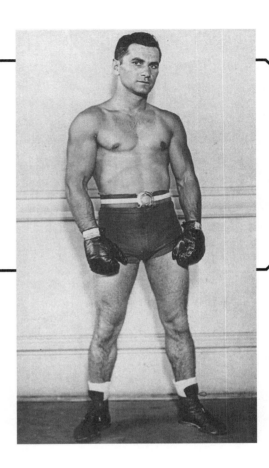

David Montrochevsky's parents fled the persecution and poverty of Czarist Russia at the turn of the last century and emigrated to, of all places, Sioux City, Iowa. There were not many Jews in Sioux City; in fact, most of its citizens had never even seen a Jewish person. David's father thought it best to anglicize the family name to "Montrose."

Young David contributed to the family budget by selling newspapers on the street corners of Sioux City. In a situation repeated countless times in other cities, he had to use his fists to discourage other newsboys from taking over his coveted corner. Many other pro fighters started out the same way. That's why so many of them had the nickname "Newsboy."

In one of his earliest amateur fights the announcer could not remember his name. It was summertime, and David, who spent most days outdoors hawking newspapers, had a deep tan.

He was introduced as "The brown-skinned newsboy . . . **Newsboy Brown.**" The name stayed with him for the rest of his career.

In 1925, three years after turning pro, Newsboy Brown transferred his base of operations to Los Angeles. In his first fight on the West Coast, Brown was matched with the 1924 Olympic flyweight champion, Fidel LaBarba. The unknown Sioux City brawler held the Olympian to a 10-round draw. Brown's excellent showing gave him instant credibility, especially after LaBarba won the National Boxing Association flyweight title only four months later.

A testament to Brown's growing popularity was his being chosen to participate on the opening card of the brand-new Olympic Auditorium in downtown Los Angeles. The Olympic was a 10,000-seat auditorium that opened in 1925. In the coming years it would acquire legendary status as California's premier arena and the West Coast's equivalent to Madison Square Garden.

Following his draw with LaBarba, Brown defeated two future flyweight champions—Frankie Genaro and Corporal Izzy Schwartz. These two victories moved him into the upper echelon of flyweight contenders.

On December 16, 1927, at Madison Square Garden, Brown dropped a close 15-round decision to flyweight champion Corporal Izzy Schwartz. Three weeks later he returned to the Olympic Auditorium in Los Angeles to challenge Johnny McCoy for California's version of the world flyweight title. In a barnburner of a fight, Newsboy edged out McCoy to win the title.

Brown defended his title for the first time on April 24, 1928, in Los Angeles against Filipino champion Speedy Dado. He stopped the game challenger in the sixth round. In August he traveled to London for a fight with Scotland's Johnny Hill. The fight was recognized as a world-title bout by California and Great Britain. After 15 hotly contested rounds, Hill's hand was raised in victory.

No longer able to make the flyweight limit, Brown returned to the ring wars in 1929 as a bantamweight. Over the next three years he lost only three of 26 fights. Two of the losses were reversed in rematches. His most impressive victories were non-title decisions over flyweight champion Midget Wolgast and bantamweight champion Panama Al Brown—two of the greatest fighters to ever hold those titles. He also defeated contenders Pablo Dano, Claude Varner,

Archie Bell, Young Tommy, and Eugene Huat. Brown was consistently rated among the top four bantamweights in the world, but was not given an opportunity to fight for that title.

By 1932 the wear and tear of his busy career was beginning to show. In June Brown dropped a 10-round nod to Mexican contender Alberto "Baby" Arizmendi, a future featherweight champion. In the rematch staged two weeks later, Brown used his superior ring savvy to outpoint Arizmendi.

The rubber match with Arizmendi took place four months later on October 18, 1932. The bout was recognized by the California State Athletic Commission as a world featherweight title bout.

Arizmendi dominated the fight and had Brown on the verge of a KO at least three times. The Associated Press reported that Arizmendi, "displaying all the speed and agility of his Aztec ancestry . . . decisively whipped his Los Angeles Jewish opponent here last night before 7,000 persons."

Six months later, in the final bout of his illustrious career, Newsboy Brown fought Baby Casanova in the El Toreo bullring in Mexico City. Over 30,000 fans watched and cheered as their national hero stopped the faded veteran in the third round. Brown never fought again.

Before he retired Newsboy was hired by a Hollywood studio to coach cowboy star Tom Mix for his fight scenes. Mix was later instrumental in getting Brown a job in the properties department of a major studio, where he worked for many years.

CHARITY BEGINS AT HOME

Established boxers were often called upon to help with charitable causes. Most responded without hesitation. On October 21, 1929, three days before the stock market crash, subway builder Sam Rosoff rented Madison Square Garden for an all-star boxing card to raise money for the beleaguered Jews living in British Mandate for Palestine. Two months earlier, on August 24, 1929, Arabs had rioted in the ancient city of Hebron and murdered 67 Jews.

The show consisted of five 10-round bouts matching Jewish boxers against five gentile opponents. Maxie Rosenbloom headlined. The four other Jewish boxers were Al Singer, Jackie "Kid" Berg, Ruby Goldstein, and Yale Okun. All five won their bouts. The show drew 16,000 spectators and raised over $75,000 (equivalent to $1 million today) for the Palestine Emergency Fund, to help Jews in the pre-state land of Israel.

An all-star 1929 boxing card at Madison Square Garden to benefit Palestine's beleaguered Jews featured five of New York's top Jewish boxers.

JOE BURMAN

Born: December 11, 1898
Died: April 1979 (Age: 80)
Hometown: Chicago, Illinois
Height: 5' 4" **Weight:** 118 lbs.
Professional Career: 1916–1924

Total Bouts	Won	Lost	Draw	ND	NC
129 (1,053 rounds)	36 (21 by KO)	3 (0 by KO)	6	49-16-12	7

Chicago's **Joe Burman** holds the record for the shortest title reign in boxing history—about 10 hours. Joe was scheduled to challenge bantamweight champion Joe Lynch at Madison Square Garden on October 19, 1923. This would have been their second meeting. Seven months earlier they had fought a 10-round non-title bout before 10,000 fans in Chicago's Dexter Park Arena. Two newspapers awarded the unofficial decision to Burman.

A few days before the title bout Lynch pulled out, claiming a shoulder injury. A physician for the New York State Athletic Commission determined the injury was not serious. Lynch disagreed and refused to fight. When he did not show up for the official weigh-in on the day of the fight, the commissioner stripped him of the title and awarded it to Burman.

Promoters put out a frantic call for a substitute. Bantamweight contender Abe Goldstein answered the call. He was in top shape, having fought three times in the previous 17 days.

The 12-round title bout was a corker, with the outcome determined by Goldstein's strong finish in the final minutes of the fight. Burman's brief reign as champion had come to an end. Adding insult to injury, his claim to the title was never recognized, since he did not win it in the ring. He fought only four more times before hanging up his gloves in 1924.

Although he did not win a world title, Joe Burman was a championship-caliber boxer. His impressive victories over Joe Lynch, Pete Herman, Charles Ledoux, and Johnny McCoy proved it. In 129 career bouts he was never knocked out.

Burman's post-boxing career included stints as a matchmaker and promoter at Chicago's Marigold Gardens. He also operated a popular men's clothing store in the city's Loop district before moving to Los Angeles.

MUSHY CALLAHAN
(Morris Scheer)
Born: November 3, 1905
Died: June 16, 1986 (Age: 80)
Hometown: Los Angeles, California
Height: 5' 7½" Weight: 140–145 lbs.
Professional Career: 1923–1930, 1932

Total Bouts	Won	Lost	Draw	ND
67 (450 rounds)	48 (21 by KO)	15 (3 by KO)	3	0-1

At the age of ten, **Morris Scheer** joined the Los Angeles Newsboys' Boxing Club. A few months later he had his first amateur fight. The youngster wanted a more-pugnacious sounding *nom de box*, so he adopted the Irish surname of the club's promoter. But Morris Callahan did not sound quite right, so he changed his first name from Morris to "Mushy," which was simply a derivative of his Hebrew name, "Moishe."

Ten years later Mushy Callahan became a bona fide welterweight contender, with impressive victories over Spug Myers, Pal Moran, James Red Herring, Ace Hudkins, and former lightweight champion Jimmy Goodrich. His progress slowed somewhat when he lost back-to-back 10-round decisions to highly ranked contenders Jack Silver and Baby Joe Gans, but those losses turned out to be a blessing in disguise. The newly crowned junior welterweight champion, Pinky

Mitchell, was encouraged by the losses, and agreed to defend his title against Callahan on September 26, 1926.

Mushy proved to be much better than Mitchell's research had indicated. He won easily, flooring Mitchell twice while romping to a 10-round decision. The new champion followed up his victory over Mitchell with four straight wins (three by knockout) before dropping a close 10-round nod to Spug Myers in a non-title bout.

In 1929 Callahan lost a close decision (non-title) to British sensation Jackie "Kid" Berg at Brooklyn's Ebbets Field. He was lured to London for a rematch with Berg after promoters offered a $10,000 guarantee to defend his title.

Mushy and Jackie crossed gloves at London's Royal Albert Hall on February 18, 1930. A head butt early in the fight closed Callahan's eye. Trying to keep pace with "The Whitechapel Windmill" with two good eyes was difficult enough; with one eye, it was near impossible. The bout was stopped in the 10th round.

After the loss of his title Callahan did not fight again for two years. In 1932 he launched a brief comeback, winning two of three fights before deciding to hang up his gloves for good.

Single throughout his boxing career, Mushy settled down in 1934 and married his Irish sweetheart, Lillian Hill, a former Ziegfeld Follies showgirl. That same year he converted to Catholicism—one of three Jewish fighters known to have converted to another religion. His son became a Jesuit priest.

Mushy worked as a physical fitness instructor for actors and actresses under contract to the Warner Brothers studio. He also served as technical director and consultant for many films with a boxing theme, coaching the actors and choreographing fight scenes. Some of the actors he worked with included Wayne Morris (*Kid Galahad*), Errol Flynn (*Gentleman Jim*), Kirk Douglas (*Champion*), Montgomery Clift (*From Here to Eternity*), Elvis Presley (remake *of Kid Galahad*), and James Earl Jones (*The Great White Hope*). Mushy played the part of referee in at least a dozen of the films he worked on. It was a role he also undertook in real life, often refereeing major fights in California.

RED CHAPMAN

(Morris Kaplan)
Born: August 16, 1901
Died: October 22, 1979 (Age: 78)
Hometown: Boston, Massachusetts
Height: 5' 5" Weight: 125 lbs.
Professional Career: 1920–1929

Total Bouts	Won	Lost	Draw	ND	NC
92 (715 rounds)	61 (21 by KO)	21 (3 by KO)	1	7-0-1	1

Red Chapman (né Morris Kaplan) was one of 10 children born to Russian immigrant parents in the Chelsea section of Boston. He began his professional boxing career in 1920, and over the next six years the redheaded fighter impressed fans and sportswriters with decisions over featherweight contenders Lew Paluso, Andy Chaney, Charlie Beecher, Babe Herman, and former champion Johnny Dundee.

When Louis "Kid" Kaplan relinquished the featherweight title in 1927, a tournament was arranged to name a successor. The two finalists were Chapman and Benny Bass of Philadelphia. The title bout took place on September 12, 1927, at Philadelphia's Shibe Park in front of 30,000 fans.

In the ninth round of an exciting seesaw battle both contestants hit the deck simultaneously after exchanging right hooks—a rare double knockdown! The startled referee began counting over both downed fighters. Benny got up first and staggered into the ropes. Chapman just beat the count and barely managed to finish the round. The 10-round decision, and the title, went to Benny. Chapman was consoled by the $25,000 he received, the largest payday of his career.

Chapman and Bass fought again on January 28, 1929. Bass was no longer champion, having lost the title to Tony Canzoneri a year earlier. The first round was barely over when Chapman claimed a foul. The referee disallowed the claim and Bass was declared the winner on a first-round knockout. It's probably best that it ended that way. Another war like their first demolition derby could have finished both fighters.

Described by those who knew him as a spry and energetic gentleman, Red was employed for many years as a court officer in Boston's Suffolk Superior Court. His son, Alan, graduated from law school and went on to become one of Boston's top criminal defense attorneys.

MICKEY COHEN
Born: June 1, 1909
Died: Unknown
Hometown: Denver, Colorado
Weight: 135–145 lbs.
Professional Record: 1926–1935

Total Bouts	Won	Lost	Draw	ND	NC
108 (751 rounds)	60 (29 by KO)	25 (KO by 6)	7	11-2-2	1

Denver's **Mickey Cohen** is often confused with another fighter with the same name who fought out of Cleveland and had a brief career as a mediocre bantamweight in the early 1930s. *That* Mickey Cohen achieved far greater notoriety as a Los Angeles gangster in the 1950s. *This* Mickey Cohen (whose real first name was David) was neither mediocre nor a gangster. He was a world-class junior welterweight boxer who was good enough to outpoint the likes of Davey Abad, Harry Dublinsky, and Mike Dundee—all highly rated contenders.

(Courtesy of J.J. Johnston)

According to contemporary newspaper reports, Cohen also took the measure of contenders Joe Glick and Tommy Grogan in no-decision bouts. He was consistently rated among the top 10 junior welterweights from 1930 to 1932.

Between 1926 and 1932 Mickey fought 101 bouts. He fought only three times in 1933 and just once in 1934. The following year, after a knockout loss to future welterweight champ Freddie "Red" Cochrane, Mickey decided it was time to hang up his gloves. Fortunately, unlike many of his contemporaries, Mickey stuck to his decision and did not launch a comeback.

AL "BUMMY" DAVIS

(Albert Abraham Davidoff)
Born: January 26, 1920
Died: November 21, 1945 (Age: 25)
Hometown: Brooklyn, New York
Weight: 145 lbs.
Professional Career: 1937–1945

Total Bouts	Won	Lost	Draw
79 (398 rounds)	65 (45 by KO)	10 (3 by KO)	4

Al Davis's nickname, "**Bummy**," was a derivation of his Hebrew name, Avrum. Friends and family affectionately called him "Vroomy." A local boxing promoter thought "Vroomy" sounded a lot like "Bummy." He told the fighter that adding the colorful nickname would create interest—which it did. The name seemed just right for a tough dead-end kid from the gritty streets of Brownsville, Brooklyn.

At age 14 Al Davis was already an experienced street fighter when he began boxing in the amateurs. From the beginning he exhibited a talent for knocking people out. A converted southpaw, Al packed a tremendous portside wallop. What he lacked in boxing technique he more than made up for with guts, durability, and that dynamite-laden left hook. He was a rough street kid with a hair-trigger temper, but when he wasn't punching people for a living, he was a good-natured, pleasant young man who did not go looking for trouble.

Davis turned pro in 1935 at the age of 15. Over the next four years he went undefeated in 35 bouts, including 19 by knockout. On

November 1, 1939, at Madison Square Garden, he ended the career of the great Tony Canzoneri with a third-round TKO. Tony was 11 years older than Davis, and a shell of the extraordinary fighter he'd been during his heyday. It was the first time in 170 professional fights that Canzoneri was knocked out. The next day, to everyone's relief, Canzoneri announced his retirement.

Six weeks after the Canzoneri fight Davis returned to Madison Square Garden to face master boxer Tippy Larkin. The crowd numbered over 17,000 fans. Bummy's left hook flattened Larkin in the fifth round. It was Larkin's first knockout loss in 72 professional bouts.

Davis was now the hottest fighter in the country and a world-rated welterweight contender. On February 23, 1940, he was back on top at the Garden for a 10-round non-title match with lightweight champion Lew Ambers, a cagey, hardened veteran of 100 bouts. The arena was packed to the rafters with a standing-room-only crowd of 21,000 exuberant fans.

Ambers (real name Louis D'Ambrosio) had recently defeated the great Henry Armstrong for the lightweight crown. To honor his hometown of Herkimer, New York, Ambers was nicknamed "The Herkimer Hurricane." He was a tireless seasoned ring tactician with an iron jaw.

The Herkimer Hurricane took Bummy to school. Actually, he did more than that. What Bummy got was a master class in the fine art of boxing. Ambers simply overwhelmed the young fighter with his vast experience. By the eighth round Davis was bleeding from his nose and mouth and both of his eyes were nearly closed, but he refused to go down, gutting it out to the last round. He won only two rounds on the judges' scorecards. Davis realized he still had a lot to learn.

To close out 1940 Bummy was in Madison Square Garden with Fritzie Zivic, who had whipped Henry Armstrong for the welterweight title five weeks earlier.

Zivic had a ton of experience (128 bouts), but he was also one of the dirtiest fighters to ever wear a crown. Zivic knew every trick in the book—both subtle and not so subtle. Most of the tricks were done so artfully that he was never disqualified. Within a minute of the first round Zivic had thumbed, butted, and raked his laces across Davis's eyes. At one point, while the ref was breaking up a clinch, Zivic stepped behind the official and belted Bummy. "He's trying to blind me!" the distressed fighter screamed at his seconds during the one-minute break between the first and second rounds.

Zivic continued the same tactics in the second round. Davis was unable to land a solid punch on his elusive tormentor. Midway through the round he decided to take matters into his own hands—Brownsville style. Davis shoved Zivic back, shouting "Okay, you son-of-a-bitch, if you want to fight dirty, let's go!" and then went completely berserk. He began winging punches aimed directly at Zivic's groin, landing six or seven shots before the referee was able to pull him off.

Davis was immediately disqualified. He responded by kicking the referee and then went

Fritzie Zivic (right) jabs Al "Bummy" Davis moments before the riotous ending.

him to fight Zivic in a return match at New York's Polo Grounds, with the proviso that his end of the purse would go to the US Army Relief Fund.

Davis had been inactive since their last bout and weighed almost 200 pounds when he began training. Zivic had kept busy, fighting at least once a month.

Both fighters were warned by the boxing commission that there would be serious consequences if they did not fight according to the rules.

Zivic behaved himself, using an incessant left jab and nimble footwork to keep Davis at a safe distance and avoid his vaunted left hook. The bout was competitive until the seventh round, when Zivic took full command and proceeded to administer a terrific beating. Davis was out on his feet when the referee intervened to stop the bout in the 10th round.

With his New York suspension still in effect, Davis remained active by fighting in other states. When the suspension was finally lifted, he returned to Madison Square Garden for the first time in three years. On February 18, 1944, he was matched with former lightweight champion Bob Montgomery. Bummy was a 4–1 underdog, but he still possessed the ability to draw in the customers. Over 18,000 fans were on hand to witness his return.

Bummy knocked out Montgomery in just 63 seconds of the first round. It was the quickest knockout ever recorded in Madison Square Garden. (Two weeks after his disastrous encounter

after Zivic again. It took a small army of police, corner men, and the Garden's security staff to restrain the wild-eyed Brownsville bomber and forcibly remove him from the arena. The 17,000 fans in attendance were in an uproar. Crumpled programs, hats, cigar butts, beer containers, and other assorted debris sailed into the ring. A full-scale riot was narrowly averted.

The next day the New York State Athletic Commission lowered the boom on Bummy. He was suspended for life and fined $2,500. But eight months later he was granted a temporary reprieve. The New York Commission allowed with Davis, Montgomery regained the light-weight title by outpointing Beau Jack in 15 rounds.)

The Montgomery win was the climax of Davis's colorful boxing career. He won nine of his next 11 bouts, but lost the important ones to Beau Jack and Henry Armstrong. Although he was only 24 years old, the Brownsville slugger had already fought 72 professional bouts. He had recently married and was considering hanging up his gloves, but could not resist the money offered him to fight the sport's latest knockout sensation, Rocky Graziano.

The highly anticipated slugfest matched Bummy's left hook against Rocky's right cross. The fans got exactly what they expected. Before the bell ended the second round, Davis and Graziano had exchanged knockdowns. In the third round Graziano knocked Davis down with a punch that landed seconds after the bell rang. It's possible Graziano did not hear the bell above the din of 17,000 screaming fans, but despite protests from Davis's corner, the referee allowed the bout to continue. Davis was still groggy when the fourth round began and was quickly floored. Bummy got up—he always did—but Rocky was teeing off on his chin. The referee stopped the fight 44 seconds into the round.

In his eight years as a pro Davis had earned a small fortune, estimated to be in excess of $200,000. He used part of the money to invest in a neighborhood tavern and two racehorses.

It will never be known if he would have continued with his boxing career. In the early-morning hours of November 21, 1945, he was talking to some friends in his Brooklyn bar when four holdup men barged in with guns drawn. The thugs had already taken about $1,400 from other bars in the previous hour.

Bummy had just sold the establishment to his friend, who now stood behind the bar, a gun pointed at his head. Bummy felt an obligation to do something. He calmly addressed the four nervous gunmen. "Why don't you leave him alone? The guy just bought this place. Give him a break." For a moment the thieves stood frozen. Then the one nearest Bummy spoke up, "Why don't you mind your own fucken' business before I blow your brains out?"

Perhaps had the punk known who he was talking to, he would have chosen his words more carefully. But the die was cast. Bummy's hair-trigger temper took over. His first left hook dropped the guy who insulted him, breaking his jaw. He then took off after the others. The hoodlums panicked and ran out the door while firing back at Bummy. A slug tore into his right arm but he kept charging. As they raced to their getaway car a bullet struck him in the neck, and another pierced his lung. Bummy collapsed and was dead before he hit the sidewalk.

The following day news of his death appeared on the front page of the *New York Times*. He was 25 years old and left a wife and two-year-old son.

(Courtesy of Jerry Fitch)

JACKIE DAVIS

Born: November 10, 1912
Died: Unknown
Hometown: Cleveland, Ohio
Height: 5' 5½" Weight: 142 lbs.
Professional Career: 1930–1935

Total Bouts	Won	Lost	Draw	ND
122 (874 rounds)	73 (16 by KO)	28 (1 by KO)	18	1-2

Jackie Davis won a Chicago Golden Gloves title in 1930. Four years later he was a rated welterweight contender, having outpointed Izzy Jannazzo, Cocoa Kid, and former lightweight champion Sammy Mandell. In addition to the above top fighters, Jackie also crossed gloves with Barney Ross, Harry Dublinsky, Wesley Ramey, Andy Callahan, Pete Nebo, and Battling Battalino.

In 1934 Jackie Davis was stopped by future lightweight champion Lew Ambers. It was his only KO loss in 122 bouts.

Davis returned to his hometown of Cleveland after he retired. He was a referee in the 1940s and '50s, and also wrote a sports column for the *Cleveland Plain Dealer*.

DAVEY DAY

(David Daitch)
Born: August 12, 1912
Died: October 2, 1990 (Age: 78)
Hometown: Chicago, Illinois
Height: 5' 6½" Weight: 130–140 lbs.
Professional Career: 1931–1941

Total Bouts	Won	Lost	Draw
74 (477 rounds)	61 (29 by KO)	9 (2 by KO)	4

One of the Windy City's best and most popular fighters in the 1930s was crack lightweight contender **Davey Day**, a stablemate of the great Barney Ross.

Day turned pro in 1931 and compiled an exceptional record, losing only five of his first 50 bouts. Other than two early prelim losses, his only setbacks were to top contenders Al Roth and Baby Arizmendi. The other loss was by split decision to lightweight champion Lou Ambers in a non-title bout. Despite rarely weighing more than 135 pounds, Davey beat many top lightweights and welterweights, and was rated in both divisions. On his way to a title shot he defeated Stanislaus Loayza, Charley Gomer, Jimmy Garrison, Joe Ghnouly, Tommy Spiegal, Bobby Pacho, Enrico Venturi, Pete Lello, and Roger Bernard.

By 1938 the only fighter standing between Day and a world championship was Henry Armstrong, the same fighter who had defeated Barney

Ross for the welterweight title 10 months earlier. The phenomenal Armstrong, then at his peak, had also recently won both featherweight and lightweight crowns, thus becoming the only fighter in history to hold three titles simultaneously.

On March 31, 1939, at Madison Square Garden, Day challenged Armstrong for his welterweight championship. As agreed beforehand, Day weighed in 1 pound over the 135-pound lightweight limit so only Armstrong's welterweight title was on the line. The challenger fought courageously in a grueling and bloody contest, but eventually succumbed to the incessant windmill attack of "Hammerin' Hank." The referee stopped the bout at 2:49 of the 12th round.

Proving you can't keep a good man down, Davey bounced back two months later with an eighth-round TKO of top lightweight contender Pedro Montanez. He then split two fights with future champ Sammy Angott. They were rematched for a third time on May 3, 1940, for the vacant lightweight title, and Angott won a close 15-round decision.

Following his loss to Angott, Davey flattened Nick Castiglione in one round and won a 10-round decision over tough Billy Marquart. In his last fight, on October 10, 1941, he was knocked out in the first round by future lightweight champion Bob Montgomery. Aside from his loss to Armstrong, it was the only time in 74 pro bouts that he was ever knocked out. Davey retired after the loss to Montgomery and opened a luggage store in the Loop district. He also operated a veteran's taxi for many years.

SAMMY DORFMAN

Born: January 1905
Died: August 1974 (Age: 68)
Hometown: New York, New York
Weight: 130–140 lbs.
Professional Career: 1925–1933, 1941

Total Bouts	Won	Lost	Draw	ND
86 (634 rounds)	60 (9 by KO)	10 (1 by KO)	13	2-1

From 1925 to 1927 **Sammy Dorfman** lost only one of 40 professional fights. He established his credentials as a top featherweight contender, with victories over Carl Duane, Dominick Petrone, and Petey Mack.

On April 4, 1929, at Madison Square Garden, Sammy faced the great former featherweight champion Tony Canzoneri. Dorfman gave it his best shot, but Canzoneri was just too good, and walked off with a 10-round decision.

Following the loss to Canzoneri, Dorfman remained undefeated in his next 17 fights, until Detroit's highly ranked Wesley Ramey ended his streak with a 10-round decision on May 15, 1931.

Sammy took great pride in the fact that no one had been able to knock him out. Toward the end of his career, in 1932, a biased referee stopped his bout with a Philadelphia boxer named Charlie Baxter because of a swollen eye. Dorfman was incensed by the referee's decision. As reported in the *New York Times*, Dorfman "went at him," and "it took half a dozen burly policemen to remove him from the ring. . . . The police and his seconds carried him to the dressing room."

Dorfman fought only three more times and then retired. Eight years later, at the age of 36, he made a short-lived comeback as a middleweight. He knocked out his opponent in the second round and then hung up his gloves for good.

THE MEDICAL COMMUNITY GIVES IT A NAME

The outward signs of neurological damage caused by repeated blows to the head had been observed in boxers ever since the sport first began, but no one had ever put a medical term to it. In 1928 Dr. Harrison Martland, a noted forensic pathologist and the chief medical examiner for Newark, New Jersey, published an article in the *Journal of the American Medical Association* that included various case studies of active and retired boxers. Some of the boxers in the study exhibited symptoms that included tremors, mental confusion, slowed movement, and problems with balance and speech—all typical of fighters who've taken too many punches to the head. He coined the phrase "punch drunk syndrome" to describe the condition. A few years later doctors renamed the condition using the more elegantly worded dementia pugilistica.

Among the theories put forth by Dr. Martland was an explanation of how it was possible that multiple concussion hemorrhages in the deeper portions of the boxer's brain could, over time, often mimic the symptoms seen in Parkinson's disease. Today these cases are referred to as Parkinsonism Pugilistica, the syndrome currently affecting former heavyweight champion Muhammad Ali. (This should not be confused with regular Parkinson's disease, which is a slowly progressive neurodegenerative disorder associated with motor and non-motor symptoms.)

Thirteen years after Dr. Martland's article appeared, an important book on the subject was published. *The Medical Aspect of Boxing* by Ernst Jokl, MD, was the first book devoted entirely to explaining the types of injuries suffered by professional boxers. Since then the subject has been further analyzed by other doctors. In 1984 the American Medical Association adopted a resolution calling for the abolition of boxing, both amateur and professional, because of "the dangerous effects of boxing on the health of participants."[26]

Over the past few years much attention has been paid to head injuries incurred by professional football players. The research currently being conducted in this regard can no doubt help to define the pathology of brain injuries suffered by boxers as well as football players, and perhaps lead to greater safety measures, although trying to solve the problem in a sport whose goal is to inflict physical damage remains problematical. The entire range of chronic head injuries originating from several different sports is now defined using the umbrella term *chronic traumatic encephalopathy* (CTE).

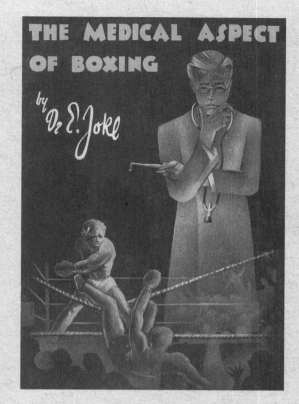

The first book devoted entirely to explaining the types of injuries suffered by professional boxers.

LEONE EFRATI

Born: May 26, 1915
Died: April 16, 1944 (Age: 28)
Hometown: Rome, Italy
Weight: 128–132 lbs.
Professional Career: 1935–1939

Total Bouts	Won	Lost	Draw
49 (401 rounds)	27 (0 by KO)	10 (0 by KO)	12

Italian-born **Leone Efrati** was one of the six million Jewish martyrs murdered in the Holocaust. Before the war he was one of Europe's finest boxers, establishing an excellent record prior to his arrival in the United States in 1938. A victory over contender Frankie Covelli (their previous bout had ended in a draw decision) led to a National Boxing Association title bout with featherweight champion Leo Rodak in Chicago. Efrati lost a very close 10-round decision.

Two weeks after his unsuccessful bid for the featherweight title, Efrati fought a 10-round draw with future contender Pete Lello. In his final two bouts in America (he had 13 altogether), Efrati lost 10-round decisions to Covelli and future featherweight champion Jackie Callura.

In 1939 Efrati was deported back to Italy, which at the time was a German ally. His supporters in the United States tried to convince State Department officials that, as a Jew, his return was tantamount to a death sentence, but to no avail. Four years later, in 1943, Efrati was arrested in Rome. He was sent to Auschwitz, where he was forced to take part in brutal boxing matches against much heavier opponents for the amusement of the sadistic guards. Efrati survived all of this, but when his brother was beaten by the guards, he came to his defense. His fists were no match against machine guns, and Leone Efrati died in Auschwitz on April 16, 1944.

IRVING ELDRIDGE

Born: 1914
Died: Unknown
Hometown: New York, New York
Weight: 135 lbs.
Professional Career: 1933–1940

Total Bouts	Won	Lost	Draw
88 (563 rounds)	62 (24 by KO)	15 (2 by KO)	11

Irving Eldridge turned pro on August 28, 1933, with a four-round decision over Johnny Mendes at Starlight Park in the Bronx. The five-foot-eight 135-pounder was a diamond in the rough, so his managers took their time polishing the young fighter's skills and getting him experience. Irving had 27 bouts before he engaged in his first eight-rounder. That fight, against highly ranked Frankie Covelli, resulted in his first loss.

Three years and 30 fights later, Irving was ready for any lightweight in the world. At various times between 1939 and 1940, *The Ring* magazine rated him as high as number eight among the top lightweight challengers. His stature was enhanced with victories over Tommy Spiegal, Jimmy Vaughn, Claude Varner, and future welterweight champion Freddie "Red" Cochrane.

In 1940 Eldridge outpointed Lenny "Boom Boom" Mancini (the father of Ray "Boom Boom" Mancini) in eight rounds. Six days later he was knocked out for only the second time in his career by top-ranked Aldo Spoldi, the same fighter who outpointed him three years earlier. Irving could have used a rest, but just two weeks later he was back in the ring for the last time, and lost a return bout to Mancini. In his entire career, up to that point, Eldridge had never suffered two consecutive losses. After 88 bouts, the 26-year-old decided it was time to hang up his gloves.

MURRAY ELKINS

Born: 1906
Died: 1959 (Age: 53)
Hometown: New York, New York
Weight: 139–150 lbs.
Professional Career: 1923–1932

Total Bouts	Won	Lost	Draw	ND	NC
48 (333 rounds)	32 (4 by KO)	8 (3 by KO)	4	1-1	2

Between 1923 and 1926 **Murray Elkins** lost only one of 26 professional bouts. Among his victims were three outstanding boxers: Bruce Flowers, Joey Silvers, and Cirilin Olano. He lost a 10-round decision to Flowers in their return bout, but rebounded with victories over Al Bryant and Young Terry. For six months between 1928 and 1930, Elkins was rated among the top ten welterweight contenders.

Murray was one of four siblings, two of whom were involved in boxing. Eddie Elkins had over 70 bouts in the lightweight division, and brother Abe was a fight manager. Ruby was not affiliated with the sport. All four brothers died of heart attacks within a few years of each other.

ARMAND EMANUEL

"The Boxing Barrister"
Born: October 22, 1905
Died: July 27, 1979 (Age: 73)
Hometown: San Francisco, California
Height: 6' ½" Weight: 178–187 lbs.
Professional Career: 1926–1932

Total Bouts	Won	Lost	Draw	ND
51 (364 rounds)	39 (13 by KO)	7 (3 by KO)	2	2-1

Armand Emanuel certainly did not fit the popular image of a professional boxer. He was a college graduate who also possessed a degree from Golden Gate Law School, class of 1927. But passing the bar and opening a law practice could not put an end to Armand's lifelong dream of one day acquiring a world boxing title.

In 1925, with only a dozen amateur fights under his belt, Armand utilized his superior speed, busy left jab, and nimble footwork to win both the Pacific Coast and National AAU heavyweight championships. The following year, while still attending law school, he turned pro under the management of his father, a successful realtor and the owner of an auto dealership in San Francisco.

Three years after turning pro Armand defeated Philadelphia contender Matt Adgie for his 27th consecutive victory. He then had a draw and a win against aging former light-heavyweight champion Mike McTigue. The following month Armand entered the Madison Square Garden ring as a 7–1 underdog against the great light-heavyweight champion Tommy Loughran. Both men weighed over the 175-pound limit, so Loughran's title was not at stake.

Fighting a mirror image of himself, Loughran was hard-pressed throughout the 10-round bout. At the conclusion it appeared that Armand had pulled off a major upset. Unfortunately the judges thought otherwise, and awarded the fight to Loughran. The 7,000 fans in attendance booed loud and long when the unpopular decision was announced.

Armand's surprising performance, combined with his unusual background, had garnered national attention. "The Boxing Barrister" appeared on the cover of *The Ring*, and he was now rated among the top 10 light-heavyweight contenders. Some sportswriters were even comparing his boxing ability to the great Benny Leonard.

Two months after the Loughran bout, on August 27, 1928, Armand's plans for a title shot were derailed by middleweight champion Mickey Walker. Although outweighed by 11 pounds, Walker, one of the greatest—and strongest—fighters of all time, knocked out Armand in the ninth round.

According to papa Emanuel, his son had been the unwitting victim of Jack Kearn's chicanery. Kearns, Walker's wily manager, made sure the ring floor had extra padding to slow down Armand's fancy footwork and make it more difficult for him to evade Walker's relentless attack.

His next important bout was against "The Nebraska Wildcat," Ace Hudkins. Hudkins had recently lost a controversial decision to Walker in a middleweight title match. That fact alone should have been some cause for concern. So it was not much of a surprise when Hudkins, one of the best fighters to never win a title, clawed his way to a unanimous 10-round decision at Los Angeles's Wrigley Field.

Armand followed the loss to Hudkins by outpointing heavyweight Jimmy Maloney and fighting to a draw with light-heavyweight contender Leo Lomski. But a surprising loss to a novice boxer named Al Morro had fight fans scratching their heads. After four more wins over obscure opponents, Armand traded in his leather boxing gloves for a leather attaché case and went to work full-time as a lawyer.

According to press reports, "The Boxing Barrister" had made over $100,000 during his five-year boxing career. Sadly, the stock market crash of 1929 wiped out his savings. In an effort to recoup some of his losses, Armand returned to the ring in 1932 to face undefeated heavyweight Steve Hamas, and was knocked out in the second round. Oddly enough, Hamas, a former collegiate football star, was one of the few active professional boxers to also hold a college degree.

The Hamas debacle sent Armand into permanent retirement. Whatever fighting he did thereafter was confined to the courtroom.

LEW FARBER
Born: April 26, 1918
Died: April 28, 1988 (Age: 70)
Hometown: New York, New York
Height: 5' 3" Weight: 118–125 lbs.
Professional Career: 1928–1938

Total Bouts	Won	Lost	Draw
84 (590 rounds)	48 (9 by KO)	27 (1 by KO)	9

During the first two years of his pro career (1928–1930), **Lew Farber** compiled a modest 17-8-3 record. In 1931 he lost two non-title decisions to the great flyweight champion Midget Wolgast. It took two more years before Farber realized his full potential and became a serious contender for bantamweight honors. Showing great improvement, in 1933 he defeated Wolgast via a split 10-round (non-title) decision, and outpointed contenders Speedy Dado and Pablo Dano. These impressive victories earned him a number-three ranking among the world's elite bantamweights.

Farber eventually outgrew the bantamweight class and fought the last three years of his career as a featherweight. He attained contender status in that division as well, but lost crucial decisions to bantamweight champion Baltazar Sangchili (non-title) and featherweight contender Filio Echevarria.

Dissatisfied with his progress and the lack of big-money fights, Farber decided to hang up his gloves at the age of 26. Lew's younger brother, welterweight Mickey Farber, was another tough Lower East Side boxer best remembered for his two memorable 10-round split-decision brawls with Brownsville's Al "Bummy" Davis.

ABE FELDMAN

Born: October 27, 1912
Died: June 1, 1980 (Age: 67)
Hometown: Schenectady, New York
Height: 5' 11" Weight: 180–186 lbs.
Professional Career: 1932–1939

Total Bouts	Won	Lost	Draw	NC
55 (348 rounds)	35 (15 by KO)	14 (2 by KO)	5	1

In the first three years of his professional boxing career **Abe Feldman** lost only two of 31 bouts, including a "no contest" with future heavyweight champion Jim Braddock. (That 1933 bout is featured in the film, *Cinderella Man*.) Abe went on to score impressive victories over Al Ettore, Steve Dudas, and Johnny Miler, and drew with Bob Olin. (In his next fight Olin won the light-heavyweight title.)

Feldman's greatest victory occurred on July 24, 1935, when he outpointed John Henry Lewis three months before Lewis took the title from Olin. The *New York Times* reported that "Lewis, after a good start, tired under Feldman's steady body punching."[27]

After defeating Lewis the National Boxing Association rated Feldman the second-best light heavyweight for 1935. But Abe could not keep the streak going, and foundered in subsequent bouts against veteran Jack Roper and former light-heavyweight champ Maxie Rosenbloom, losing decisions to both men. The once-promising boxer began a downward spiral in 1936, losing 10 of his last 17 bouts. Most of his losses were to good boxers with winning records.

Abe rarely weighed more than 184 pounds. He was a strong and durable boxer who liked to fight at close quarters where his superior strength was a factor when facing light-heavyweight opponents. He also thought nothing of taking on heavyweights—a disadvantage when facing powerful maulers such as Tony Galento and Leroy Haynes, who outweighed him by 20 and 37 pounds, respectively. In 55 professional bouts, only Galento and Haynes were able to stop him.

LEW FELDMAN

Born: November 5, 1908
Died: May 11, 1983 (Age: 74)
Hometown: Brooklyn, New York
Height: 5' 5" Weight: 122–135 lbs.
Professional Career: 1927–1941

Total Bouts	Won	Lost	Draw
188 (1,516 rounds)	115 (10 by KO)	55 (5 by KO)	18

Lew Feldman was one of the most active and durable fighters of the 1930s. His first pro fight was a four-round draw with Sammy Farber on November 14, 1927. Over the next 13 years, fighting in both the featherweight and lightweight divisions, Feldman engaged in 187 additional contests, including 25 times against 12 different world champions—eight of whom he defeated. Like many fighters of his era, Feldman developed slowly against steadily improving competition. Although his managers were careful not to overmatch him, very few of his opponents had losing records.

On August 25, 1932, Feldman outpointed the reigning NBA featherweight champion, Tommy Paul, in a 10-round non-title bout. Six weeks later he was knocked out by the great Kid Chocolate in the 12th round of a featherweight title bout sanctioned by the New York State Athletic Commission. This was not the first time Feldman lost to Chocolate. He previously dropped two hotly contested decisions to the Cuban wonder.

In 1938 Feldman challenged the great Henry Armstrong for the welterweight championship. Lew was past his prime, Armstrong at his peak. Armstrong was one of the ring's all-time great fighters and had previously stopped Feldman in the sixth round of a non-title fight six months earlier. This time he needed just one round to end the fight.

In addition to Tommy Paul, the other world champions that Feldman outpointed were Petey Sarron, Mike Belloise (twice), Lew Jenkins, Chalky Wright (twice), Midget Wolgast, Bat Battalino, and Freddie "Red" Cochrane.

JACKIE FIELDS
(Jacob Finkelstein)
Welterweight Champion 1929–1930, 1932–1933
Born: August 2, 1909
Died: June 3, 1987 (Age: 79)
Hometown: Los Angeles, California
Height: 5' 7½" Weight: 126–152 lbs.
Professional Career: 1925–1933

Total Bouts	Won	Lost	Draw	ND	NC
86 (633 rounds)	72 (31 by KO)	9 (1 by KO)	2	2	1

Boxing, like any other art form, has its share of child prodigies. Before he left Chicago young Jake Finkelstein was instructed in the finer points of the sport by trainer and former ring great Jack Blackburn—the same man who taught Joe Louis everything he knew about boxing.

When Jake and his family moved to California, he continued his boxing instruction at the Los Angeles Sporting Club under the watchful eye of another master trainer, George Blake. The 13-year-old's natural talent and instinct for the sport riveted Blake. Further exciting the experienced trainer's enthusiasm was the realization that the boy's obvious talent was wedded to tremendous confidence and determination.

Three years and 50 amateur fights later, 16-year-old **Jackie Fields** (at some point during his amateur career, "Finkelstein" became "Fields") was in Paris, representing the United States at the 1924 Olympic Games.

Fighting in the 126-pound featherweight division, Jackie defeated five foreign opponents before qualifying for the gold-medal bout against fellow countryman, Joe Salas. (At the time Olympic boxing rules allowed two entries per nation.) After three rounds of torrid, nonstop action, Jackie Fields's hand was raised in victory. At 16 years of age, he became the youngest boxer ever to win a gold medal in the Olympic Games.

Jackie Fields, the son of a kosher butcher, was a young man in a hurry. Turning pro five days before his 17th birthday, he racked up five wins in six fights, including one draw. Nine months after his first professional fight Jackie was matched with future ring great Jimmy McLarnin. He was not ready for a fighter of McLarnin's caliber and experience, but the $5,000 he was guaranteed for taking the match pushed logic aside.

McLarnin floored him four times en route to a second-round KO victory. Adding injury to insult Jackie suffered a broken jaw. It was the only time in his 86 professional fights that Fields was ever knocked out.

Over the next three years Jackie grew into a 145-pound welterweight, compiling a 36-2 record with one no-decision. His only losses were to ring greats Louis "Kid" Kaplan and Sammy Mandell.

On March 25, 1929, Jackie fought Young Jack Thompson for the vacant National Boxing Association World welterweight title. Thompson, a masterful ring tactician who some people were already comparing to the legendary Joe Gans, was outpointed over 10 rounds. (California law did not permit professional fights beyond 10 rounds.) It was Thompson's second loss to Fields.

Baltimore's Joe Dundee was recognized by the powerful New York State Athletic Commission as world welterweight champion. A unification fight was arranged for July 25, 1929, at the State Fairgrounds in Detroit, Michigan. Twenty-five thousand fans anxiously awaited the opening bell.

Fields, a 2–1 favorite to win, dominated his opponent from the opening bell. After being floored four times in the second round, Dundee, on the verge of being knocked out, deliberately hit Fields below the belt, causing an automatic disqualification. In 1970 Fields told author Peter Heller that Dundee's manager had bet Dundee's entire purse of $50,000 on their fighter, with the provision that if the fight ended in a disqualification, all bets would be called off. Dundee denied the punch was intentional, explaining to boxing officials that

in his befogged state he didn't know what he was doing, but rumors persisted that he'd fouled out to save his $50,000 payday.

On February 22, 1930, in San Francisco, Fields suffered his first defeat in two years when he lost a 10-round decision to Young Corbett III. Corbett's southpaw style had bothered him, and by the time he figured out how to adjust his strategy, it was too late. Since Corbett had weighed two pounds over the welterweight limit, Fields's title was not at stake. Jackie rebounded from the Corbett defeat with a TKO over future welterweight champion Tommy Freeman in Cleveland.

On May 9, 1930, at the Olympia Arena in Detroit, Fields defended his undisputed title for the first time against former opponent Young Jack Thompson. The challenger put on a brilliant boxing exhibition over the last five rounds of the 15-round bout and was awarded the decision.

Two years later Fields challenged Lou Brouillard for the welterweight title. The tough French-Canadian southpaw had recently dethroned Young Jack Thompson. Jackie wasn't impressed. He outboxed Brouillard and regained the title with a unanimous 10-round decision. He even managed to floor the rock-jawed Canadian in the eighth round.

In 1932 Jackie was involved in an automobile accident outside of Louisville, Kentucky, that resulted in a severe injury to his eye. He should have quit, but the Depression had wiped out nearly all of the $500,000 he had earned in the ring. He wanted at least one more big payday before hanging up his gloves. Although very few people knew it, Jackie had only partial vision in the affected eye.

When he was offered $45,000 to defend his title against former conqueror Young Corbett III on March 22, 1933, Jackie readily accepted the challenge, even though the bout would be fought in Corbett's hometown of San Francisco.

The decision was close enough to have gone either way, but when the bell rang ending the final round, the referee raised Corbett's hand in victory.

Nine weeks later, in the final bout of his career, Jackie won a 10-round decision over Young Peter Jackson at the Olympic Auditorium in Los Angeles. Jackie would have continued fighting, but fearing injury to his good eye convinced him to retire.

In his post-boxing life Jackie followed his Los Angeles neighbors Mushy Callahan and Newsboy Brown into the movie business, working for Twentieth Century Fox in various capacities.

In 1957 Jackie moved to Las Vegas, Nevada, and became part owner of the Tropicana Hotel. He eventually sold his interest in the hotel but continued to work as the hotel's public relations director. During the 1960s he also served as chairman of the Nevada State Athletic Commission.

Jackie Fields fought 12 world champions, 19 times. He never shied away from the best fighters in his division. The majority of his fights were against quality opponents. He easily ranks among the greatest Jewish boxers of all time.

AL FOREMAN

Born: November 3, 1904
Died: December 23, 1954 (Age: 50)
Hometown: Montreal, Canada
Height: 5' 5" Weight: 125–135 lbs.
Professional Career: 1920–1933

Total Bouts	Won	Lost	Draw	ND
130 (947 rounds)	99 (64 by KO)	20 (2 by KO)	10	1-0

Al Foreman was orphaned at the age of four. For the next 10 years he lived in a home for Jewish orphans outside London. At the age of 14, with World War I still raging, he ran away and tried to join the army. The recruiting officer told him he was too young to serve in a combat unit, but if the orphanage would give its permission, he could serve as a drummer boy in the famous Black Watch infantry regiment. Permission was granted, but the war abruptly ended, and Al's outfit was assigned to occupation duty. It was at this time that he first laced on a pair of boxing gloves.[28]

Foreman's success as an army boxer convinced him that he had a future in the ring. His first documented bout occurred in 1920. Over the next six years he compiled a 49-12-7 record that included 30 wins by knockout.

In 1924 he moved to Canada and eventually became a citizen. Foreman's prime as a fighter was 1927 to 1932. During that time he lost only four out of 53 fights. The losses were to former featherweight champion Louis "Kid" Kaplan, future junior lightweight champion Johnny Jadick, and contenders Billy Townsend and Nel Tarleton— all superb fighters.

During the last four years of his career Al won the Canadian, British, and British Empire lightweight championships. He was a highly rated contender in both the featherweight and junior lightweight classes, earning that status by defeating George Rose, Carl Tremaine, Leo "Kid" Roy, Phil McGraw, title claimant Maurice Holtzer, and former champions Johnny Dundee and Mike Ballerino.

Al Foreman had a cast-iron chin. He was stopped only twice in 130 professional fights. As far as can be determined he was never counted out. His final fight occurred on June 29, 1934, in Washington, DC—a split-decision loss to future featherweight champion Petey Sarron.

During his career Foreman had studied photography in his spare time. After hanging up his gloves he got a job with the *Montreal Standard*, one of Canada's largest weekly national newspapers. It wasn't long before the quality of his work earned him recognition as one of the best news photographers in the business.[29]

At the outbreak of World War II Al volunteered for service and was commissioned as a turret gunner with the Royal Air Force. His unit, "The Damn Busters," became famous for dropping 22,500-pound bombs—the most powerful conventional weapon of the war—that destroyed the Ruhr dams in Germany. In all he made 37 operational flights, including one mission where his turret was hit by flak and his crewmates found him hanging from the fuselage, his feet jammed in the wreckage. In recognition for his service he was awarded the Distinguished Flying Cross.[30]

Upon his return to civilian life Al opened his own portrait studio in Montreal. He died of a heart attack in 1954 at the age of 50.

KID FRANCIS

(Francesco Buonaugurio)
Born: October 7, 1907
Died: 1943 (Age: 35)
Hometown: Marseille, France
Height: 5' 4" Weight: 118–126 lbs.
Professional Career: 1923–1935

Total Bouts	Won	Lost	Draw	NC
124 (1,069 rounds)	95 (22 by KO)	14	13	2

Francesco Buonaugurio fought as "**Kid Francis**" to honor his first trainer, Al Francis. The star-crossed boxer was born in Italy but raised in Marseille, France. Between 1928 and 1932 he was a top-rated bantamweight and featherweight contender. Francis fought in Europe, South America, and the United States, including 27 times in New York City. His picture appeared on the cover of *The Ring* magazine in June 1931.

Kid Francis had a fan-friendly style. He bored in aggressively and rarely took a backward step. His attack featured a heavy emphasis on body punching. He defeated such outstanding ring men as Andre Routis, Archie Bell, Pete De Grasse, Eugene Huat, and former flyweight champion Fidel La Barba. He also lost a return bout to La Barba. In his only title fight he lost a controversial split decision to the phenomenal bantamweight champion Panama Al Brown in 1932 (one of three losses to Brown).

The following year Francis lost a 10-round decision to former champion and fellow Frenchman, Victor "Young" Perez. No one could have imagined that 10 years later both Perez and Francis would meet the same tragic fate as Holocaust victims. In 1943 Kid Francis was arrested by the Germans in Paris and deported to Auschwitz, where he was murdered.

BERNIE FRIEDKIN

"Schoolboy Friedkin"
Born: March 16, 1915
Died: January 18, 2007 (Age: 91)
Hometown: Brooklyn, New York
Height: 5' 3" Weight: 125–136 lbs.
Professional Career: 1935–1940

Total Bouts	Won	Lost	Draw
76 (487 rounds)	49 (10 by KO)	11 (2 by KO)	16

Bernie Friedkin began his professional boxing career while still in high school—ergo his nickname, "Schoolboy." A smart boxer who relied more on speed and technique than punching power, Bernie is best known for his famous "grudge match" with Brooklyn rival Al "Bummy" Davis. Both fighters were hugely popular in their Brownsville neighborhood, and it was inevitable that they would eventually meet to settle who was best. On July 21, 1938, at Madison Square Garden, Bummy answered the question when he knocked out Bernie in the fourth round.

In subsequent bouts Friedkin drew with former featherweight champions Kid Chocolate, Mike Belloise (twice), and Petey Scalzo. He was outpointed by Scalzo in their rematch. Other notable opponents were Al Reid, Joey Fontana, Everett Rightmire, and Pat Foley. Bernie had one of the highest ratios of draws to total fights—16 out of 76.

After hanging up his gloves he took a job with the Ronzoni Macaroni Company, and later worked as a dispatcher at Kennedy Airport.

SAILOR FRIEDMAN

(David Edelman)
Born: June 18, 1899
Died: January 6, 1968 (Age: 68)
Hometown: Philadelphia, Pennsylvania
Height: 5' 8" Weight: 135–156 lbs.
Professional Career: 1916–1928

Total Bouts	Won	Lost	Draw	ND	NC
119 (1,004 rounds)	29 (16 by KO)	21 (1 by KO)	4	33-24-5	3

Sailor Friedman (or "Freedman," as it was sometimes spelled in newspapers) was a fine fighter, but his personal life was often mired in controversy due to his affiliation with gamblers and bootleggers.

Friedman ran away from home at the age of 14. The following year he joined the United States Navy. During his three-year tour he served on the battleship USS *Michigan*. In 1915 he won the navy bantamweight championship, but shortly thereafter received a one-year suspension for fighting with a doctored glove.*

Sailor turned pro in 1916. His manager was Philadelphia's Max "Boo Boo" Hoff, a notorious Jewish Prohibition-era bootlegger who also managed some of the city's best prizefighters. After he retired in 1928, Sailor remained close to Hoff and served as his bodyguard.

In his prime Friedman was one of the toughest competitors in both the lightweight and welterweight divisions. He was a persistent pressure fighter with a chin that was virtually dent-proof. In 118 professional bouts Friedman was stopped only once, very early in his career.

Friedman fought at least once a month, except for a six-month gap in 1922. That year, instead of facing opponents in the ring, he found himself in a Chicago courtroom facing a prosecutor who was trying to send him to the electric chair. He and two other men were accused of murdering Abraham Rubin, a taxicab driver, who was said to have ties to the bootleg liquor trade as a transporter. The first trial ended in a deadlock. Friedman was exonerated in a second trial and resumed his boxing career. He also continued to work as an enforcer for Hoff.

In 1925 Friedman fought two no-decision bouts with the great welterweight champion Mickey Walker in Newark, New Jersey.

---

* A "doctored" glove is one that has been illegally tampered with to make it more damaging to an opponent. It is a serious breach of the rules.

Newspapers awarded the unofficial verdicts to Walker.

Friedman retired in 1928. In his post-boxing life he continued to work for Philadelphia racketeers, most notably Nig Rosen (Harry Stromberg). Sailor faded from public view after 1934, and additional information as to whatever became of him is unknown.

DANNY FRUSH

Born: 1895
Died: March 21, 1961 (Age: 66)
Hometown: Cleveland, Ohio
Height: 5' 7" **Weight:** 125–133 pounds
Professional Career: 1917–1928

Total Bouts	Won	Lost	Draw	ND	NC
81 (510 rounds)	52 (30 by KO)	13 (7 by KO)	3	9-1-2	1

London-born **Danny Frush** was managed by the famous theatrical impresario Sam Harris. In his first important bout in America, Danny lost a 15-round decision to Jackie "Kid" Wolfe. Over the next three years he defeated fringe contenders Andy Chaney, Artie O'Leary, Freddie Jacks, and Al Shubert, but was stopped in the seventh round (non-title) by featherweight champion Johnny Kilbane.

On August 15, 1922, at Brooklyn's Ebbets Field, over 15,000 fans were on hand to see Frush and Johnny Dundee compete for the vacant world featherweight title (as recognized by the New York State Athletic Commission). Dundee stopped Frush in the ninth round. Two fights later Frush was knocked out by future featherweight king, Louis "Kid" Kaplan. Proving you can't keep a good man down, in his next bout Frush scored an eighth-round knockout over former champion Eugène Criqui in Paris, France.

After hanging up his gloves in 1928, Danny opened a health spa in Baltimore. He also studied to become a licensed physical therapist, eventually going into that field full-time.

JOE GLICK

Born: February 22, 1903
Died: September 5, 1978 (Age: 75)
Hometown: Brooklyn, New York
Height: 5' 8" Weight: 125–154 lbs.
Professional Career: 1921–1934

Total Bouts	Won	Lost	Draw	ND	NC
244 (2,049 rounds)	129 (26 by KO)	68 (10 by KO)	31	7-4	5

After he dropped out of school in the ninth grade, **Joe Glick** was employed as a buttonhole maker in Williamsburg, Brooklyn. Seeing no future in this, Joe became a professional boxer at the age of 16. Over the next three years he lost only four of 68 fights.

On January 29, 1926, in his 99th pro fight, Joe appeared in his first Madison Square Garden main event, outpointing the aging ring legend, Johnny Dundee. Glick's end of the purse was $10,000. That adds up to a lot of buttonholes. The fight was the first of nine Garden main events for Joe.

His victory over Dundee led to a title bout later that year with junior lightweight champion Tod Morgan. Although Glick was game, Morgan was just too slick, and outboxed the challenger, winning at least 11 of the 15 rounds.

Among Joe's 244 opponents were scores of top contenders and 14 past, present, or future world champions. Incredibly, he went through all of this with only one functioning eye!

The only persons who knew his secret, other than his family, were trainer Ray Arcel and manager Harry Alberts. Glick was born with a condition known as "amblyopic syndrome." In layman's terms it meant the muscles of his right eye had failed to develop. He passed the State Athletic Commission's physical exam by memorizing the eye charts.

In spite of his handicap Joe developed into a fine boxer, renowned for his left hook to the body, competitive drive, and better-than-average defense.

Among the top fighters Glick defeated were Danny Kramer, Ray Miller, Baby Joe Gans, Andre Routis, Mike Dundee, Bobby Garcia, and Luis Vicentini. He lost a decision to future welterweight champion Jimmy McLarnin and fought two draws with former featherweight champion Mike Ballerino.

In November 1928 Glick outpointed the number-three lightweight contender, Baby Joe Gans, before 19,000 fans in Madison Square

Garden. It was a huge win for the 23-year-old boxer. Baby Joe Gans was an exceptional boxer and dangerous puncher. He was scrupulously avoided by many other contenders.

Two months later Glick returned to the same venue to face Jimmy McLarnin for the second time. McLarnin had already knocked out several top Jewish fighters, so the usual Irish vs. Jewish rivalry was even more pronounced for this bout. A standing-room-only crowd jammed Madison Square Garden to see the highly anticipated battle.

McLarnin won the 10-round decision, but many fans disagreed with the verdict. The return bout took place six weeks later, and once again the Garden was packed to the rafters. This time Glick was not going to leave the result up to the judges. He intended to knock out McLarnin.

Glick rushed out of his corner and carelessly ran into a terrific left hook to the head. He staggered back and was relentlessly pursued and pummeled by McLarnin for the remainder of the round. In the second round McLarnin dropped his still-dazed opponent twice before knocking him out with a picture-perfect right cross to the jaw. It was only the third time in 164 professional fights that Glick had been stopped.

If not for the extraordinary depth of talent in both the junior lightweight and lightweight divisions, Joe Glick most assuredly would have won a championship. But the field was just too crowded with great fighters. Louis "Kid" Kaplan, Benny Bass, Jackie "Kid" Berg, Tony Canzoneri, and Young Corbett III outpointed him, frustrating his drive to win a world title.

As his career wound down in the early 1930s, Joe lost 18 of his last 25 fights. Add to that number at least a dozen decisions levied against him that could have gone the other way, plus seven disqualifications for questionable low blows, and the real meaning of those 68 defeats on his record can easily be misinterpreted—unless placed in proper context.

In Glick's last two fights—typically spaced just one month apart—he was knocked out by future middleweight champions Ceferino Garcia and Freddie Steele. Joe was way past his prime at this point in his career.

Many of his later fights took place on the West Coast, where he became a fan favorite. After hanging up his gloves Joe moved to Los Angeles and began to get work in pictures as a bit player. He eventually retired with a pension from the Screen Actors Guild.

Joe Glick was not quite good enough to defeat the greatest fighters of his era, but considering the competition he faced and his relentless, nonstop schedule, coming in second best was quite an accomplishment. One has to wonder what he could have achieved with two good eyes.

HOLLYWOOD AND BOXING

Boxing is a sport of drama, excitement, romance, and physicality—qualities that filmmakers have mined to the fullest. Boxing-themed motion pictures have even included musicals and Westerns. The industry's love affair with boxing goes back to the very beginning of motion pictures. In 1894 Thomas Edison, co-inventor of the motion picture camera, paid heavyweight champion James J. Corbett $5,000 plus royalties for the rights to distribute a film of Corbett sparring with another boxer. Three years later Corbett's title fight with Bob Fitzsimmons became the first heavyweight championship to be filmed.[31]

Since the 1890s nearly 500 boxing-themed movies have been produced—more than all baseball, football, and basketball films combined.[32] Some of Hollywood's greatest directors have been drawn to the sport. They include Alfred Hitchcock (*The Ring*, 1927), King Vidor (*The Champ*, 1931), Rouben Mamoulian (*Golden Boy*, 1939), Raoul Walsh (*Gentleman Jim*, 1942), Robert Wise (*The Set-Up*, 1949, and *Somebody Up There Likes Me*, 1956), Stanley Kubrick (*Day of the Fight*, 1951, a documentary), John Huston (*Fat City*, 1972), and Martin Scorsese (*Raging Bull*, 1980).

If a boxing film adheres to historical reality, it will usually include a recognizable Jewish character depicted as a boxer, trainer, or manager. Sylvester Stallone created Rocky's fictional Jewish trainer, "Mickey Goldmill" (brilliantly acted by Burgess Meredith) as a not-so-subtle homage to Charley Goldman, the trainer of undefeated heavyweight champion Rocky Marciano. *Cinderella Man* (2006) depicts the life of Depression-era Irish-American heavyweight champion James J. Braddock. The film accurately portrays the prevalence of Jewish boxers at that time. Early scenes show Braddock in the ring with two of the five Jewish opponents he faced during his career.

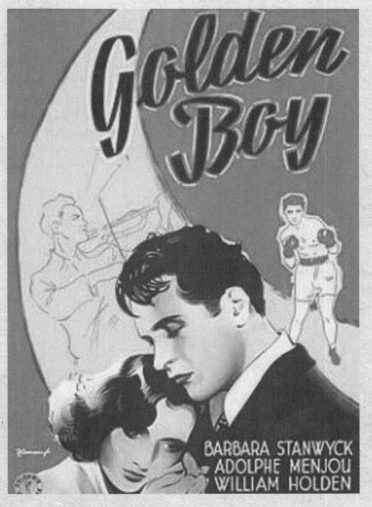

Golden Boy was the most popular boxing movie of the 1930s.

(Courtesy of PhillyBoxingHistory.com)

MARTY GOLD

(Martin Goldberg)
Born: July 15, 1904
Died: December 15, 1958 (Age: 54)
Hometown: Philadelphia, Pennsylvania
Height: 5' 3" Weight: 112 lbs.
Professional Career: 1921–1933

Total Bouts	Won	Lost	Draw	ND
131 (1,009 rounds)	43 (16 by KO)	49	11	12-7-9

Marty Gold paid his dues in the highly competitive flyweight division of the 1920s. His apprenticeship included bouts against contenders Black Bill, Dave Adelman, Eddie Leonard, Benny Schwartz, and future champions Frankie Genaro, Midget Wolgast, Johnny McCoy, and Panama Al Brown. He learned valuable lessons from all of them.

By 1930, after nine years in the pro ranks, all the hard work and experience was about to pay off. That year he defeated top flyweight contenders Black Bill and Frenchy Belanger—victories that were particularly gratifying, as he had lost to both in previous years. Between 1930 and 1931 Gold was rated among the top 10 flyweight contenders.

Gold often went into a popular fighter's backyard, which meant a good payday but often resulted in a "hometown" decision for his opponent. It is highly probable that half (or more) of his losses out of town were the result of biased or crooked officiating. But win or lose, in 131 professional fights, no opponent could ever put Marty down for the count.

BENNY GOLDBERG

Born: December 25, 1919
Died: September 10, 2001 (Age: 81)
Hometown: Detroit, Michigan
Height: 5' 5" Weight: 116–122 lbs.
Professional Career: 1935–1946

Total Bouts	Won	Lost	Draw	NC
43 (303 rounds)	38 (16 by KO)	2 (0 by KO)	2	1

In the 1930s and '40s, every fighter hailing from Detroit fought in the shadow of the great Joe Louis. In spite of this, several other Motor City clouters were good enough to gain international recognition. One of the best was **Benny Goldberg**, a classy hard-punching southpaw who ranked among the top bantamweight contenders for almost five years.

Benny was born in Warsaw, Poland, and came to America with his parents when he was two years old. The family settled in Detroit, where Benny turned pro in 1937 after compiling an outstanding amateur record. In 1936, in a specially arranged amateur match, he defeated Olympic gold medalist and future world featherweight champion Jackie Wilson.

The young fighter credited Barney Ross for his success in the ring. Benny studied and analyzed Ross's classic boxing style and patterned himself after the great boxer. His dedication paid off. Benny's rise in the pros was meteoric. Among his victims were contenders Tony Olivera, Abe Denner, and former featherweight champion Joey Archibald. Those victories earned him a shot at the bantamweight championship held by California's Manuel Ortiz. Five and a half years earlier Goldberg had defeated Ortiz in a four-round preliminary bout when both were just starting out as pros.

Manuel Ortiz is recognized as one of the greatest bantamweight champions of all time. He held the title for eight years and defended it 21 times. In a hard-fought 15-rounder Ortiz proved to be a shade better and won the decision. Undeterred by the loss, Benny defeated his next seven opponents, including a decision over fifth-ranked Luis Castillo.

Benny's last 11 bouts took place in southern California. He liked the climate and decided to make his home in Los Angeles. For many years he worked for the movie studios as a bodyguard for actors. Among his clients were Tony Curtis, Vince Edwards, and Robert Blake.

ABE GOLDSTEIN

(aka, Abe Attell Goldstein)
Bantamweight Champion: 1923–1924
Born: October 9, 1898
Died: February 12, 1977 (Age: 78)
Hometown: New York, New York
Height: 5' 5" Weight: 118 lbs.
Professional Career: 1916–1927

Total Bouts	Won	Lost	Draw	ND	NC
134 (1,202 rounds)	70 (35 by KO)	16 (4 by KO)	7	31-6-3	1

In boxing, as in life, it pays to be in the right place at the right time. On October 17, 1923, only two days before he was scheduled to defend his title against Chicago's Joe Burman at Madison Square Garden, bantamweight champion Joe Lynch insisted on a postponement, claiming a shoulder injury. The champion was summoned to the New York State Athletic Commission office. A staff physician examined him and stated the injury was not that serious. Lynch disagreed and refused to fight. The Commission then stripped him of the title and awarded it to Burman, who seven months earlier had won a newspaper verdict over Lynch in a 10-round non-title bout.

Promoter Tex Rickard sent out an emergency call for a substitute. Bantamweight contender **Abe Goldstein**, a 24-year-old veteran of 103 professional fights, answered the call. Goldstein was in great shape. He'd already fought three times in the previous 17 days.

Abe was not about to squander a golden opportunity. He staged a furious rally in the closing moments of the fight and was awarded the 12-round decision and the title.

Previous to his title-winning effort, Abe had proven his mettle against the likes of Johnny Buff, Young Montreal, Frankie Genaro, Kid Williams, Earl Puryear, and Pete Zivic. His most impressive victory had been a 15-round drubbing of future flyweight champion Pancho Villa in 1922. In a rematch the ferocious little Filipino—one of boxing's all-time greats—outpointed Goldstein. But the defeat did not alter Abe's status as a leading contender for bantamweight honors.

Goldstein, like many other fighters of his era, fought once or twice a month in a highly competitive environment overflowing with extraordinary talent.

The next big moment for Abe came five months after winning the title. On March 21,

1924, at Madison Square Garden he outboxed Joe Lynch and won a unanimous 15-round decision. The victory was sweet revenge. Lynch, a great fighter, had knocked him out in the 11th round three and a half years earlier.

Goldstein successfully defended his title twice, outpointing Charles Ledoux and Tommy Ryan in 15-round bouts. His reign as bantamweight champion came to an end on December 19, 1924, when Brooklyn's Eddie "Cannonball" Martin won a razor-thin 15-round decision.

As an ex-champ Goldstein continued to mix it up with the world's best bantams. In 1926, 10 years after turning pro, he won a decision over future champion Panama Al Brown. One year later Abe lost a 10-round decision to Bud Taylor, who was only six weeks away from winning the vacant bantamweight title in a bout with Tony Canzoneri. Goldstein had fought on the undercard of the Taylor vs. Canzoneri bout. He fought an up-and-coming Filipino named Ignacio Fernandez and was stopped in the seventh round. Abe decided it was time to retire. To his credit he never attempted a comeback.

RUBY GOLDSTEIN
"The Jewel of the Ghetto"
Born: October 7, 1907
Died: April 23, 1984 (Age: 76)
Height: 5' 5" Weight: 130–145 lbs.
Hometown: New York, New York
Professional Career: 1924–1933, 1937

Total Bouts	Won	Lost	Draw
60 (219 rounds)	54 (38 by KO)	6 (6 by KO)	0

If boxers were judged on physical appearance alone, then frail, sickly-looking **Ruby Goldstein** would have been given little chance to succeed. But boxing is not a bodybuilding or strong-man contest, and looks can be deceiving. Despite his somewhat fragile appearance, very few boxers have ever entered the ring with as much natural talent and raw punching power as "The Jewel of the Ghetto."

Although Goldstein never weighed more than 145 pounds during his prime, he was known to drop light heavyweights in the gym while wearing

16-ounce training gloves! Yet punching power was not his greatest asset. In the ring, perfectly balanced and gliding effortlessly as if on ice, he resembled ballet star Rudolf Nureyev with boxing gloves. Ruby's darting jabs set up a destructive right cross that was delivered with uncanny speed and extraordinary power. His natural ability was enhanced under the tutelage of master trainer Hymie Cantor who took Goldstein under his wing and prepared his entry into the professional ranks.

Almost from the outset of his career Goldstein was referred to by newspaper reporters as "the world's greatest prospect," and the logical heir apparent to recently retired lightweight champion Benny Leonard.

Ruby had won 19 amateur fights before turning pro on December 30, 1924, with a second-round KO of Al Vano at the Pioneer Sporting Club in New York. Over the next 17 months he chalked up another 22 straight victories, 11 by knockout. "The Jewel of the Ghetto" caught the public's imagination. He was wildly popular, and often fought before standing-room-only crowds.

It wasn't long before big-time mobsters also took an interest in Ruby. Waxey Gordon (Irving Wexler), one of New York's major Jewish bootleggers, bought into Ruby's contract, becoming a 50 percent partner in his management. Newly rich bootleggers liked to collect beautiful women, promising prizefighters and fast racehorses to show off to their friends. The Mob guys often bet heavily on Ruby, and he did not let them down.

He appeared well on his way toward winning the lightweight championship.[33]

Nobody saw it coming, but the bubble was about to burst.

On June 25, 1926, more than 15,000 fans jammed the Coney Island Stadium to watch Ruby continue his march to the lightweight championship. His opponent was little-known Ace Hudkins, aka, "The Nebraska Wildcat." The soubriquet was an accurate description of Hudkins's vicious fighting style. He was an aggressive hell-for-leather type who could not be discouraged no matter how hard he was hit. Oddsmakers were not impressed. They made Ruby the 4–1 favorite to win.

Hudkins's record was a decent 36-8-11, with 15 wins by KO, but most of his fights had taken place on the West Coast, so he was hardly known to New York fight fans, except for the fact that speed demon Sid Terris had easily outpointed him a year earlier in Chicago.

The fight was scheduled for six rounds, since both Goldstein (age 18) and Hudkins (age 20) were below the legal age of 21, required to fight a 10-round bout in New York. Ruby was nervous but confident. He knew that Waxey Gordon and his cohorts had placed huge bets on him to knock out Hudkins.

Within a minute of the first round, Ruby, as expected, floored Hudkins with a tremendous right-hand punch to the jaw. It was the first time "The Nebraska Wildcat" was ever knocked down. He lay flat on his back and seemed dead to the world. As the crowd cheered, Ruby turned and walked to a neutral corner, fully expecting another easy win. But at the count of seven Hudkins stirred and, using the ropes to aid his ascent, just beat the count.

Ruby was wild with his follow-up punches, allowing Hudkins to survive the remainder of the first round. Hudkins came out fresh in the next round and took the offensive, landing damaging punches to Ruby's body. Ruby desperately tried to land another haymaker. His frustration grew as his inability to knock out his stubborn opponent continued into round three. In the fourth round Ruby was outboxing Hudkins when the Nebraskan suddenly rushed him to the ropes. Goldstein never saw the sweeping left hook that landed on the point of his chin. The lower ring rope broke Ruby's fall before he slid to the canvas, where he was counted out for the first time.

"The Jewel of the Ghetto" was devastated that he'd let down his army of fans, many of whom had bet money they could ill afford to lose. The next day a headline in the *New York Evening Journal* read: "$400,000 Changed Hands." The paper listed many of the biggest losers, including two of notorious gambler Arnold Rothstein's lieutenants, who were reported to have dropped a total of $35,000 between them. Waxey Gordon, part owner of Goldstein, lost close to $45,000. Even Al Jolson, a big rooter for Goldstein, was said to have dropped $5,000. One bettor, the paper reported, took the short end and wound up a big winner. Professional gambler Nick the Greek won approximately $80,000 betting on Hudkins.[34]

It seemed to Ruby that the entire Jewish population of the Lower East Side went into mourning after his defeat—which wasn't far from the truth. For an 18-year-old kid, the pressure was too much to bear. Too embarrassed to face his fans, Ruby took a train out of New York and didn't get off until he arrived in California.

A few months later he returned to New York and tried to rebuild his career. He would lose only five of his next 38 fights. But something had gone out of Ruby after the loss to Hudkins. Yes, there were impressive wins over Jack Zivic, Cuddy DeMarco, and former lightweight champion Jimmy Goodrich, but there were also huge losses when it counted most—to Sid Terris (KO by 1) and Jimmy McLarnin (KO by 2).

Goldstein was never outpointed. His final stats were 54 wins (38 by KO) and six losses. All six losses were by knockout. Although he continued to show flashes of the old Ruby, he always seemed to lose the big ones. Perhaps if Goldstein had been an older and more mature boxer when he fought Hudkins, he could have handled the defeat better, but that scenario was not in the cards. Like more-recent boxing prodigies Mike Tyson and Gerry Cooney, Goldstein never overcame the psychological effect of that first disastrous knockout loss. His entire boxing career was defined by that one crushing defeat.

In retirement Ruby became a highly respected referee. He officiated in 39 world championships and hundreds of other important fights. If you never saw Ruby fight you could still get an idea of his extraordinary ability as a fighter by watching his impeccably balanced footwork as he quickly glided and shifted about the ring as if on skates. His reputation as an honest arbiter was enhanced in 1947 when he cast the lone dissenting (and accurate) vote for Jersey Joe Walcott in his bout with Joe Louis.

When he wasn't refereeing, Ruby was employed for many years as a salesman for the Schenley Liquor Company.

In 1962 Ruby's reputation as a referee was marred when he was accused of a late stoppage in the Benny "Kid" Paret vs. Emile Griffith title fight. Paret died 10 days later from injuries sustained in that fight. Despite the blame heaped on Ruby, Paret was really the victim of boxing's irregular medical supervision. He came into the ring for his final fight neurologically damaged from a series of brutal fights, capped off by a terrible beating he had received just three months earlier against middleweight champion Gene Fullmer, yet no medical tests were ordered, nor was Paret's license suspended. He was an accident waiting to happen. While Ruby took the brunt of the blame, the entity most responsible was the negligent New York State Athletic Commission. Ruby worked one more fight after that tragic incident and never refereed again.

In the final analysis, Ruby Goldstein was a credit to the sport of boxing, both as a fighter and a referee.

CHARLEY GOMER

Born: 1911
Died: May 2, 1992 (Age: 81)
Hometown: Baltimore, Maryland
Weight: 135 lbs.
Professional Career: 1930–1941

Total Bouts	Won	Lost	Draw	NC
159 (1,198 rounds)	90 (36 by KO)	53 (6 by KO)	14	2

Among **Charley Gomer**'s 159 opponents were 5 world champions and a slew of world-class contenders. His first major victory occurred in 1935 when he split two decisions with top-ranking lightweight Eddie Cool. For the next six years Charley fought on average once or twice a month. Opponents included world champions Mike Belloise, Chalky Wright, Kid Chocolate, Benny Bass, and Freddie "Red" Cochrane.

Although just a step below the best lightweight fighters of his era, Gomer was always capable of upsetting the odds. In 1940, nearing the end of his prolific 11-year career, he won decisions over featherweight contenders Everett Rightmire and Abe Denner. Charley fought all over the United States, but he was most popular in his hometown of Baltimore, where 45 of his 159 bouts took place.

JOEY GOODMAN
Born: 1910
Died: Unknown
Hometown: Richmond, Virginia
Weight: 136–144 lbs.
Professional Career: 1925–1935

Total Bouts	Won	Lost	Draw	ND	NC
98 (672 rounds)	71 (21 by KO)	14 (0 by KO)	8	4	1

The career of **Joey Goodman** presents a textbook case of how boxers of the Golden Age learned their trade. Joey, a 16-year-old 130-pounder, turned pro in 1925. Over the next four years he was brought along slowly, trading jabs and hooks with other ambitious youngsters like Willie Siegel, Jackie Cohen, Buster Brown, Frankie DeAngelo, Al Ridgeway, Maxie Strub, and Lope Tenorio. By the end of 1929 Joey had compiled a respectable 42-11-5 record, including 15 wins by knockout. He was now ready to challenge any lightweight in the world.

On February 3, 1930, in his sixtieth pro bout, Joey took on lightweight champion Sammy Mandell. The contract stipulated that both men weigh over 135 pounds, so Mandell's title would not be at stake if he lost. The precaution was not warranted. Mandell, one of the finest boxers in the history of the division, had no trouble outboxing Goodman and winning the decision.

Undeterred by the defeat, Joey lost only one of his next 13 contests. His only other loss that year was to junior lightweight champion Benny Bass (non-title). His excellent showing against

Bass, a former featherweight champion, boosted Joey's stock considerably.

In 1931 Joey fought his way into the junior welterweight top 10 with victories over Tommy Grogan and Jack Portney. Despite his fine record Goodman never received a title shot. Perhaps it was all too frustrating, but for reasons unknown, he had only one fight each in 1934 and 1935 before deciding to hang up his gloves at the age of 25.

In an era of intense competition in both the lightweight and welterweight divisions, this rock-jawed boxer was never stopped, and established an enviable record of only 14 losses in 98 fights.

AL GORDON
PHILADELPHIA

AL GORDON

Born: September 3, 1903
Died: November 2, 1983 (Age: 80)
Hometown: Philadelphia, Pennsylvania
Weight: 130–135 lbs.
Professional Career: 1921–1932

Total Bouts	Won	Lost	Draw	ND	NC
122 (905 rounds)	60 (21 by KO)	19 (3 by KO)	10	22-9-1	1

Al Gordon established his impressive professional credentials against the likes of Bobby Wolgast, Rosey Stoy, Joe Ryder, Frankie Rice, and future featherweight champion Benny Bass.

A temporary setback occurred in 1924 when Ray Miller tagged Gordon with his powerful left hook and stopped him in the second round. It was the first of only three knockout defeats for Gordon in 122 bouts.

Gordon returned to the win column by outpointing Canadian champion Leo "Kid" Roy and top contenders Joe Glick, Basil Galiano, and Maurice Holtzer. In 1928 *The Ring* rated him the world's number-four junior lightweight contender.

Al was past his prime when Philadelphia neighbor Harry Blitman flattened him in the first round in 1931. After losing three of his next five bouts, Al knew it was time to retire. He purchased a hack license and drove a cab for many years in Philadelphia.

JACK GROSS

Born: August 1, 1905
Died: 1988 (Age: 82)
Hometown: Philadelphia, Pennsylvania
Height: 6' 1" Weight: 205 lbs.
Professional Career: 1927–1932

Total Bouts	Won	Lost	Draw	ND	NC
56 (317 rounds)	45 (31 by KO)	8 (4 by KO)	1	1-0	1

(Courtesy of PhillyBoxingHistory.com)

After turning pro in 1927, Philadelphia's **Jack Gross** went through 29 fights without a defeat. The southpaw's first loss was to master boxer Tommy Loughran. He would lose to Loughran twice more, but each bout was hard-fought and closely contested. (Loughran accounted for three of Gross's eight career losses.) Gross won ten of his next 11 fights, including victories over Emmett Rocco, Al Walker, and Murray Gitlitz. In May 1929 he was rated the number-nine heavyweight in the world by *The Ring* magazine. He was bounced from the ratings after being stopped by the formidable black heavyweight contender George Godfrey. In subsequent contests he defeated Roberto Roberti and won a 10-round decision over Godfrey. His efforts to reclaim a top-10 rating were stymied when he dropped a close 10-round decision to Ernie Schaaf and, in his next bout, was stopped by future heavyweight champion Primo Carnera in the seventh round at Brooklyn's Ebbets Field. It was his second knockout loss to Carnera. Gross retired and moved to New Jersey, where he became a justice of the peace and a Bridgeton City magistrate.

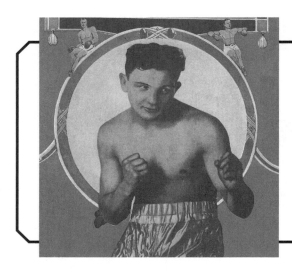

IZZY GROVE
(Eddie Poplick)
Born: 1909
Died: Unknown
Hometown: New York, New York
Height: 5' 6" Weight: 145–160 lbs.
Professional Record: 1926–1932

Total Bouts	Won	Lost	Draw	ND
73 (473 rounds)	33 (4 by KO)	30 (10 by KO)	7	3

Izzy was born Eddie Poplick on the Lower East Side of New York. As he explained it, "One night at a boxing show in the New York Athletic Club, they called out a name, Isaac Van Groven. He wasn't there, so I went up. I figured he'd come later, and if he didn't, I could handle myself . . . I'm **Izzy Grove** ever since."[35]

His first pro fight, in 1926, resulted in a four-round draw with Marty Shapiro. Over the next two years Izzy fought 38 times. On October 6, 1928, he outpointed former welterweight contender Hilario Martinez. Seven weeks later he appeared in a 10-round co-feature at Madison Square Garden against future middleweight champion Vince Dundee. The more-experienced Dundee won a close but unanimous decision. They split two subsequent bouts, with Izzy winning the first and Dundee the rubber match.

In 1929 Izzy scored a major upset by defeating third-ranked middleweight contender Harry Ebbets. They fought twice more, with Ebbets winning both times. It was during this time that Izzy appeared on the cover of *The Ring* magazine and was briefly rated the number-eight welterweight in the world.

Other notable opponents included Georgie Levine, My Sullivan, Johnny Indrisano, Paul Pirrone, and future middleweight champion Gorilla Jones. All of Izzy's losses were to fighters with winning records. He retired in 1932 after losing a 10-round decision to Eddie Whalen. After hanging up his gloves, Izzy became a theatrical booking agent in New York City.

WILLIE HARMON

(Herman Eisman)
Born: April 20, 1899
Died: Unknown
Hometown: New York, New York
Weight: 147 lbs.
Professional Career: 1918–1928

Total Bouts	Won	Lost	Draw	ND	NC
95 (790)	65 (25 by KO)	13 (3 by KO)	5	8-1-2	1

In 1926 **Willie Harmon** was rated among the top five welterweights in the world. That same year he was offered a golden opportunity—a title fight with the recently crowned welterweight champion Pete Latzo. A year earlier Latzo had lost a 10-round decision to Harmon. At the weigh-in for the second bout, Latzo scaled 153 pounds—6 pounds over the welterweight limit. Needless to say, Harmon was upset. He was giving away almost 9 pounds, and the title would not be at stake. New Jersey boxing officials talked Harmon into going through with the bout by assuring him the title would still be up for grabs.

Latzo's weight advantage may have been a factor in Harmon's defeat. He was knocked out at 2:50 of the fifth round. The loss was one of only three knockouts suffered by Harmon in 94 bouts.

After a four-month layoff Willie returned to the ring with a vengeance. Hoping for another crack at the title, he went undefeated in his next 10 fights. The winning streak was broken on August 1, 1927, when he was outpointed in 10 rounds by future middleweight champion Vince Dundee.

Harmon then won seven of his next eight bouts, including decisions over Jack Zivic and Hilario Martinez. In his last fight, on March 3, 1929, he was knocked out by future welterweight champion Tommy Freeman. Even though he was only 28 years old and still a rated contender, Willie decided to call it a career.

GUSTAVE HUMERY

Born: December 17, 1908
Died: July 6, 1976 (Age: 67)
Hometown: Paris, France
Height: 5' 4" Weight: 132–140 lbs.
Professional Career: 1927–1942

Total Bouts	Won	Lost	Draw
85 (467 rounds)	59 (36 by KO)	26 (18 by KO)	0

There was rarely a dull moment when France's **Gustave Humery** began trading blows with opponents. In 59 of 85 professional fights, either he or his opponent wound up on the canvas. Humery had 36 knockout victories to his credit, but suffered the same fate himself 18 times. Typical was his 1935 fight with England's fine lightweight contender Harry Mizler. He floored the Englishman five times and was on the verge of stopping him when Mizler, in desperation, caught his charging antagonist with a swift left-right combination that staggered Humery and turned the fight in Mizler's favor. In the eighth round Humery's corner, realizing their man was out on his feet, threw in the towel.

On his good nights he was *very* good. Between 1927 and 1937 Humery won the featherweight and lightweight titles of France, in addition to winning the European lightweight title. His record is studded with the names of many world-class boxers, including the likes of Panama Al Brown, Johnny Cuthbert, Cleo Locatelli, Harry Corbett, Jackie "Kid" Berg, Harry Mizler, and Ernie Roderick. Even past his prime he continued to challenge the top men in his weight class. In the last fight of his 18-year career he was stopped by France's legendary future middleweight champion, Marcel Cerdan, who at the time had only one loss in 64 pro fights.

ABIE ISRAEL
(Morris Israel)
Born: January 11, 1913
Died: January 16, 1972 (Age: 59)
Hometown: Portland, Oregon
Weight: 110–130 lbs.
Professional Career: 1929–1938

Total Bouts	Won	Lost	Draw
92 (424 rounds)	58 (26 by KO)	24 (6 by KO)	10

Abie Israel was only 16 years old when he embarked on a pro career in 1929. Most of his fights took place in Seattle, Washington, where he remained a top attraction for over 10 years. The converted southpaw attempted to follow in the footsteps of previous Jewish featherweight champions Abe Attell, Kid Kaplan, and Benny Bass when he challenged the current champion Freddie Miller on July 11, 1933, at Seattle's Civic Ice Arena. The scheduled 15-round bout was Seattle's first world boxing championship.

Three months earlier Abie had outpointed Miller in a six-round non-title bout. The upset had catapulted Abie into the ratings and led to a return bout with Miller for the title. But the rematch produced a vastly different result. Miller dropped Abie twice en route to a fourth-round knockout.

Fourteen weeks later Abie met former featherweight champion Tommy Paul, who had lost the title to Miller 10 months earlier. In another case of biting off more than he could chew, Abie was TKO'd in the eighth round.

In subsequent bouts Abie drew with contender Pete DeGrasse, but lost decisions to Henry Woods, Al Spina, and former flyweight champ Midget Wolgast. The losses spelled finis to his title aspirations.

BEN JEBY

(Benjamin Jebaltowsky)
Middleweight Champion 1933
Born: December 27, 1909
Died: October 5, 1985 (Age: 75)
Hometown: New York, New York
Height: 5' 10" Weight: 150–160 lbs.
Professional Career: 1924–1934, 1936

Total Bouts	Won	Lost	Draw	NC
73 (546 rounds)	54 (22 by KO)	14 (2 by KO)	4	1

In 73 professional fights **Ben Jeby** never looked for an exit. He always took the fight to his opponent. Constantly moving forward, he outhustled and outfought bigger punchers and better boxers who were disconcerted by his endless energy, fighting spirit, and their inability to discourage or hurt him. This is not to imply that Jeby was easy to hit. No top fighter of his era could survive if he was easy to hit. Even on the attack Jeby always maintained a tight defensive posture.

Jeby turned pro in 1927 at the age of 19. Over the next two and a half years he lost only four of 25 fights. In his prime he outpointed former champion Joe Dundee and top middleweight contenders Harry Ebbets and Len Harvey. In September 1931 Ben managed a 10-round draw with the division's number-one contender, Dave Shade, at the Queensboro Stadium in Long Island City. Madison Square Garden put them together for a rematch 24 days later. This time Shade won

a 12-round decision. Jeby rebounded by finishing the year with four straight wins, including a decision over Jackie Aldare and a third-round knockout of veteran Eddie Whalen.

A setback occurred in 1932 when he was knocked out in the first round by unheralded Frank Battaglia, one of the hardest punchers in the middleweight division. Although terribly disappointed by the loss, Jeby did not become overly discouraged. With the dogged determination that was his hallmark as a fighter, he set about restoring his reputation, and returned to action four months later with a third-round knockout of tough club fighter Billy Kohut. After outpointing Roscoe Manning, he knocked out three opponents in a row, including contender Paul Pirrone, who was dropped seven times before the bout was stopped in the sixth round.

Jeby's victory over Pirrone was a quarter-final match of a tournament sponsored by the New

York State Athletic Commission, designed to find a successor to world middleweight champion Mickey Walker, who had relinquished the title several months earlier to campaign as a light heavyweight.

After defeating Chick Devlin in the semifinals, Jeby squared off against former foe Frank Battaglia for the vacant middleweight title. The fight presented a golden opportunity to not only win the crown, but also to gain revenge for his embarrassing loss to Battaglia.

Fighting as if his life depended on the outcome, Jeby completely dominated his former conqueror, winning almost every round until referee Jack Britton intervened and stopped the one-sided contest in the 12th round. It was only the second time in 58 bouts that Battaglia had been stopped.

On March 17, 1933, Jeby defended his title for the first time against his number-one contender, Vince Dundee. The bout generated enough interest to entice 11,000 fans into Madison Square Garden. Three years earlier Dundee had easily outpointed Jeby. This time the fight was far more competitive. At the end of 15 close rounds the bout was judged a draw. Four months later Jeby successfully defended his title against Young Terry in 15 rounds at Newark's Dreamland Park.

Jeby put his title up for grabs for the third time when he faced the great southpaw Lou Brouillard at New York's Polo Grounds. Brouillard, a former welterweight champion, held victories over two boxing legends, Mickey Walker and Jimmy McLarnin. He was an extremely strong and durable fighter. When these two baby bulls met, something had to give. In the seventh round Brouillard connected with a powerful left hook that landed flush on the jaw of the defending champion. Ten seconds later Jeby was an ex-champ.

Although he was only 25 years old, Jeby's career began to falter after the loss of his title. In 1934 he lost five of eight contests, all to highly ranked fighters, including a 10-round non-title bout to old nemesis Vince Dundee, who four months earlier had relieved Lou Brouillard of his middleweight crown.

Jeby sat out 1935. He scored two minor victories the following year and then retired. A few years after his last bout, Jeby received a plumber's license and worked in that field for most of his life.

GOLDEN GLOVES FOR A GOLDEN ERA

In 1927 the *New York Daily News* sponsored the first Golden Gloves tournaments for amateur boxers living in New York City's five boroughs and surrounding suburbs. Any amateur boxer between the ages of 16 and 25 could enter. There were so many applications that first year organizers were forced to limit the number of entrants to 2,300. The Golden Gloves quickly became an annual institution in New York, and the largest citywide amateur boxing tournament in the nation. After six weeks of elimination matches across the city the championship matches were staged at Madison Square Garden on March 28, 1927. Nearly twenty-two thousand fans turned out for the finals, with another ten thousand turned away.

By 1930 over 200 other cities from coast to coast were hosting their own Golden Gloves tournaments, sponsored by a local newspaper or radio station. The amateur bouts provided experience and publicity for many future professionals. The various regional winners in each weight category would then meet to determine national champions. Inter-city competitions were also very popular, especially the New York vs. Chicago rivalry that continued into the early 1960s.

The Golden Gloves has two categories: "Sub-Novice" for amateurs with less than 11 bouts going into the tournament, and "Open Division" for boxers with more-extensive amateur experience. Flyweight Terry Roth, representing the Lower East Side's Seward Gymnasium, became the first New York Golden Gloves champion in 1927 when he won the 112-pound flyweight open title. Roth turned pro that same year. Barney Ross of Chicago and Bob Olin of New York were the first two Golden Gloves winners from their respective cities to win a professional title.

Over the past 30 years Golden Gloves tournaments have mirrored the downsizing of the sport. Budgetary constraints and a general lack of interest have caused many cities to discontinue the tournaments. In New York only about 400 applicants sign up to enter the annual competition, including a new women's division. The age limit was rescinded in the 1980s. Anyone over the age of 16 can enter the tournament if physically fit. (The names of the 32 Jewish New York Golden Gloves champions appear in the appendix.)

ANDRE JESSURUN

Born: November 21, 1914
Died: May 24, 1976 (Age: 61)
Hometown: New York, New York
Height: 5' 7½" Weight: 147–154 lbs.
Professional Career: 1934–1941

Total Bouts	Won	Lost	Draw
112 (930 rounds)	67 (10 by KO)	32 (4 by KO)	13

Andre Jessurun's ancestors, Spanish Jews, left Spain for Portugal in the 15th century to escape the Inquisition. When Portugal initiated its own Inquisition against the Jews, the family fled to Holland, and eventually moved to Dutch Guiana (now Suriname), in South America. In 1919, when Andre was four years old, the family emigrated to New York City's Lower East Side.

As an amateur boxer Andre made it to the finals of the New York City Golden Gloves welterweight open championship in 1934. That same year, in the Inter-City Golden Gloves tournament, he represented New York and won a second division title, also at welterweight.

In his first three years as a pro Andre fought 58 times, the majority against quality opposition. Jessurun had a busy and aggressive style that required him to be in top condition for every contest, since he almost always set a terrific pace. He was good enough to win two out of four bouts against the great welterweight contender, Cocoa Kid. Andre also defeated Nat Bor, the

Jewish 1932 Olympic Games bronze medalist. At the time Bor had lost only two of 31 professional bouts.

Despite fighting the toughest welterweights of his era, Andre continued his amazing pace without letup, averaging 18 bouts a year from 1939 to 1941. In 1939 he lost a split decision to highly ranked Steve Mamakos. After winning two of his next three bouts, Andre was outpointed by number-one welterweight contender Holman Williams, one of the greatest boxers to never win a title.

Jessurun was an iron man, but even iron has a breaking point. To say that he was abused and mismanaged is an understatement. His handlers threw him in against every tough fighter, with little time off to rest and recover between bouts. Adding insult to injury, he later found out that his crooked manager had been shortchanging him for years.

Even in the twilight of his hectic career Andre was capable of defeating the likes of Ralph Zannelli,

Steve Belloise, Ossie Harris, and Jerry Fiorello. Mixed in with those victories were losses to Izzy Jannazzo and Antonio Fernandez. In a return bout with Belloise he was KO'd in the seventh round.

Six months before he retired Andre lost a 10-round decision to old foe Cocoa Kid. In his last professional fight, on November 7, 1941, at the Chicago Stadium, he was stopped by Shorty Hogue.

Andre was married to the sister of featherweight contender Al Reid. After his loss to Hogue she insisted that he quit the ring and, fortunately,

he listened. Andre was just two weeks shy of his 27th birthday, but he was already a well-worn veteran of 112 professional fights.

Although he volunteered to serve in the military during World War II, the many injuries he had sustained during his boxing career precluded that option, so he took a job as a welder at the Brooklyn Navy Yard. After the war Andre supported his wife and two children by working as a long-haul truck driver for Swift Line Transfer. He was still on the job when he suffered a fatal heart attack at the age of 61.

LOUIS "KID" KAPLAN
"The Meridian Buzzsaw"
Featherweight Champion 1925–1927
Born: October 10, 1901
Died: October 26, 1970 (Age: 69)
Hometown: Meriden, Connecticut
Height: 5' 2" Weight: 126–140 lbs.
Professional Career: 1918–1933

Total Bouts	Won	Lost	Draw	ND	NC
164 (1,504 rounds)	108 (28 by KO)	22 (3 by KO)	13	13-0-3	5

Louis "Kid" Kaplan was a rip-roaring, hell-for-leather, nonstop punching machine who defeated some of the greatest featherweights and lightweights of all time. In 1958 the sport's preeminent boxing historian, Nat Fleischer of *The*

Ring, named Kaplan the 10th-greatest featherweight boxer of the modern gloved era.

Kaplan was born in 1901 in Kiev, Russia. When he was five years old the family left Russia and settled in Meriden, Connecticut, where his father went into the junk business to support his wife and five children.

Young Louis saw no future for himself in the junk business. It was his intention to earn his living as a prizefighter. After a four-year apprenticeship in the amateur ranks, the 17-year-old turned pro in 1918. Four years later Kaplan had established his credentials as a top-rated featherweight contender, with victories over Danny Frush and Jimmy Goodrich, and several draw decisions with Babe Herman.

Kaplan's unusual strength, whirlwind style, and seemingly endless reserves of stamina overwhelmed most of his opponents. His low KO percentage (28 KOs in 167 fights) was due in part to his style of fighting, which did not allow him to set down on his punches, and to the fact that from the very beginning of his storied career, he consistently fought the best fighters of his era.

In a 1925 tournament authorized by the New York State Athletic Commission to crown a new featherweight champion, Kaplan scored two knockouts and one decision before facing top-rated Danny Kramer in the finals.

Kramer, an 8–5 favorite, was a hard-punching Philadelphia southpaw. He was also a Mob-managed fighter. Rumors abounded that gamblers had gotten to the judges, and the fix was in for Kramer to win a decision. Kaplan knew that if the rumors were true, the only way he was sure to win the title was by a knockout. But Kramer had only been stopped twice in 128 previous bouts.

The *New York Times* described the Kaplan vs. Kramer title bout as "one of the season's hardest and most sensational battles . . . every minute of every round was crowded with exciting, spectacular action." Kaplan fought as if possessed. Kramer desperately sought to slow the Kid's furious assault by landing powerful body punches, but every time Kaplan was hit, he came back stronger and more determined. In the ninth round Kaplan landed a series of blows that had Kramer staggering around the ring. Many in the crowd of 10,000 spectators were screaming at the referee to stop the fight. Finally, Kramer's corner took matters into their own hands and threw a towel into the ring, signifying defeat. Louis "Kid" Kaplan became the first boxer from the Nutmeg State to win a world boxing title.

On August 27, 1925, Kaplan made the first defense of his title against Babe Herman, a clever stylist whose record against the champion showed one victory and three draws. The fight, staged in Waterbury, Connecticut, attracted 20,000 spectators and gate receipts of $60,000, setting a new state record. The 15-rounder ended in yet another draw decision. It was later revealed that Kaplan had fractured his right big finger in the eighth round, and from then on used his right arm only defensively. Kaplan's share of the gate was $19,685, while Herman received $9,892.

In a rematch four months later at Madison Square Garden, Kaplan outfought Herman, flooring him four times en route to winning a unanimous 15-round decision.

In 1927 Kaplan announced that he could no longer comfortably make the 126-pound featherweight limit, and intended to relinquish the championship to campaign in the lightweight division. Racketeers offered him a $50,000 bribe if he would postpone his move into the heavier division, and agree instead to lose the featherweight title to a fighter under their control. He was going to give up the title anyway, so why not throw the fight and reap a huge payoff? He didn't even have to concern himself with making 126 pounds, he was told, as the scales would be fixed as well.

Unwilling to be tainted by even a hint of scandal, Kaplan refused the offer, reporting the bribe to the New York State Athletic Commission. "Sure, I could use the cash," he said. "But every time I fight, my friends bet plenty on me, and what about their dough? I wouldn't do a thing like that to them for a million bucks."[36]

Over the next five years three successive champions—Sammy Mandell, Al Singer, and Tony Canzoneri—refused to give Kaplan a shot at the lightweight crown. Sportswriters began calling him "the uncrowned lightweight champ."

While campaigning for a shot at the lightweight crown, Kaplan defeated Joe Glick, Phil McGraw, Johnny Jadick, Maurice Holtzer, Bat Battalino, Jack Portney, and Harry Dublinsky—all top-rated fighters. The great Jimmy McLarnin was one of only three fighters able to stop him in 164 professional fights. He never got a return with McLarnin, but in 1928 Kaplan avenged his KO loss to Billy Wallace with a 10-round decision at Madison Square Garden. Nearing the end of his career Kaplan was knocked out by lightweight contender Eddie Ran.

Shortly after he retired in 1933, Kaplan revealed that the vision in his right eye had been failing for several years, and that he could no longer see out of the damaged orb.

During the course of an extraordinary boxing career, Louis "Kid" Kaplan defeated eight men who were either past, present, or future world champions. He also whipped dozens of rated contenders. Despite the passage of time, Kid Kaplan's star has not dimmed. He is still considered by knowledgeable boxing historians to be one of the greatest fighters of boxing's Golden Age.

MIKE KAPLAN

Born: January 7, 1917
Died: May 10, 1990 (Age: 73)
Hometown: Boston, Massachusetts
Height: 5' 7" **Weight:** 135–147 lbs.
Professional Career: 1936–1942

Total Bouts	Won	Lost	Draw	ND
61 (461 rounds)	46 (11 by KO)	7 (3 by KO)	6	3

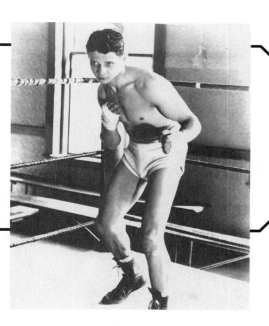

Boston's **Mike Kaplan** broke into the welterweight "top ten" in 1939 by outpointing third-ranked Jimmy Leto. Even more impressive was his victory and draw against highly ranked Cocoa Kid. To show he was no flash in the pan, Mike continued his streak with decisions over Joe Ghnouly, Leonard Del Genio, and Eddie Brink, all tough, seasoned veterans.

In 1940 Kaplan lost a split 10-round decision to Fritzie Zivic. It was his only loss in 11 fights that year. Despite the loss he remained among the upper echelon of challengers, with decisions over Tommy Cross, Milt Aron, and future welterweight champion Freddie "Red" Cochrane.

On April 18, 1941, Kaplan fought a return bout with Zivic at the Boston Garden. Three months earlier Zivic had defeated Henry Armstrong for the welterweight championship of the world. Unfortunately for Kaplan, Zivic was not willing to risk his recently acquired title, so by agreement both men weighed 1 pound over the welterweight limit of 147 pounds. Zivic's caution was justified. He lost a unanimous 10-round decision.

Kaplan then traveled to Philadelphia's Shibe Park where he took on future lightweight champion, Bob Montgomery. After losing most of the early rounds to Kaplan, the great "Philadelphia Bobcat" staged a dramatic comeback and won a unanimous 10-round decision.

With his opportunity to fight for a title fading, Kaplan began to think of retirement. His title chances were further diminished when he was stopped by "California" Jackie Wilson in the third round. The bout was automatically halted when one of Kaplan's corner men entered the ring after he had been knocked down twice. Other than a cut-eye TKO loss, this was only the second time in 53 bouts that Kaplan had been stopped. In the last bout of his career Kaplan won a 10-round unanimous decision over former lightweight champion Lew Jenkins.

In the 1950s Kaplan relocated to Florida and managed a hotel's spa and health club in Miami Beach. He subsequently moved to Las Vegas, where he continued in the same business.

"KO" PHIL KAPLAN

Born: April 19, 1902
Died: August 1, 1983 (Age: 81)
Hometown: Newark, New Jersey
Height: 5' 9½" **Weight:** 150–170 lbs.
Professional Career: 1921–1931

Total Bouts	Won	Lost	Draw	ND	NC
102 (743 rounds)	66 (34 by KO)	14 (1 by KO)	4	10-4-3	1

"KO" Phil Kaplan turned pro at the age of 19 without any amateur experience. His apprenticeship took five years in the professional ranks before he achieved contender status. Kaplan's powerful left hook was his weapon of choice. He used it to score 34 knockouts. A four-fight series of hotly contested battles with "The Pride of Harlem," Jack McVey, proved beyond doubt that he was a force to be reckoned with in the middleweight division. McVey, a great black welterweight and middleweight contender, is barely remembered today, but he was one of the best boxers of the 1920s.

Kaplan and McVey split their first two bouts. They met for a third time on March 27, 1926, at New York's Commonwealth Sporting Club. The judges awarded the 12-round decision to Kaplan. His only loss in 11 fights that year was to the irrepressible future light-heavyweight champion, "Slapsie Maxie" Rosenbloom.

In 1928 Kaplan won his fourth encounter with Jack McVey via a disputed 10-round decision. The *New York Times* described a "savagely waged" contest.[37] That same year Kaplan knocked out Abie Bain and Vince Forgione. In a tournament designed to certify the top challenger for Mickey Walker's middleweight title, Kaplan lost a 10-round decision to Belgium contender Rene DeVos at Madison Square Garden. He returned to the Garden six weeks later and was disqualified for landing a low blow in the fourth round against highly rated Harry Ebbets.

After his loss to Ebbets, Kaplan seemed to lose interest. He had only six bouts in 1929 and 1930. The following year, competing as a light heavyweight, he struggled to outpoint tough journeyman Billy Kohut, and was held to a six-round draw by the veteran Billy Alger. Realizing he had passed his peak as a fighter, "KO" Phil wisely decided to retire at the age of 28.

Kaplan was stopped only once in 102 fights. The loss, in his fifth bout, was caused by an injury to his hand.

HERBIE KATZ

Born: November 24, 1919
Died: June 1, 1987 (Age: 66)
Hometown: Brooklyn, New York
Height: 5' 11" **Weight:** 175 lbs.
Professional Career: 1935–1947

Total Bouts	Won	Lost	Draw
91 (493 rounds)	64 (33 by KO)	24 (10 by KO)	3

Jewish fight fans thought they had another light heavyweight champion in **Herbie Katz**, a hard-socking bruiser out of Brooklyn, New York. As an amateur Katz racked up an impressive 48-4 record, including 35 wins by KO. After turning pro in 1935, he won 27 of his first 31 bouts, including 13 by KO.

Herbie fought in both the middleweight and light-heavyweight divisions. In 1937 Katz defeated former middleweight contender Paul Pirrone and lost an eight-round decision to future light-heavyweight champion Gus Lesnevich at Madison Square Garden. In addition to Lesnevich, Katz fought four other past or future world champions—Melio Bettina, Solly Krieger, Joey Maxim, and Harold Johnson.

Although he rarely weighed more than 175 pounds, Katz had no qualms about venturing into the heavyweight division. In a bout with "Two Ton" Tony Galento in 1943, he gave away 48 pounds and was stopped in the first round. He retired four years later after a first-round KO loss to future light-heavyweight champion Harold Johnson.

LEW KIRSCH

(Lew Kirschenbaum)
Born: April 6, 1907
Died: July 1982 (Age: 75)
Hometown: New York, New York
Height: 5' 6" Weight: 133–145 lbs.
Professional Career: 1925–1929, 1932, 1937

Total Bouts	Won	Lost	Draw
51 (280 rounds)	47 (19 by KO)	3 (1 by KO)	1

Lew Kirsch turned pro in 1925, and over the next three years was undefeated in 33 fights. His first loss was a 10-round decision to highly rated lightweight contender Tommy Grogan. The following year he had only one bout and then remained idle for two years. His comeback, in 1932, resulted in seven consecutive wins, including an eight-round decision over fourth-ranked junior lightweight Joey Costa.

Kirsch was a good fighter, but one had to be much better than good to enter the pantheon of ring greats that stood at the pinnacle of the sport in the 1930s. On September 29, 1932, at the Queensboro Stadium in Long Island City, Kirsch finally faced his moment of truth in the person of Tony Canzoneri, one of the greatest pound-for-pound fighters who ever lived.

Canzoneri, a veteran of 105 pro fights, was the lightweight champion of the world when he and Kirsch crossed gloves for their scheduled 10-round non-title bout. Nine weeks earlier

Canzoneri had lost an upset split decision to junior welterweight champion Johnny Jadick. To some it was an indication that Canzoneri might be slowing down.

Kirsch's management, in a classic case of wishful thinking, thought their boy just might pull off another upset. Unfortunately for Kirsch, reality intruded, and Canzoneri's great talent overwhelmed him in three rounds. A hard left hook to the body started his downfall. As reported by the *New York Times*, "Kirsch remained on his feet throughout the battle but was reeling and groggy and holding Canzoneri tenaciously when the referee ended the proceedings."

The young fighter was emotionally devastated by his first (and only) knockout loss, and decided to retire. Six and a half years later he returned to the ring and won seven of eight bouts against ordinary opposition before hanging up his gloves for the last time.

DANNY KRAMER

Born: November 22, 1900
Died: March 1971 (Age: 70)
Hometown: Philadelphia, Pennsylvania
Height: 5' 3" **Weight:** 125–130 lbs.
Professional Career: 1917–1930

Total Bouts	Won	Lost	Draw	ND
179 (1,100 rounds)	93 (34 by KO)	31 (5 by KO)	20	30-4-1

On January 2, 1925, at Madison Square Garden, **Danny Kramer** and Louis "Kid" Kaplan met to determine a new featherweight champion of the world. Kramer vs. Kaplan was one of 12 title bouts in which both boxers were Jewish.

Kramer was managed by Max "Boo Boo" Hoff, a "connected" (read: mobster) Philadelphia fight manager with gambling and bootleg interests. Rumors of a fix in favor of Kramer were rampant. Kaplan, aka "The Meridian Buzzsaw," got wind of the rumors and decided not to leave matters up to the judges' decision.

In a sensational seesaw battle Kramer was unable to slow down or halt Kaplan's incessant attack. By the ninth round Kramer was in obvious distress. With ringsiders screaming at the referee to halt the bout, Kramer's seconds, in the traditional gesture of surrender, threw a towel into the ring, automatically ending the bout and awarding the title to Kaplan

Kramer had 16 additional fights in 1925. He returned to the Garden just 49 days after his brutal fight with Kaplan to take on Canadian featherweight champion Leo "Kid" Roy in a 12-rounder. He knocked out Roy in the eighth round. His most satisfying victory that year was a first-round knockout of previous conqueror George "KO" Chaney.

Danny's career began to wind down in 1927. The following year he lost to Joe Glick, King Tut, Santiago Zorilla, Red Chapman, and Leo "Kid" Roy. He sat out 1929 and then returned to the ring for one last fight in 1930 against journeyman Eddie O'Dowd. Kramer won via a fourth-round KO and called it a career.

SOLLY KRIEGER

Middleweight Champion 1938–1939
Born: March 28, 1909
Died: September 9, 1964 (Age: 55)
Birthplace: Brooklyn, New York
Height: 5' 8" Weight: 159–180 lbs.
Professional Career: 1928–1941

Total Bouts	Won	Lost	Draw
113 (741 rounds)	82 (54 by KO)	25 (3 by KO)	6

There was never a dull moment when **Solly Krieger** fought. He employed the type of aggressive bob-and-weave style made famous by former heavyweight champion Jack Dempsey. Like Dempsey, Solly's best punch was an explosive left hook out of a weave. He was an excellent infighter and relentless body puncher.

As an amateur Krieger won the New York Golden Gloves welterweight championship (sub-novice) in 1928. He turned pro that same year. By 1936 he was a seasoned middleweight with 53 pro fights under his belt, and was ready to make his move. Krieger started off the year in dynamic fashion by knocking out previous conquerors Young Terry and Jackie Aldare. Subsequent victories over Roscoe Manning, Frank Battaglia, and Oscar Rankins earned him a rating among the world's top 10 middleweights.

To maintain his rating in the brutally competitive middleweight division, Solly had to compete against other top contenders. In 1937 he lost 10-round decisions to cagey ex-champion Teddy Yarosz and future champion Fred Apostoli. Undeterred, Krieger rebounded with one of his greatest victories by pounding out an impressive 12-round decision over future light-heavyweight champion Billy Conn.

On November 1, 1938, Solly challenged Al Hostak for the National Boxing Association middleweight title. Hostak, out of Seattle, Washington, was one of the division's hardest punchers. He came into the fight having knocked out his last 16 opponents. But Solly was no softie in that department, either, having flattened 45 of 92 opponents. Nevertheless, Hostak was the 7–1 favorite.

Concentrating on a body attack, Krieger was ahead on the scorecards when he floored the champion in the 14th round. It was the first time Hostak had ever been knocked down in 56 pro fights. Despite the champion's hometown advantage (the fight took place in Seattle's Civic Auditorium), the judges awarded the title to Krieger on a split 15-round decision.

Krieger had struggled to make 160 pounds for Hostak. Knowing that his days as a middleweight were coming to an end, he moved up to the light-heavyweight division for a rematch with Billy Conn. But in the year since their last meeting Conn had improved and was nearing his peak as a great fighter. This time he was able to outpoint Krieger and win a unanimous 12-round decision.

Still not convinced, Krieger asked for a rubber match with "The Pittsburgh Kid." On May 12, 1939, he lost a decisive 12-round decision to Conn at Madison Square Garden. Two months later Conn won the light-heavyweight championship.

Six weeks after his loss to Conn, Krieger defended his middleweight title in a return match with Al Hostak. But sweating down to the 160-pound weight limit had drained him. A newspaper account of the fight described Krieger as "a shadow of his former self in making weight for the fight." He was knocked down four times before the referee, former heavyweight champion Jim Braddock, stopped the fight in the fourth round.

That fight should not have happened. Solly had outgrown the middleweight division and never fought at 160 pounds again. In his next fight, eight months later, he weighed 181½ pounds.

Solly Krieger (right) vs. Billy Conn, Madison Square Garden, May 12, 1939.

During his prime Solly Krieger was competitive with some of the best fighters to ever hold the middleweight title. One of those fighters, Freddie Steele, lost only 6 of 139 professional fights. In 1974 he told author and historian John D. McCallum that Solly was the toughest opponent he ever fought. "He could take a punch and could throw a punch," said Steele. "Solly was very hard to nail as he fought out of a shell and in a crouch. Always dangerous, he was the one-punch-and-out type of slugger and could turn the tables on you damn fast."[38]

ART LASKY

Born: November 16, 1908
Died: April 2, 1980 (Age: 71)
Hometown: Minneapolis, Minnesota
Height: 6' 4" **Weight:** 190–203 lbs,
Professional Career: 1930–1936, 1938–1939

Total Bouts	Won	Lost	Draw	ND
58 (336 rounds)	39 (33 by KO)	7 (5 by KO)	6	4-2

On March 22, 1935, **Art Lasky** was just one victory away from challenging Max Baer for the heavyweight championship of the world. All he had to do was defeat an over-the-hill fighter named James J. Braddock. The 3–1 odds favored Lasky.

Braddock, a former light-heavyweight contender, had been on the skids. He had come off the relief rolls a year earlier and was now in the midst of a startling comeback. Against Lasky the New Jersey Irishman fought an inspired fight. The *New York Times* described "a savage, grueling struggle that thrilled a crowd of 11,000 onlookers."[39] Braddock's right hand landed hard and often enough to take a close 15-round decision.

Three months later 10–1 underdog Jimmy Braddock pulled one of the biggest upsets in boxing history by outpointing Max Baer in 15 rounds to win the heavyweight championship of the world.

Braddock's victory over Baer played out like a real-life fairy tale. The likable and unassuming former dockworker was an everyman whose hard road from relief to riches lifted the spirits of an entire Depression-weary nation. He was immortalized as boxing's "Cinderella Man."

For Art Lasky there was no glory or immortality. In the following months he was stopped by heavyweight contenders Ford Smith and Charley Retzlaff. He won three of his next five contests and then lost to journeyman Jack Roper on a seventh-round TKO (technical knockout).

Early in his career Art Lasky had looked like the real goods. From 1930 to 1934, the six-foot-four, 197-pound heavyweight lost only four of 43 pro bouts. His knockouts of Tiger Jack Fox and Fred Lenhart tabbed Lasky as a fighter to watch. In 1934 he earned a top-10 rating after outpointing heavyweight contenders Lee Ramage and King Levinsky. A controversial loss to highly rated Steve Hamas and a draw with Levinsky kept him in the mix. But Lasky's defeat by Braddock and several subsequent losses ended his title aspirations.

In 1936 he stopped Johnny Paychek in the fifth round. During the bout Lasky was thumbed in the eye and suffered a detached retina. Despite being blind in one eye he made a comeback in 1938 and had two draws in southern rings. The following year Lasky had one more fight and then retired.

ROY LAZER

Born: December 27, 1911
Died: December 1988 (Age: 76)
Hometown: Paterson, New Jersey
Weight: 205 lbs.
Professional Career: 1931–1940

Total Bouts	Won	Lost	Draw	ND
67 (450 rounds)	51 (20 by KO)	12 (4 by KO)	3	1-0

A rugged heavyweight and crowd-pleasing performer, **Roy Lazer** has the distinction of being one of four Jewish opponents of the incomparable Joe Louis. On April 12, 1935, two years before he won the heavyweight title, the undefeated "Brown Bomber" stopped Lazer in the third round for his 14th knockout victory in 17 fights. Prior to that defeat Lazer had lost only two of 39 professional fights.

In a 10-year career spanning 67 bouts, Roy defeated quality heavyweights such as Babe Hunt, Ben Foord, Dutch Weimer, Leroy Haynes, and future champion Jersey Joe Walcott. He also fought competitively with contenders Patsy Perroni, Paul Cavalier, Buddy Knox, and "Two Ton" Tony Galento. In 1935 Roy traveled to England, Scotland, and Wales, where he won six of nine fights.

During World War II, Roy enlisted in the US Army and saw action in France, Belgium, and Germany. After recovering from wounds received in combat, he staged boxing bouts in rest camps for US servicemen. Roy was elected to the New Jersey Boxing Hall of Fame.

RAY ARCEL—TEACHER EXTRAORDINAIRE

Ray Arcel instructing a student.

The trainer with the longest career in boxing was Ray Arcel. The first world champion he trained, Abe Goldstein, captured the bantamweight crown in 1923. At age 24, Ray was a year younger than his fighter. He worked his last fight 59 years later, in 1982. In between those years Arcel built a stellar reputation as boxing's most revered teacher-trainer, and one of its finest ambassadors.

Arcel trained nearly 2,000 fighters, including 22 world champions, but he is best known for his work with the great lightweight champion, Roberto Duran. In 1971 he and another great teacher, Freddie Brown, began training the young Panamanian. The two Jewish trainers had over eighty years of boxing experience between them. Under the dynamic duo's tutelage Duran's rise was nothing short of phenomenal. Within one year he captured the lightweight championship of the world. Arcel and Brown continued to train Duran for the next nine years.

Ray Arcel was born in Terre Haute, Indiana, on August 30, 1899. His father was a Russian-Jewish immigrant, and his mother was born in Brooklyn. Ray was born to boxing. He was a teenaged amateur boxer when he decided his true calling was to become a master trainer. Arcel spent almost every day at Grupp's Gym on 116th Street, where he was fortunate to be mentored by Frank "Doc" Bagley and Dai Dollings. Bagley was a brilliant trainer and corner man. Dollings, a Welshman and former bare-knuckle fighter, was known for his ability to bring a fighter to the peak of condition.

"I used to follow them around like a little puppy dog," said Arcel. "I watched them, I worked with them, and they let me take care of fighters. If they couldn't come to the gym they'd ask me to look after the fighters, and tell me what to watch for. . . . In those years there was so much talent around that it rubbed off on anybody who wanted to watch and learn."[40]

Arcel obviously learned his lessons well. Less than a year after his success with Abe Goldstein, he was training Charley Phil Rosenberg for a shot at the bantamweight crown. Ten weeks before the fight Rosenberg arrived at training camp 38 pounds overweight. Not only did Arcel train his fighter down to the 118-pound bantamweight limit in time, but Rosenberg was also able to maintain his strength and stamina throughout the 15 round bout. The boxing community took notice. By the end of the decade Ray Arcel's special talents were in demand throughout the country. He couldn't handle all the offers coming his way, so he decided to join forces with another well-known trainer, Whitey Bimstein, and share the work. Their partnership lasted a decade.

Beloved by his boxers and respected by his peers, Arcel's persona was more like that of an articulate and refined college professor than a boxing trainer. "I never considered myself a trainer," said Arcel. "I considered myself a teacher."[41] He was described by author A. J. Liebling in his book, *The Sweet Science*, as "severe and decisive, like a teacher in a Hebrew school." The lessons he imparted went beyond boxing. At a 1988 dinner honoring Arcel, former middleweight champion Billy Soose spoke for all those who came in contact with the great teacher: "He not only taught me boxing, he taught me values."

In the early 1950s Arcel branched out into promoting. He saw an opportunity to use the new medium of television to benefit boxing and renew the interest that seemed to be waning in postwar America. As always, his approach was to be honest in his dealings with fighters and managers, and to consider the positive impact his promotions would have on the sport. Ray's weekly Saturday-night fights televised on the ABC network drew excellent ratings, but the criminal faction that was in competition with Ray wanted to control all of the television pie. In 1953, attempts were made to undermine Ray's successful promotions through the use of intimidation and threats. Ray, however, refused to compromise his principles.

Studying the action are two of boxing's finest teachers, Ray Arcel (left) and Freddie Brown. In the 1970s they co-trained the great Roberto Duran.

On September 19, 1953, Arcel was standing outside a Boston hotel, having just returned from Yom Kippur services, when someone approached him from behind and struck him over the head with a lead pipe. He suffered a concussion and spent 19 days in a hospital under police protection. The attack prompted a congressional investigation that eventually contributed to the breakup of the Mob-controlled International Boxing Club and the jailing of its criminal overlords. Unfortunately, the person who attacked Arcel was never identified.

In 1955, while mulling over an uncertain future in an uncertain sport, Arcel was offered an executive position in private industry by his longtime friend Harry Kessler, a highly successful entrepreneur who was also one of the country's top referees. For the next seventeen years Ray forged a successful career as a purchasing agent for the Meehanite Metal Corporation. The opportunity to train Roberto Duran drew him back to boxing in 1971.

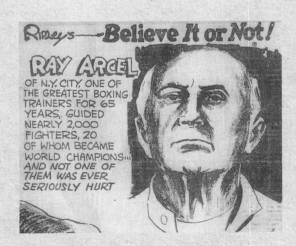

After he retired in 1982, Ray Arcel retained his "elder statesman" status. He was often called upon by reporters for quotes on a variety of topics pertaining to the sport.

While Ray Arcel loved boxing as few have, he was realistic in his assessment of the troubled sport. "Boxing can bring out the worst evil in people," he told journalist Jerry Izenberg. "It can be cruel. Fighters sweat and bleed and usually die broke. Nobody cares. It shouldn't be that way. The good ones are artists. The very art form is self-defense. But there are so many people that kill it for them."[42]

The man who lived the entire length of boxing's rise and decline in the twentieth century, and was so much a part of its history, died on March 6, 1994, at the age of 93.

Recognition of Ray Arcel's amazing career came from many different sources. (Copyright 2015 Ripley Entertainment Inc.)

GEORGIE LEVINE

Born: 1901
Died: Unknown
Hometown: New York, New York
Height: 5' 8" **Weight:** 147–153 lbs.
Professional Career: 1917–1929, 1932

Total Bouts	Won	Lost	Draw	ND	NC
111 (810 rounds)	54 (5 by KO)	31 (2 by KO)	13	4-2-1	6

Georgie Levine began his pro career at the age of 16. Almost immediately he was thrown in with more-experienced boxers, resulting in a number of losses. In 1922 he was rushed into a bout with perennial welterweight contender Dave Shade, and was stopped in the 14th round. Over the next three years Levine steadily improved. By 1925 he was holding his own with such top-tier fighters as Sergeant Sammy Baker, Panama Joe Gans, Paul Doyle, Jack McVey, and future welterweight champion Pete Latzo.

On July 9, 1926, Levine challenged Pete Latzo at New York's Polo Grounds for the welterweight championship. It was Latzo's second defense of the title he had won in May from Mickey Walker. The title fight ended abruptly in the fourth round after Levine landed a low blow and was disqualified.

Over the next few years Levine remained a viable contender with victories over Sylvan Bass,

Izzy Grove, and Andy DiVodi. He also held the formidable Canada Lee to a draw. During one of those fights Levine suffered an eye injury. The damaged eye continued to deteriorate, and he had it secretly removed and replaced with a glass eye. Levine never told the boxing commission about the operation, and he was able to pass the rudimentary pre-fight physical exams given before each fight by memorizing the eye chart. He finally retired in 1929 after a 10-round points loss to future welterweight champion Tommy Freeman. Levine returned for one more fight three years later and never fought again.

During his career Levine fought 39 times in California. After hanging up his gloves he moved to Los Angeles permanently, and purchased two bars in Hollywood that he operated for the next 30 years.

KING LEVINSKY

Aka, "Kingfish Levinsky"
(Harry Krakow)
Born: September 9, 1910
Died: September 30, 1991 (Age: 81)
Hometown: Chicago, Illinois
Height: 5' 11" Weight: 182–200 lbs.
Professional Career: 1928–1939

Total Bouts	Won	Lost	Draw	ND
118 (786 rounds)	75 (40 by KO)	35 (5 by KO)	7	0-1

Viewed from outside of the ring **King Levinsky**'s awkward and seemingly undisciplined style made him look easy to beat. But as many quality boxers found, to their chagrin, it was a mistake to underestimate him. The Kingfish wasn't much of a boxer, but he was strong and durable, had good fighting instincts, and possessed a powerful right-hand wallop.

As the story goes, it was Harry Krakow's idea to rename himself "Kingfish Levinsky" out of deference to his hero "Battling Levinsky," the great Jewish light heavyweight of a generation earlier, and to combine it with the name of his favorite character in the popular *Amos and Andy* radio show. Still others say the name derived from his father's job as a fish peddler in the local market. The press would variously refer to him as both "King" and "Kingfish." Whatever the origin, the name fit Levinsky's guileless and happy-go-lucky personality to a tee.

Levinsky was born and raised in Chicago's Maxwell Street Jewish ghetto. Thick-bodied and strong, the five-foot-11, 175-pound teenager thought he might have a future in boxing. He turned pro in 1928, shortly before his 18th birthday. In the late 1920s Chicago was churning with boxing activity. Over a dozen fight clubs regularly showcased weekly or bimonthly shows. Over half of Levinsky's 118 professional bouts took place in Chicago.

Given his comedic persona, the Kingfish would have been the perfect foil for a reality-based TV show. Early in his career his older sister, Lena Levy, thought her kid brother was being shortchanged by greedy managers and promoters. So the headstrong Lena fired his handlers and applied for a manager's license. Lena explained her strategy: "What you have got is a big punch and I am going to find the bums for you to practice it on. Between us we will make a lot of dough and it will stay in the family."[43]

King Levinsky and his sister Lena Levy. Lena took command of her brother's career when she thought he was being shortchanged by greedy managers and promoters.

Lena turned out to be a savvy bargainer for Levinsky's services. His growing bank balance soon showed the results of her efforts. The only promise she did not live up to was providing him with "the bums" to practice on. The popular fighter had a loyal following, but no one was going to part with their Depression-era dollars to watch him flatten a bunch of tomato cans. The real money would only be possible by fighting the top contenders.

By 1932 the Kingfish had filled out to a solid 200 pounds. That year he stifled Jack Dempsey's comeback attempt by clearly outpointing the 37-year-old ex-champ in a four-round exhibition bout that broke the Chicago Stadium attendance record. Five months later Levinsky lost a 20-round decision to future heavyweight champion Max Baer. It was his second loss to Baer. But victories over the tough Basque contender Paulino Uzcudun and former champions Tommy Loughran and Jack Sharkey kept him in the ratings.

Even though Lena was the manager, the chauvinistic boxing commissions would not allow her into the ring between rounds, so she would sit on the steps just beneath Levinsky's corner and scream encouragement. From her perch the King's big sister would jump up and down so often and with such energy that sportswriters dubbed her "Leapin' Lena."

On December 28, 1934, heavyweight champion Max Baer came to Chicago for a four-round exhibition with Levinsky. It was their third meeting. Both men were guaranteed a nice payday for what was intended to be a glorified sparring session.

Just before the bell rang to start the first round, the King's sister whispered in his ear that if he made a good showing, it would improve his chances for a title shot with Baer. Levinsky misconstrued the advice. He thought that Lena meant he should go all out for a knockout. Lena was horrified to see her brother begin to slam home rights with the intention of separating Max from his senses. Baer was taken totally by surprise and was shaken up by several solid shots to his chin. The wild first round ended with a furious Max Baer glaring at Levinsky and vowing to flatten him in the next round.

At the bell to start the second round Baer charged across the ring. Two minutes later Levinsky was stretched out on the canvas, knocked out for the first time in his career. Upon regaining consciousness Levinsky would not believe that he had been knocked out until he saw the pictures in the next day's newspapers.

Lena attempted to rebuild her brother's confidence after the Baer fiasco. She arranged a series of bouts against mediocre opponents. The Kingfish won his next 12 outings, including 11 by knockout. The only fighter to last the distance was tough journeyman Babe Hunt.

Next up was an opponent everyone remembers but Levinsky wished he could forget. On August 7, 1935, he faced the undefeated heavyweight sensation, Joe Louis.

Louis was two years away from winning the heavyweight championship, but even at this early stage of his career he was being compared to Jack Dempsey in terms of his destructive hitting power. Lena was at first reluctant to take the match—until Louis's promoter, Mike Jacobs, offered to pay her brother $30,000. "For that money we will fight anyone," she answered. "Where's the contract?"[44]

Louis was coming off his recent knockout victory over former heavyweight champion Max Baer. He seemed unstoppable. The Louis vs. Levinsky bout drew 40,000 fans to Chicago's Comiskey Park, with another 100,000 people (mostly Louis supporters from Chicago's poor black neighborhoods) gathered outside. The odds favored Louis, but many fans in the stadium thought Levinsky just might score an upset if he could connect with his powerful right cross.

The problem for Levinsky was that he began to believe Louis's press notices (not that they weren't true), and by fight time his confidence was wrecked. His seconds had to literally shove him out of the corner to begin the fight.

Levinsky threw only two punches and both missed their intended target. After sampling a few of "The Brown Bomber's" bombs, Levinsky quickly went on the defensive in a futile attempt to avoid being knocked out. It didn't help. Louis floored a passive Levinsky four times en route to a first-round knockout victory.

Lena was crushed by the humiliating defeat and urged her brother to retire. When he refused she sold his contract and washed her hands of the fight game. The Kingfish fought 22 more times but never appeared in a Chicago ring again.

Levinsky's last important fight took place on January 5, 1937, at the Olympic Auditorium in Los Angeles. He lost a 10-round decision to former light-heavyweight champion "Slapsie Maxie" Rosenbloom.

Over the next two years Levinsky fought sporadically, losing six of seven fights. The once-durable Chicago fishmonger, who in 112 previous battles could only be knocked out by the murderous hitting duo of Max Baer and Joe Louis, was halted by four ordinary opponents. The $250,000 Levinsky earned in the ring was quickly depleted by bad investments and three failed marriages. His first wife was fan dancer Roxanne Carmine (née Rosie Glickman). In September 1934 Carmine/Glickman sought a divorce on grounds of cruelty. They had been married only five weeks.

In 1960 Levinsky relocated to Miami Beach, Florida. He supported himself by selling ties out of a suitcase. Whether you were just happy to help him out or were annoyed by his high-pressure sales technique (delivered as he wrapped a tie around a customer's neck as if to perform a strangulation), it was difficult to refuse the King-fish. Whenever Sinatra was in town he made sure to buy a caseload of the King's ties.

Sadly, with age came the inevitable price to be paid for his many years in the ring. His speech became increasingly slurred and his memory turned fuzzy. But self-pity was not part of the King's makeup. The good-natured ex-contender sold his ties with a smile and a wink, all the while telling stories about his colorful boxing career until he could no longer remember them.

King Levinsky (right) barrels into heavyweight champion Max Baer in the first round of their exhibition match in 1934.

NAT LITFIN

Birth and death dates unknown
Hometown: Pittsburgh, Pennsylvania
Height: 5' 7" Weight: 121–135 lbs.
Professional Career: 1929–1942, 1944

Total Bouts	Won	Lost	Draw	ND
115 (727 rounds)	73 (KO 21)	36 (KO 2)	5	1-0

Many of **Nat Litfin**'s early prizefights remain undocumented, the reason being he fought under various spellings of his name. But the 115 bouts that *have* been documented provide more than enough information to evaluate his career.

Nat fought five world champions. He defeated future featherweight champions Joey Archibald and Jackie Wilson, but lost decisions to Petey Scalzo and Willie Pep. The loss to Pep came three months before Pep won the featherweight championship.

On June 25, 1934, future bantamweight champion Georgie Pace knocked Litfin out in the first round. In 115 professional fights only one other opponent was able to stop him. Four years later Litfin scored the greatest victory of his career when he won a split decision over the reigning bantamweight champion, Sixto Escobar. Both fighters weighed over the 118-pound limit, so the title was not at stake, and Escobar retained his title.

After defeating Escobar *The Ring* magazine ranked Litfin the number-two bantamweight in the world. Over the next few years he stayed in the mix of challengers, but eventually lost his high ranking after being outpointed by Pep, Scalzo, Lulu Costantino, and Al Reid.

SAMMY LUFTSPRING

Born: May 14, 1916
Died: September 27, 2000 (Age: 84)
Hometown: Toronto, Canada
Weight: 147 lbs.
Professional Career: 1936–1940

Total Bouts	Won	Lost
40 (287 rounds)	32 (14 by KO)	8

Before he turned pro in 1936, Toronto's **Sammy Luftspring** established an outstanding amateur record. He was Canada's best hope for a gold medal at the upcoming Olympics in Berlin, Germany. But instead of participating, Luftspring and his buddy, Norman "Baby" Yack, another outstanding Canadian Jewish boxer, decided to boycott the Nazi Olympics to protest Germany's treatment of its Jewish population.

After their decision was made public, both Luftspring and Yack were invited to participate in an alternate Olympic Games planned for Barcelona, Spain. They were on their way to Barcelona when the event was abruptly canceled due to the outbreak of the Spanish Civil War. Luftspring returned to Canada and turned pro.

From 1936 to 1938 Sammy won 23 of 27 bouts, including the Canadian welterweight title. Two years later he was ranked among the top five welterweights in the world, and was on a fast track to a title bout with Henry Armstrong when disaster struck. In a tune-up bout against Steve Belloise at the Bronx Coliseum, he was unintentionally thumbed in the left eye. Despite fighting half blind for seven rounds against the murderous punching Belloise, Luftspring pressed the action and appeared to have won. But two of the three judges voted for Belloise.

The loss to Belloise was a serious setback for Luftspring, but worse news was in store for the 24-year-old fighter. Luftspring had suffered a detached retina and within weeks lost total vision in the eye. The injury was permanent. Sammy Luftspring's career as a professional fighter was suddenly over.

The now ex-prizefighter needed to find a career that could support his wife and growing family. After a few false starts he eventually found his niche as a partner in a successful Toronto supper club. With Luftspring acting as its congenial host, "The Mercury Club" became a popular destination for locals, tourists, and visiting celebrities. The club operated successfully for over 20 years.

Referee Sammy Luftspring retaliating after being slugged by boxer Humberto Trottman in 1970.

While running the club Sammy remained involved with the boxing world as a referee. It's estimated that he officiated in more than 2,000 amateur and professional bouts. One bout in particular stands out. In 1970 he was the referee for a fight between Canadian welterweight champion Clyde Gray and a Panamanian fighter named Humberto Trottman. During the course of the fight Trottman became angered at what he thought was Luftspring's biased officiating. Just before the start of the sixth round, he suddenly took a swing at Luftspring and connected with a right-hand punch to the ref's jaw. Luftspring was stunned but did not go down. He responded instinctively, dodging the next punch thrown at him and then landing several punches of his own before they were quickly separated. The 54-year-old warrior had definitely won the impromptu match.[45]

Luftspring remained a very popular figure in his native Toronto for the rest of his life. In 1985 he was elected into the Canadian Boxing Hall of Fame.

GEORGIE MARKS

Birth and death dates unknown
Hometown: Los Angeles, California
Weight: 118 lbs.
Professional Career: 1917–1926

Total Bouts	Won	Lost	Draw	ND
98 (549 rounds)	70 (5 by KO)	11 (0 by KO)	15	0-2

Georgie Marks never avoided the tough ones. Among his 98 opponents were champions Abe Goldstein, Frankie Genaro, and Tony Canzoneri. Only six weeks after his second bout with Genaro, he dropped a 10-round decision to bantamweight contender Pete Sarmiento at the Olympic Auditorium in Los Angeles.

Both Georgie and his brother Benny, a flyweight, were popular Los Angeles boxers during the 1920s. Georgie came closest to winning a title. In 1924, following victories over California Joe Lynch and Willie Darcey, he was matched with the great Filipino flyweight champion Pancho Villa for a 15-round title bout in Madison Square Garden. At the weigh-in on the day of the fight, Georgie came in several pounds over the 112-pound limit, so the title was not up for grabs. It didn't matter, as Villa won a unanimous 15-round decision.

In 1926 Marks won the Pacific Coast Bantamweight Title via a 10-round decision over Chuck Hellman in Portland, Oregon. But his reign as West Coast champion was short-lived. One month later he was rematched with Hellman and lost a controversial 10-round decision. Following that defeat Marks retired.

HARRY MASON

Born: March 27, 1903
Died: August 27, 1977 (Age: 74)
Hometown: Leeds, England
Weight: 135–148 lbs.
Professional Career: 1920–1937

Total Bouts	Won	Lost	Draw	ND
216 (2,565 rounds)	146 (KO 26)	53 (KO 10)	15	1-1

Today's pro fighters consider themselves busy if they fight four times in one year. In November 1930 **Harry Mason** fought four times in two weeks. Three of the fights went 15 rounds, the other, 12 rounds. He was back in the ring 22 days later for another 12-rounder. In all, Mason fought 19 times that year. During the course of his 17-year career, Harry fought over 200 bouts, 98 of which went 15 or 20 rounds.

Harry fought in both the lightweight and welterweight divisons. He was an accomplished violinist, ergo, his nickname, "The Little Fiddler." In an odd sort of psychological warfare the colorful battler would sometimes play the violin before fights in an attempt to unsettle opponents. On occasion he would address the crowd and recite poetry from inside the ring.

Mason took great pride in his defensive skills, and boasted that no fighter was capable of disturbing his carefully parted hair. According to British boxing scribe Gilbert Odd, Mason was "an accomplished boxer, and when he chose could put on a brilliant exhibition of scientific ring craft." Mason also had a reputation as a fashion plate and was always immaculately dressed.

Harry turned pro at 16. Four years later he won both the British and European lightweight championships. In 1924 he went to America to test his skills against the world's top lightweights and welterweights. Harry made three trips to the States, winning five of 12 fights, including one draw. Two of the losses were to future welterweight champions Tommy Freeman and Joe Dundee.

Returning to England, Harry won the British welterweight title from Scotland's Johnny Brown in 1925. He drew with future ring great Len Harvey in his first defense, then lost the crown in 1926 to Jack Hood on a highly disputed decision. All of the bouts were 20-rounders. Eight years later he recaptured the British title by defeating Len "Tiger" Smith.

Mason also held victories over such top-notch fighters as Harry "Kid" Brown, Herb Brodie, Jack Casey, Archie Sexton, Alf Mancini, and James "Red" Herring. He retired in 1937 after his 216th bout.

During the course of his long career Harry fought several times in South Africa and became a fan favorite. Following his retirement he accepted an offer to manage a hotel in South Africa, where he remained for the rest of his life.

JOEY MEDILL

Born: December 25, 1907
Died: Unknown
Hometown: Chicago, Illinois
Height: 5' 3½" **Weight:** 135–145 lbs.
Professional Career: 1925–1932, 1936

Total Bouts	Won	Lost	Draw	ND
55 (409 rounds)	35 (3 by KO)	9 (4 by KO)	4	4-3

Joey Medill's clever boxing style emphasized speed and tactics over power—not unlike that of another Chicago boxing star, the great triple champion Barney Ross. Both men were managed by the crackerjack team of Sam Pian and Art Winch, premier handlers of Chicago's best boxers.

In the late 1920s Medill defeated Mike Dundee, Tommy Grogan, Patsy Ruffalo, Billy Wallace, and Stanislaus Loayza to earn a number-four ranking in the junior welterweight division. He appeared headed for a title shot but was sidetracked after losing a 10-round decision to the former featherweight king, Louis "Kid" Kaplan. One month later he outpointed Billy Townsend at the Olympic Auditorium in Los Angeles, but in a return match two weeks later Medill was knocked out in the first round. He took the next five months off and returned to action against junior welterweight contender Jack Brady. Floored five times, Medill could not answer the bell for the fifth round. The loss effectively ended Medill's contender status. He had only two more fights before calling it a career.

Left to right: Abie, Benny and Hymie Miller.

BENNY MILLER

Birth and death dates unknown
Hometown: Los Angeles, California
Weight: 160–180 lbs.
Professional Career: 1926–1934

Total Bouts	Won	Lost	Draw
44 (295 rounds)	28 (8 by KO)	15 (4 by KO)	1

Pictured here are the three fighting Miller brothers. Seated left to right are Abie, **Benny**, and Hymie **Miller**. Hymie was the 1928 National AAU Flyweight champion, and that same year represented the United States in the Amsterdam Olympics. In his first Olympic bout he appeared to be an easy winner over a fighter from Belgium. When the decision went to the other fighter, 16-year-old Hymie burst into tears. His teammates were so outraged by the injustice they requested permission to withdraw from the Games. The president of the United States Olympic Committee, Major-General Douglas MacArthur, denied their request, stating, "Americans never quit."[46]

Hymie turned pro the following year and had 38 bouts before deciding to retire. Brother Abie was also a main bout fighter, but his pro career was undistinguished. Benny, the oldest of the three brothers, won several service championships in the mid-1920s while serving in the US Navy. He was the only brother to achieve contender status.

In 1931 Benny outpointed Bert Colima, Marty Sampson, Jack Rosenberg, and Jackie Aldare. Those victories earned him a number-nine rating among the top 10 middleweight contenders, according to *The Ring* magazine. Benny remained in the ratings for four months before losing to Chick Devlin and Frankie O'Brien.

Benny finished his career in the light-heavyweight division. He defeated Henry Firpo and KO Christner, but was stopped by Steve Hamas and Art Lasky.

RAY MILLER

Born: October 5, 1905
Died: March 31, 1987 (Age: 81)
Hometown: Chicago, Illinois
Height: 5' 5" Weight: 135 lbs.
Professional Record: 1922–1933, 1936

Total Bouts	Won	Lost	Draw	ND	NC
126 (887 rounds)	67 (33 by KO)	28 (0 by KO)	4	12-8-6	1

Ray Miller's powerful left hook accounted for one of the most shocking upsets of the 1920s. On November 30, 1928, at Detroit's Olympia Stadium, Miller, a 5–1 underdog, became the only fighter to ever stop the great Jimmy McLarnin.

Over 15,000 fans witnessed the upset. McLarnin was tagged early and barely made it past the first round. Despite heroic efforts to turn the tide, he was simply unable to halt Ray's aggressive two-fisted assault over the next six rounds. When Jimmy staggered back to his corner after the seventh round, Pop Foster, his trusted manager, signaled to the referee that he was stopping the fight.

Less than four months later McLarnin avenged the defeat by outpointing Miller at Madison Square Garden in front of a standing-room-only crowd of 22,000. The rematch did not come close to matching the fireworks of their first encounter. Both fighters appeared reluctant to lead and risk being nailed by a counterpunch. By the fifth round fans were booing the slow action. McLarnin responded with a body attack in the last four rounds that clinched his victory.

Miller's potent left hook accounted for 33 knockout victories in 127 bouts. His KO percentage would have been higher but for the extraordinary caliber of opposition he faced. Nevertheless, many of the fighters he stopped were first-class boxers. The list includes Sid Terris, Johnny Jadick, Jimmy McNamara, and Solly Ritz—all taken out in the first round. Lope Tenorio, Tommy Grogan, Mike Sarko, and Georgie Day did not make it past the fourth round.

In other important bouts he won, lost, and drew with Billy Petrolle and dropped a 10-round decision to future champion Barney Ross. Ray was ranked among the world's top 10 featherweight and lightweight contenders for 41 months by *The Ring*, but never received a title shot. He was stopped just once, in a preliminary bout during his first year as a pro.

After he retired Ray became a sales rep for a major liquor distributor. In the 1950s he became a licensed referee in New York State and officiated in many important bouts.

HARRY MIZLER

Born: January 22, 1913
Died: 1990 (Age: 76)
Hometown: London, England
Weight: 135–144 lbs.
Professional Career: 1933–1943

Total Bouts	Won	Lost	Draw
79 (642 rounds)	61 (20 by KO)	16 (4 by KO)	2

Before turning pro in 1933 **Harry Mizler** established a record as one of England's greatest amateur boxers. He won a gold medal in the bantamweight division at the inaugural British Empire Games in 1930, and then won national championships at lightweight in 1932 and 1933. He also represented Great Britain in the 1932 Los Angeles Olympic Games. He was outpointed in his first Olympic bout by American Nat Bor, who also happened to be Jewish.

Harry's two brothers, Judah and Morris, were also boxers. Judah, the oldest, did not turn pro. Morris established a fine pro record at the local clubs, but never achieved contender status. All three brothers helped their parents run a kosher fish stall in London's East End neighborhood. That meant getting up at 5 a.m. and pushing the barrow to the fish market and back. The chore doubled as roadwork for Harry.

Harry made his pro debut at London's famous Blackfriars Arena in 1933. Less than five months later he won the British Lightweight title via a 15-round decision over Johnny Cuthbert. It was only his 10th professional bout. The new champion successfully defended his title in August against Billy Quinlan in Wales, but lost it three months later when he was stopped in the 10th round by the vastly more experienced Jackie "Kid" Berg. The following year Mizler went undefeated in eight fights, including a dramatic come-from-behind eighth-round TKO of France's Gustave Humery.

In 1937 Harry defeated American contender Al Roth but lost a 10-round decision to NBA featherweight champion Petey Sarron. In a return bout five months later, Sarron was disqualified in the first round for landing a low blow. As both fighters weighed over the 125-pound featherweight limit, Sarron's title was not at stake.

Mizler always wore a Star of David and the Union Jack on his boxing shorts. His pleasant personality and classy boxing style would have made him very popular in America, but the only time he fought outside of the British Isles was for his second fight with Sarron, which took place in Johannesburg, South Africa.

During World War II Harry joined the Royal Air Force and served for the duration. After the war he became a successful garment-center entrepreneur.

YOUNG MONTREAL

(Morris Billingkoff)
Born: October 10, 1897
Died: June 28, 1978 (Age: 80)
Hometown: Providence, Rhode Island
Height: 5' 3" Weight: 118–125 lbs.
Professional Career: 1916–1931

Total Bouts	Won	Lost	Draw	ND	NC
134 (1,309 rounds)	64 (14 by KO)	37 (2 by KO)	8	8-12-2	3

With his pipestem arms and skinny frame, **Young Montreal**'s physique belied a hidden strength and durability not visible to the naked eye. He was stopped only twice in 134 documented bouts. Both losses occurred when he was well past his prime.

Young Montreal remained a viable bantamweight contender for nearly a decade. He fought nine world champions a total of 17 times. Unfortunately, only one of those fights was for a title. On February 28, 1921, he fought a 10-round no-decision bout with bantamweight champion Joe Lynch. Newspapers reported Lynch edging Montreal in a very close fight. In a rematch two months later (non-title), newspapers named Montreal the winner.

Sandwiched in between those contests was a 10-round no-decision bout with highly regarded Joe Burman. At least one paper named Montreal the winner. That same year he twice outpointed number-one contender Pete Herman in officially scored 10-round bouts. Two months after their second fight, Herman outpointed Lynch to win the bantamweight championship. Both Lynch and Herman are rated among the greatest bantamweight champions. For a time Montreal was called "the uncrowned bantamweight champion."

In the late 1920s, nearing the end of his illustrious career, Montreal won decisions over future champion Bushy Graham and highly ranked contender Johnny Farr. On April 10, 1929, in the last important win of his career, Montreal decisioned former champion Bud Taylor. The victory was sweet revenge, as Taylor had knocked him out two years earlier.

They didn't come much tougher than Young Montreal. He once insisted on finishing a bout despite having broken his ankle. Other than his loss to Taylor, the only other knockout he suffered was in his very last fight.

YALE OKUN

(Julius Okun)
Born: February 28, 1907
Died: May 1978 (Age: 71)
Hometown: New York, New York
Height: 5' 11" Weight: 171–182 lbs.
Professional Career: 1923–1932, 1934–1935

Total Bouts	Won	Lost	Draw	ND
103 (781 rounds)	59 (13 by KO)	25 (5 by KO)	7	5-6-1

Yale Okun put on his first pair of boxing gloves at the Educational Alliance, the legendary settlement house located in the heart of New York City's Lower East Side. In 1926, three years after turning pro, Yale lost two consecutive 10-round decisions to master boxer (and future light-heavyweight champion) Tommy Loughran. On the plus side, Yale outboxed contenders Bob Lawson, Matt Adgie, and Martin Burke, and had draw decisions with Allentown Joe Gans, Eddie Huffman, and Joe Sekyra.

From 1928 to 1932 Yale floated in and out of *The Ring* magazine's top-10 light-heavyweight ratings. Victories over Harry Smith, Tiger Jack Payne, Tony Cancela, Corn Griffin, and future heavyweight champion Jim Braddock were interspersed with losses to Smith, Joe Knight, Leo Lomski, Joe Manley, and Lee Ramage—all quality boxers.

On December 12, 1929, Okun fought number-one light-heavyweight contender "Slapsie Maxie" Rosenbloom in a 12-round bout at Madison Square Garden. Four years earlier, when both were just starting out, they had fought a six-round draw. This time the irrepressible Maxie was able to slap, dodge, and duck his way to a unanimous decision. Six months later Rosenbloom won the light-heavyweight championship.

Two of Okun's most important bouts were against future light-heavyweight champion John Henry Lewis. In 1932 Okun dropped a 10-round decision to the brilliant prodigy. In a return bout two years later, he was stopped by Lewis in the third round. Lewis, a forgotten ring great, won the championship the following year.

After Okun retired in 1935, he invested $75,000 of his hard-earned ring wages in a golf course. Within a few years the golf course was bankrupt, and so was he. For the next several decades Yale worked as a waiter in New York City before moving to Florida in the 1970s. The money he earned as a waiter may not have matched his ring earnings, but it provided for his family and enabled him to pay for his son's dental school education.

BOB OLIN

Light-Heavyweight Champion 1934
Born: July 4, 1908
Died: December 16, 1956 (Age: 48)
Hometown: New York, New York
Weight: 171–183 lbs.
Professional Career: 1928–1939

Total Bouts	Won	Lost	Draw
86 (605 rounds)	55 (25 by KO)	27 (4 by KO)	4

In 1928 **Bob Olin**, another of the Lower East Side's Educational Alliance alumni, won the New York Golden Gloves light-heavyweight championship. He turned pro that same year and won 17 of his first 18 fights, including 13 by knockout.

As his career progressed Olin developed into a seasoned boxer, but he was not wholly consistent when facing top-tier competition. He won two of four bouts against top light-heavyweight contender Al Gainer, but then dropped back-to-back decisions to former welterweight champion Lou Brouillard. He rebounded with solid wins against Charley Massera, "Unknown" Winston, and Bob Godwin.

On November 16, 1934, at Madison Square Garden, Olin challenged "Slapsie Maxie"

Rosenbloom for his light-heavyweight title. After 15 lackluster rounds Olin was awarded the decision. Rosenbloom had appeared totally disinterested. Rumors of a fix were rampant but never proven.

Eleven months later Olin lost the championship to his former conqueror, the great John Henry Lewis. Olin tried with all his might to hold on to his title, but simply could not match the speed and skill of Lewis. Battered unmercifully for the better part of 15 rounds, Olin stubbornly refused to quit. Reporting on the fight for the *St. Louis Post Dispatch*, sports editor Ed Wray wrote the following: "Never in my forty years of covering fights have I seen a man take the kind of punishment Bob Olin took from Lewis."[47] Olin may not have been a great champion, but he certainly had the heart of one.

On a trip to London in 1936, Olin lost a controversial decision to heavyweight contender Tommy Farr, despite knocking down the rock-jawed Welshman twice. The following year Olin was knocked out by the great Tiger Jack Fox, but in his next bout won a 10-round decision over heavyweight Gunnar Barlund. Three months later Olin tried to win the title back from John Henry Lewis and was knocked down three times before the bout was stopped in the eighth round.

Olin retired in 1939 and never attempted a comeback. After service in the Coast Guard during World War II, he worked for a Wall Street Brokerage firm and also owned a successful restaurant in Manhattan. Bob Olin succumbed to a fatal heart attack in 1956 at the age of 48.

VICTOR "YOUNG" PEREZ

(Victor Perez)
Flyweight Champion 1931–1932
Born: October 18, 1911
Died: January 21, 1945 (Age: 33)
Hometown: Paris, France
Height: 5' 1" Weight: 112–118 lbs.
Professional Career: 1928–1938

Total Bouts	Won	Lost	Draw	NC
133 (1,106 rounds)	89 (27 by KO)	25 (5 by KO)	7	5-6-1

One of the most heroic and tragic stories is that of **Victor Perez**, who fought under the *nom de box* of "**Young Perez**." As a child Victor dreamed of someday winning a world championship and becoming rich and famous. His older brother Benjamin "Kid" Perez had won the flyweight championship of North Africa in 1928, but could not make the leap to contender status. Victor knew his dreams would never have a chance to be realized unless he left his home in French Tunisia and traveled to Paris. So after clearing out the local flyweight competition, the 17-year-old sailed for Paris in the winter of 1928.

Perez's first bout in the City of Lights resulted in an eight-round draw with Lucien Beauvais. It was an auspicious beginning. Over the next two years, fighting almost exclusively in Paris, Victor lost only two out of 26 professional fights. His aggressive style won him a large following among Parisian fight fans, and he was quickly elevated to main-bout status.

On June 4, 1931, in his 54th professional bout, the 21-year-old boxer outpointed Valentin Angelmann in 15 rounds to win the French flyweight title. Four months and two fights later, at the Palais des Sports in Paris, Victor realized his dream of winning a world title when he knocked out America's Frankie Genaro in the second round, thus becoming the youngest French citizen ever to win a world boxing title.

Victor made the most of his fame. He was the toast of Paris and reveled in the perks that came with the crown. He loved to party, and was often seen in the company of the famous French movie actress Mireille Balin.

But the handsome young champion did not allow his busy social calendar to interfere with his active boxing schedule. After winning the title Perez fought 18 times over the next 12 months. Even though he lost two of the fights, they were contested above the 112-pound flyweight limit, so his title was not at risk.

One year and five days after winning the flyweight crown, England's Jackie Brown dethroned Young Perez via a 13th-round technical knockout at King's Hall in Manchester. Perez did not seek a rematch, as he was finding it difficult to make the 112-pound flyweight limit. Henceforth, he would campaign for a shot at the bantamweight crown (maximum weight 118 pounds).

On February 19, 1934, Perez challenged the great bantamweight champion Panama Al Brown. At five-foot-11, Brown was the tallest fighter to ever hold the bantamweight crown. He was a superb boxer and powerful puncher who knew how to make the most of his unusual height and reach. Brown was as thin as a string bean, but very strong and durable. In 162 professional fights he was never knocked out.

As the referee called both men to the center of the ring for pre-fight instructions, the five-foot-one challenger's head was level with Brown's chest.

Victor never stopped trying, but he could not overcome Brown's huge physical advantages and ring craft. At the end of 15 hard-fought rounds

Brown was still the bantamweight champion of the world.

Eight months after their first meeting Brown granted Victor another shot at his title. The bout ended unsatisfactorily when Perez was counted out after claiming he had been fouled in the 10th round and refused to continue fighting.

Perez vowed to stay in Paris and continue his quest for another shot at the title, but a far bigger battle was looming on the horizon. On September 1, 1939, World War II began with Germany's invasion of Poland. In May 1940, Paris fell to the Germans. Caught up in events beyond his control, Victor found himself trapped behind enemy lines.

In 1943 he was arrested by the *Milice Française*, a collaborationist French paramilitary force created by the Vichy regime that specialized in rounding up Jews and members of the French Resistance. In October Perez was deported with 1,000 other Jews on "Transport 60" from the French concentration camp at Drancy to the Auschwitz death camp in Poland. One year later only 31 of the original 1,000 men, women, and children were still alive.

Perez was placed in Auschwitz III/Monowitz, a sub-camp that was used to supply slave labor for the I. G. Farben synthetic rubber factory.[48] It was a temporary reprieve. The prisoners were literally worked to death. Those who became too weak to continue the backbreaking labor were either returned to Auschwitz II to be gassed or were shot on the spot. New prisoners arrived daily to take their places.

The sadistic commandant of the slave labor camp, upon learning that a former world-champion boxer was among the prisoners, had Victor removed from the forced-labor detail. Victor was told he was going to box for the amusement of the camp's SS officers and staff, who enjoyed betting on the outcome of the fights.

Among the other prisoners ordered to fight were a group of Jewish men who had also been amateur or professional boxers before the war, including the former Greek champions Salamo Arouch and Jack Razon. (The film *Triumph of the Spirit* was based on their true stories.) Another prisoner-boxer was former bantamweight contender Kid Francis. Perez and Francis had fought each other 10 years earlier in Paris. Kid Francis was murdered in Auschwitz several months before Perez's arrival.

The fights were held twice a week. The prisoner-boxers were given upgraded sleeping quarters and one day off from their work. Each night they received an extra bowl of soup. They needed whatever strength their meager extra rations could provide in the hopes of prolonging their survival for as long as possible.

In his first fight Perez knocked out a Jewish heavyweight who was a foot taller and outweighed him by 50 pounds. Over the next 15 months he fought twice a week and reportedly won 140 consecutive bouts. During this time he was assigned to work in the kitchen of Auschwitz III. Victor used his access to the food supply to regularly steal a 50-liter container of soup and distribute it to the starving inmates.

Israeli journalist Noah Klieger, who was a prisoner and boxer at Auschwitz, remembers that Victor's friends warned him that he would be hanged if discovered. He never forgot the courageous fighter's response: "Human beings were created in order to help others. We live in order to help!"[49]

Klieger also remembered that Perez attempted to escape from Auschwitz but was captured and tortured for two weeks in the infamous "standing room," a tiny cell with no space to lie down, in which inmates were made to spend the night while still working as slaves during the day.

With the Soviet Army rapidly approaching, the Nazis abandoned Auschwitz in January 1945. They took with them 57,000 prisoners who were barely alive and forced them to march westward toward Germany in freezing temperatures. Fewer than 20,000 would survive the ordeal. Victor Perez was not among them.

As related in Yossi Katz's book, *A Voice Called: Stories of Jewish Heroism*, Perez died according to his credo, "Human beings were created in order to help others." Katz interviewed Noah Klieger, who survived the death march and gave the following eyewitness account:

On January 21, 1945, the fourth day of the death march, the starving, exhausted and freezing Jewish prisoners were stopped outside the Gleiwitz concentration camp near the Czech border. Victor had snuck away from the group and entered the abandoned German camp and found a large sack of bread in the kitchen. Perez put the sack on his shoulders and rushed back to feed his friends. As he approached the group and stood in front of a small ditch, a German guard pointed his machine gun at Perez and ordered him to halt. Victor tried to explain to the guard, "These are my friends and they are starving, I'm just bringing them some bread," but the Nazi insisted Perez not move. He ignored the SS guard and leaped across the ditch, hoping to give the sack of bread to his starving friends, but the Nazi aimed his machine gun at Perez and fired several shots, killing the former champion instantly.[50]

In 2013 a French biographical film based on the life story of Young Perez was released. Perez is portrayed by Brahim Asloum, a French boxer who won a gold medal (light-flyweight division) in the 2000 Olympics.

THE MACCABIAH GAMES

Poster for the first Maccabiah games in 1932. (Courtesy of The Joseph Yekutieli Maccabi Sports Archive)

The Maccabiah Games, otherwise known as "the Jewish Olympics," officially began in 1932 in Tel Aviv, with 400 athletes competing. The second Maccabiah took place in 1935 and included 1,350 Jewish athletes from 28 countries, including the United States. Despite Nazi Germany's order warning them not to attend, a delegation of 134 Jews from Germany traveled to Tel Aviv and participated in the games. The contingent refused to fly the German flag during the opening ceremonies.

Many of the athletes from Germany and other European countries who competed in the 1935 games chose to remain in Israel. Ben Bril, an Olympic boxer (1928) and eight-time Dutch national amateur champion, who won a gold medal at the Maccabiah, returned to Holland. The following year he boycotted the 1936 Munich games. During the German occupation of the Netherlands he was deported to Germany and imprisoned in the Bergen-Belsen concentration camp. Ben Bril and a younger brother survived, but four of his brothers and a sister did not. Bril died in 2003 at the age of ninety-one.

The Maccabiah was reborn with the independent State of Israel. In 1950, 19 countries sent a total of 800 hundred athletes to Israel. The opening parade and track and field events were held in the new 50,000-spectator stadium in Ramat Gan, a suburb of Tel Aviv. In an emotional opening ceremony Prime Minister David Ben-Gurion told the competitors, "Existence in our ancestral home requires physical might no less than intellectual excellence."[51]

Over the past 60 years thousands of Jewish athletes, including dozens of Olympic Games medalists and world record holders, have competed in the quadrennial Maccabiah Games. The tournament is organized in full cooperation with the International Sports Federations. It is the third-largest international sporting event in the world after the Olympics Games and FIFA World Soccer Cup. Competition is open to Israeli citizens regardless of religion and to Jewish athletes from all over the world. The 2009 Games were the first to be televised beyond Israel's borders. In 2013 the 19th Maccabiah Games hosted 7,500 athletes competing in 34 events, including chess. Boxing, a staple in previous games, was not included.

BILL POLAND

Born: October 14, 1917
Died: February 4, 2005 (Age: 87)
Hometown: Bronx, New York
Height: 6' 2" Weight: 200 lbs.
Professional Career: 1937–1943, 1946–1947

Total Bouts	Won	Lost	Draw
50 (235 rounds)	39 (29 by KO)	8 (4 by KO)	3

Bill Poland attended high school in the Bronx where he was an all-around athlete, winning letters in football and swimming. He started boxing to keep in condition during the off-season, and quickly realized he had a natural aptitude for the sport. Following a successful amateur career, Bill turned pro in 1937. The six-foot-two, 200-pound heavyweight could box and punch. Four years after his pro debut Poland's record showed only two defeats in 36 fights, including 22 wins by knockout. Following impressive KOs over Harry Bobo and Eddie Blunt, it appeared he was headed for a top-10 contender slot, but he was sidetracked when stopped by Bobo in the sixth round of their rematch. A subsequent eight-round draw with future contender Joe Baksi was followed by a ninth-round KO at the hands of highly rated Lee Savold.

After hanging up his gloves in 1947, Poland entered the nightclub business in New Jersey, but eventually moved to Las Vegas, where he was employed by the Riviera Hotel.

JACK PORTNEY

Born: June 27, 1909
Died: February 1991 (Age: 81)
Hometown: Baltimore, Maryland
Height: 5' 5" **Weight:** 145 lbs.
Professional Career: 1927–1938

Total Bouts	Won	Lost	Draw	ND	NC
126 (1,034 rounds)	95 (24 by KO)	19 (6 by KO)	6	3-2	1

In its heyday as a boxing metropolis, the city of Baltimore produced several world-class Jewish boxers. One of the best was Russian-born southpaw **Jack Portney.**

After compiling a 29–1 amateur record, Portney turned pro in 1927. Three years later he earned a top-10 rating in the lightweight division by outpointing former world champion Louis "Kid" Kaplan. Portney eventually grew into a welterweight and achieved a number-three rating in that division after defeating Andy Divodi, Wesley Ramey, Herb Bishop, and former champions Benny Bass and Johnny Jadick.

Frustrated when he couldn't land a title shot in 1934, Portney wrote to a promoter in Australia and received an invitation. He fought three 15-round bouts within 33 days in Australia, including a win over former junior lightweight champion Tod Morgan.

Portney continued to fight past his prime. In 1936 he outpointed Phil Furr, but lost two close decisions to the Cocoa Kid, a highly ranked welterweight contender. The following year he was stopped by Cocoa in the 12th round of a scheduled 15-rounder. Portney won five of his next six fights, but then lost a 10-round decision to future ring great Holman Williams.

Portney finally hung up his gloves in 1938, but kept his hand in the game for a number of years by promoting boxing shows at the Baltimore Garden Athletic Club. He also owned and operated pool halls in Baltimore before opening Jack Portney Sporting Goods, a retail establishment. In the 1950s he expanded to a successful wholesale business that specialized in the sale of billiard and bowling supplies.

AUGIE RATNER

Born: May 20, 1894
Died: May 14, 1979 (Age: 84)
Hometown: New York, New York
Height: 5' 8" **Weight:** 160 lbs.
Professional Career: 1915–1926

Total Bouts	Won	Lost	Draw	ND	NC
104 (1,024 rounds)	34 (14 by KO)	21 (1 by KO)	6	31-7-4	1

Before he turned pro in 1915, **Augie Ratner** won both the New York State and National AAU 145-pound titles. In 1917 he was drafted into the US Army during World War I. Augie took part in the Meuse-Argonne Offensive in the fall of 1918. The 47-day battle was the largest in United States military history. It involved 1.2 million American soldiers and brought the war to a close.

During his 10-year boxing career Ratner fought seven men who at one time or another held a world title. On March 17, 1920, he challenged middleweight champion Mike O'Dowd in O'Dowd's hometown of St. Paul, Minnesota. As the fight was "no decision," the only way Ratner could win the title was by a knockout. It was a tall order. Augie was not a great puncher, and the iron-chinned O'Dowd had never been knocked out.

The bout went the full 10 rounds. The *Chicago Tribune* scored the fight for O'Dowd, explaining that Ratner was on the defensive until the last two rounds.

In a follow-up bout Ratner won a newspaper decision over future middleweight champion Bryan Downey, but then lost two officially scored 15-round decisions to Downey. In spite of the setbacks Augie maintained his contender status with a 15-round decision over former welterweight kingpin Ted "Kid" Lewis.

Ratner consistently took on the cream of the middleweight division. Opponents included Mike Gibbons, Dave Rosenberg, Jock Malone, Dave Shade, Lou Bogash, and Frankie Schoell. Stepping up in weight, he also crossed gloves with two future light-heavyweight champions, getting an eight-round draw with Paul Berlanbach and a one-round KO over Jack Delaney. In a rematch one year later he lost a 12-round decision to Delaney.

On January 1, 1925, Ratner challenged the peerless middleweight champion Harry Greb in a non-title bout. They had fought a 20-round bout seven years earlier, with Greb taking the decision. This time the relentless "Pittsburgh Windmill" gave Ratner one of the worst beatings of his career, but was unable to stop him. Ratner kept his record intact of never having been KO'd or stopped in over 100 professional fights. That enviable record was shattered four months later, when future light-heavyweight champion Jimmy Slattery knocked him out in the second round to become the first and only fighter to stop him. Augie had only five more fights before hanging up his gloves in 1926.

In an interview that appeared in the February 1967 issue of *Boxing Illustrated*, Ratner was asked who he considered his toughest opponent. He stated that it was a toss-up between Harry Greb and Ted "Kid" Lewis. "Both were great," said Ratner. "Ted 'Kid' Lewis could box and hit. Greb was not as other men. He started his fights at a fast pace and accelerated it as the fight wore on. . . . He was blazingly fast, throwing punches from every angle. You had to be in perfect conditon."[52] Ratner rated Mike Gibbons the best boxer he ever fought.

AL REID
(Abe Reibman)
Born: January 28, 1915
Died: 1993 (Age: 78)
Hometown: Bronx, New York
Height: 5' 5" Weight: 126–130 lbs.
Professional Career: 1935–1941

Total Bouts	Won	Lost	Draw
100 (720 rounds)	57 (2 by KO)	30 (4 by KO)	13

Al Reid was a tough and tenacious gamecock of a fighter. The Bronxite threw a hailstorm of leather, rarely pausing long enough to set himself for a solid punch, which accounts for his low KO percentage.

In 1938, four years after turning pro, Al Reid was ranked the number-three featherweight in the world by *The Ring*. Yet despite impressive victories over the likes of Maxie Shapiro, Sal Bartolo, Bernie Friedkin, Joey Fontana, Nat Litfin, and Mickey Farber, he never received a title shot. Al fought seven men who at one time or another held a world title. He defeated Bartolo, fought two draws with Mike Belloise, but lost to Kid Chocolate, Leo Rodak, Petey Scalzo, Chalky Wright, and Beau Jack. Only Beau and Chalky were able to stop him. His two other losses inside the distance were the result of cuts over his left eye.

Al was not the most carefully managed boxer. Over the course of his 100-bout career he was thrown in with everybody and given little time off between bouts. The constant activity against tough competition eventually burned him out, and his career was over in just six years.

After hanging up his gloves in 1941, Al enlisted in the US Coast Guard a few weeks before the Japanese attack on Pearl Harbor and served for the duration of World War II.

After the war Al was employed as a shipping foreman for a plastics manufacturer in Long Island City. He also worked as a licensed boxing judge. For many years Al was active with the New York veteran boxers' association in that organization's efforts to help indigent former prizefighters.

CHARLEY PHIL ROSENBERG

(Charles Green)
Bantamweight Champion 1925–1927
Born: August 15, 1902
Died: March 12, 1976 (Age: 73)
Hometown: New York, New York
Height: 5' 4" Weight: 114–133 lbs.
Professional Career: 1921–1929

Total Bouts	Won	Lost	Draw	ND
70 (623 rounds)	33 (7 by KO)	18 (0 by KO)	9	7-2-1

In 1902 Rachel Green was six months pregnant with her ninth child when her husband, a laborer in a garment factory, was accidentally crushed to death in an elevator shaft. The distraught widow tried to support her brood by peddling items from a pushcart, but it was an impossible task. In order to cope she placed three of her sons in Manhattan's Hebrew Orphan Asylum. But Charley, her infant son, was too young for the orphanage, so during the day she placed him in a basin under her pushcart where she could keep an eye on him while trying to eke out a living.

When Charley was about five years old his mother decided to move her brood from the

Lower East Side to Harlem, then a mixed ethnic neighborhood that also included a significant Jewish population.

Charley grew up tough—and hungry. "I was a rough kid in the streets, like all kids 50 years back were rough kids," he recalls. "I worked when I could. I went out and took other things when I couldn't, that's all. I mean, it was nothing for me to go into a grocery store and steal a dozen rolls or something because we were hungry. Nine kids and nobody to help us. We had a very tough bringing up."[53]

In 1921 Charley was earning $6 a week working as an errand boy for a millinery shop when a fellow employee, a part-time boxer named Phil Rosenberg, had to pull out of a scheduled match. After learning his coworker would be giving up $15 if he failed to show, Charley offered to take his place using Phil's boxing license. The rest, as they say, is history. Charley launched his professional boxing career as "**Charley Phil Rosenberg.**" The name had a nice ring to it.

A year later he was matched with the Olympic flyweight champion Frankie Genaro at the Commonwealth Sporting Club in New York City. Although he lost the 12-round decision, Rosenberg gave Genaro a tough fight. This was no small accomplishment, as Genaro was a master boxer and would eventually win the world flyweight title.

Rosenberg followed up his loss to Genaro with impressive victories over hot prospects Sammy Butts and Henny Catena. Another 12-round barnburner with Genaro five months after their first fight returned the same result, but Rosenberg continued to show improvement.

In 1923 Rosenberg earned in excess of $20,000 for a total of 14 bouts. He was earning more money than he could have dreamed of, but what he wanted more than anything was a shot at the title. That opportunity came two years later. On March 20, 1925, in Madison Square Garden, Charley Phil met bantamweight champion Eddie "Cannonball" Martin (Edward Martino).

The fight crowd knew that Rosenberg was having trouble making the 118-pound limit. But Charley Phil had a secret weapon in master trainer Ray Arcel. Under Arcel's supervision Rosenberg lost 37 pounds in two months. Still, oddsmakers doubted he could maintain his strength in the later rounds. "Cannonball" entered the ring a 4–1 favorite to retain his crown.

Arcel did his job well. Charley Phil was in superb condition and took the fight to the champion. He even appeared to get stronger as the bout progressed. The unanimous 15-round decision went to Rosenberg.

Over the next two years Rosenberg fought 19 times (mostly in non-title bouts) in various locales outside of New York. "I'll tell you this, I was a bad boy when I was boxing," Charley Phil told author Peter Heller in an interview. "Every town I went to I started trouble in. I went somewhere in Ohio, Toledo or somewhere, and some fellow kept hollering, 'Kill the Jew bastard,' and I turned around, took a mouthful of water and blood, and I spit it right in his face. It was the mayor of Toledo!"[54]

In 1927 Rosenberg was stripped of his title because he could not make weight for a title defense against Bushy Graham (Angelo Geraci). At the weigh-in on the day of the fight Rosenberg was four and a half pounds over the bantamweight limit of 118 pounds. Nevertheless, the New York State Athletic Commission decided not to cancel the fight that evening. Commissioner William Muldoon ordered that if Graham won, he would be recognized as world champion. If Rosenberg won, the title would be declared vacant.

Charley won the 15-round decision but left the ring an ex-champion. There was more bad news. The commission had uncovered information of a secret agreement between the fighters not to make weight. Both Graham and Rosenberg were suspended for a year. Rosenberg always maintained that no secret agreement had ever existed.

Tired of the training grind and the shenanigans of his crooked manager, Charley fought only four more times before announcing his retirement in 1929.

In the late 1930s Charley became an insurance salesman, remaining in that field for the next 30 years.

DAVE ROSENBERG
Middleweight Champion 1922
Born: May 5, 1901
Died: February 1, 1979 (Age: 77)
Hometown: Brooklyn, New York
Height: 5' 8½" Weight: 152–160 lbs.
Professional Career: 1919–1925

Total Bouts	Won	Lost	Draw	ND
65 (611 rounds)	38 (12 by KO)	10 (0 by KO)	5	6-3-3

New York's **Dave Rosenberg** entered the pro ranks with an outstanding pedigree. In 1919 he won both the New York State and National AAU amateur welterweight titles.

On November 25, 1921, only two years after turning pro, Dave moved up to contender status by defeating Bert Colima at Madison Square Garden. He kept the momentum going with a 12-round draw against perennial contender Soldier Bartfield, and then outpointed, in quick succession, Augie Ratner, Marty Cross, and Zulu Kid (Giuseppe Di Melfi). A loss to Phil Krug in Newark, New Jersey, was followed 18 days later with a win over Italian Joe Gans at Brooklyn's Broadway Arena.

On August 14, 1922, Rosenberg won a 15-round unanimous decision over Phil Krug for the world middleweight championship as recognized by the New York State Athletic Commission. It was the high point of Rosenberg's career. Three and a half months later he was an ex-champ, having lost the title by an eighth-round disqualification to Mike O'Dowd.

Rosenberg remained idle for nine months after losing the title. In his next bout he stopped ancient Soldier Bartfield. He fought only sporadically over the next three years. After retiring in 1925, Rosenberg worked for many years as a garment-center salesman in New York City.

MAXIE ROSENBLOOM
"Slapsie Maxie," "The Harlem Harlequin"
Light-Heavyweight Champion: 1930–1934
Born: November 6, 1904
Died: March 6, 1976 (Age: 71)
Hometown: New York, New York
Height: 5' 11" Weight: 165–190 lbs.
Professional Career: 1923–1939

Total Bouts	Won	Lost	Draw	ND	NC
297 (2,765 rounds)	207 (19 by KO)	39 (2 by KO)	26	16-5-3	1

Maxie Rosenbloom averaged 18 fights a year for 16 straight years! In the two years before he won the title, Maxie had 46 fights—the equivalent of an entire ten- to 15-year career for the majority of today's world champions. Maxie is among the handful of boxers that have approached or exceeded 300 career bouts. Other members of this exclusive club include ring immortals Sam Langford, Battling Levinsky, Jack Britton, Ted "Kid" Lewis, Johnny Dundee, Harry Greb, Freddie Miller, and Fritzie Zivic. It takes a very special athlete to achieve what these men have accomplished. "Slapsie Maxie" Rosenbloom was very special.

Maxie was born in Connecticut but raised on the Lower East Side of New York City. At the age of 14, after a short stint in reform school, he began boxing in local amateur tournaments. He did not take naturally to the sport. The learning process was slow and painful. Maxie lost 20 of his first 25 amateur bouts. The 145-pound youth was physically strong and had a chin of granite, but he was having a rough time adjusting his wild street-fighting instincts to that of a disciplined boxer. But he refused to give up, and within a year began posting more wins than losses.

After about 200 contests as a simon-pure, Maxie was ready to turn pro. He was 19 years old and had filled out to a solid 165 pounds. Under the direction of his manager-trainer Frank Bachman (who would remain with him throughout his entire career), the young light heavyweight began his professional apprenticeship.

In his second year as a pro Rosenbloom met a murderous punching southpaw named Hambone Kelly, who had knocked out 32 of 36 opponents. For the first three rounds Maxie got the worst of it, but he kept battling back. In the fourth round he landed a left hook that broke Kelly's nose. The next two rounds saw Maxie outpunch the puncher and win a six-round decision. Kelly's face and chest were covered with his own blood. The defeated boxer was taken to a hospital to treat his severely broken nose.

The fight was an important turning point for Rosenbloom. Against his better judgment he had let himself be drawn into a slugging match against a dangerous opponent. Maxie won the fight, but the bruises and aching hands he incurred, plus the damage he caused to Kelly, got him to thinking there had to be a less-strenuous way to win. He had another fight scheduled just eight days later. What if he was the one who suffered the broken nose and had to pull out of his forthcoming match and forfeit a payday?

According to his manager Frank Bachman, after the Kelly fight Rosenbloom altered his fighting style. He became a cautious counterpuncher and incorporated a bob-and-weave defensive technique that made him a difficult and elusive target.[55]

Bachman was asked why his fighter had adopted the new style. "I guess he started to get smart. He began to realize he'd last longer the other way."[56] Maxie answered the same question with one of his colorful malapropisms, saying that his old fighting style could lead to "a conclusion of the brain." Maxie was a grade-school dropout, but, as he was to prove time and again, his boxing IQ registered in the genius range.

Over the next 14 years Maxie's innovative style of fighting entertained audiences (or bored them—depending on your point of view) with his highly effective slap-and-weave style. Maxie appeared to enjoy his work as he darted about, hands dangling at his sides, bending, ducking, slapping, and weaving to and fro as his opponents became ever more frustrated in their futile attempts to land a haymaker. The slapdash style had a clownish quality, an image that was reinforced after journalist Damon Runyon dubbed him "Slapsie Maxie."

Rosenbloom's unusual technique was admired and analyzed by a young trainer named Cus D'Amato who, according to his protégé Teddy Atlas, used it as the basis for his invention of the "peekaboo" style he taught to future champions Floyd Patterson, Jose Torres, and Mike Tyson. When Atlas asked D'Amato why, if Rosenbloom was such a good defensive fighter, he sported so much scar tissue over his eyes, Cus answered that

Maxie, shown with actress Arline Judge, received star billing in this 1941 film, *Harvard, Here I Come*. Note the cauliflower ear.

his slap-happy style and apparent lack of knockout power. The popular conception was that Maxie couldn't punch, which is understandable given the fact that he knocked out only 19 of 297 opponents. But Maxie could punch when he wanted to, or had to; it just wasn't often, or necessary.

It may sound like a contradiction considering his profession, but Rosenbloom was actually a nonviolent boxer. Going for a knockout entails risk, as it leaves the aggressor vulnerable to a counterpunch. And to hit with power necessitates punching with a tightly closed fist. A fighter's hands—the tools of his trade—take a lot of punishment, and are often injured when thrown with full force. An injury to the delicate bones and ligaments of the hand can take a long time to heal. With Maxie's busy fight schedule (averaging a fight every three weeks), he could not risk a postponement due to an injured mitt, which would result in a missed payday.

One look at Maxie's solid physique and powerful arms was proof enough that he possessed the natural power, if not the inclination, to score many more knockouts. But throwing with full power could damage his hands; cuffing or slapping an opponent with an open glove would prevent the type of hand damage that so often plagues boxers. Maxie's brilliant boxing style was intended to cause the least amount of damage to himself and to his opponents, but still allow him to come away with a win.

Fighters who thought Maxie had no punch and that they could walk through his open-handed blows quickly realized how incredibly

it was acquired early in his career, during the early learning process. Maxie was never cut or severely punished during his prime fighting years.

Although he had the reputation of a playboy, Maxie always entered the ring in top shape. His constant fighting kept him in great condition. All he had to do between fights was some light gym work. He was also an inveterate gambler and big spender, and was often seen in the company of beautiful women. He avoided alcohol, however, and always found time to do his roadwork. To sportswriters who said he did not take his profession seriously enough, Maxie had a ready retort: "I don't drink, I don't smoke, and I don't leave the dames alone."

Maxie made for colorful copy in or out of a boxing ring. His witticisms and malaprops, nightclub escapades and zany behavior, were duly reported in the daily press. But his genius as a fighter was not fully appreciated or understood by contemporary writers, who were not impressed by strong he was. They felt the power even in his slaps. His quick counters were thrown with speed and accuracy and from every angle. On the rare occasion when an opponent did manage to land a solid punch, Maxie would ball his fist and rap them with a good shot to put them back in line. He then would pick up where he left off and continue to slap them silly.

It didn't happen often, but when he was struck by a haymaker, Maxie's iron jaw withstood the impact. He was stopped only twice in 297 bouts.

By the time he won the light-heavyweight title in 1930, "The Harlem Harlequin" was a thoroughly accomplished boxer, and one of the three or four greatest defensive masters who ever lived.

Incredibly, despite his 297 fights, no film of Maxie in action exists. Several of his title fights were filmed but none have survived (or perhaps they have yet to be rediscovered). All that we have is a brief "sparring session" in a Hollywood film made in 1939 called *The Kid from Kokomo*. It was one of Maxie's first movie roles in a career that would eventually encompass over 100 film and TV appearances. In the scene he steps into the ring with actor Wayne Morris for about half a minute of sparring. Of course it's a staged fight, but Maxie is seen going through his moves.

The short sequence is quite revealing. Maxie moves around with his hands down. He avoids punches by slipping, ducking, and weaving away from them. He never loses his balance and always remains in range to counter (usually with an open-handed slap) when his opponent least expects it. Blows aimed at his head miss by mere inches. Maxie is constantly in motion as he steps in and out of range or from side to side.

Rosenbloom easily ranks with the greatest light-heavyweight champions of all time. It would not be out of the question to place him in the number-one spot. Very few boxers of any weight division have come close to matching the type of brutal competition he faced year after year. Among the best fighters he defeated are Mickey Walker, Jimmy Slattery, Dave Shade, Tiger Jack Fox, Al Gainer, Pete Latzo, Frankie Schoell, Tiger Flowers, Jack McVey, Ace Hudkins, Harry Ebbets, Johnny Wilson, Fred Lenhart, and Leo Lomski, to name just a few.

In 1930 Maxie outpointed Jimmy Slattery to win the light-heavyweight title, gaining revenge for a previous loss. He defeated Slattery again the following year at Brooklyn's Ebbets Field. Of all his ring foes, Rosenbloom considered Slattery the smartest fighter he ever faced.

Rosenbloom's easy 15-round decision over Adolph Heuser, Germany's light-heavyweight champion, in Madison Square Garden in March 1933, was embarrassing to the Nazi regime in Germany. It was considered a factor in Hitler's decision to ban Germany's athletes from competing with Jewish athletes, "to avoid contradictions of the Nazi claim of superiority over non-Aryans."[57]

During his four-year reign as light-heavyweight champion Maxie had 108 fights, including 8 title defenses. He lost the title on a controversial decision to Bob Olin on November 16, 1934, at Madison Square Garden. Despite Maxie's suspiciously sluggish performance, a majority of sportswriters covering the bout still thought he deserved to win.

17 days later, as if to prove a point, he was back in action, outpointing Al Gainer, the number-one light-heavyweight contender. Less than a year later, in a non-title fight, Rosenbloom outpointed the new light-heavyweight champion, John Henry Lewis, who only a month earlier had defeated Bob Olin for the title. It is highly conceivable that had Rosenbloom not been robbed (or agreed to be robbed) of his title, he might have remained champion for another four years.

Throughout his career Rosenbloom was an equal-opportunity boxer. He fought 70 black fighters at a time when many top white boxers scrupulously avoided the best black fighters. He was more than willing to go into an opponent's hometown for a decent payday. As a result he lost so many outrageous decisions, he would ask out-of-town promoters in advance, "If I win, can I get a draw?" Maxie's record shows 26 draws, most of which were outside of New York and should have been scored in his favor.

From 1937 to 1939, ex-champ Rosenbloom campaigned successfully as a heavyweight, tipping the scales at 190 pounds. He won decisions over Kingfish Levinsky, Roscoe Toles, Lee Ramage, and Bob Nestell. In 1938, after outpointing Lou Nova and fighting a 10-round draw with Bob Pastor, Maxie became the fifth-ranking heavyweight contender in *The Ring*'s ratings. That same year he boldly issued a challenge to the great heavyweight champion Joe Louis. But the Brown Bomber's management wanted nothing

to do with him. They were confident Joe would win, but were less sure he would look good in the process. Anybody, even Joe Louis, could be made to look foolish when faced with Rosenbloom's unorthodox and troublesome style. Rosenbloom's challenge to the most-feared fighter in the world was in keeping with his supreme confidence.

When Maxie finally retired in 1939, a few months shy of his 35th birthday, he was still a world-class competitor and ranked among the top 10 heavyweight contenders. That same year he married 22-year-old USC graduate Muriel Faeder.

Maxie might have continued fighting except for the fact that his budding career as a Hollywood character actor was taking off. A few bit parts in movies had led to a contract with the Warner Brothers Studio. It was indeed fortunate that he had another career to fall back on, as he continued with his extravagant spending habits and habitual gambling. In 1947 a costly divorce from his wife of eight years ate up much of his ring earnings.

Maxie's movie roles increased as he approached the end of his boxing career. He was often cast in the role of a not-too-bright ex-pug. The *New York Times* described his on-screen persona: "A Damon Runyonesque character with a flattened nose and a cauliflower ear, he spoke in the dese-and-dems jargon of the boxing fraternity and was the master of the twitch and the double take." He used to joke that Jack Warner, head of the studio, sent him to Max Reinhardt's acting school to study diction. "I met Marlon Brando there," said Maxie. "He talked exactly like me."

Mr. and Mrs. Maxie Rosenbloom attend the 1939 movie premiere of *Babes in Arms* with Mickey Rooney and Judy Garland. (Los Angeles Public Library)

Maxie had a fruitful career in Hollywood, appearing in over 100 movie and television roles. In several movies he even received top billing. People sometimes wondered if he was acting or just playing himself. But off-screen Maxie was anything but a dim bulb. He was a highly intelligent and creative individual.

In his mid-sixties Maxie began to exhibit the debilitating effects of his long career as a boxer. The punches incurred in 297 professional fights finally caught up to the great fighter, and he was diagnosed with dementia pugilistica. Maxie also suffered from Paget's disease, a degenerative bone disorder. His last years were spent in a convalescent home, where ongoing care and treatment was paid for by the Motion Picture and Television Fund.

"Slapsie Maxie" Rosenbloom, an American original . . . and a boxing immortal . . . passed away on March 6, 1976, at the age of 71.

BARNEY ROSS

(Beryl David Rasofsky)
Lightweight Champion 1933–1934
Junior Welterweight Champion 1933–1935
Welterweight Champion 1934, 1935–1938
Born: December 23, 1909
Died: January 18, 1967 (Age: 57)
Hometown: Chicago, Illinois
Height: 5' 7" Weight: 135–144 lbs.
Professional Career: 1929–1938

Total Bouts	Won	Lost	Draw	ND
81 (622 rounds)	72 (22 by KO)	4 (0 by KO)	3	2-0

In 1905 Isadore Rasofsky and his wife Sarah fled the pogroms and poverty of Russia for the golden land of America. They settled in the Lower East Side of Manhattan with their two young children. Six years later the family moved to the Maxwell Street district of Chicago. By then two more children had been born, including a son they named Beryl David. Outside of his home, on the streets of Chicago, the name Beryl was Americanized to "Barney."

Barney Ross was brought up in an Orthodox Jewish home. His father was a Talmudic scholar with high hopes his son would follow in his footsteps. But when Barney was 15 years old his father was shot and killed during a holdup of the small grocery store his parents owned.

The tragedy devastated the family. Ross's mother suffered a nervous breakdown and was sent back east to live with her sister. Barney's three younger siblings were placed in an orphan asylum. Barney was taken in by an aunt.

Filled with anger and resentment and disdaining his religious upbringing, young Barney took to the streets and for a short time even worked as a messenger boy for Chicago crime lord Al Capone. Fortunately, after a friend brought him to a boxing gym, Barney became infatuated with the sport. The boxing ring channeled his anger and the discipline required of a boxer kept him off the streets. He began to compete in local amateur tournaments under the name Barney Ross. His goal was to eventually turn pro and earn enough money to reunite his family.

Barney fought in the amateurs for five years, pawning the medals he won for the few dollars they would bring. In four years Ross amassed some 250 bouts. The qualities that made him stand out as an amateur boxer (and later as a professional) were athletic intelligence, quick hands, a rock-solid chin, and tremendous fighting heart.

In 1929 Ross won both the Chicago and Inter-City Golden Gloves featherweight championships. He turned pro that same year under the very capable management team of Sam Pian and Art Winch. In 1933, four years after turning pro, Ross won the lightweight and junior welterweight titles via a split 10-round decision over the great Tony Canzoneri.

In a rematch three months later, in New York's Polo Grounds, Ross won another split decision in a hard-fought 15-round battle. Ross's fast and accurate left jabs, deft footwork, and furious rallies proved to be the decisive factor. (After he retired Ross evaluated all of the great fighters he encountered during his 81-bout career. He named Canzoneri as the finest all-around fighter he'd ever faced.)

For retaining his crown Ross received $35,000, the largest payday of his career up to that time. He used the money to make good on his promise to reunite his mother (since recovered from her nervous breakdown) and three younger siblings. He moved them into a fashionable apartment on Chicago's West Side.

Over the next nine months Ross earned an additional $150,000 through endorsements, personal appearances, and in seven successful defenses of his junior welterweight title. It was around this time that he returned to his religious

Two boxing legends square off in 1933: Barney Ross (left) and Tony Canzoneri.

roots, taking his late father's collection of biblical texts with him to training camp, where he was often seen studying them after his workouts. He even began wearing *tzitzit*, a garment with ritual fringes worn by observant Jews, under his custom-made suits.[58]

The highlights of Ross's brilliant boxing career were his three epic fights with the great welterweight champion Jimmy McLarnin. The first bout took place on May 28, 1934, in front of 60,000 fans at the Madison Square Garden Bowl in Long Island City, New York. The promotion brought in $210,000, a remarkable amount considering the Great Depression was in full swing.

The new champ is given a parade down Chicago's LaSalle street in 1933. With Ross is his mother and Chicago mayor Ed Kelly (hatless, lower left). (Courtesy of Douglas Century)

After 15 rounds of nonstop action, Ross was awarded the welterweight title via a split decision. The victory was especially sweet for New York's Jewish fans, as the magnificent Irish boxer had previously knocked out seven top Jewish boxers, including the great Benny Leonard in the final bout of his ill-advised comeback.

The return bout with McLarnin six months later resulted in yet another split decision—this time for McLarnin. Not everyone agreed with the verdict. Twenty-two of 28 sportswriters had Ross the winner. It didn't help that the judges and the referee were all of Irish descent.

The final installment of their historic trilogy took place in front of 45,000 fans at the Polo Grounds exactly one year after their first fight. This time there were no dissenting scores. Both judges and the referee gave Ross the verdict.

Ross had accomplished everything he set out to do in boxing. But he was still the sole support of his mother and three younger siblings. His finances were complicated by the fact that while champion he had developed an obsessive gambling habit, betting on horses. Ross was introduced to the sport of horse racing by singer Al Jolson. It was not unusual for Barney to drop thousands of dollars in a single day at the track. One of the reasons he fought so often was to pay off mounting gambling debts. As noted by biographer Douglas Century, "Ross was by nature a compulsive personality, with a weakness for alcohol, cigarettes, and women—but worst of all he developed a pathological addiction to gambling."[59]

After regaining the welterweight title Barney won 18 fights, including three brutal encounters with the great Filipino fighter Ceferino Garcia. A week before his final bout with Garcia, Ross broke his left hand while sparring. He swore his trainer and managers to secrecy and, despite their protestations, insisted on going through with the fight, telling them, "I can lick Garcia with one hand." He did just that and managed to win a unanimous decision by faking and blocking with his left while scoring most points with his uninjured right hand. It was a remarkable exhibition of skill and guts. But 45 rounds with the very tough Filipino had taken more out of Barney than he realized.

As often happens, the wear and tear of a tough boxing career catches up to a fighter without warning. After 250 amateur and 80 professional fights, the superb fighting machine had finally worn out. The worst time for that to happen is in the midst of a fight against a top-notch opponent. It was Barney's misfortune that the realization came to him while facing one of the most destructive fighters who ever lived.

On May 31, 1938, at the Madison Square Garden Bowl, Ross was mauled by the great triple champion Henry Armstrong and lost a unanimous 15-round decision. Ross had endured a terrible beating but refused to go down. By the 11th round many in the crowd of 35,000 were screaming for the bout to be stopped. Ross implored the referee, Arthur Donovan, not to stop the fight. In between the 11th and 12th rounds Ross told Pian and Winch he would never speak to them again if they threw in the towel. He somehow made it to the final bell, although Armstrong later admitted he eased up for the final three rounds, out of respect for Ross. The decision and the title went to Armstrong, but Ross kept his record intact of never having been stopped.

As the bruised and battered ex-champion left the ring for the last time and walked down the aisle toward his dressing room, the crowd became eerily silent. Ross was puzzled at first and then realized what was happening: "I suddenly realized that this unbelievable, fantastic silence was the most wonderful tribute I had ever received. It spoke louder, a thousand times louder, than all the cheers I had heard since the day I put on a pair of boxing gloves and won my first fight . . ."[60]

In keeping with a promise he had made to his mother—that he would only take one real beating—Ross announced his retirement. Promoters tried to entice him back into the ring, but Ross would have none of it. He did not want to wind up like so many ex-champs who compromised their health and hard-won reputations by fighting beyond their prime.

Shortly after he retired Barney opened a restaurant in Chicago's Loop district. But the restless ex-champion was not cut out for the life of a restaurateur. When World War II broke out he enlisted in the US Marine Corps. As a celebrity he could have been assigned work as a morale booster or training new recruits, but Barney always liked to be where the action was, so he requested combat duty. He was 32 years old.

On November 4, 1942, Ross's outfit, the 2nd Marine Division, landed on Guadalcanal. Two weeks later, while on patrol with three other marines, Barney found himself in a foxhole fighting for his life. For the next 13 hours he single-handedly protected his marine buddies who were too badly wounded to fire their own weapons. During the battle Ross lobbed over 20 hand grenades at enemy machine-gun positions and fired 400 rounds. When he ran out of bullets for his Browning automatic rifle, he picked up the other men's weapons and, as they handed off the ammunition to him, continued to fire.[61]

By dawn one of his marine buddies was dead. Out of ammunition and wounded in the leg and foot, the 140-pound Ross picked up his 230-pound comrade and carried him to safety, placing him next to the other wounded marine. When reinforcements arrived they counted 22 dead Japanese soldiers surrounding his foxhole. Ross, whose helmet had more than 30 shrapnel dents, was awarded the Silver Star for heroism.[62] He was cited for saving the life of two marines and halting an enemy advance.

After recovering from his wounds Barney was sent back to the front lines five more times. The stress of combat turned his hair white. He also contracted malaria and had to be hospitalized. While he was recuperating, well-meaning medical corpsmen gave him doses of morphine to ease his pain. He eventually developed a dependency on the drug, and by the time he returned to the States in 1943, Ross was a full-blown junkie with a $500-a-day heroin habit.

In 1946 his wife threatened to divorce him unless he overcame his addiction. Ross voluntarily entered the US Public Health Service Hospital in Lexington, Kentucky, intent on beating his addiction. Barney went public with his story, and the news made headlines throughout the world.

A harrowing description of his four-month struggle to kick his heroin habit is described in Ross's 1957 autobiography, *No Man Stands Alone*. That same year a movie was released that dealt almost exclusively with his life as a drug addict. *Monkey on My Back* starred Cameron Mitchell as Barney. Movie marquee posters showed the actor sticking a needle into his arm with the words "The Barney Ross Story! Junkie! It Means Dope-Fiend! The Hottest Hell on Earth!"

The marketing campaign for the movie was embarrassing to Barney and his family. Ross was even more upset with the movie itself. He had been hired as a consultant, but the Hollywood version of his story was not what he had envisioned. He denounced the movie as "filth, bilge, and cheap sensation."[63] Ross threatened to sue United Artists for $5 million, but settled out of court for $10,000.

Ross was tireless in his efforts to steer young people away from drug addiction. He even testified before Congress on the nation's narcotics problem, telling legislators that the profit motive

Barney Ross, in Marine Uniform, celebrates the Passover Seder with his family, April 1944 at his mother's home. Left to right: George Rasof, brother; Rabbi Strauss; Sam Rasof, brother; Mrs. Sarah Rasof, mother; Barney; his wife Cathy; Audrey Kaplan, niece; Irving Kaplan, brother in-law. (Courtesy of Douglas Century)

should be taken out of the drug trade; that incurable addicts should be considered sick people, and be given free injections at clinics under careful supervision. He was also adamant that the government enforce the death penalty for big-time dope dealers.

Barney spoke often at inner-city high schools, explaining to students the horror and futility of drug addiction firsthand. He also took addicts under his wing, giving them personal support and encouragement.

There was yet another fight that Barney was ready to give his all for—the fight to establish a homeland for the Jewish people.

In 1947 Ross was actively involved with Peter Bergson's "American League for a Free Palestine," which sought to rally support for the creation of a Jewish state. He helped to raise hundreds of thousands of dollars for the future state of Israel. Barney was also involved in activities that smuggled arms and men into the region. Throughout his life he remained a strong and committed supporter of Israel.

Ross's final battle was one he could not win. He'd been a chain smoker for years, and in 1966 was diagnosed with throat cancer. When the news became public, thousands of get-well cards and letters poured into his home in Chicago.

Ross signs up for the George Washington Legion, a group of Jewish war veterans who volunteered to fight for the new state of Israel. (Courtesy of Douglas Century)

His many friends in show business and boxing staged a number of testimonials and benefits on his behalf. Barney fought the disease with all the strength left within him, but finally succumbed on January 17, 1967, at the age of 57.

BARNEY ROSS AND HANK GREENBERG—A PAIR OF ACES

In 1934 two of America's most popular Jewish sports heroes—boxing champion Barney Ross and baseball's home-run slugger Hank Greenberg—refused to perform in their respective sports on a Jewish High Holiday.

Ross and Greenberg were active at a time when anti-Semitism in America was on the rise. The world was in the throes of the Great Depression, and bigots were coming out of the woodwork to blame the Jews for America's economic woes. Hank was the star first baseman for the Detroit Tigers. Detroit was also home to one of the country's most influential anti-Semites, the radio priest, Father Charles E. Coughlin. His weekly harangues over the radio, in which he railed against "Jewish conspirators" and "moneychangers," won him a vast following throughout the country.

Hank Greenberg was to become the first Jewish player elected to the National Baseball Hall of Fame. In only his second year in the major leagues he had become immensely popular with the Motor City fans. He carried himself like an all-American hero both on and off the field. Handsome and intelligent, the 6'4", 215-pound super athlete was an imposing figure and a powerful and fierce competitor.

Although he was not religiously observant, Hank Greenberg chose not to play on Yom Kippur, the holiest day on the Hebrew calendar. Instead he spent the entire day at Detroit's Shaarey Zedek synagogue. When Greenberg entered the synagogue, services stopped and he was greeted with applause by the congregants. The great baseball player's decision to publicly acknowledge his faith made every Jew in America proud.

Meanwhile, in New York City, Barney Ross, one of America's most popular boxers, was scheduled to defend his welterweight title against Irish Jimmy McLarnin at an outdoor venue on September 6, 1934. Rain on the day of the fight forced a postponement. A new date was planned, but Ross told the promoters he would not fight on September 10, as he planned to observe Rosh Hashanah (first of the Jewish High Holidays) that day and attend synagogue services, as he did every year. The fight was rescheduled for September 17, three days before Yom Kippur.

The story of Ross's adamant refusal to fight on Rosh Hashanah was reported in the media but was deemed less newsworthy than Greenberg's decision not to play on Yom Kippur, and received far less attention. In fact, some newspaper reporters, instead of commending Ross's genuine piety, took a more-cynical approach. According to the *Chicago Tribune*, the

Hank Greenberg was the first major league ball player to enlist following the attack on Pearl Harbor. (Courtesy of National Baseball Hall of Fame Library, Cooperstown, NY)

Barney Ross receives an award for being the outstanding recruit in his company during Marine basic training at camp Pendleton.

bout's promoters knew that New York's Jews would decline to attend on the Jewish New Year, so it made sense to find a more suitable date. The cynicism was understandable in light of the perceived differences between professional baseball and professional boxing. The public, although still very enthusiastic about boxing, understood that it was a dangerous and sometimes disreputable "ghetto" sport. On the other hand, the clean sport of baseball—the national pastime—was an idealized reflection of American society.

However, it should be noted that years before Hank Greenberg picked up a baseball, the first heroes for Jewish immigrants and their children were ghetto boxers, not baseball players. If Hank Greenberg had come along without having been preceded by scores of Jewish boxing champions and contenders, his accomplishments would have been viewed as an athletic anomaly and an exception to the stereotype that Jews lacked the ability and toughness to make it in sports. Jewish boxers had already punched holes in that stereotype; Hank Greenberg, in his role as a baseball superstar, knocked it out of the park.

Barney Ross and Hank Greenberg had something else in common besides their refusal to compete on a Jewish High Holy Day. They both enlisted in the United States armed services at the outbreak of World War II. Ross was 32 and had retired a few years earlier. Greenberg was 30, and still in his prime as an athlete. Both could have served as athletic directors but instead volunteered for combat duty.

Ross joined the Marines and saw combat on Guadalcanal. He was awarded the Silver Star for stopping an enemy advance and saving the lives of two marine buddies. Greenberg had originally been drafted into the peacetime army in 1940, and was honorably discharged just two days before the Japanese attack on Pearl Harbor. A few days later he reenlisted with the Army Air Forces, becoming the first major league player to volunteer for service. He was promoted to captain and had a distinguished record while serving with a B-29 bomber group in the China-Burma-India Theater.

AL ROTH

Born: September 22, 1913
Died: September 16, 1982 (Age: 78)
Hometown: Bronx, New York
Height: 5' 4" **Weight:** 128–141 lbs.
Professional Career: 1931–1941

Total Bouts	Won	Lost	Draw
90 (634 rounds)	47 (12 by KO)	30 (2 by KO)	13

Al Roth won the New York Golden Gloves 118-pound amateur championship in 1931. He turned pro a few months later, and over the next 10 years faced brutal competition in both the featherweight and lightweight divisions. But win or lose, Al Roth rarely took a backward step. He fought grueling battles with top contenders Davey Day, Pedro Montanez, Petey Hayes, Eddie Cool, Aldo Spoldi, and, in non-title bouts, world champions Lew Ambers and Baby Arizmendi—none of whom could stop him.

On October 4, 1935, at Madison Square Garden, Roth faced the great Tony Canzoneri for the lightweight championship of the world. Canzoneri was much the superior boxer but, in typical fashion, Roth took everything the champion dished out, and never stopped throwing leather. Hopelessly behind after 11 rounds, Al's right fist finally landed on the tiring champion's chin and staggered him. Although bloodied and exhausted, Canzoneri's experience, guts, and greatness pulled him through to the final bell. After 15 rounds of nonstop action, Canzoneri was awarded a unanimous decision.

Nearing the end of his career Roth was stopped for the first time in 88 bouts when he suffered a fractured rib in a bout against the formidable Billy Marquart, a fighter he'd beaten two years earlier. Roth was not allowed to answer the bell for the seventh round. Two fights later, on August 14, 1941, Roth met future lightweight champion Beau Jack at Ebbets Field. The referee stopped the bout at the end of the fifth round after both of Roth's eyes were swollen shut. It was the last fight of his career.

TED SANDWINA

Born: January 25, 1906
Died: July 17, 1997 (Age: 91)
Hometown: Sioux City, Iowa
Height: 6' 1" Weight:195–208 lbs.
Professional Career: 1926–1933

Total Bouts	Won	Lost	Draw
86 (519 rounds)	49 (41 by KO)	31 (14 by KO)	6

Ted Sandwina's mother was the famous Kate Sandwina, a circus performer known as "The Lady Hercules." In the early twentieth century she was billed as "The World's Strongest Woman," and was a featured attraction with the Ringling Bros. and Barnum & Bailey Circus. By her own account she defeated the internationally acclaimed strongman Eugene Sandow in a weightlifting contest in New York. According to Katie, she lifted 300 pounds over her head, while Sandow only managed to lift it to his chest. She then adopted the stage name "Sandwina," becoming a feminine version of Sandow.

During one of her European tours Katie met her husband of 52 years, Max Heymann. As part of her act she would lift her 165-pound husband over her head with one hand.

On January 25, 1909, Katie gave birth to a son whom she named after President Theodore Roosevelt. Ted Sandwina grew up in the circus and spent his formative years touring Europe with his mother and father.

While still a teenager Ted decided to become a professional boxer. His first recorded bout was a four-round draw against Max Diekmann in 1926. The muscular six-foot-one, 195-pound heavyweight won 17 of his next 21 bouts, including 12 by knockout.

In 1929 Ted launched an American tour that he hoped would lead to a fight for the heavyweight championship. His colorful background created a lot of buzz, and expectations were high for the Jewish strongman.

After knocking out five of seven opponents, Ted was matched with Italian heavyweight

Riccardo Bertazzolo at Madison Square Garden. Ted won an easy 10-round decision over an inept foe who was described in the *New York Times* as "deplorably unschooled." His next fight two months later was more competitive, and resulted in a 10-round draw with "Napoleon" Jack Dorval.

In June 1930 Sandwina was rated the 10th-best heavyweight in the world, and that same month he appeared on the cover of *The Ring* magazine. But subsequent losses to Tony Galento, Ernie Schaaf, and Stanley Poreda pushed him out of the ratings. He was also plagued by various training injuries. The last two years of Sandwina's career were all downhill as he lost 19 of 20 fights (eight by knockout), including a fourth-round stoppage to future champion Primo Carnera.

Ted retired in 1933 and lived out the rest of his life in his adopted hometown of Sioux City, Iowa.

"The Lady Hercules" Kate Sandwina—world's strongest woman and the mother of heavyweight boxer Ted Sandwina.

JOEY SANGOR
(Julius Joseph Singer)
Born: May 4, 1903
Died: January 1982 (Age: 78)
Hometown: Milwaukee, Wisconsin
Height: 5' 6" Weight: 125–130 lbs.
Professional Career: 1921–1930

Total Bouts	Won	Lost	Draw	ND
76 (669 rounds)	18 (6 by KO)	14 (5 by KO)	2	24-11-7

In the late 1920s Milwaukee's **Joey Sangor** was tearing up the competition in the featherweight and junior lightweight divisions. He outpointed contenders Santiago Zorilla, Young Nationalista, and Sammy Dorfman, and had two non-title wins over bantamweight champion Bud Taylor.

In 1929 Sangor challenged junior lightweight champion Tod Morgan. The bout took place in Sangor's hometown of Milwaukee. Unfortunately Wisconsin still adhered to the no-decision rule, so Sangor had to win by a knockout or a foul to dethrone the champion. The bout went the full 10 rounds. If judged officially the decision could have gone either way, although most reporters covering the bout had scored it for Sangor. It was a tough break for the hometown favorite.

Five weeks after his bout with Morgan, Sangor crossed gloves with ex-featherweight champion Tony Canzoneri. Near the end of the second round Canzoneri's right fist found Sangor's chin.

The referee's count reached seven when the bell rang. In those days a fighter could be saved by the bell, so Sangor was dragged back to his corner where his seconds administered smelling salts and doused him with water, restoring him to consciousness. The plucky challenger somehow lasted into the seventh round before Canzoneri dropped him again and the fight was stopped. In effect Sangor was actually knocked out twice in one fight.

After a 10-month layoff Sangor returned to the ring and lost two of his next three bouts. He was only two weeks shy of his 27th birthday, but decided his career had run its course and it was time to retire.

After hanging up his gloves Sangor operated a drugstore in Milwaukee in partnership with his brother, Lew, who also managed his ring career.

In 1967 Joey's hometown honored him with induction into the Wisconsin Athletic Hall of Fame.

MORRIE SCHLAIFER

Born: April 1, 1894
Died: March 1, 1978 (Age: 83)
Hometown: Omaha, Nebraska
Weight: 147–150 lbs.
Professional Career: 1920–1927

Total Bouts	Won	Lost	Draw	ND	NC
96 (758 rounds)	42 (25 by KO)	29 (5 by KO)	3	7-11-2	2

If you were good enough to get past tough **Morrie Schlaifer**, odds are you had what it took to become a contender or world champion. Although the 150-pound Omaha mauler was never quite good enough to grab the brass ring, like so many other tough journeyman fighters, he was always dangerous and capable of pulling a major upset. Among the better fighters Morrie upset were Panama Joe Gans, Paul Doyle, Bermondsey Billy Wells, future welterweight champ Pete Latzo, and faded boxing legend Jack Britton.

On the other hand, Morrie could never outduke master boxers Dave Shade (five losses) and Frankie Schoell. He also lost a return bout to Latzo, and was outpointed by England's Tommy Milligan and Philadelphia's Sailor Friedman. The closest Morrie came to a title bout was a 1923 encounter with the great welterweight champion Mickey Walker. "The Toy Bulldog" stopped him in the sixth round. After 60 fights the wear and tear of his give-and-take style of fighting had taken its toll, and he began losing to second-rate opponents. Morrie finally got the message and retired in 1927 after losing six of his last seven fights.

BENNY SCHWARTZ

Born: May 4, 1903
Died: March 1984 (Age: 80)
Hometown: Baltimore, Maryland
Weight: 118 lbs.
Professional Career: 1920–1933

Total Bouts	Won	Lost	Draw	ND
137 (1,140 rounds)	80 (8 by KO)	37 (6 by KO)	7	9-3-1

Benny Schwartz (right) and his manager.
(Courtesy of Thomas Scharf)

Bantamweight **Benny Schwartz**, who began his career as "Young Mendel," was one of Baltimore's most popular fighters during the 1920s. In his first two years as a pro Benny lost only seven of 46 bouts. One of those losses, on November 24, 1922, was to world bantamweight champion Joe Lynch at Memorial Hall in Springfield, Ohio. Lynch was far too experienced and knocked out his young challenger in the fifth round.

Over the next 10 months Schwartz ran up a string of victories and was rewarded with a title bout against the great flyweight champion Pancho Villa at the 5th Regiment Armory in Baltimore. The match was promoted by Benny's manager, Benny Franklin, who also worked his corner during the fight. At the end of 15 hard-fought rounds the unanimous decision went to the dynamic Filipino fighter.

In 1927 Schwartz fought a 12-round non-title bout with bantamweight champion Charley Phil Rosenberg. Schwartz lost the decision but rebounded with impressive victories over Joe Ryder and Pinky May before losing a decision to future bantamweight king Panama Al Brown.

Schwartz continued to fight past his prime, with varying degrees of success, for another five years, until a knockout loss to future featherweight champion Petey Sarron convinced him to retire.

CORPORAL IZZY SCHWARTZ

(Isadore Schwartz)
Flyweight Champion 1927–1929
Born: October 23, 1900
Died: 1988 (Age: 87)
Hometown: New York, New York
Height: 5' 1" Weight: 110–115 lbs.
Professional Career: 1921–1930, 1932

Total Bouts	Won	Lost	Draw	ND	NC
130 (1,210 rounds)	64 (7 by KO)	32 (4 by KO)	12	10-5-6	1

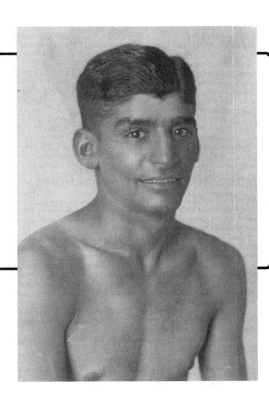

Orphaned at the age of two, **Izzy Schwartz** spent his childhood years in New York's Hebrew Orphan Asylum. In 1917, the year America entered World War I, he enlisted in the army. After thrashing a much larger soldier in an impromptu barracks brawl, Izzy was persuaded by the company commander to join the camp's boxing squad. His boxing talent was obvious from the beginning. The following year Izzy won the All-Army flyweight title and was promoted to corporal.

Izzy was always on the move, using his considerable speed, busy left jab, and slick footwork to pile up points. But what Izzy lacked in punching power he more than made up for with his classy boxing skills and fighting heart. In 130 fights he was stopped only 3 times. One of those losses was due to a broken hand and the other from a foul punch. The only other time he failed to go the distance was in his very last fight.

After the sudden retirement of flyweight champion Fidel LaBarba in 1927, the New York State Athletic Commission set up a tournament to determine a new champion. Izzy defeated four opponents to make it to the finals. On December 16, 1927, in Madison Square Garden, he outpointed Newsboy Brown over 15 rounds to win the title.

Five months later Izzy moved up a division and challenged Bushy Graham for the bantamweight championship of the world. After 15 rounds Graham was awarded the decision. Izzy then defended his flyweight title twice before putting it on the line against Newark's Willie LaMorte.

LaMorte copped the 15-round decision, but when it was revealed the next day that both boxers were under contract to the same manager (a conflict of interest, and clear violation of the rules), the New York Commission refused to recognize LaMorte as champion. Another tournament was arranged to determine a new champion. This time Izzy did not make it to the finals, losing a 10-round decision to French champion Eugene Huat.

Izzy was typical of the majority of Jewish fighters who were able to maintain a stable and productive life after their boxing careers ended.

He was married to his wife Sarah for over 60 years, and together they raised two fine sons. For many years he worked as a motion-picture projectionist, eventually becoming financial secretary of the Motion Picture Projectionists' Union Local 306. Throughout his life he maintained close ties to boxing through his affiliation with Ring #8 of the New York Veteran Boxers' Association.

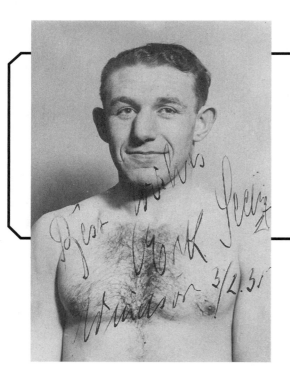

ERICH SEELIG

Born: July 15, 1915
Died: January 19, 1984 (Age: 78)
Hometown: Atlantic City, New Jersey
Weight: 160 lbs.
Professional Career: 1931–1940

Total Bouts	Won	Lost	Draw	ND
63 (544 rounds)	41 (8 by KO)	14 (3 by KO)	7	1-0

Erich Seelig began his professional boxing career in Germany in 1931 and won both the middleweight and light-heavyweight titles of that country. When the Nazis came to power in 1933 the government ordered all Jewish national champions stripped of their titles. Threatened by the Nazis and barred from defending his title, Erich and his parents fled to France. He resumed his career and continued to box in France, Belgium, and England before emigrating to the United States in 1935.

Seelig fought just about every top middleweight contender of his era. In Europe he defeated Kid Tunero and lost close decisions to Gustave Roth and Marcel Thil. In America he outpointed contenders Paul Pirrone, Carmen Barth, Glen Lee, and future champion Ken Overlin. A draw with Teddy Yarosz and split-decision losses to Fred Apostoli and Billy Conn did not hurt his standing. At one point he was ranked the number-five middleweight in the world by *The Ring* magazine.

On December 11, 1939, at the Cleveland Arena, Seelig challenged NBA middleweight champion Al Hostak for the title and was knocked out in the first round. He had two more fights and then retired.

Seelig's wife Greta was also a Jewish refugee from Nazi Germany. She had been a world-class hurdler but was barred by the German government from competing in the 1936 Olympic Games. The couple eventually settled in Atlantic City, New Jersey, where they operated a chicken farm.

Erich Seelig was elected to both the New Jersey Boxing Hall of Fame and the International Jewish Sports Hall of Fame.

SOLLY SEEMAN

Born: February 26, 1902
Died: March 11, 1989 (Age: 87)
Hometown: New York, New York
Weight: 5' 7" Weight: 135 lbs.
Professional Career: 1920–1929

Total Bouts	Won	Lost	Draw	ND	NC
81 (569 rounds)	47 (9 by KO)	10 (0 by KO)	13	6-3	2

Solly Seeman was 14 years old when he threw his first left jab in a boxing class at Manhattan's Young Men's Hebrew Association on East 92nd Street. Over the next four years he established a brilliant amateur record, winning the New York State flyweight championship, Metropolitan bantamweight championship, and, in 1920, the National AAU featherweight title. Solly also qualified for the 1920 Olympics by winning four fights in one night at New York's 71st Regiment Armory, but decided to forgo the games and turn pro instead.

As a pro Solly outpointed Joey Silvers and Johnny Ceccoli, won a newspaper decision over former lightweight champion Jimmy Goodrich, and drew with Chilean contender Luis Vicentini. But the depth of talent in the lightweight division of the 1920s was extraordinary. Even though Seeman was one of the finest pure boxers of his era, the occasional defeat was to be expected. In 1925 Chicago's future champion Sammy Mandell traded jabs and feints with Seeman in two bouts and edged him both times. That same year Benny Valgar (considered by some experts to be on a par with the great Benny Leonard as a boxer) won a convincing 10-round decision over Seeman.

Solly retired in 1929 at the age of 27. After 81 professional fights his face bore few scars, a tribute to his excellent boxing technique and the fact that he quit before his skills began to erode.

In 1935 Jimmy Braddock hired Seeman to advise him how to defeat heavyweight champion Max Baer. Evidently the lessons paid off as Braddock—a 10–1 underdog—jabbed Max silly and won the title.

Solly was smart both inside and outside of the ring. For over 30 years he operated a successful machine shop that eventually expanded to three plants with headquarters in Jamaica, New York. He and his wife Rose raised two boys, both of whom graduated law school and forged successful careers of their own.

BENNY SHARKEY

Born: May 19, 1911
Died: 1975 (Age: 64)
Hometown: Newcastle, England
Weight: 125 lbs.
Professional Career: 1928–1940

Total Bouts	Won	Lost	Draw
196 (1,970 rounds)	128 (54 by KO)	51 (6 by KO)	17

Benny's father, Leon, had boxed in England as "Tom Sharkey" (not to be confused with the famous American boxer of the same name). An older brother fought as "Willie Sharkey." The actual family name is Goldwater. Benny decided to keep the family's boxing tradition going and used the name "**Benny Sharkey**" throughout his career.

In his first year as a pro Benny fought 30 times. He continued that incredible pace, averaging over 15 fights a year for the next 11 years, eventually amassing a total of 196 professional bouts. Benny defeated former world champions Emile Pladner and Teddy Baldock and won an impressive 10-round decision (non-title) over the reigning bantamweight champion, Baltazar Sangchili. Other top opponents included featherweight contenders Nel Tareton, Dick Corbett, Johnny King, Benny Caplan, and Johnny McMillan. He also drew with featherweight title claimant Maurice Holtzer, and twice defeated Venezuelan champion Simon Chavez. In one of the few knockout losses of his career, Sharkey was caught cold in the first round of a 1934 non-title bout with featherweight champion Freddie Miller.

The Ring rated Sharkey among the top 10 bantamweights in the world for three months in 1931. He returned to the ratings in February 1938 as the number-seven featherweight in the world.

In September 1939, at the outbreak of World War II, Benny joined the Royal Air Force. After the war he drove a taxi in London for a number of years before becoming an ambulance driver in the 1950s.

(Courtesy of Ronald Silverberg)

PINKY SILVERBERG

(Pincus Silverberg)
Flyweight Champion 1927
Born: April 5, 1904
Died: January 16, 1964 (Age: 59)
Hometown: Ansonia, Connecticut
Weight: 112–122 lbs.
Professional Career: 1920–1934, 1937

Total Bouts	Won	Lost	Draw	ND	NC
89 (714 rounds)	33 (7 by KO)	33 (1 by KO)	15	4-2	2

The 1920s was a Golden Age for the flyweight division. The field was crowded with outstanding boxers from a variety of countries. Popular champions such as England's Jimmy Wilde, Filipino Pancho Villa, and America's Fidel LaBarba drew thousands of people to major league ballparks for their title fights. Among the scores of talented contenders vying for a shot at the title was Connecticut's **Pinky Silverberg**.

Pinky began his pro career in 1920 when he was 16 years old. His older brother, Herman Silverberg (aka, Herman "Kid" Silvers), a featherweight, turned pro about the same time, and was a main-event boxer in the New York clubs.

In 1927 Silverberg won the vacant NBA flyweight title when his opponent, Ruby "Dark Cloud" Bradley, was disqualified for landing a low blow in the seventh round. In a ceremony a week after the fight, the NBA commissioner presented Pinky with his championship belt.

The top flyweight contenders lined up for a shot at the new champion and Pinky was ready to accommodate them, but through a strange set of circumstances he never got a chance to defend his title.

Seven weeks after winning the title Silverberg and Bradley met for a return match. Silverberg weighed in slightly over the flyweight limit, so his championship was not on the line. This time Bradley won a unanimous 10-round decision.

A few days after the fight the National Boxing Association took the title away from Silverberg. The reason given was "an unsatisfactory showing" in his second bout with Bradley. The action was unprecedented. It is the only time in boxing history that a champion was shorn of a legitimately won championship due to a poor performance in a subsequent non-title match.

Although it was later revealed that Silverberg had fought Bradley with a broken hand, the organization's decision stood. The reason for the NBA's stubborn refusal to restore his title appears to have involved a bureaucratic power struggle within the organization's hierarchy. Adding to the confusion were the disparate claims by fighters recognized as champion by New York State and the European Boxing Union. During the 1920s over a dozen fighters were recognized as flyweight champions by these organizations. The situation did not completely resolve itself until 1935, when Scotland's Benny Lynch won undisputed recognition.

Pinky outgrew the flyweight class and for seven years campaigned as a bantamweight. He fought the best of his era, including Midget Wolgast (four times), Panama Al Brown, Black Bill, Nel Tarleton, Pete Sanstol, Archie Bell, and future featherweight champion Petey Sarron.

There were few soft touches on Silverberg's boxing résumé. He fought 85 documented bouts and was stopped only once, by top contender Willie LaMorte in 1926. Problems with his oft-broken hands hampered many of his performances.

After he retired Pinky supported his wife and two children by working for an aircraft parts manufacturer in Ansonia, Connecticut. In 2007 he was inducted into the Connecticut Boxing Hall of Fame.

PAL SILVERS

Birth and death dates unknown
Hometown: New York, New York
Weight: 140–185 lbs.
Professional Career: 1925–1941, 1945–1946

Total Bouts	Won	Lost	Draw	NC
121 (721 rounds)	74 (19 by KO)	36 (15 by KO)	10	1

Pal Silvers was one of three talented fighting brothers (along with Joey and Marty) who were fixtures in the New York City boxing scene for nearly two decades. Beginning his career in 1925, Pal eventually fought in every weight class from junior lightweight to heavyweight. He was at his best in the late 1920s when he outpointed welterweight contenders Nick Testo and future thespian Canada Lee. Pal also defeated highly rated middleweight Vince Forgione twice, but lost decisions to future champions Gorilla Jones and Vince Dundee. In December 1928 *The Ring* listed him at number eight among the top 10 welterweight challengers.

Silvers is best remembered for a controversial 1931 bout with the legendary former lightweight champion Benny Leonard. After Leonard's fortune was wiped out in the stock market crash of 1929, he launched a comeback. The bout with Silvers was his first in over seven years. Described as "a pudgy, slow-footed old man of 35" by the UP wire service, the formerly peerless master boxer was being pummeled when suddenly, Silvers did a swan dive to the canvas in the second round and was counted out. The obvious fix fooled no one.

Pal tried to wash away the memory of his poor acting by winning eight of his next 10 fights, but he was soon past his prime and became a stepping-stone for young fighters on the way up.

ABE SIMON

Born: January 1, 1913
Died: October 24, 1969 (Age: 56)
Hometown: Richmond Hill, New York
Height: 6' 4" Weight: 255 lbs.
Professional Career: 1935–1942

Total Bouts	Won	Lost	Draw
47 (251 rounds)	36 (25 by KO)	10 (4 by KO)	1

Abe Simon attended John Adams High School in Richmond Hill, New York, where he was a star lineman for the school's football team and an "A" student. In 1932 Yale University offered the six-foot-four, 260-pound athlete a football scholarship. Abe turned down the scholarship when an enterprising manager told him he could earn a fortune as a heavyweight boxer. It wasn't long before Abe was training to be a boxer under the sponsorship of millionaire Jock Whitney and his silent partner, former heavyweight champion Gene Tunney.

In his first two years as a pro Abe won 16 of 17 bouts, including 14 by knockout. He lost for the first time on August 30, 1937, when the more-experienced Buddy Baer (another giant, at six-foot-six and 245 pounds) stopped him in the third round.

Following the Baer debacle a change of management ensued, and his career was taken over by the influential promoter Jimmy Johnston, who hired the excellent trainer Freddie Brown to sharpen his boxing skills. Johnston and Brown guided Abe through a number of important bouts, including a sixth-round knockout of future heavyweight champion Jersey Joe Walcott. Additional victories over contenders Eddie Blunt, Gunnar Barlund, and Roscoe Toles added to his prestige. By 1940 the vastly improved boxer was rated the sixth-best heavyweight in the world.

On March 21, 1941, at Detroit's Olympia Stadium, Abe challenged heavyweight champion Joe Louis. The fight was scheduled for 20 rounds. The "Brown Bomber" was still in his prime and considered unbeatable. Abe, a 20–1 underdog going into the fight, surprised the 18,000 fans in the stadium (and the millions listening on radio) by putting up stubborn resistance.

Abe was knocked down for the first time in his life in the opening round and was floored again in the third round. Yet despite the battering he refused to give up, and even managed to stagger Louis in the seventh round. By the beginning of the 13th round the champion's left eye had closed up. Louis, determined to end the bout, floored Abe twice. Upon arising from the second knockdown Simon was staggered again by another powerful blow to his jaw. The referee stopped the fight at 1:20 of the 13th round. After the fight Louis praised Simon: "For a big guy he was pretty good and just about as tough as they come."[64]

Abe's gutsy showing—he was only the third boxer to last past the 10th round with Louis—earned him a rematch almost a year to the day after their first bout. This time the venue was Madison Square Garden. America had entered World War II less than four months earlier, and there was a patriotic fervor among the standing-room-only crowd of 19,000 fans. Sergeant Joe Louis (he'd recently enlisted in the army) was defending his title for the 21st time. Joe weighed 207 to Simon's 255¼ pounds.

Joe Louis was always devastating in rematches, and this fight was no different. Big Abe was sent to the canvas in the second and fifth rounds after absorbing horrific punishment. Showing tremendous fortitude and resilience, the lumbering giant somehow managed to win the fourth round by taking the fight to Louis and scoring with body punches at close quarters.

The inevitable ending came at the beginning of the sixth round. Simon was knocked down by a volley of punches and was counted out by referee Arthur Donovan. Upon arising Abe protested vigorously to Donovan that he was up at "nine" and had beaten the count.

In an article for *Esquire* magazine, written several years after he retired, Simon revealed that he had suffered terribly from chronic headaches after his two punishing fights with Louis. Despite lucrative offers from promoters, he realized that continuing with his career would lead to further damage, so he wisely retired after his second go-round with Louis. His wife, a registered nurse, was instrumental in persuading him to retire.

To all who knew him outside of the ring, Abe Simon was a gentle giant who was nothing like the menacing characters he occasionally played in movies and television. Abe appeared in *Requiem for a Heavyweight* (1962), *Never Love a Stranger* (1958), and *Singing in the Dark* (1956). But his most memorable movie role was playing a hulking thug in the classic movie, *On the Waterfront* (1954).

Abe was only 56 years old when he suffered a fatal heart attack while working as a security guard at Yonkers Raceway in New York.

AL SINGER

(Abraham Singer)
"The Bronx Beauty"
Lightweight Champion 1930
Born: September 6, 1906
Died: April 20, 1961 (Age: 54)
Hometown: New York, New York
Height: 5' 4½" Weight: 128–135 lbs.
Professional Career: 1927–1931, 1935

Total Bouts	Won	Lost	Draw
73 (410 rounds)	62 (26 by KO)	9 (4 by KO)	2

The few existing films of **Al Singer**'s fights reveal a graceful boxer of inordinate skill. Singer's speed, his flashing combinations, balletic footwork, and accurate power punches were reminiscent of Benny Leonard in his prime. Within a few short years of turning pro he was drawing thousands of fans to New York's arenas and ballparks.

Singer had been an outstanding all-around athlete in high school, where his favorite sport was basketball. His father, a small garment manufacturer, did well enough to move his wife and five children out of the Lower East Side to the Bronx, at the time a fashionable borough of New York City.

Al displayed a natural affinity for the sport, amassing an impressive array of amateur trophies, including the Metropolitan AAU (Amateur Athletic Union) featherweight title. He was undefeated in his first two years as a pro. The

19-year-old phenom soon drew the attention of Prohibition gangsters interested in owning "a piece" of a promising fighter. What happened next remains a mystery to this day. According to Singer, two men posing as detectives took his manager, Harry Drucker, downtown to "headquarters." The manager was never heard from again.

Singer, like virtually all professional fighters, had no control over who managed him, and always denied any involvement with the Mob. Yet the rumors persisted that he was a "connected" boxer and that several of his early fights were fixed.

His first important match was against former featherweight champion Tony Canzoneri on December 14, 1928. The match sold out Madison Square Garden. Although a heavy underdog, Al surprised the oddsmakers by holding his more-experienced opponent to a 10-round draw. The fight was a thriller from start to finish. James Dawson, writing for the *New York Times*, tagged Singer "The New Benny Leonard." It was the highest compliment any young boxer could receive. Al's impressive showing thrust the 20-year-old boxer onto the world stage.

Over the next 14 months "The Bronx Beauty" cut a swath through the lightweight division. He scored back-to-back second-round knockouts of European champion Gaston Charles and world featherweight champion Andre Routis (non-title). He then outpointed Joe Ryder, Davey Abad, and Dominick Petrone. A victory over former bantamweight champion Bud Taylor moved him firmly into the upper echelon of lightweight contenders vying for a shot at the title.

A temporary setback occurred when he was knocked out by Ignacio Fernandez. Al blamed his defeat on an eye injury incurred in a previous fight that was not given enough time to heal. He also lost a disputed 12-round decision to the great Cuban featherweight Kid Chocolate. But in his final bout of 1929, he flattened tough Pete Nebo in one round.

Singer began 1930 in top form by winning a 10-round decision over the rugged Chilean contender Stanislaus Loayza, and then knocked out Eddie "Kid" Wagner in three rounds. He also avenged his previous loss to Ignacio Fernandez with a unanimous 10-round decision.

On July 17, 1930, Singer faced lightweight champion Sammy Mandell at Yankee Stadium in front of 40,000 fans. The odds favored Mandell, one of the savviest boxers of his generation. The champion's record showed only seven defeats in 92 fights. Singer came into the ring with six defeats in 59 fights, including 25 wins by knockout.

In a startling upset Mandell was knocked out in 1:46 of the first round. It was the fastest exchange of a title on record, up to that time. Singer, who was paid $75 for his first pro fight less than four years earlier, received over $20,000 for the abbreviated contest. There was talk that gamblers had fixed the fight and that Mandell had taken a dive, but the allegations were never proven.

On September 11, 1930, Singer returned to Yankee Stadium to face the great Jimmy McLarnin in a non-title fight. After outboxing McLarnin in the first two rounds, Singer was nailed by a right cross in the third round that dropped him hard. He was up at nine but was floored again and failed to beat the count. Fortunately for Singer, his title was not at stake, as both fighters had weighed above the 135-pound lightweight limit.

Two months later Singer was back in Madison Square Garden for a title defense against his former foe, Tony Canzoneri.

Singer was favored to outbox Canzoneri, but the challenger upset the odds. Canzoneri flattened Singer in just 1:06 of the first round, breaking the record for the fastest exchange of a title set only four months earlier in the Singer vs. Mandell fight.

Al came back with four straight wins in 1931, including a 10-round decision over contender Lew Massey and a second-round KO of former bantam champ Eddie "Cannonball" Martin. But in his last fight of the year he suffered a second-round knockout loss to featherweight champion Bat Battalino (non-title). It was Al's 68h professional bout. The loss convinced the 22-year-old boxer to hang up his gloves. A brief comeback in 1935 resulted in four wins against nondescript opponents.

When America entered World War II Singer enlisted in the army. But the same eye problems that had plagued him during his career eventually resulted in his receiving a medical discharge.

In his post-boxing life Al dabbled in real estate, cabaret ownership, and had various sales positions. In 1955 he was appointed a boxing judge by the New York State Athletic Commission.

On April 20, 1961, Al Singer was found dead in his apartment, victim of a heart attack. He was 54 years old.

LEW TENDLER

Born: September 28, 1898
Died: November 15, 1970 (Age: 72)
Hometown: Philadelphia, Pennsylvania
Height: 5' 6" Weight: 135–154 lbs,
Professional Career: 1913–1928

Total Bouts	Won	Lost	Draw	ND	NC
172 (1,219 rounds)	59 (39 by KO)	11 (1 by KO)	2	87-5-6	2

In 1958 uber boxing historian Nat Fleischer, the venerable publisher and editor of *The Ring*, ranked **Lew Tendler** the ninth-greatest lightweight of all time. His choice is not hard to fathom. Lew's remarkable record speaks for itself. It lists only 11 official losses (including two dubious disqualifications) out of 172 professional fights. Three of those losses were to boxing legends Benny Leonard, Mickey Walker, and Johnny Dundee (whom Tendler defeated in a return bout). Five occurred when he was past his prime. According to the International Boxing Research Organization, an investigation of Lew's 98 no-decision bouts reveals that only four newspaper verdicts favored his opponents.

Lew Tendler came from the same South Philly ghetto neighborhood that spawned many outstanding Jewish boxers during the first three decades of the last century. His first job was selling newspapers on a Philadelphia street corner. He was six years old.

Philadelphia had eight daily newspapers, and competition for a prime location could sometimes turn violent. Circulation wars were common. Older boys would often bully their way onto a busy street corner already occupied by a younger and smaller newsboy. It was an asset for a newsboy to be good with his fists. Lew hawked papers for nine years and was a fierce defender of his turf. Even if he didn't always win, the young tyro put up such a determined effort that the older boys thought it less punishing to find another location and leave the little wildcat alone.

Lew had not yet celebrated his bar mitzvah when he began fighting in amateur bouts. He eventually graduated to tournaments that were often held in the city's burlesque houses. The bouts took place in between the acts. A flood of good fighters were developed in these tournaments. After a lengthy amateur career Lew turned pro in 1913 at the age of 15.

At the time Philadelphia had an ordinance that restricted all professional boxing matches to not more than six rounds. Limiting a fight to six rounds had the effect of speeding up the action. It also provided a young fighter with the opportunity to fight often and gain experience without being subjected to a grueling 10- or 20-round bout. Philadelphia had seven arenas running weekly boxing shows. There were also additional fight clubs in neighboring cities. It was in these clubs that Lew, fighting once or twice a month, established a reputation as a powerful and aggressive body puncher with an unorthodox southpaw style. Within two years of turning pro the ex-newsboy had become one of Philadelphia's most popular boxers.

Lew received his "boxing PhD" against the likes of Johnny Dundee, Eddie O'Keefe, Benny Kaufman, Phil Bloom, Frankie Callahan, George KO Chaney, Ever Hammer, Willie Jackson, Joe Welling, Frankie Britt, and Rocky Kansas.

By the age of 23 he was a top-rated lightweight contender and a seasoned veteran, with 113 professional fights under his belt. A showdown with the great lightweight champion Benny Leonard was inevitable.

The first Leonard vs. Tendler match took place in Jersey City on July 22, 1922. The bout attracted 55,000 fans to the same huge stadium built a year earlier for the Jack Dempsey vs. Georges Carpentier heavyweight title fight.

New Jersey still adhered to the "no decision" rule, which meant the only way Tendler could win the title was by a knockout. Lew was confident he could accomplish what most observers considered an impossible task. The 3–1 odds favored Leonard, who was considered invincible at 135 pounds. The champion, in the fifth year of his reign, predicted a seventh-round knockout (the bout was scheduled for 12 rounds).

Knowing he had to win by a knockout to acquire the title caused Lew to pressure Leonard relentlessly, in hopes of creating openings for his vaunted left cross. Midway through the eighth round the challenger landed his best punch when a left to the jaw caused Leonard's knees to sag. The champion was in obvious distress, but his steel-trap mind quickly shifted into overdrive. Momentarily frozen by the punch, and a sitting duck for Tendler's follow-up punches, Leonard suddenly spoke to Tendler. To some it looked like he was telling Tendler to "Keep your punches up, Lew," although the punch that hurt him had landed nowhere near foul territory. Others claimed he spoke to Tendler in Yiddish in order to confuse him. Whatever was said (and it was never made clear by either fighter), Lew was provoked to answer Leonard with a few choice words of his own. Tendler's reaction gave Leonard the few seconds he needed to regain his equilibrium and make it to the end of the round.

In the following rounds the momentum shifted back to the champion, but going into the 12th round, it was still anybody's fight. In the final minute Benny closed with a furious rally and appeared to have won the round. The faces of both champion and challenger bore the telltale signs of a bruising contest.

The following day the *New York Times* reported that Leonard had won "by the scantest of margins." Most other newspaper reports agreed, although some declared the fight a draw.

Of course a rematch was called for to settle the matter. So on July 24, 1923, 63,000 fans came to Yankee Stadium anticipating another great fight. The attendance and gate receipts (over $450,000) set a record for a lightweight title bout that stood for over 50 years. It was also the first championship fight held in the brand-new "House that Ruth Built."

In the intervening year between the first and second fight Leonard had studied and analyzed Lew's southpaw style. The end result was a fight that bore very little resemblance to their first highly competitive encounter. In what may have been his greatest performance ever, Leonard completely outboxed and outpunched Tendler, dominating practically every round. As the bout drew to a close Leonard opened up with every combination in his huge repertoire in an attempt to end the fight. Only Lew's great heart and chin kept him upright in the last two rounds. It was the worst beating he'd ever taken. The unanimous decision in Leonard's favor was a foregone conclusion. Of some comfort to Lew was the $116,000 he received for his share of the record gate.

On June 2, 1924, Lew received his third opportunity to win a world title when he challenged Mickey Walker for the welterweight championship. Weighing 142¾ to Walker's 147, Tendler attempted to keep Walker, a strong infighter, at long range. At the end of seven rounds the fight was even. In the eighth round Walker was able to work his way inside and began scoring with damaging body punches. Lew tried his best to hold off "The Toy Bulldog," but the youth, strength, and skill of the great welterweight champion were just too much to cope with, and he lost a close but unanimous 10-round decision.

It was no disgrace to lose to Walker, a legendary fighter who would go on to win the middleweight crown, but Lew had been fighting for 11 years, and the decline of his skills was inevitable. Nevertheless, he still managed to win 28 of his next 33 fights and remain competitive with the world's top welterweights. The only time he was ever stopped occurred one year after the Walker fight, when Jack Zivic scored a TKO in the fifth round. Tendler's seconds had thrown in the towel after he had gone down twice and was being pummeled by Zivic. Five months later Lew avenged the loss by defeating Zivic over 10 rounds.

In retirement Lew fared better than most ex-fighters. Hugely popular in his hometown of Philadelphia, Tendler opened a restaurant in the city and named it—what else?—"Lew Tendler's." For many years it was a magnet for tourists, professional athletes, celebrities, and politicos. Two branches of the restaurant, in Atlantic City and Miami Beach, were also successful. On a personal note, Lew was married to the former Celia Lasker for over 50 years and they had three sons.

With or without a championship belt, the life and career of this great fighter defined the real meaning of the word "champion."

SID TERRIS
"The Ghetto Ghost"
Born: September 26, 1904
Died: December 1974 (Age: 70)
Hometown: New York, New York
Height: 5' 10" Weight: 130–135 lbs.
Professional Career: 1922–1931

Total Bouts	Won	Lost	Draw	ND
118 (910 rounds)	94 (13 by KO)	13 (5 by KO)	4	6-0-1

Sid Terris may have been the fastest lightweight boxer of all time. His hand and foot speed seemed almost superhuman. Like a pugilistic Michael Jordan, the five-foot-ten, 133-pound speed demon seemed to defy the physical boundaries of gravity. Old-timers were in awe of his phenomenal speed and agility. Legendary trainer Cus D'Amato claimed that he once saw Terris distract an opponent by jumping off the canvas, and in the fraction of a second when both feet were in midair, he landed three left jabs!

Before he turned pro in 1922 Terris had a brilliant amateur career, winning 50 consecutive bouts. He won the New York State, Metropolitan, and National AAU lightweight championships in a 10-month span.

Terris's rise in the professional ranks was highlighted by decisions over former featherweight champion Johnny Dundee and future lightweight champions Jimmy Goodrich and Rocky Kansas. Although he went as high as number one in the lightweight ratings, Terris never received a title shot.

One of his most memorable victories was a bout that brought together the world's two fastest lightweights. In 1924 Sid Terris faced off against the great "French Flash," Benny Valgar. Over 14,000 excited fans paid their way into Brooklyn's Henderson Bowl (formerly the Coney Island Stadium) to see the highly anticipated contest.

Both Valgar and Terris were experienced and consummate boxing artists, but it was Terris's edge in speed that carried him to victory. The *New York Times* praised his "remarkable speed and cleverness," and cited his performance as "one of the most skillful exhibitions of boxing seen here in recent years." An interesting but not surprising sidelight is that six of the eight boxers who appeared on the undercard were also Jewish.

Terris was considered the favorite to replace the recently retired lightweight champion Benny Leonard. But in a 1925 tournament to name Leonard's successor, he lost a close decision to another master boxer—future lightweight champion Sammy Mandell. Their previous fight, a year earlier, had ended in a 10-round draw.

Over the next two years Terris lost only two of 30 bouts. Among the top men he defeated were Billy Petrolle, Babe Herman, Ace Hudkins, and former junior lightweight champ Jack Bernstein. In a Polo Grounds match that attracted over 50,000 fans, he met ghetto rival Ruby Goldstein. Terris was tagged by Ruby's powerful right cross in the first round and was floored for a nine-count. As Ruby, "The Jewel of the Ghetto," rushed to flatten Terris, "The Ghetto Ghost" landed a perfectly timed right to Ruby's jaw that put him down for the full count.

In 1928 Terris was knocked out in the first round by Jimmy McLarnin. There was no disgrace in losing to McLarnin, an all-time great fighter, but two months later Sid's fans became alarmed when young Ray Miller duplicated McLarnin's feat.

Terris was a veteran of over 100 bouts and appeared to be past his prime. This was confirmed when other opponents who a year earlier could not hit him with a bucketful of rice were now able to get close enough to score. In 1931— his last year as a pro—he struggled against two mediocre opponents. If Terris continued fighting he would be fodder for up-and-coming youngsters wanting to build their reputation with a victory over the once-great "Ghetto Ghost."

At age 27 he knew it was time to hang up his gloves and dancing shoes. After he retired, the popular and personable ex-prizefighter secured a job as headwaiter at one of New York City's premier restaurants.

PHIL TOBIAS

"The Hebrew Boxer"
Born: February 4, 1906
Died: May 31, 1981 (Age: 75)
Hometown: New York, New York
Height: 5' 2" Weight: 118 lbs.
Professional Career: 1926–1933

Total Bouts	Won	Lost	Draw	ND	NC
79 (575 rounds)	34 (7 by KO)	29 (2 by KO)	10	1-1	4

On November 19, 1928, in his 43rd professional bout, New York's **Phil Tobias** entered the golden circle of top 10 challengers for the flyweight title by outpointing future champion Midget Wolgast. That victory was Tobias's greatest achievement as a boxer. Unfortunately, his flaw as a fighter was an inability to remain consistent against top competition—including Wolgast, who he lost to twice in five outings. (The other two bouts with Wolgast consisted of a no-decision and a draw.) Yet, just when it seemed he would be dropped from the ratings, Tobias would bounce back with an impressive victory over a tough contender, as he did against Ruby Bradley and Johnny McCoy. The results of those fights point to a world-class fighter who was better than his overall record would indicate.

In 1931, with his career winding down, Tobias traveled to Caracas, Venezuela, and lost a close 10-round decision to future bantamweight champion Sixto Escobar. He finished out his career in South America, winning seven of his last 15 bouts.

BENNY VALGAR

"The French Flash"
Born: September 24, 1898
Died: October 1972 (Age: 74)
Hometown: New York, New York
Weight: 125–135 lbs.
Professional Career: 1916–1932

Total Bouts	Won	Lost	Draw	ND	NC
215 (1,954 rounds)	91 (18 by KO)	25 (0 by KO)	8	67-12-7	5

In a 1935 article that appeared in the *New York Enquirer,* Ray Arcel, the dean of American boxing trainers, stated the following: "When it came to all-around ring generalship, **Benny Valgar** was on a par with Benny Leonard, though Leonard packed the better punch." I interviewed Ray Arcel in 1978. He still reserved the highest praise for both fighters. "I've seen every great fighter from 1915 to the present, and to me, [Benny] Leonard was the best," said Arcel. "He was, without question, the fastest-thinking fighter I ever saw. I class one other fighter with him as far as cleverness, and that was Benny Valgar."

Benny's parents had emigrated to France from Russia in 1894. In 1913 his widowed mother took Benny and his four siblings to New York City.

Valgar turned pro in 1916 following a successful amateur career that included winning the national AAU bantamweight title. Four years later he received his first and only title shot when he fought the great featherweight champion Johnny Kilbane in an eight-round no-decision bout in Newark, New Jersey. (New Jersey boxing regulations did not permit bouts beyond eight rounds.) The following day 11 of 13 newspaper reporters who witnessed the bout wrote that Valgar had narrowly outpointed the champion. But their opinion did not matter. The only way the title could have changed hands was by a knockout.

In 1925 Valgar was considered the heir apparent to recently retired lightweight champion Benny Leonard. He was the favorite among 50 top lightweights invited to compete in a tournament to find a successor to Leonard. In his first three tournament bouts Valgar dazzled audiences with easy victories over Alex Hart, Basil Galiano, and Solly Seeman, each one a highly regarded contender. But his 12-round semifinal resulted in a surprise loss to Jimmy Goodrich (the eventual tournament winner).

"The French Flash" had proven his superiority over Goodrich in a previous fight, and the upset puzzled fans and sportswriters. The *New York Times* reported that Valgar's showing "was far below the form expected of him." Up to that time the only fighter to win a clear points victory over Valgar was the famed "Ghetto Ghost," Sid Terris, perhaps the only lightweight in the world faster than Valgar.

Even as his career wound down, Valgar's superb defensive skills—he was a master at blocking and parrying blows—kept him from taking the type of ruinous punishment so common to his profession. Other than a slightly flattened nose, his face bore none of the facial scars prevalent among his contemporaries. His official ledger shows 215 documented professional bouts, although the actual number is believed to be higher. He is one of only two fighters with more than 200 bouts to have never been knocked out or stopped (the other is Jewish boxer Harry Stone). Recognition of Benny Valgar as one of the greatest boxers of all time is long overdue.

After he retired in 1932, Valgar and his wife settled in Brighton Beach, Brooklyn, and opened a dress shop in the Brownsville section of that borough.

SAMMY VOGEL

Born: July 28, 1902
Died: Unknown
Hometown: New York, New York
Weight: 135–142 lbs.
Professional Career: 1920–1928

Total Bouts	Won	Lost	Draw	ND	NC
65 (552 rounds)	43 (11 by KO)	15 (3 by KO)	3	2-1	1

Sammy Vogel was another outstanding Jewish boxer out of New York's Lower East Side. As an amateur bantamweight he represented the United States at the 1920 Antwerp Olympic Games, where he lost a decision in his second tournament bout. Expectations were very high for the young boxer when he turned pro two months later. *The Ring* magazine called him a "pocket edition of Benny Leonard." As a pro he scored impressive victories over Mike Dundee, Billy Petrolle, Mickey Travers, and Bucky Lawless. But his road to a title shot was stymied by losses to future lightweight champion Jimmy Goodrich and top contenders Hilario Martinez and Bruce Flowers (three times).

(Courtesy of PhillyBoxingHistory.com)

EDDIE "KID" WAGNER

Born: October 21, 1900
Died: October 30, 1956 (Age: 56)
Hometown: Philadelphia, Pennsylvania
Weight: 135 lbs.
Professional Career: 1915–1931

Total Bouts	Won	Lost	Draw	ND	NC
175 (1,435 rounds)	53 (13 by KO)	36 (7 by KO)	9	50-16-8	3

Over the course of his 16-year career Philadelphia's **Eddie "Kid" Wagner** faced seven world champions 12 times. Ring greats who crossed his path include Jack Bernstein, Johnny Dundee, Louis "Kid" Kaplan, Sammy Mandell, and Sid Terris.

In 1925 Wagner was one of 50 lightweight boxers invited to participate in a tournament to determine a successor to retired champion Benny Leonard. His first bout against Jimmy Goodrich at Madison Square Garden ended in a 10-round draw. Officials ordered two more "overtime" rounds. Goodrich was awarded the decision and went on to win the tournament four months later.

The only fighter able to KO Wagner in his prime was the great Billy Petrolle, who stopped him in the 10th round in 1926. Just one month later Wagner fought a 10-round non-title draw with featherweight champion Louis "Kid" Kaplan.

Wagner's career began winding down in the late 1920s. But, like most fighters, he continued to fight on and paid the price. Between 1929 and 1931 Wagner won only two of 17 fights. In the last three months of his career he was knocked out by highly rated contenders Harry Dublinsky, Tony Herrera, and future lightweight champion Al Singer. Five of Wagner's seven knockout defeats took place during the last two years of his career.

ARCHIE WALKER

(Irving Wolkow)
Born July 26, 1902
Died: Unknown
Hometown: Brooklyn, New York
Weight: 135–140 lbs.
Professional Career: 1921–1927

Total Bouts	Won	Lost	Draw	ND	NC
66 (533 rounds)	39 (11 by KO)	17 (3 by KO)	3	3-2-1	1

In 1922, just three years after turning pro, **Archie Walker** was rushed into bouts against top lightweight contenders Benny Valgar, Phil Salvadore, Clonie Tait, and Jack Bernstein. He lost to all except Bernstein, who he managed to outpoint in their first bout, but who then beat him in two subsequent rematches.

With added experience Walker continued to improve, and was victorious over the likes of Mel Coogan, Andy Chaney, and Johnny Shugrue. In 1924 he fought a 10-round no-decision bout with future lightweight champion Sammy Mandell. All four newspapers covering the bout reported a draw.

In 1927 Archie traveled to London, where he lost a 15-round decision to former British welterweight champion Harry Mason. All of Walker's 17 losses were to outstanding boxers with winning records.

After he retired Archie worked for a Wall Street clearinghouse. In later years he was employed by the Ford Motor Company.

EDDIE "KID" WOLFE

Born: March 3, 1910
Died: Unknown
Hometown: Memphis, Tennessee
Height: 5' 6" Weight: 135–145 lbs.
Professional Career: 1927–1936

Total Bouts	Won	Lost	Draw	ND	NC
97 (874 rounds)	61 (12 by KO)	21 (2 by KO)	12	2-0	1

Unlike most other Jewish pugilists, **Eddie "Kid" Wolfe** did not begin his boxing career in a major East Coast city. Eddie was born and raised in Memphis, Tennessee, where he had his first professional fight in 1927. In less than two years he established a reputation as one of the finest lightweight boxers in the South. Eddie fought 40 main events in New Orleans when that city was a hotbed of boxing activity. His rythmic fluid boxing style appealed to the "Big Easy" locals.

In 1929 former contender Phil McGraw and ancient ring legend Johnny Dundee were imported to New Orleans to test the undefeated youngster. Eddie was way too fast for the aging veterans, and outpointed both. Wolfe's handlers then decided to match him with Tony Canzoneri, the recently dethroned featherweight champion. Canzoneri walked off with a unanimous decision.

Next up was another former featherweight champion, Louis "Kid" Kaplan, who was rated the number-three lightweight in the world. "The Meridian Buzzsaw" overwhelmed Wolfe and stopped him in the seventh round.

Undeterred by his first knockout defeat, Wolfe continued with his career and gained valuable experience. He eventually achieved a top-10 rating in both the lightweight and welterweight divisions by defeating Matt Brock, Joe Glick, King Tut, Harry Dublinsky, Eddie Ran, and Tracey Cox. He also had two draws with Baby Joe Gans and Mike Dundee. Nearing the end of his career, he went 1-1-1 (win, loss, and draw) against future middleweight champion Teddy Yarosz.

In 97 pro fights, only two opponents were able to stop him: the aforementioned Louis "Kid" Kaplan and hard-punching lightweight contender Billy Wallace. After his active boxing career was over, Eddie kept his hand in the sport by working as a boxing judge and referee.

NORMAN "BABY" YACK

(Benjamin Norman Yakubowitz)
Born: December 25, 1915
Died: January 11, 1987 (Age: 71)
Hometown: Toronto, Canada
Height: 5' 5" Weight: 118–124 lbs.
Professional Career: 1936–1939

Total Bouts	Won	Lost	Draw
37 (293 rounds)	23 (4 by KO)	13 (1 by KO)	1

Toronto's **Norman "Baby" Yack** was one of Canada's greatest amateur boxers. The Russian-born bantamweight won 90 of 100 bouts before earning a place on the Canadian National boxing team that was to compete in the 1936 Berlin Olympic Games. But Norman and his parents were deeply distressed by the German government's treatment of Jews, and decided to boycott the Nazi Olympics. Joining in the boycott was his friend and teammate Sammy Luftspring.

After their protest was made public, both fighters were invited to represent Canada in an alternate Olympic games in Barcelona, Spain. They were in southern France, waiting for a boat to take them to Barcelona, when the games were canceled due to the outbreak of the Spanish Civil War.

Baby Yack turned pro in September 1936. Less than a year into his pro career he won the Canadian bantamweight title by outpointing Frankie Martin. He defeated Martin in a return bout, and then won two out of three against Henry Hook, a vastly more experienced bantamweight contender. The following year he whipped fourth-ranked Indian Quintana. The series of victories moved him into the upper echelon of title challengers.

Achieving a top-10 rating in those days was never easy, but staying there was even tougher. In 1938, following two decisions over Spider Armstrong, he lost to former flyweight champion Small Montana and highly rated contender Georgie Pace. After scoring a KO over Lefty Gwynne, Yack was knocked out by featherweight contender Bobby Ivy (the only KO defeat of his career).

The following year he lost two out of three bouts to Lou Transparenti, and was outpointed by Nicky Jerome and Harry Jeffra (Jeffra won the featherweight title in his next fight).

Perhaps his quick burnout was due to being brought along too fast against extremely tough competition. Most of his opponents were seasoned journeymen or world-ranked contenders. Nevertheless, in his brief three-year pro career, Baby Yack established an impressive record against some of the best fighters of his era.

After he retired Yack is believed to have worked as a cab driver in Montreal.

CHAPTER 5

WAR AND PEACE: 1941–1963

We will win this war because we are on God's side.
—HEAVYWEIGHT CHAMPION JOE LOUIS, MADISON SQUARE GARDEN, WAR BOND RALLY, 1942

The war in Europe and Asia had been raging for more than two years when Japan launched a surprise air attack on the US naval base at Pearl Harbor, Hawaii. The attack killed over 2,300 Americans and destroyed or damaged 20 warships and over 300 aircraft. The next day Congress declared war on Japan. Within days Japan's ally, Germany, declared war on the United States. The conflict was now global.

Over the next four years 16 million Americans answered the call to duty and took part in the monumental effort to defeat Nazi Germany and Japan. Included among these fighters for freedom were 550,000 American Jews, including women, who served in the armed forces. The boxing community did its part. Over 4,000 professional prizefighters, in addition to many trainers and managers, interrupted their careers to serve in various branches of the military.

On the home front boxing was a popular diversion for the civilian population. In every city, fans flocked to arenas in hopes of taking their minds off the war for a few hours. But as the months turned into years, increasing numbers of young men were being drafted or volunteering for service, including many established boxing stars. In addition, four world champions had their titles frozen for the duration of the war while they served in the armed forces.

Bill Goodman, a former licensed corner man and a student of the boxing scene for over 60 years, believes the shortage of talent eventually led to lowered fan appreciation for the art of boxing. Goodman comments:

In my opinion after America entered the war, the sport began its downward slide in terms of the quality and quantity of fighters. Matchmakers and promoters had major problems keeping a show together because so many talented prospects were in the service and no longer available. The ones left were lesser-caliber fighters who didn't have the talent—or if they did have the talent, they weren't being nurtured and taught as they had been prior to the war. As a result many unschooled club fighters advanced to main-bout status. The fans got used to seeing a less-sophisticated style of boxing—crude, but with plenty of slam-bang action. It was no longer necessary to be the stylist that it was prior to that period. The quality went down, and the public got used to it.

For every accomplished boxer who headlined a card during the war, there were scores of other less-talented club fighters who achieved the very same goal.

Fans wanted to see the Rocky Graziano and Beau Jack style of fighter, the action guys that kept going, kept punching, and looked for that knockout. For the first time posters began advertising fighters with phrases like "He never stops punching from bell to bell."

I'm not knocking Beau Jack. He was an interesting, colorful fighter and a hell of a campaigner, always trying, but nevertheless, he wasn't the classic boxer we saw in the prewar years. As good a fighter as Beau was, he wasn't on the level of a Barney Ross, Tony Canzoneri, Sammy Mandell, or Kid Chocolate. Of course, not everyone could measure up to these great fighters, but you had an endless number of outstanding fighters in the 1920s and '30s.

Very few outstanding boxers were developed during or after World War II. Most of the great fighters from that era began their careers prior to the war, and that includes the great black fighters from the 1940s, such as Ezzard Charles, Charley Burley, Archie Moore, Holman

Williams, Eddie Booker, Lloyd Marshall, and Jimmy Bivins. Even after the end of the war, they were not developing the same type of talent that they did before the war. There were some good fighters—I won't say there weren't good fighters—but as far as I'm concerned, they weren't as good as the fighters developed in the 1910s, '20s, and '30s. Yes, here and there you had an outstanding guy, but for the most part, they were not up to those fighters quality-wise.[1]

A positive result of the boxing scene in the United States at this time was that it opened doors to a few outstanding African-American boxers who were finally getting a chance to appear in feature bouts at major venues, including Madison Square Garden. But, as noted by Bill Goodman, for every quality boxer who shared top billing, there were also scores of less-talented pugs being promoted to main events that in normal times would not have merited the honor.

Boxing's continuing popularity on the home front made promoters think that the end of the war would boost the sport's fortunes even more, as name boxers returned to civilian life and took up where they had left off. But this optimistic view turned out not to be true.

THE LAST HURRAH
Nobody could see it coming, but the immediate postwar years would turn out to be the last hurrah for boxing's great Golden Age of talent

and activity. At the end of World War II the US Congress enacted the GI Bill of Rights that made it possible for millions of returning veterans to get low-cost mortgages and cash payments of tuition to acquire a college education or technical training. The GI Bill accelerated the entrance of returning vets into the economic mainstream and, combined with a booming postwar economy, was responsible for jump-starting the modern middle class in America.[2] Nevertheless, a large portion of America's African-American population was still struggling to attain their piece of the American dream.

In the 1930s the rise of Joe Louis and Henry Armstrong had opened up greater acceptance and opportunities for black fighters. That trend would be reinforced in subsequent decades by the social and demographic changes that significantly reduced the number of white boxers. By 1948 nearly half of all contenders were black. Most cited Joe Louis as their inspiration. Ten years earlier Italian Americans were the dominant contender group. Now they were in second place, followed by Mexican Americans.[3]

The mass exodus to the suburbs by the emerging middle class (including about a third of American Jews) that began in the late 1940s and continued through the 1950s took with it many of boxing's core customers, thereby hurting the network of small urban arenas that relied on their patronage to stay in business. Arenas that had been accustomed to drawing $4,000 to $5,000 per show on a regular basis saw revenues drop to $1,000 or less.

"No longer is there a stream of young fighters flowing into the ring," wrote *New York Times* reporter John R. Tunis in 1949. "The lifeblood of boxing is thinning out, perhaps temporarily, but it is thinning out, nevertheless. In my own state, Connecticut . . . fighting is poorer in quality and quantity today than before the war."[4]

By the end of the 1950s, the ranks of professional boxers in the United States had been depleted by 50 percent as compared to figures before the war. The retirement of the great but aging heavyweight champion Joe Louis in 1949 was symbolic. Boxing was in desperate need of a charismatic heavyweight champion to boost interest, but there was none on the horizon. Fan interest was waning, the public's tastes were changing, and there was growing competition from other sports. Boxing's image was also tainted by extensive press coverage of congressional investigations concerning infiltration by organized-crime figures and allegations of fixed fights.

Bill Goodman witnessed the changes firsthand: "[Boxing] wasn't something a guy wanted to be a part of anymore. And the people in the neighborhoods didn't make fighters heroes like they had in the past, with the Jewish and Italian fighters who came from the Lower East Side, Brooklyn, or the Bronx."[5]

TELEVISION TAKES OVER

Just in the nick of time, the new medium of television arrived to save the day. Television and boxing were made for each other. The shows were relatively easy and inexpensive to produce.

The camera only had to focus on the small space occupied by the ring, and commercials could conveniently be inserted during the one-minute break between rounds.

Television rejuvenated the sport and created millions of new fans almost overnight. By 1952 televised boxing was reaching 5 million homes, representing 32 percent of the available audience. In 1955 the figure had climbed to 8.5 million homes. From 1949 to 1955 boxing reportedly sold as many television sets as Milton Berle, and it rivaled *I Love Lucy* in the ratings. Fight fans could now watch all-time greats such as Joe Louis (attempting his comeback), Sugar Ray Robinson, Ezzard Charles, Rocky Marciano, Jake LaMotta, Archie Moore, Ike Williams, Willie Pep, and Sandy Saddler from the comfort of their living rooms.[6]

New stars emerged and quickly became household names. Kid Gavilan, Chuck Davey, Ralph "Tiger" Jones, "Irish" Bob Murphy, Carmen Basilio, "Hurricane" Jackson, Gene Fullmer, Joey Giardello, and Bobo Olson developed huge followings based on their frequent TV appearances.

But there was a downside to televised boxing. The greedy moguls and their mobster affiliates used the new medium to exploit boxing for all it was worth. They ended up killing the golden goose by saturating the airwaves with boxing almost every night of the week.

In 1949 the Mob-riddled International Boxing Club (IBC) became the sport's major promotional arm, acquiring exclusive TV contracts with the NBC and CBS networks. The networks agreed to pay $90,000 a week for the right to broadcast IBC fights. The titular head of the organization was James D. Norris, the wealthy scion of a family with huge real estate and commercial holdings that included major arenas and racetracks. Early on, Norris had reluctantly decided it would be easier to run his boxing empire with the Mob's cooperation, since they already controlled (through front managers) many top fighters desirable to television. Before he made his pact with the devil, several Mob-controlled fighters claiming injuries had pulled out of Norris's televised promotions shortly before they were scheduled to appear, causing him to scramble for substitutes. Needless to say, sponsors were not happy.

In order to avoid future disruptions, Norris agreed to a silent partnership with the notorious underworld boxing czar Frankie Carbo and his chief lieutenant, Frank "Blinky" Palermo, thereby gaining access to many of the sport's biggest names. But there was a huge trade-off: With Mob cooperation came loss of control. Everyone in the boxing industry knew the real powers pulling the strings of the IBC operation were Mafia hoodlums Carbo and Palermo. Their association with Norris granted them even more influence to fix fights and buy or muscle their way into the management of top contenders and world champions.

From 1949 to 1953 the IBC monopoly controlled the promotional rights to 36 of 44 championships staged in the United States, including all of the title fights in the very popular heavyweight and middleweight divisions. Carbo's role in the IBC had escalated to the point where he was in complete control.[7]

Competition from other promotional groups was not tolerated, especially if attempts were made to infringe on the TV money pie. Fighters who refused to give up control of their careers to the underworld bosses of the IBC were blacklisted from participation in lucrative television bouts.

On the local level, many independent promoters who operated neighborhood arenas that showcased up-and-coming talent found it impossible to compete with the sheer volume of free televised fights. For decades these venues had functioned as boxing's farm system for developing new talent. Once there were more than 400 fight clubs in the United States. Many had been operating continuously since the early 1920s. The changing times and the advent of televised boxing decimated their ranks. By the late 1950s only a handful were left. Professional boxing has never fully recovered from this devastation of its traditional infrastructure.[8]

It wasn't long before the dwindling supply of boxing talent could no longer keep up with the demands of the ravenous TV schedule. Many promising young fighters, fresh out of the prelim ranks, were rushed into televised main events only to have their careers short-circuited after taking a bad beating from a more-experienced opponent. Some became discouraged and quit; others continued, but were too damaged to ever achieve their full potential.

In 1954 the *New York Times*'s sports columnist Arthur Daley made the following observation: "It seems utterly ironical that there should be more fans and more interest in boxing than ever before in history while there is a shrinkage in sites, competitors, and caliber of performances."[9] Televised boxing, once seen as a savior for the sport, had now become a major force in its destabilization.

With most of the neighborhood fight clubs out of business, many established trainers and managers were finding it increasingly difficult to make a decent living. All but a few left the sport to either retire or find gainful employment elsewhere. Unfortunately, what they took with them was the knowledge and experience accumulated over decades. The loss of this irreplaceable resource created a disconnect in the passing of valuable lessons to a new generation of managers, trainers, and boxers.

The problems facing boxing were of no concern to the hoodlums running the IBC, who were still raking in the TV money. Eventually their brazen behavior caught up to them and brought about the organization's destruction. In 1957 the Justice Department found the IBC in violation of the Sherman Antitrust Act by engaging in a conspiracy to control world-championship boxing matches. Three years later Carbo and Palermo were convicted of extortion and menacing after trying to take control of welterweight champion Don Jordan. Both received lengthy prison terms.

The breakup of the IBC and the jailing of its criminal overlords was welcome news to everyone who had boxing's best interests at heart. But tremendous damage had already been done. The overexposure of televised bouts and the lack of new and exciting stars of equivalent stature to replace the Old Guard had taken a heavy toll on the sport.

In 1962 boxing was down to just one nationally televised show per week. That year welterweight champion Benny "Kid" Paret suffered fatal injuries in a brutal knockout loss to Emile Griffith. The fight was telecast nationally. The tragedy no doubt contributed to the ABC network's decision to cancel its *Fight of the Week* programming two years later. Boxing would not return to network television on a regular basis for another 12 years.

GOING . . . GOING . . . GONE

While all of this was happening, other major sports were moving inexorably forward. Professional basketball, which wasn't even on the radar screen until the creation of the National Basketball Association in the late 1940s, was slowly but surely gaining in popularity. Professional football, barely noticed in previous decades, was about to begin its greatest era. Baseball also grew stronger in the postwar years. The national pastime not only retained its importance in popular culture, but also expanded its franchises to other cities in the 1950s and '60s. Interest in professional hockey and tennis was also accelerating, and within a decade would reach unprecedented levels of popularity.

So while other professional sports reported steady growth in the decades following World War II, boxing took the opposite track by devolving and contracting in four major categories: public interest (number of fans); active participants (boxers); schools and performance sites (gyms and arenas); and qualified mentors (trainers and managers).

In his 1958 autobiography, *50 Years at Ringside*, Nat Fleischer, the esteemed boxing historian and publisher of *The Ring* magazine, observed: "Prior to World War II the difficulty in ranking fighters lay in selecting 10 from an outstanding field of possibly 15 or more prominent performers. Today's headache comes from trying to find a sufficient number of worthies in any division after the first three or four have been listed."[10]

A generation earlier thousands of Jewish boxers from New York, Chicago, Philadelphia, and other major cities had inundated the sport. By the early 1950s the Lower East Side of Manhattan—the neighborhood that had once churned out more outstanding Jewish prizefighters than anywhere else on the planet—was down to its final few holdouts. Joey Varoff, Danny Bartfield, Henry Winchman, Hy Meltzer, Irving Palefsky, Harold (Izzy) Drucker, Leo Center, Artie Diamond, Leo Zipkin, Tony Arnold, and Joey Klein were among the last of a vanishing breed. Demographic changes affecting the Bronx also severely affected that borough's output of Jewish boxers. Among the last of the Bronx battlers were welterweights Harvey and Moe Weiss, identical twins who had interrupted their promising boxing careers to volunteer for service with the Marine Corps during World

The Weiss twins, Harvey (left) and Moe were promising boxers out of the Bronx, New York. Harvey, who survived combat while serving with the Marines in the South Pacific, died of injuries sustained in a bout in April 1946. (Courtesy of Michael P. Capriano)

War II. In a tragic irony, Harvey Weiss survived intense combat in the South Pacific only to die of injuries sustained in a boxing match less than a year after his return to civilian life.

Outside of New York City there was Detroit's Allie Gronik, New Jersey's Johnny Kamber, and an Israeli-born boxer named David Oved. All were solid main-bout boxers but not "top ten" title contenders. Overseas, the East End London boxing scene, a hotbed of activity before the war, was virtually bereft of Jewish boxers.

The last bastion of the Jewish prizefighter in America was Brownsville, Brooklyn—home to the venerable Beecher's Gym. In 1925 the Jewish population of Brownsville and adjacent East New York neighborhood had increased to 285,521, making it the largest concentration of Jewish population in the city, exceeding the Lower East Side's 264,178. Brownsville's inhabitants had left the crowded streets of the East Side in search of cleaner, healthier, and more-spacious living.[11]

Brooklyn had scores of outstanding Jewish boxers in the 1920s and '30s. Many received their undergraduate training at Beecher's Gym. Among its honored alumni were Solly Krieger, Al "Bummy" Davis, Lew Feldman, Joey "Kid" Baker, "Schoolboy" Bernie Friedkin, Herbie Katz, Curley Nichols, Paul Klang, Marty Goldman, Izzy Redman, Lou Schwartz, and Yussel Goldstein.

The mean streets of Brownsville, once home turf for the Jewish troops of gangland's "Murder, Inc." hit squad, were still capable of producing good Jewish prizefighters into the late 1940s. Harold Green, Artie Levine, Herbie Kronowitz, Morris Reif, Georgie Small, and Ruby Kessler headlined at Madison Square Garden. Other postwar main-bout Brooklyn bruisers included Julie Bort, Harry Diduck, Milt Kessler, Davey Feld, George Kaplan, Irwin Kaye Kaplan, Marvin Dick, and Sid Haber.

Beecher's Gym changed ownership several times during the 1950s. It closed in 1962. Within one year boxing had lost three of its most important monuments to the Golden Age of boxing—Stillman's Gym, St. Nick's Arena, and Beecher's Gym. Plans were already in progress to tear down Madison Square Garden III and replace it with another arena 17 blocks south, above the old Pennsylvania Station at 33rd Street and 8th Avenue.

The contenders and champions featured in this section represent the last vestiges of the Golden Age of the Jewish boxer.

Danny Bartfield	Vic Herman	Herbie Kronowitz	Maxie Shapiro
Robert Cohen*	Danny Kapilow	Artie Levine	Georgie Small
Harold Green	Joey Klein	Al Phillips	Allie Stolz
Alphonse Halimi*	Julie Kogon	Morris Reif	

* world champion

DANNY BARTFIELD

Born: January 14, 1920
Died: January 19, 2012 (Age: 92)
Hometown: New York, New York
Height: 5' 8" **Weight:** 135–142 lbs.
Professional Career: 1940–1948

Total Bouts	Won	Lost	Draw
46 (280 rounds)	41 (13 by KO)	5 (1 by KO)	0

Danny Bartfield's uncle was the great Jacob "Soldier" Bartfield, a perennial welterweight contender of the early 1900s. Soldier's nephew did not achieve the heights of his more-famous uncle, but he did manage to land three Madison Square Garden main events in the mid-1940s, and for eight months was rated by *The Ring* magazine among the top 10 lightweight challengers.

Bartfield won 36 of his first 38 pro fights, including two decisions over dangerous fringe contender Morris Reif. He was a good boxer but was plagued by hand injuries throughout his career. Bartfield broke his right hand in a Madison Square Garden bout against the brilliant welterweight Willie Joyce. The injury forced a two-year hiatus to allow his injured mitt to heal. He returned to the ring in 1947 and won five of six fights, losing only to future lightweight champion Paddy DeMarco.

Danny retired in 1948. For many years he was employed as a salesman for a liquor company. In the 1950s and '60s he worked part-time as a referee for professional wrestling matches in New York.

DAVID "MICKEY" MARCUS: A SOLDIER FOR ALL HUMANITY

World War II hero and former West Point intercollegiate boxing champion David Marcus became Israel's general.

The number of Jewish collegians who boxed is small, but one in particular stands out and deserves special mention. David "Mickey" Marcus was born on New York's Lower East Side in 1902, the fifth child of poor Jewish immigrants from Romania. A top student and outstanding athlete while attending Boys High School in Brooklyn, Marcus was accepted to the United States Military Academy at West Point in 1920. In his junior year he joined the West Point boxing team and won the intercollegiate championship. Graduating in 1924 at the top of his class, Marcus was offered a Rhodes Scholarship to Oxford University in England, but he declined the offer in order to be near his fiancée, Emma, whom he was soon to marry.[12]

After fulfilling his army commitment Marcus enrolled in law school, attending classes at night while holding down a full-time job during the day. Later he worked for the US Attorney General's office and the New York City Department of Corrections. In 1940 Mayor Fiorello La Guardia appointed him commissioner of corrections.

When the United States entered World War II Marcus left his job and returned to the army as a lieutenant colonel. His first assignment was commander of the Ranger School in Oahu, Hawaii. In 1943 he was transferred to the European Theater, where he was appointed a divisional judge advocate. He volunteered to join the 101st Airborne Division assault force that parachuted into Normandy on D-Day, despite having no previous training as a paratrooper. His service earned him several major United States and British decorations, including the Bronze Star and Distinguished Service Medal.[13]

Marcus retired from the army in 1947 with the rank of colonel. A few months later he volunteered to help the new state of Israel defend itself against five invading Arab armies intent on annihilating the fledgling country. Marcus served as Prime Minister David Ben-Gurion's personal military advisor during the 1948 Arab-Israeli war. His tireless efforts included training recruits, organizing schools for officers, writing military manuals, and teaching the effective use of various types of armaments. Marcus was appointed the supreme commander of the Jerusalem front and was given the rank of *alluf* (the Hebrew term for "general"), thus becoming the first Jewish general in Israel in two thousand years.[14]

On June 10, 1948, a few hours before the ceasefire was to take effect, Marcus was tragically killed by friendly fire while inspecting the perimeter of his military headquarters in the village of Abu Ghosh. He was buried at West Point with full military honors. His gravestone at West Point reads: "Colonel David Marcus—A Soldier for All Humanity." In 1966 actor Kirk Douglas produced and starred in *Cast a Giant Shadow,* a film based on the life of Mickey Marcus.

ROBERT COHEN

Bantamweight Champion 1954–1956
Born: November 15, 1930
Hometown: Paris, France
Height: 5' 3½" Weight: 118 lbs.
Professional Career: 1951–1956, 1959

Total Bouts	Won	Lost	Draw
43 (355 rounds)	36 (14 by KO)	4 (2 by KO)	3

In 1951, the year **Robert Cohen** became a professional prizefighter, Algeria was home to approximately 140,000 Jews. Robert's father, a barber in the port city of Bone, was an Orthodox Jew who obeyed the biblical commandment to be fruitful and multiply. By the time he finished fulfilling his duty, there were 10 additional Cohens, including Robert, the youngest.

When he was 14 years old, Robert was brought to a local boxing gym by an older brother and immediately became infatuated with the sport. His dedication matched his enthusiasm. Like all Algerian fighters he idolized the great French-Algerian middleweight champion Marcel Cerdan, who won the title from Tony Zale in 1948 and tragically died in a plane crash a year later.

The young fighter studiously copied Cerdan's aggressive infighting style. With hands held high and elbows in close, Robert stepped in behind a hard left jab, slipping past punches to gain the inside position where he would belabor his opponents with combinations to body and head—just like Cerdan. It was a crowd-pleasing style that won the five-foot-three-and-a-half, 118-pound bantam an enthusiastic following.

After he won the Algerian amateur bantamweight championship, Robert moved to Paris and turned pro in 1951. Two years later he won both the French and European bantamweight championships. Among his victims were top-ranking contenders Theo Medina, Jean Sneyers, Henry "Pappy" Gault, and Mario D'Agata.

In keeping with his Orthodox upbringing Robert always found time to pray in the local synagogue and observe the strict dietary laws that required him to eat only kosher food, even when traveling to another country.

On September 19, 1954, in Bangkok's National Stadium, before an audience of 70,000 that included the King and Queen of Thailand, Cohen challenged local hero Chamroen

Songkitrat for the bantamweight championship of the world. Utilizing his greater experience, Cohen hammered out a close 15-round victory.

In 1956 Robert defended his title against Italy's Mario D'Agata at the Stadio Olimpico in Rome. In the sixth round he was cut over his left eye. The referee ruled the cut too severe for him to continue and halted the bout. Mario D'Agata was declared the winner, becoming the first totally deaf person to win a world boxing title.

After the loss of his title Cohen had only one more fight and then retired. He moved to the Belgian Congo where he began working in his father-in-law's textile business. Wanting to keep his hand in boxing, Cohen also opened a gymnasium. When the unstable political situation in the Congo became untenable, Robert and his wife moved to Cape Town, South Africa, where they have lived for the past 50 years.

HAROLD GREEN
Born: October 24, 1924
Died: September 2001 (Age: 76)
Hometown: Brooklyn, New York
Height: 5' 9" Weight: 147–160 lbs.
Professional Career: 1942–1951

Total Bouts	Won	Lost	Draw
88 (573 rounds)	71 (23 by KO)	14 (4 by KO)	3

Harold Green exchanged punches with four world champions, fought nine main events at Madison Square Garden, and was a top-10-rated contender in both the welterweight and middleweight divisions for nearly two years. The only losses he sustained in a career spanning 88 fights were to other world-class pros.

Harold came out of Brooklyn's tough Brownsville neighborhood—home turf of the notorious Murder, Inc. gang, and fertile spawning ground for sluggers like Al "Bummy" Davis, Morris Reif, Georgie Small, and, more recently, Riddick Bowe, Mark Breland, and Mike Tyson. But unlike those power punchers, Green was an accomplished boxer as he proved by outpointing former welterweight champion Fritzie Zivic and future middleweight champion Rocky Graziano, twice.

His third match with Graziano, on September 28, 1945, nearly caused a riot in Madison Square Garden. Green was outboxing Rocky when he caught a right to the jaw in the third round and collapsed face-first to the canvas. As the count reached 10, he suddenly jumped to his feet and began arguing with referee Ruby Goldstein that he'd beaten the count. Goldstein ruled otherwise. Green then tore across the ring to get at Graziano and continue the fight. The 19,000 fans were in an uproar as handlers from both corners tried to keep the fighters apart. Order was finally restored when police entered the ring and escorted both fighters back to their dressing rooms. Green later apologized, but the New York Commission punished him with a year's suspension.

The incident was a rare out-of-control moment for Green, who was usually a calm and collected ring technician. Years later he claimed in an interview with *The Ring* that mobsters had promised him a title shot if he threw the fight. Green told the interviewer that he had changed his mind at the last moment.

Harold returned to Madison Square Garden in 1947 and outpointed middleweight contender Pete Mead. Two months later he was back in the Garden to face future champion Marcel Cerdan, who stopped him in the second round.

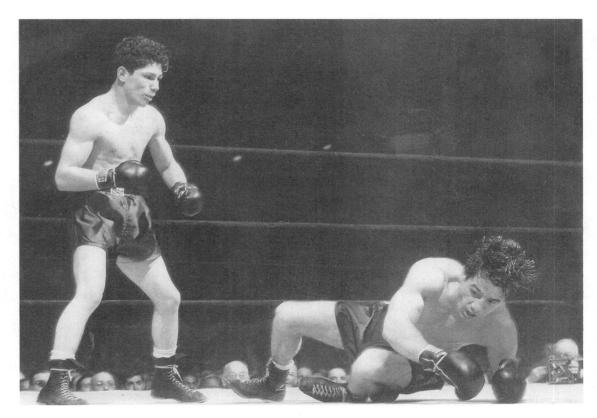

Harold Green scores a knockdown over future middleweight champion Rocky Graziano.

In 1950, nearing the end of his career, Green knocked out 20-year-old Joey Giardello in the sixth round. Their rematch two years later resulted in a 10-round decision for Giardello. Harold retired after that fight. Giardello would eventually win the middleweight title in 1963.

After hanging up his gloves Green opened a marine equipment supply business in Brooklyn.

THE SHANGHAI GHETTO

In 1936 Chaim Weizmann, Zionist leader and statesman (and the future first president of the state of Israel) wrote, "The world seemed to be divided into two parts—those places where Jews could not live and those where they could not enter."[15] The previous year Nazi Germany had passed the infamous Nuremberg Laws that stripped Jews of citizenship, barred them from employment as doctors, lawyers, or journalists, and prohibited them from using state hospitals, public parks, libraries, and beaches. Hitler's annexation of Austria in March 1938 brought an additional 185,000 Jews under Nazi control, and they too were expelled from all cultural, economic, and social life.

Amid the disaster that was unfolding, most of the world's countries had shut their doors to Europe's endangered Jewish population. One of the few places that remained open to Jewish refugees was Shanghai, a Chinese city under Japanese occupation. Between 1936 and 1941 an estimated 20,000 Jews from Germany and Austria found a safe haven in Shanghai. Most lived in the northeastern Hongkou district.

Although the occupation forces were in complete control, they did not molest Shanghai's mixed European and Chinese population. No doubt the presence of the well-established International Settlements in Shanghai, which included many English, French, and American citizens, had prevented the type of mass slaughter by the Japanese military that took place one month later in the then Chinese capital of Nanking.

The Jewish community in Shanghai became remarkably self-sufficient. A variety of social networks were established that included synagogues, newspapers, aid programs, medical services, schools, and cultural activities. American-based Jewish philanthropic organizations, most notably the Joint Distribution Committee (JDC), provided much-needed financial assistance through their representatives in Shanghai.

In a further effort to normalize their lives, the Jews of Shanghai formed athletic clubs. Sport competition was considered vital to the community's well-being. Aside from keeping people occupied, the activities contributed to the health of the community and lifted the spirits of both spectators and participants. There was competition in soccer, boxing, field hockey, table tennis, handball, gymnastics, and chess. Many of the athletes, both men and women, had been members of Jewish sporting clubs during the interwar years in Europe. A good number were also involved with Betar, the militant Zionist organization begun by Ze'ev

Jabotinsky prior to World War II. As such, athletic competition had a political purpose in preparing these young men and women for the fight to establish the Zionist dream of a Jewish homeland.[16]

Jewish boxers in Shanghai were among the city's best. The first refugee matches were organized in July 1939 by Max Buchbaum, a refugee and former German amateur champion. The top refugee boxers were Sam Lewko (Lewkowitz), Eli "Kid" Ruckelstein, and Alfred "Laco" Kohn.[17] Lewko and Ruckelstein were both experienced boxers. Kohn, a teenager, had never boxed, but under Buchbaum's expert coaching, he would eventually develop into a formidable light-heavyweight boxer. (After the war Kohn emigrated to America, and in 1948 won a New York City Golden Gloves championship.)

Sam Lewko had over 100 amateur bouts before coming to Shanghai, and was billed as the Maccabi champion of Berlin. That summer Lewko and Ruckelstein defeated the best of Shanghai's Japanese, French, and American fighters. Jewish boxers trained at the American Marine Club and were very popular with all the nationalities inhabiting Shanghai's International Settlements. Crowds numbering several thousand flocked to the stadium to see up to eight fights per night. Sam Lewko created a sensation when he knocked out a Japanese professional heavyweight brought especially from Tokyo to demonstrate the power of the nation of the conquerors.[18]

The outbreak of war between the United States and Japan after the attack on Pearl Harbor made relief efforts more difficult. Food and medical supplies dwindled. Under pressure from its Nazi ally, the Japanese military governor passed a law confining Hongkou's Jewish population to a "Restricted Area for Stateless Refugees." In early 1943 the Japanese occupiers of Shanghai relocated the 23,000 Jewish immigrants to the poorest section of the city. Unsanitary living conditions and rampant undernourishment in the ghetto took a toll.[19] Hundreds of refugees were at the point of starvation. Others died from typhoid, malaria, and other diseases.

Shanghai was liberated by Chinese forces on September 3, 1945. Over the next four years most of the refugees went to the United States, Israel, and Australia. By 1957 only 100 Jews remained in Shanghai.

Sam Lewko, best of the Shanghai refugee boxers. (Courtesy of Inga Lewkowitz)

ALPHONSE HALIMI

Bantamweight Champion 1957–1959
Born: February 18, 1932
Died: November 12, 2006 (Age: 74)
Hometown: Paris, France
Height: 5' 3" Weight: 118 lbs.
Professional Career: 1955–1964

Total Bouts	Won	Lost	Draw
51 (403 rounds)	42 (21 by KO)	8 (3 by KO)	1

Alphonse Halimi's background was similar to that of bantamweight champion Robert Cohen. Like Cohen, Alphonse was born in Algeria to Orthodox Jewish parents and was the youngest of 13 siblings. Halimi also had a distinguished amateur career. Before turning pro in 1955, he fought 189 amateur bouts and was the French national bantamweight champion three years in a row. He always fought with a Star of David sewn onto his boxing trunks.

Halimi's ascent in the professional ranks was meteoric. He won his first seven fights by knockout, five in the first round. In his 11th pro fight, he won an upset 10-round decision over the highly ranked American contender Billy Peacock.

On April 1, 1957, in Paris, Halimi challenged world bantamweight champion Mario D'Agata. Many fans and sportswriters thought the undefeated challenger was not yet ready to take on the champion. Halimi had only had 18 pro fights.

D'Agata, the only totally deaf person to ever win a world boxing title, had had almost three times as many fights, and had not lost in four years

Halimi upset the odds by outboxing D'Agata and won a unanimous 15-round decision. In less than three years, two Algerian Jewish fighters—Cohen and Halimi—had won the bantamweight championship.

On November 6, 1957, Halimi traveled to Los Angeles for a unification title bout with Raul "Raton" Macias of Mexico. Macias was recognized as champion by the National Boxing Association. New York, Britain, and the European boxing authorities recognized Halimi. The fight, staged in Wrigley Field before 20,000 spectators, went the full 15 rounds. Macias was one of the best bantamweights of the 1950s, but Halimi proved to be just a bit too versatile and ring-wise for the tough Mexican fighter, and won a split decision. The $50,000 purse for Halimi was the largest of his career up to that point. Upon his return to Paris, Halimi was awarded France's *Légion d'honneur* by President Charles de Gaulle.

Over the next 17 months Halimi defeated six opponents in non-title fights. During that time another young Mexican fighter, Jose Becerra, was cutting a swath through the bantamweight division. An explosive puncher, Becerra had knocked out 37 opponents while losing only four of 68 fights. Halimi agreed to defend his title against Becerra on July 8, 1959. The 8–5 odds favored Halimi.

Their fight drew 15,000 fans to the Los Angeles Sports Arena. After seven rounds neither man had established a clear advantage. Two of the judges had the fight even up to that point. Then, midway through the eighth round, Becerra trapped the champion against the ropes and dropped him with a devastating left hook to his jaw. Halimi arose on unsteady legs at the count of four. A barrage of punches sent Halimi to the canvas again, but this time he failed to beat the count.

Seven months later Halimi returned to Los Angeles, hoping to take the crown back from the only fighter to have ever knocked him out. For eight rounds the 32,000 fans in the Los Angeles Memorial Coliseum saw Halimi skillfully outbox Becerra. All three officials had Halimi in the lead. Then the roof caved in. Halimi did not see the left hook that found his jaw in the ninth round. He struggled to get up but was unable to beat the referee's count. It was a dramatic ending to what, up to then, had been a very competitive and interesting fight.

Halimi launched his comeback five months later. He won eight fights in a row, including a 15-round decision over Scotland's Freddie Gilroy for the European bantamweight title. The following year, in London, he lost the title to England's Johnny Caldwell. A rematch with Caldwell produced the same result.

On June 26, 1962, Halimi outpointed Italy's Piero Rollo in 15 rounds to regain the European title. The bout has historic significance because it took place in Tel Aviv. It was the first professional boxing match ever held in the State of Israel.

Halimi retired in 1964. He settled in France, and after briefly managing a cafe in Paris, he was employed as a trainer by the French National Sports Institute. Alphonse was the seventh and last Jewish bantamweight champion, and a worthy successor to Harry Harris, Monte Attell, Abe Goldstein, Charley Phil Rosenberg, Pinky Silverberg, and Robert Cohen.

VIC HERMAN

Born: December 2, 1929
Died: March 7, 2002 (Age: 73)
Hometown: Glasgow, Scotland
Weight: 112–118 lbs.
Professional Career: 1947–1954

Total Bouts	Won	Lost	Draw
57 (404 rounds)	38 (21 by KO)	16 (1 by KO)	3

Vic Herman—boxer, artist, and bagpiper—was born in Manchester, England. While still a toddler his Russian immigrant father, a cabinetmaker, moved the family to Glasgow, Scotland. In his teenage years Vic pursued an amateur boxing career as a member of the Jewish Lads' Brigade, a national Jewish youth organization based in the United Kingdom. Herman's success as an amateur encouraged him to turn pro in 1947. Within a few years he achieved a top-10 rating in both the flyweight and bantamweight divisions. For a time he was ranked the number-two flyweight in the world by *The Ring* magazine. The boxing style of this powerfully built baby bull can best be described as relentlessly aggressive.

In 1951 Herman won a 12-round decision over Norman Tennant for the Scottish Area flyweight title. Five months later he attempted to add the British flyweight title to his laurels, but was outpointed over 15 rounds by London's Terry Allen. Other highly rated opponents included Peter Keenan, Henry Carpenter, Norman Lewis, and Joe Cairney.

In 1953 Herman toured the Far East, where he lost a 10-round decision to bantamweight contender Chamroen Songkitrat in Bangkok, Thailand. Five weeks later, in Tokyo, Japan, flyweight champion Yoshio Shirai knocked him out in the 10th round of a non-title fight. It was his first and only knockout loss in 57 fights.

After two more fights Herman retired and, with his wife and two children, moved to New York's Greenwich Village to devote the rest of his life to his first love—art. Over the next several decades Vic Herman, former world-class boxer, became a world-class artist. His paintings have been exhibited in galleries across America and Europe. But his early years as a struggling artist were very difficult, and eventually cost him his first marriage. After the divorce Vic moved to California, where his artistic career took off, thanks to the millionaire Daniel Solomon, who not only bought his early works but also ensured that around 100 of his paintings were exhibited and sold in American art galleries.[20]

Vic Herman, a renaissance man of many talents, was also an accomplished bagpipe player in his youth and on several occasions had entered the ring for a fight playing the pipes. After he returned to London in the late 1960s, he used the woodworking skills learned from his father to begin another career, as a bagpipe maker, while his services were still in demand as a portrait painter.

DANNY KAPILOW

Born: March 16, 1921
Died: February 26, 2010 (Age: 88)
Hometown: New York, New York
Height: 5' 7½" Weight: 142–150 lbs.
Professional Career: 1941–1948

Total Bouts	Won	Lost	Draw
67 (445 rounds)	48 (16 by KO)	12 (1 by KO)	7

Danny Kapilow waited until after he'd graduated from New York's James Madison High School before making his pro debut on January 7, 1941. Over the next 19 months he compiled an outstanding 29-2-3 record. Six months after America entered World War II Danny joined the US Coast Guard. He managed to squeeze in a few bouts during weekend furloughs, including a 10-round draw with future middleweight champion Rocky Graziano.

Danny was discharged from the Coast Guard in September 1945. One month later, on October 24, 1945, he lost an unpopular 10-round decision to former lightweight champion Sammy Angott. In follow-up bouts he knocked out welterweight contender Gene Burton in the first round, but lost another decision to Angott. Danny came back with an upset 10-round decision over Philadelphia's Wesley Mouzon.

Two weeks after defeating Mouzon, on March 15, 1946, Danny appeared in Madison Square Garden against welterweight contender Willie Joyce, one of the finest boxers of his era. The 10,000 fans were treated to a superb boxing match between two clever exponents of the sweet science. The judges voted the 10-round bout a draw. Kapilow retained his high ranking with subsequent victories over Dorsey Lay and Aaron Perry.

Five months after their first meeting Kapilow fought a return bout with Willie Joyce at Madison Square Garden. Joyce was slightly better and copped the 10-round decision. Seventeen days later Danny was in Griffith Stadium, in Washington, DC, trading punches with former lightweight champion Beau Jack. After ten rounds of nonstop action the judges gave the decision to Beau.

Having fought 60 bouts in 67 months, Kapilow was due for some well-deserved R & R. He took the next six months off. In his return to the ring, on February 18, 1947, he faced future welterweight champion Johnny Bratton in that fighter's hometown of Chicago. The flashy Bratton and the methodically proficient Kapilow delighted the audience in the Chicago Stadium with another example of classic boxing technique. In a fight that resembled a violent chess match Bratton was awarded a split 10-round decision.

In his last bout of 1947 he was outpointed by slick Gene Burton, the same fighter he'd knocked out two years earlier.

Danny considered hanging up his gloves. He was only a month shy of his 27th birthday, and had been lucky so far. Superb boxing skill had kept him from taking a sustained beating in the ring. But his well-connected manager, Al Weill, told him to reconsider, as he could guarantee a good payday if he agreed to take on welterweight champion Sugar Ray Robinson in a non-title bout.

Danny took about one minute to decide. He realized there was no chance that he could defeat the greatest fighter of all time. Also influencing his decision was the fact that he was about to be married. Danny retired and never regretted not fighting a prime Sugar Ray Robinson.

After hanging up his gloves he took a job with the Teamsters Union and eventually became the head of a local chapter. Kapilow was also very involved with veteran boxers' associations. With his lifelong friend, Charley Gellman, an ex-fighter who was the director of two New York City hospitals, care was provided for many former professional fighters suffering from neurological impairment and other physical ailments. Danny was more fortunate than most other ex-pros. He remained sharp and active into his early eighties.

BOXING IN THE DP CAMPS

Following the defeat of Germany in World War II, the homeless, tortured, and starved remnant of European Jewry that survived the slaughter of the Holocaust converged upon makeshift camps designated for "displaced persons" (DPs). The DP camps were administered by the US Army and were located in the American Zone of Occupation in southern Germany. Approximately 12 of these camps housed between 150,000 and 250,000 Jewish refugees. Most of the refugees were forced to remain in the DP camps on the "accursed German soil" for three years, until the doors to the future state of Israel, or the United States, became open to them.

In January 1946 representatives from the DP camps formed a committee to set up self-governing institutions. Financial support and medical care were provided by the United Nations Relief and Rehabilitation Administration (UNRRA), the American Jewish Joint Distribution Committee (JDC), and several other Jewish relief organizations. The goal of the organizers was to revitalize political, religious, and cultural life in the DP camps. As part of the program the Association of Jewish Sports Clubs was created to set up tournaments in soccer, track and field, swimming, basketball, table tennis, volleyball, and boxing. It was hoped that sports could be one of the activities that would aid in the mental and physical recovery of the survivors.

By early 1947 the DP camps had 16,000 young Jewish athletes representing 105 different teams (including 20 teams that refused to engage in sports activities on the Sabbath). Most of the athletes had been members of Jewish sports clubs in their countries of origin before the war.

The various athletic events often drew hundreds—and sometimes thousands—of spectators. Although soccer was the most popular sport, organizers also encouraged participation in boxing. They were of the opinion that boxing might help to prepare young Jews for the impending battle for the future state of Israel. Indeed, many of the DP camp athletes would be at the forefront in the coming struggle to establish a Jewish homeland.[21]

The first championship tournament took place in Munich in January 1947. It included more than 50 Jewish boxers in every weight class. All of the boxers wore the Star of David on their shorts. Over 2000 spectators filled the arena, while hundreds more, unable to gain entry, waited outside. In attendance were many American military officers and officials of the various Jewish agencies. The tournament was filmed, and a Hebrew-language newsreel (with subtitles) of the event exists and can be viewed on the website of the Steven Spielberg Jewish Film Archive.[22]

The moving opening ceremonies had an air of solemnity as the orchestra played "Hatikvah" and the American National Anthem. At the conclusion of the tournament the 16 champions were awarded specially designed silver cups. The runners-up received engraved certificates. As noted by author Phillip Grammes, the championships "meant a kind of return to normality after the long, dark years of the Holocaust."[23]

JOEY KLEIN

Born: January 5, 1933
Hometown: New York, New York
Weight: 147–150 lbs.
Professional Career: 1951–1955, 1957

Total Bouts	Won	Lost	Draw
44 (294 rounds)	24 (5 by KO)	15 (4 by KO)	5

Joey Klein has the distinction of being the last Jewish fighter out of the Lower East Side to appear on network TV. On February 7, 1955, Joey lost a unanimous 10-round decision to welterweight contender Chico Vejar at Brooklyn's Eastern Parkway Arena. The bout was televised over the old Dumont network.

Joey turned pro in January 1951, around the same time televised boxing was inundating the airwaves with fights nearly every night of the week. Within a few years television's demand for new talent began to outrun the supply. Young boxers who showed any promise were rushed into televised main events. Joey had 42 bouts in four years, appearing in televised fights nine times, often against more-experienced opponents. In an earlier era he would have been matched more carefully and taken whatever time was necessary to develop his full potential. Klein scored impressive victories over Gerald Dreyer, Rocky Casillo, Freddie Herman, Vic Cardell, and Pat Manzi, but was outpointed by Tony Pellone, Al Andrews, Jed Black, Carmine Fiore, and Danny Giovanelli. Most were rising stars or experienced veterans.

After his loss to Vejar, Joey took a two-year hiatus from boxing. He returned for two more bouts in 1957 and then retired.

JULIE KOGON

Born: April 4, 1918
Died: December 20, 1986 (Age: 68)
Hometown: New Haven, Connecticut
Height: 5' 7" Weight: 135 lbs.
Professional Career: 1937–1950

Total Bouts	Won	Lost	Draw	NC
142 (1049 rounds)	85 (38 by KO)	38 (1 by KO)	18	1

Julie Kogon (sometimes spelled Kogan) was a classic stand-up boxer with a style reminiscent of the great Benny Leonard. He also possessed a solid chin (only one KO loss in 142 bouts) and sufficient power to flatten 38 opponents. Throughout his career Julie proudly wore the Star of David on his trunks, with his initials "J.K." imprinted above the star.

Before turning pro in 1937 Julie had compiled an outstanding 85-2 amateur record. Both Julie and his twin brother Harry were among the top amatuer boxers in Connecticut.

Julie was undefeated in his first 27 professional bouts. He quickly developed an enthusiastic fan base in his home state, appearing in New Haven rings 70 times, often in front of sold-out audiences. Julie won the New England lightweight championship in 1947, but never fought for the world title. Among his 142 opponents were five world champions: Petey Scalzo, Willie Pep, Bob Montgomery, Ike Williams, and Jimmy Carter. Julie defeated Scalzo but lost to the other four great fighters.

It is a testament to his fine defensive skills that despite an intense schedule, Kogon's face was virtually unmarked. On those rare occassions when he was tagged Julie proved he could take a solid punch. The only knockout loss on his record—to future lightweight champion Jimmy Carter—occurred near the end of his career, in his 133rd professional fight.

Shortly before he retired Julie purchased a luncheonette in New Haven which he operated successfully for many years. After selling the luncheonette Julie worked as a salesman for a Ford dealership. The personable ex-fighter also coached for the Yale University Intramural Boxing program. In 2009 he was elected to the Connecticut Boxing Hall of Fame.

HERBIE KRONOWITZ

(Ted Kronowitz)
Born: September 23, 1923
Died: November 9, 2012 (Age: 89)
Hometown: Brooklyn, New York
Height: 5' 10" Weight: 160 lbs.
Professional Career: 1940–1942, 1946–1950

Total Bouts	Won	Lost	Draw
83 (551 rounds)	55 (10 by KO)	23 (2 by KO)	5

Herbie Kronowitz's real first name is Ted. At the age of 17 he was too young to turn pro, so he borrowed his older brother Herbert's birth certificate to obtain a professional boxing license. He managed to squeeze in 40 bouts over the next two and a half years before joining the US Coast Guard in 1943. A year later he was about to be transferred overseas for duty aboard a Coast Guard cutter when he received word that his brother Albert had been killed in the Battle of the Bulge. Since his other brother was serving with the army in the Pacific, Herbie was ordered stateside for the remainder of the war.

Kronowitz resumed his career in May of 1946, and over the next 22 months won ten of 11 bouts. He preferred to box at long range and utilize his fine left jab and mobile footwork to outmaneuver opponents, but if the situation called for it, he was more than willing to mix it up on the inside. Among the quality fighters listed on his record are Artie Levine, Harold Green, Pete Mead, Joey De John, Rocky Castellani, Laverne Roach, Sonny Horne, Lee Sala, and Johnny Greco. Most of his losses were by split decision to good fighters. *The Ring* magazine ranked him number nine among the world's top 10 middleweights for two months in 1947. That was no small accomplishment back when the middleweight ratings included the likes of Tony Zale, Jake LaMotta, Charley Burley, Bert Lytell, Marcel Cerdan, Steve Belloise, Rocky Graziano, and Artie Levine.

On March 7, 1947, Kronowitz fought Artie Levine in the last Madison Square Garden main event between two Jewish boxers. After 10 furious rounds Levine won a close but unanimous decision that was roundly booed by the crowd of 12,000 fans.

Three months later Herbie decisioned Harold Green for the "middleweight championship of Brooklyn." The bout attracted 15,000 fans to Ebbets Field.

After hanging up his gloves in 1950, Herbie purchased two New York City taxi medallions. Countless times passengers would recognize his name on the license placard and ask if he was the same person they had seen fight.

The former contender never strayed far from his boxing roots. He became an active member of the Veteran Boxers' Association and was a licensed referee on the staff of the New York State Athletic Commission from 1955 to 1984. Light on his feet, Herbie seemed to glide around the ring, a reminder of the excellent footwork of his ring days.

He always put the safety of the boxers first, and was respected for his competence and impartiality.

Reflecting on the positive aspects of his boxing career Kronowitz told an interviewer: "The thing about boxing is that it gave every one of us everything we have. I don't mean just money. It taught us how to live, how to act, how to eat, how to be physically fit. It opened doors to places that we never could have gotten into. Some made more money than others, but every boxer looks at his career as the most important experience in his life."[24]

ARTIE LEVINE

Born: January 25, 1925
Died: January 13, 2012 (Age: 86)
Hometown: Brooklyn, New York
Height: 5' 8" **Weight:** 160–170 lbs.
Professional Career: 1941–1949

Total Bouts	Won	Lost	Draw
72 (437 rounds)	52 (36 by KO)	15 (4 by KO)	5

"I knew about **Artie Levine**," said the former welterweight and middleweight champion Sugar Ray Robinson. "Six weeks before I outpointed Tommy Bell for the title I boxed Levine in Cleveland. He clipped me with a left hook to the jaw that flopped me like a fish in the fifth round, or so I've been told."[25] That quote appeared in Sugar

Ray Robinson's 1970 biography. The great fighter staggered to his feet at the count of nine. He fought on pure instinct for the next two rounds. Robinson did not fully recover his senses until the eighth round. The terrific battle ended when Robinson, fighting desperately, knocked Levine out with only 19 seconds left in the 10th round.

THE HARRY HAFT STORY

During World War II the average life span of a prisoner in a Nazi slave labor camp was measured in weeks. Inmates succumbed to disease, starvation, hard labor, and the brutality of the guards. In 1943, Harry (Herschel) Haft, an 18 year-old Polish Jew, was imprisoned at the Jaworzno slave labor camp in Poland. Jaworzno was one of the many sub-camps of Auschwitz providing forced labor for the German war industry. Before his arrival in Jaworzno Harry had been interned at four other slave labor camps where he was beaten and starved, yet the Germans could not destroy his will to survive.

Haft was among a group of prisoners forced to fight other Jewish inmates in bare-knuckle brawls for the perverse entertainment of SS officers who placed bets. The bouts ended when one man could no longer stand on his feet. Harry fought 75 bare-knuckle fights to a finish. At the end of every match he was the only one left standing.

With the approach of the Soviet Army, the Germans evacuated the camp at Jaworzno and fled westward, taking the camp's prisoners with them. The death march back to Germany lasted for weeks. Of the several thousand Jews who left Jaworzno, only about 200 men made it to a train station where the soldiers loaded them into a single boxcar. Several days later the train arrived in Germany. When the doors were opened, only 30 men were still alive.

Harry and a friend made a break and dashed into the forest, hoping to escape. The guards opened up with machine guns. His friend was hit and fell forward into a ditch. Harry jumped in beside him. As guards approached the ditch, he heard one tell the other, "Don't waste any more bullets; they're already dead."

Haft waited until he was sure the guards had left before crawling out of the ditch. Wandering in the Bohemian forest, he saw an SS uniform hanging on a branch. A German soldier was bathing in a river. His handgun and rifle lay between the boots. Harry grabbed the rifle, aimed and fired. The shot missed and the soldier came running toward him. Harry reached for the handgun and emptied the contents of the chamber into his target. Blind with rage, he then battered the dead man's skull with the butt of the rifle.

Harry removed his bloody clothing and put on the uniform, which hung loosely on his 110-pound frame. Later he approached a farmhouse where an

Harry Haft. (Courtesy of Alan Scott Haft)

elderly German couple, thinking he was a German soldier, allowed him into their home and gave him food, but the husband became suspicious and kept badgering him with questions. Fearing they had seen through his disguise, Harry drew his weapon and shot them both. He continued hiding in the forest until the war's end.

In 1945 he joined other Jewish survivors in a Displaced Persons (DP) camp run by the US Army. There he made contact with relatives who told him what they knew about his family's fate. Two brothers had vanished and were believed to have been killed while fighting with partisans. A third brother was drafted into the Russian army and had risen to the rank of colonel, but was killed in the Battle of Berlin. Harry's mother and his two sisters were murdered in the Treblinka death camp.

In an effort to help rehabilitate the survivors, various programs were arranged at the DP camp. One of the activities organized by the American servicemen was a Jewish boxing championship. By the time Harry decided to enter the tournament in January 1947, he had put on 50 pounds and resembled the strapping youth he was before his nightmare began. Harry won the Amateur Jewish Heavyweight Championship and was named the outstanding boxer in the tournament. He was awarded a trophy by an American general.

In 1948 Harry emigrated to the United States, where he was taken in by an uncle. He then embarked on a brief professional boxing career that included bouts with unbeaten Roland LaStarza and future heavyweight champion Rocky Marciano. Harry retired after losing to Marciano on a third-round TKO. His professional record was 13-8, with 8 knockouts.

Harry eventually married and raised a family, but he was haunted by his wartime experiences for the rest of his life. When asked why he chose to become a professional boxer after all the physical abuse and torture he had endured in the concentration camps, he would answer, "After all I have been through, what harm could a man with gloves on his hands do to me?"

Harry's son, Alan Haft, authored a riveting biography of his father's life, entitled *Harry Haft: Survivor of Auschwitz, Challenger of Rocky Marciano.*[26]

Robinson often said that Artie Levine hit him with the hardest punch of his 202-bout career. In 2000 the *Cleveland Plain Dealer* named the Robinson vs. Levine fight the most exciting in the city's history.

Levine's 50 percent KO ratio was among the highest in the middleweight division. But he wasn't just a slugger. He was also an excellent boxer, which made him even more dangerous. Artie was always looking to create an opening for his murderous left hook.

In the late 1940s Levine earned a top-10 rating in both the middleweight and light-heavyweight divisions. His best wins were over Sonny Horne, Jimmy Doyle, Vic Dellicurti, Billy Walker, and Herbie Kronowitz. All except Kronowitz were KO victims.

Artie retired in 1949 following consecutive losses to Chuck Hunter and Dick Wagner. He was only 24. Artie had become dissillusioned with boxing. He felt abused and disgusted by the criminal element that had taken over management of his career. He wisely decided it was time to hang up his gloves. Always smart and ambitious, Artie became a successful sales manager at one of the largest car dealerships in the country.

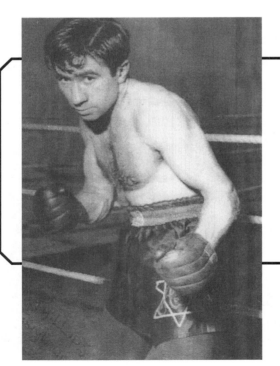

AL PHILLIPS

"The Aldgate Tiger"
Born: January 25, 1920
Died: February 7, 1999 (Age: 79)
Hometown: London, England
Height: 5' 4½" Weight: 125 pounds
Professional Career: 1939–1951

Total Bouts	Won	Lost	Draw
90 (600 rounds)	73 (33 by KO)	14 (3 by KO)	3

For 44 months, between 1943 and 1951, London's **Al Phillips** was rated among the top 10 featherweight contenders by *The Ring* magazine. As his nickname "The Aldgate Tiger" implied, Phillips was an all-action, two-fisted pressure fighter with a hefty wallop. Slick stylists gave him the most trouble. Liverpool's great master boxer Nel Tarleton was one such opponent. Tarleton survived some rough moments to outpoint Phillips in a bout for the British Empire featherweight title in 1945.

Over the next two years Phillips won 14 of 16 bouts, culminating with a 15-round decision over Cliff Anderson for the vacant Empire and British featherweight titles. Six weeks later, on May 27, 1947, he added the European featherweight championship to his collection after his opponent, Ray Famechon, was disqualified in the eighth round. Just one month later he lost all three titles when outpointed by Ronnie Clayton over 15 rounds.

In the final months of his career Phillips outpointed Clayton in a non-title 10-rounder, but lost the 15-round rubber match.

After he retired Phillips became a successful matchmaker and promoter in England.

MORRIS REIF

Born: February 16, 1923
Died: December 2013 (Age: 90)
Hometown: Brooklyn, New York
Height: 5' 7" Weight: 145 lbs.
Professional Career: 1940–1950

Total Bouts	Won	Lost	Draw
64 (293 rounds)	51 (34 by KO)	12 (6 by KO)	1

Morris Reif turned pro in 1940 and won his first 18 bouts, 11 by knockout. In his next bout he took on 61-bout veteran Mickey Farber and was stopped in the seventh round. Over the next three years Reif acquired experience to go along with his powerful punch. Interestingly, he lost his first two Madision Square Garden main events to Jewish boxers Danny Bartfield and Harold Green. Both outpointed Reif in hard-fought battles. Next up was Willie Joyce, one of the finest boxers to never win a title. Once again Morris failed to land his big left hook and lost the decision.

The Garden's promoters decided at this point to match Reif with someone he would not have to chase. On January 4, 1946, Reif went head-to-head with the great former lightweight champion Beau Jack, a tireless swarmer who threw 10 punches for every one thrown by an opponent. The 15,000 fans in attendance expected a great

BOXING IN ISRAEL

Sports have always been an important part of Israeli society, even in pre-state days. Soccer, and later basketball, became the two most popular sports. For the young pioneers participation in sports was considered more than just a recreational activity. As Hebrew University professor Anat Helman observes, "Zionists sought to replace the 'old Jew' of the diaspora—a stock figure in Israeli discourse, depicted as passive, cowardly, sickly and weak—with the antithetical 'new Jew' who was active, brave, healthy and strong. . . . Sports was regarded in the *Yishuv* [Jewish communities in pre-state Israel] as one of the instruments for creating this new Jew and imparting discipline for future military service."[27]

Although the country's athletic achievements do not match its remarkable accomplishments in technology and medical research, Israel has managed to produce its share of world-class athletes. Israeli athletes have won seven medals in the Olympic Games—in judo, canoeing, and windsurfing. The Maccabi Tel Aviv basketball team has won the European Championship six times since 1977. Other Israelis have won international competitions in figure skating, gymnastics, wrestling, fencing, and track and field. Despite ongoing political problems a growing number of Israeli-Arab athletes have joined sports teams, including at least five players on the Israeli national soccer team.

The various athletic associations received a big boost in 1989 when Russian premier Mikhail Gorbachev allowed Jews to leave the Soviet Union and emigrate to a country of their choice. Over the next seven years close to one million former citizens of the Soviet Union came to Israel. Among the immigrants were many highly trained athletes and coaches from various sports who brought their knowledge and culture of athleticism with them. It was during this time that a number of boxing gyms sprang up in Tel Aviv, Haifa, and Ashkelon. Today the Israel Boxing Association, the organization that supervises amateur boxing tournaments, has about 2000 registered members. (By contrast, the Israel Football [soccer] Association represents some 30,000 soccer players.)

In recent years the two most successful Israeli boxers have been Yuri Foreman and Ron Nakash. Foreman, a junior middleweight, was born in Russia, grew up in Israel, and now makes his home in New York City. The former Golden Gloves champion won a professional title in 2010 but lost it the following year. Nakash, a 200-pound cruiserweight, has compiled a 26-1 record, with 18 knockouts. He turned pro at the age of twenty-seven, a late start for a boxer. He is chief commander and head instructor of the Israel Defense Forces' Krav Maga Instructional Division.

The Israel Boxing Association's general director, Dr. William Shihada, is making a noble attempt to use the amateur boxing program to build bridges between young Arabs and Jews in Israel. Jews and Israeli Arabs train and spar with each other in the same gyms. "In 20 years of my experience in running Israel's boxing league, I have never seen any ethnic, racial, or religious tension among our kids," says Dr. Shihada "Education for coexistence is at least as important, if not more important, than training fighters, as far as we're concerned. For me promoting coexistence is the most important thing."[28] Most of the IBA's members in Dr. Shihada's program are teens and young adults (both male and female). Not surprisingly, the boxers come from the poorest segments of Israeli society, with about 70 percent coming from Arab villages, and the rest from inner-city neighborhoods populated by Russian and Ethiopian Jewish immigrants. All of the boxers are Israeli citizens.

fight. They were not disappointed. The *New York Times* called it "one of the most exciting battles of recent years in New York."[29] In the fourth round, in the midst of a hot exchange, Beau landed a right uppercut under Reif's heart that put the Brownsville slugger on the canvas for the 10-count.

Following his loss to Beau Jack, Reif won his next seven fights, six by knockout. In his last attempt at breaking into the ratings, he fought future welterweight champion Johnny Bratton at the Chicago Stadium on January 24, 1947. Bratton, too quick and skillful, won a unanimous 10-round decision.

Reif's explosive left hook flattened 34 opponents, but more than punching power was necessary to get past the top welterweight contenders of the mid- to late-1940s. Like his famous Brownsville stablemate, Al "Bummy" Davis, Reif relied too much on his punch and less on boxing technique to achieve victory. Nevertheless, he was a feared puncher and a force to be reckoned with in the talent-laden welterweight division.

After he retired Morris worked as a house painter, and then took a job as a truck driver for the airlines. In the early 1970s he relocated his wife and three children to Los Angeles, where he worked in a youth center teaching boxing.

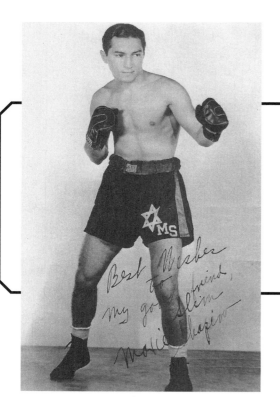

MAXIE SHAPIRO

Born: April 12, 1913
Died: November 22, 1997 (Age: 84)
Hometown: New York, New York
Height: 5' 6½" **Weight:** 135 lbs.
Professional Career: 1938–1948, 1951

Total Bouts	Won	Lost	Draw
125 (908 rounds)	88 (26 by KO)	30 (6 by KO)	7

Maxie Shapiro was the last great Jewish lightweight to come out of New York City's Lower East Side neighborhood. Bobbing like a cork in a stormy ocean, Maxie ducked and slipped punches with remarkable ease and countered with an array of combination punches. Except for a broken nose his face was unmarked, despite having engaged in 125 professional fights.

A GOLDEN AGE FOR BOXING MOVIES

Six of the greatest boxing movies ever made were produced between 1942 and 1956: *Gentleman Jim, Body and Soul, Champion, The Set-Up, The Harder They Fall,* and *Somebody Up There Likes Me*. Jewish actors John Garfield (*Body and Soul*) and Kirk Douglas (*Champion*) received Academy Award nominations. Six years before it was made into a movie, Rod Serling's *Requiem for a Heavyweight* debuted as a live TV production on the *Playhouse 90* series of great dramas. Former boxer Jack Palance starred as the fictionalized broken-down ex-pug, Mountain McClintock. The 1962 movie version starred Anthony Quinn, in an equally impressive performance. (In deference to Quinn's Mexican-American heritage, the main character's name was changed to Mountain Rivera. Jackie Gleason and Mickey Rooney costarred.)

Of the films mentioned above, only *Body and Soul* (1947) clearly identified the lead character as Jewish. Garfield portrays the fictional Charlie Davis, a boxer from the Lower East Side of New York, who fights his way out of poverty to become middleweight champion of the world. His ethnicity is revealed in a scene in which his widowed mother (Anne Revere) applies for welfare benefits. The interviewer asks her religion and she replies, "Jewish." In a key scene later in the film, Shimon, the local grocer, speaking with an unmistakable Yiddish accent, tells Mrs. Davis, "Over in Europe the Nazis are killing people like us just because of their religion, but here Charlie Davis is a champion." It is one of the first references in a Hollywood film to the Holocaust.

Abraham Polonsky, who wrote the screenplay for *Body and Soul*, would later become a victim of the McCarthy-era Hollywood blacklist, as would John Garfield (born Jacob Julius Garfinkle).

The main character of the 1947 movie *Body and Soul* was a Jewish boxer from the Lower East Side.

Shapiro had a late start in boxing. After two years in the amateurs he turned pro in 1938 at the age of 25, and won his first 37 bouts before dropping a close decision to Al Reid. Four months later he outpointed Reid in a return match. After losing a split 10-round decision to future featherweight champion Jackie Wilson at the Baltimore Arena, Maxie won six in a row, including impressive wins over contenders Everett Rightmire and former featherweight champion Leo Rodak. Rodak was one of five past or future world champions Shapiro defeated. The others were Bob Montgomery, Jackie Callura, Sal Bartolo, and Phil Terranova.

On September 19, 1941, at Madison Square Garden, Maxie faced the great Sugar Ray Robinson. Even at that early stage of his career, Robinson, with only 23 fights on his professional résumé (to Maxie's 58), was considered an extraordinary talent. Robinson at five-foot-11 was nearly five inches taller than Shapiro.

For two rounds Shapiro was competitive with Robinson. But after landing a hard right cross to Robinson's jaw in the second round, it was all downhill. Sugar Ray's almost super-human athleticism combined with his tremendous punching power overwhelmed Maxie. Referee Arthur Donovan stopped the bout in the third round after Shapiro had been floored four times.

One year after the Robinson fiasco Maxie scored the biggest victory of his career with a decisive 10-round drubbing of future lightweight king Bob Montgomery in the latter's hometown of Philadelphia. Their return bout two months later, also in Philadelphia, saw Montgomery win a close 10-round decision.

Maxie Shapiro is one of only three boxers to have fought both Sugar Ray Robinson and Henry Armstrong, two of the greatest fighters who ever lived. Armstrong, past his prime and in the midst of an ill-advised comeback, took him out in seven rounds, but the authenticity of that knockout remains questionable.

Shapiro was in and out of the lightweight ratings for about five years but never received a title shot. He retired in 1948, returning for one more bout in 1951 before hanging up his gloves.

MAKE MINE A MOGEN DAVID!

In the early 1950s, as televised boxing saturated the airwaves, manufacturers of products aimed at male consumers, such as beer, automobiles, cigars, and razor blades, all clambered to get on board the TV bandwagon and advertise their products to millions of potential customers.

In 1952 the Mogen David wine company became a sponsor of the Dumont Network's *Fight of the Week* series broadcast from Brooklyn's Eastern Parkway Arena. (*Mogen David*, Hebrew for "Shield of David," refers to the six-pointed Star of David.) The company manufactured kosher wines and hoped to appeal to a broader audience beyond its Jewish clientele, which may explain the reason the word "kosher" is never uttered by the velvet-voiced actor describing the wine's virtues during the live commercials aired between rounds.

> *Remember the good old days when this time of the year was the signal for a good healthy dose of Grandma's homemade spring tonic? That's the kind of memory that really takes you back through the years. . . . Mogen David wine is a real taste of those good old days, rich with the same sweet Concord grape flavor of long ago [sips]. You know, even the warm ruby-red glow of Mogen David wine gleaming in the glass or your decanter seems to speak of a pleasant, peaceful world of yesterday. And Mogen David appeals to so many folks that it's the biggest-selling wine of its kind in the world.* [Translation: biggest-selling *kosher* wine of its kind in the world.]
>
> *Mogen David wine is always in good taste, whether your party's a church social, card game, formal dinner, or an old-fashioned family get-together [sips]. This spring treat yourself to a memory. Enjoy the home-sweet-home wine like Grandma used to make.*[30]

Although it's doubtful that many church socials featured Mogen David kosher wine, the salesman's pitch is indicative of boxing's large and eclectic audience—Jewish and non-Jewish alike—during the golden age of televised boxing.

GEORGIE SMALL

Born: June 30, 1926
Died: October 31, 1999 (Age: 73)
Hometown: Brooklyn, New York
Height: 5' 8" **Weight:** 160 lbs.
Professional Career: 1945–1952, 1954–1955

Total Bouts	Won	Lost	Draw
58 (363 rounds)	44 (20 by KO)	13 (2 by KO)	1

Hard-luck **Georgie Small**, a fearless two-fisted puncher out of Brownsville, Brooklyn, was a rising star in the middleweight division until a tragic event changed everything.

On February 22, 1950, Georgie and Lavern Roach were scheduled for a 10-round main event at the St. Nicholas Arena in Manhattan. Roach, a World War II US Marine veteran with movie-star looks, was on the comeback trail. Two years earlier he'd been overmatched in a bout with the great French middleweight, Marcel Cerdan. Roach was knocked down eight times in eight rounds before the bout was mercifully stopped.

After a brief retirement, the 24-year-old Texan resumed his career and won three bouts against minor opposition, bringing his record to 27-4 (11 by KO). Georgie Small's record showed only six losses in 44 bouts (17 by KO). The 6–5 odds favored Roach.

Both fighters had previously worked out in the same gym and became friendly. But boxing is a business, and friendship or not, the match was made.

Roach, as expected, was the superior boxer, and was ahead in the scoring going into the 10th round. About halfway into the round Small landed a hard right to Roach's chin that floored the Texan. He arose on unsteady legs and was promptly knocked down by another right. The referee ended the bout at this point. Roach got up but collapsed a few seconds later and was carried out of the ring on a stretcher. He was rushed to a nearby hospital but never regained consciousness, and died the following day.

Small was devastated by the tragedy, but decided to continue with his career. Three months later he appeared in a televised Madison Square Garden main event against future welterweight champion Kid Gavilan. The great Cuban fighter administered a savage beating and won a unanimous 10-round decision. Small seemed tense throughout the bout and was unable to launch a sustained attack, as if fearing he might injure Gavilan.

Contemplating retirement, Small did not fight again for another year. When he came back the results were mixed. Often, when he had an opponent in trouble, he would hold back. The memory of his bout with Roach was stifling his natural aggressiveness. Nearing the end of his troubled career Small lost decisions to middleweight contender Pierre Langlois and future champion Joey Giardello. In his final fight he was stopped by Argentina's Eduardo Lausse, one of the division's hardest punchers.

Fifteen years after his tragic fight with Roach, Small told journalist Jimmy Breslin that he was still tormented by guilt over the death of his friend.

Not yet 50, Small began to experience memory and balance problems related to the punishment he took in the ring, making him unable to hold a job that could support his wife and young son. He ended his days in an adult-care facility in Arizona, where he passed away at the age of 73.

ALLIE STOLZ

Born: September 2, 1918
Died: September 4, 2000 (Age: 82)
Hometown: Newark, New Jersey
Height: 5' 6½" Weight: 135 lbs.
Professional Career: 1937–1946

Total Bouts	Won	Lost	Draw
75 (521 rounds)	63 (KO 21)	10 (KO 4)	2

From the age of 10 **Allie Stolz** had a burning desire to become a professional boxer and emulate his idols, former lightweight champions Benny Leonard and Al Singer. He devoted the next 18 years of his life to accomplishing that goal.

On the night of May 15, 1942, at Madison Square Garden, 23-year-old Allie Stolz appeared to have realized his lifelong dream. After flooring lightweight champion Sammy Angott for a nine-count in the third round, Allie controlled the pace of the fight while consistently peppering Angott with his accurate jabs and well-timed counterpunches. Angott fought back stubbornly, but it was obvious to the 16,000 fans in attendance, and the sportswriters sitting at ringside, that on this night Allie was the superior boxer.

When the decision was given to Angott the crowd was stunned. The referee had scored for Stolz but was outvoted by the two judges. Rumors spread quickly that the decision was

Allie Stolz (left) in title fight with lightweight champion Sammy Angott. Allie's refusal to accept Mob management cost him the championship. (AP Photo)

fixed and that both judges had been bribed by organized-crime figures after Stolz had refused to drop his manager and replace him with a Mob-controlled flunky.

Stolz, a slight underdog going into the fight, was crushed by the defeat. He would obsess about the injustice for the rest of his life.

In his campaign for a return bout with Angott, Stolz defeated featherweight champion Chalky Wright (non-title) and third-ranked lightweight contender Willie Joyce. He was subsequently outpointed by Chalky's successor, the great Willie Pep, and was stopped by future champions Beau Jack and Tippy Larkin. Stolz won 10 of his

next 11 fights (his only loss by split decision to Willie Joyce), thereby earning another shot at the lightweight championship.

Sammy Angott had since relinquished the title to campaign as a welterweight. This time Allie's opponent was the famed "Philadelphia Bobcat," Bob Montgomery. They fought before 11,000 fans at Madison Square Garden on June 28, 1946.

Fighting in his 75th pro bout (the last of his career), Allie displayed flashes of his old brilliance, but it was not enough. In a bout the *New York Times* called "one of the greatest lightweight battles," the game challenger was floored six times, and finally counted out in the 13th round.

THE PIANO MAN PACKS A PUNCH

The proliferation of televised boxing ensured that the sport would continue to maintain its position in American popular culture throughout the 1950s. Training in a neighborhood gym or sparring with friends was still a rite of passage for many Jewish boys. In 1951, 16 year-old Allen Konigsberg, a resident of Brooklyn, was one of those young men. Konigsberg was a good athlete who enjoyed baseball, basketball, and boxing. He was intent on entering the New York City Golden Gloves tournament. Allen began training at a local gym under the watchful eye of a coach, but the aspiring boxer's dreams were dashed when his mother found out about his secret ambition. She refused to sign the release form, abruptly terminating his nascent boxing ambitions. The young man later gained fame as a world-renowned comedian and filmmaker under the name Woody Allen.[31]

Legendary comedian Jackie Mason claimed to have fought professionally, although it's more than likely Jackie mined that fantasy for its comic value. "You know, in a fight I might go down," says Jackie, "but one thing about me . . . I don't get up. Why should I get up? I get up again, he hits me again . . . then I'm down again . . . what, do I have to make three trips to the same place? I figured I'm not that busy, I'll lay around a while. I noticed another thing . . . while I was lying there he wasn't hitting me. I figure if I could have come in lying down I never would have had this whole problem."[32]

Perhaps the most successful American Jewish performer of recent vintage with an authentic boxing background is singer, pianist, and composer Billy Joel. Growing up on Long Island, New York, Joel became interested in boxing and joined a local gym at the age of 16. Over the next three years he won 22 of 26 amateur bouts, including a Golden Gloves competition. Two of his losses were by decision and two by knockout. "I think about it now and I must have been out of my mind," said Billy. "But I really enjoyed it while I was doing it."[33]

Billy never intended to take his interest in boxing beyond the amateur stage. "Being able to defend myself gave me a certain level of self-confidence, but I was never a violent guy. . . . Boxing got me in the best shape of my life, and it required much the same discipline as piano playing—you have to put in the work. But I also think you have to have a killer instinct to excel at it, and I didn't have that. I just wanted to take care of myself.

"I can't even watch the sport anymore. I used to be a boxing fan, and now I can't stand the violence of it. Because I know what it feels like to get hit. But I also know what it takes to get back up."[34]

CHAPTER 6

NOT YOUR GRANDFATHER'S SPORT: BOXING FROM THE 1960S TO THE PRESENT

I don't have to be what you want me to be. I'm free to be who I want.

—CASSIUS CLAY, AFTER WINNING THE HEAVYWEIGHT TITLE FROM SONNY LISTON IN 1964

If a great heavyweight champion is symbolic of his era—as Sullivan, Corbett, Jeffries, Johnson, Dempsey, Louis, and Marciano were of theirs—then Muhammad Ali was the perfect representative of the turbulent 1960s. Ali was boxing's equivalent of the Beatles, the phenomenal British rock band that arrived on the scene at the same time. The presence of both was a harbinger of seismic cultural changes that went beyond music and sports. When Cassius Clay (soon to change his name to Muhammad Ali) took the heavyweight championship from Sonny Liston in February 1964, it signaled the dawn of a new era for boxing—the Muhammad Ali era. The heavyweight championship was still the most important title in the world of sports, so when Ali spoke, people paid attention.

Outside of the ring, the brash and confident champion announced that he was aligned with the controversial black separatist organization known as "The Nation of Islam." When he refused induction into the army in 1967, citing his opposition to the Vietnam War, he became even more of a polarizing figure. Ali claimed conscientious-objector status based on his religion. The federal government was not convinced. He was convicted of draft evasion and sentenced to five years in prison. Ali was free on bail while his case was appealed, but state boxing commissions would not allow him into the ring for the next three and a half years. In June 1971 the Supreme Court overturned his conviction.

Before his enforced layoff Ali's magnificent athleticism and boxing skills enabled him to "float like a butterfly and sting like a bee" as he defeated one challenger after another. But he was not the only boxer grabbing all the headlines—at least not on the sports pages. In addition to

Ali the 1960s saw an entirely new crop of boxing stars dominate the sport, most of whom were either black or Latino. Joe Frazier, Bob Foster, Dick Tiger, Jose Napoles, Emile Griffith, Luis Rodriguez, Carlos Ortiz, Nocolino Loche, Antonio Cervantes, and Eder Jofre were among a score of outstanding boxers who could have held their own with the best of any previous era. The same could be said of 1970s stars Roberto Duran, Rubin Olivares, Sugar Ray Leonard, Thomas Hearns, Aaron Pryor, Alexis Arguello, Carlos Monzon, Marvin Hagler, Rodrigo Valdez, and Larry Holmes.

The decades that followed were not devoid of great boxers, but their numbers were steadily reduced to a mere handful when compared to the depth of talent and greatness that was the hallmark of the Golden Age. It was during this time that New York City and Madison Square Garden lost their preeminent positions, and the gambling hot spots of Las Vegas and Atlantic City became the sport's central venues for championship contests.

Those fans hoping for a Jewish world champion would not have much to cheer about until Mike Rossman and Saoul Mamby battled their way to the top in the late 1970s.

Rossman, whose real last name is DePiano, is the son of an Italian Catholic father and a Jewish mother. His father suggested he use his mother's maiden name to attract Jewish fans.

Mike had a pleasing and technically proficient boxer-puncher style that featured excellent footwork, intelligent use of the left jab, counterpunching skills, and knockout power in his right fist. His greatest triumph was winning the light-heavyweight title in 1978 with a stunning 13th-round TKO upset of Argentina's formidable Victor Galindez. In conquering Galindez, Rossman defeated one of the best light heavyweights of the past 50 years. Rossman was also the first Jewish-American boxer in 40 years to win a world boxing title. But his tenure as champion was short-lived. Seven months later Galindez stopped him in the ninth round to regain the title. Rossman retired in 1983 with a 44-7-3 (27 KOs) record.

Saoul Mamby is the son of a mother of Spanish descent who converted to Judaism. His father is from the Caribbean Island of Jamaica. Saoul became a bar mitzvah at the Mount Horeb congregation in the Bronx. After service in the army that included a year in Vietnam, he embarked on a brief amateur boxing career and compiled a 25-5 record. Saoul turned pro in 1969, and 11 years later won the light-welterweight title. He made seven successful defenses before losing the title on a controversial decision to Leroy Haley.

Saoul was a highly skilled but cautious boxer who emphasized defense above all. He was stopped only once in 85 pro fights (at the age of 45), and is one of the few fighters to last the full 10 rounds with a prime Roberto Duran. But his safety-first style and lack of aggression cost him many decisions. Even so, the fact that he is one of only three boxers in the entire history of the sport to have fought throughout five decades is an amazing achievement. Saoul fought his last bout in 2008 when he was 60 years old! The bout took place in the Cayman Islands (one of the few places that would sanction a professional fight involving a 60-year-old boxer). He lost a 10-round decision to a 31-year-old boxer with a dismal record. As usual Saoul emerged unscathed. His final stats: 45-34-6 (19 KOs).

Rossman and Mamby were among the last fighters to win a championship before the proliferation of organization title belts in the 1980s made the words "world champion" virtually meaningless.

Another highly rated Jewish boxer was Moroccan-born Nessim Max Cohen, who won the middleweight championship of France in 1971. Five years later, in his only attempt at a world title, he was stopped by the great Colombian knockout artist Rodrigo Valdez. Tunisian-born Felix Brami won France's super bantamweight title in 1972 and was a rated contender for 22 months, although he never fought for a world title. Flyweight contender Henry Nissen, the son of Holocaust survivors, was born in a DP (Displaced Persons) camp in Germany in 1948. One year later his family settled in Australia, where Henry became a professional boxer in 1970. Within 14 months of turning pro he won both the Australian and Commonwealth (British Empire) flyweight titles. He retired shortly after losing the Commonwealth title in 1974.

Despite the paucity of Jewish boxers in the 1980s and '90s, a few standouts managed to achieve a measure of success, and therefore deserve mention. New Jersey's Kenny Bogner briefly attained contender status in the lightweight division. France's Gilles Elbilia was both the European and French welterweight champion when he lost to Detroit's Milton McCrory for the WBC world welterweight title in 1984. Gary Jacobs, a highly rated Jewish boxer from Scotland, challenged welterweight champion Pernell Whitaker in 1994, but despite a fine effort he came up short after 12 rounds. Dana Rosenblatt was a top-10 contender in the middleweight division and finished out his career with only one loss in 40 pro fights.

By the time Fabrice Bénichou, who is believed to be of Spanish-Hebrew heritage, captured the IBF super bantamweight title (aka, junior featherweight) in 1989, at least four other sanctioning organizations had anointed their own champions in that new weight class. Fifty years earlier boxing fans and governing authorities had correctly rejected the 122-pound weight class as superfluous and unnecessary, since only a few pounds separated it from the well-established bantamweight (118-pound) and featherweight (126-pound) divisions.

KOSHER KLOUTERS

If one searches hard enough, there are still a handful of Jewish boxers to be found today. The most prominent are Yuri Foreman and Dmitriy Salita. Both are Russian-born immigrants who arrived in America during the 1990s.

Salita and Foreman are Orthodox Jews who strictly adhere to the kosher dietary laws and will not fight on the Sabbath. Salita is affiliated with the Lubavitcher Hasidim. Foreman is studying to be a rabbi. The journey these men have taken mirrors that of their Golden Age counterparts. They came to America as poor immigrants and used boxing to improve their economic and social status. The main difference is in their learning curve as boxers. Each had less than 30 fights when they challenged for a title. The total number of rounds was 176 for Salita and 166 for Foreman. Back in 1925, the average numbers for a challenger were 84 fights and 644 rounds.[1]

Salita, a welterweight, is a former New York Golden Gloves champion. He turned pro in 2001 and has lost only two of 38 bouts. Foreman is also a former New York Golden Gloves champion. In 2009 he won the WBA super welterweight title belt, but lost it seven months later to former champion Miguel Cotto of Puerto Rico. He retired in 2014 and is continuing his rabbinical studies.

The Foreman-Cotto bout was the first boxing championship staged at the brand-new Yankee Stadium. Ironically, the very first championship match staged at the original Yankee Stadium 87 years earlier featured not one but *two* Jewish boxers in the main event—Benny Leonard and Lew Tendler.

THE TIMES ARE A-CHANGIN'

According to Larry Lawrence, an erudite memorabilia collector and sports maven, if a dedicated sports fanatic had fallen into a Rip Van Winkle sleep back in 1955 and woke up in the twenty-first century, his first words would probably be "What the hell happened to boxing?"

Indeed, no other professional sport has changed as much as boxing, especially over the past three decades.

The most obvious manifestation of boxing's altered landscape is the ridiculous title situation. In 1955 there were eight weight divisions ruled by eight undisputed world champions. Boxing fans could easily name every world champion. Even housewives and schoolchildren knew that Rocky Marciano was the heavyweight champion of the whole wide world. Today there are about 100 world champions distributed among 17 weight divisions. That is more than twice the number of weight divisions and more than *ten times* the number of world champions in 1955. Most people today would have difficulty naming even one of them, including the two current heavyweight champions (as of 2014).

The reason why boxing has spun out of control is because it is the only professional sport that operates without a national commissioner, or any semblance of centralized authority to enforce rules, consolidate title claims, create credible rankings, and ensure that the best fighters advance in the sport. The control of the sport is in the hands of a few dominant promoters and four so-called "sanctioning organizations" that certify title fights and issue monthly rankings of top contenders.

With no effective oversight in place, the quasi-official sanctioning organizations make up their own rules and then break them when it suits their purposes. They place the needs of a few powerful promoters ahead of the welfare of boxers and the sport. Exploitation, incompetence, and conflict of interest are standard operating procedure. Even casual fans of the sport know the monthly ratings of the World Boxing Council (WBC), World Boxing Association (WBA), International Boxing Federation (IBF), and World Boxing Organization (WBO) are not to be trusted.

"Everyone in boxing knows the sanctioning bodies that issue the ratings have no legitimacy," wrote investigative journalist Jack Newfield in 2001. "They force champions to pay huge sanctioning fees for the right to defend their titles. They strip champions of their titles if they don't go along with the sport's backroom politics. They assign incompetent judges to fights. They are more like bandits than regulators."[2]

Over the past few years the rotten reputation of these boxing parasites has finally begun to diminish their influence over the sport. Boxing fans hoped the situation would improve and the sport would finally gain some coherence, leading to the recognition of one undisputed champion for each weight division, but that has not been the case. The major promoters who use these easily corrupted organizations to their benefit began to circle the wagons and came up with a novel way to retain their hegemony over the sport. Don King, Bob Arum, and Golden Boy Promotions (a new group headed by Oscar De La Hoya and partners) decided to only promote title fights that involve boxers under their control. In other words, each promotional outfit has become a boxing universe unto itself. The promoter

decides who among his stable of contenders will challenge one of his champions. So no matter who wins, everything remains in-house, and the promoter maintains control of the fighters. What this does is guarantee that the best contenders and champions under exclusive contract to one promotional group will probably never face the best boxers from a rival group. If baseball were run like boxing, there would be at least four separate World Series champions. Since the promoters decide who fights for their inter-organization title belts, any rating system for boxers is rendered irrelevant.

The sanctioning organizations (known collectively to sportswriters and fans as "The Alphabet Boys" for the initials that identify them) still remain useful to promoters and television by granting an "official" imprimatur to the scores of title fights that take place every year under their jurisdiction. In this way total chaos is avoided and television can advertise every fight as being for some kind of title.

As they have done for the past 35 years, these organizations continue to extort "sanctioning fees" charged to every champion and challenger who competes for the privilege of fighting for one of their title belts. Earlier sanctioning organizations, such as the National Boxing Association and the European Boxing Union, operated quite efficiently without charging fees. The Alphabet Boys base their fees on a percentage of the fighter's earnings. The fees can run into five or six figures for a televised fight. That is why the banditos who run these organizations found it useful to create seven additional weight divisions. Additional weight divisions translate into more title fights, and therefore more sanctioning fees. It is estimated that just one of these organizations, the Mexican-based World Boxing Council (WBC), has taken in over $20 million in sanctioning fees. As a foreign entity with headquarters outside of the United States, the WBC has never had to account for what happened to all that money.

From the 1920s to the 1960s there were never more than 35 title fights per year. In 1978, one year after television executives recognized the authority of the WBC and WBA, and sanctioning fees became part of the landscape, there were 68 title fights. Five years later the number increased to 83. In 2012, nearly 200 "championship" bouts requiring the fighters to cough up fees were sanctioned by the WBC, WBA, IBF, and WBO. The confusion grows worse year by year as additional titles are invented ("Intercontinental," "Interim," "Emeritus," "Honorary," "Supreme"), all with the sole purpose of increasing the flow of sanctioning fees.

Repeated efforts to clean up boxing have failed mainly because of the unregulated nature of the sport and the fact that change would not be in the interest of the small circle of promoters, sanctioning organizations, and high-profile boxers who benefit from maintaining the status quo.

THE AGE OF GOLD

Although the current state of boxing is not a "Golden Age" in terms of the depth of talent and activity, it is most definitely an "Age of Gold" for the sanctioning organizations who over the past 37 years have raked in millions of dollars off the blood and sacrifice of every fighter who contends for one of their championship belts. (The WBC even has the gall to charge the fighter for their oversized tin-and-plastic trinket.) Yet, in spite of the millions these organizations have collected, the rank-and-file boxer is still without a union, pension plan, or health benefits. If there is any constant that remains from the old days, it is that boxers are still the most vulnerable and easily exploited of all professional athletes.

Aside from their questionable rankings, exorbitant sanctioning fees, and general corruption and stupidity, the Alphabet Boys have demystified what it means to be a world champion. Jim Brady, author of *Boxing Confidential: Power, Corruption, and the Biggest Prize in Sport*, put the title mess in historical perspective: "In the 1950s, there were approximately 5,000 fighters worldwide. There were generally eight weight divisions, with one champion in each. That breaks down to one champ every 625 boxers. Today, with just the major sanctioning bodies and not counting the whackos, you have about one 'world champion' for every 69 pros. It's ridiculous. Championship belts used to mean something. Now all they're good for is holding up your pants."[3]

It is impossible for a fan to keep up with the endless procession of belt holders. The only recognizable names are those fighters capable of capturing the public's attention and whose skill and charisma make them stand out from a pack of mediocre pretenders. The short list includes

Mike Tyson, Evander Holyfield, Manny Pacquiao, Oscar De La Hoya, Roy Jones Jr., Bernard Hopkins, and Floyd Mayweather Jr. As of 2015 all except Mayweather and Pacquiao have retired.

Boxing fans who complain about the sport's lack of integrity, loss of coherence, and the glut of mostly obscure belt holders need look no further than promoters Don King and Bob Arum and their toadies in the sanctioning organizations to understand why, except for the occasional megafight, boxing has become a marginalized and debased fringe sport.

Those who state that Golden Age promoters Tex Rickard and Mike Jacobs were just as ruthless and greedy as their modern-day counterparts are missing the main point. Yes, the business of professional boxing is a rough dog-eat-dog business, and Rickard and Jacobs were certainly no angels, but at least they left the sport better off than when they found it. The same cannot be said of Don King or Bob Arum.

I have often wondered who did more *lasting* damage to my favorite sport. Certainly the greed and predatory behavior of the old-style mobsters who controlled professional boxing in the 1950s contributed to its demise as a mainstream sport; of that there is no doubt. But in spite of the corruption they inflicted and the damage that they caused, boxing still managed to maintain a semblance of structure that oversaw the orderly succession of champions in the eight traditional weight divisions. The damage was not permanent. What was left of the sport after the dissolution of the monopolistic International Boxing

Club could have been salvaged and improved upon by right thinking people.

Instead, staying true to boxing's less than honorable antecedents, beginning in the late 1970s rival promoters Don King and Bob Arum, responding to television's desire to broadcast only title fights, formed separate alliances with the two main sanctioning groups in order to further their own monopolistic hold over the sport. As long as ratings remained strong, TV executives were not concerned that dozens of horrendous mismatches were being foisted on the public in order to safeguard a popular champion's title. But the result was the destruction of a system that while certainly not perfect, at least encouraged competitive matches between legitimately ranked contenders.

The huge number of world champions with multiple title belts has also contributed to a distortion of boxing's history. During the Golden Age it was considered extraordinary for a fighter to win a title in more than one weight division. In 70 years (1900 to 1970), only five boxers accomplished this feat. Over the past three decades (1984 to 2014), dozens of fighters have won multiple titles in three or more weight divisions. Most of today's fans are either unaware or just ignore the fact that seven additional weight classes—combined with a plethora of rival organizations that recognize their own world champions—makes it far easier to win a title in more than one weight class.

"To people who don't know boxing history—and even to many who do—a guy who won two or three titles years ago is no big deal," comments Tony Arnold, a boxing historian and former professional boxer. "You won two or three titles back in the 1930s? So what? The average guy today is wearing multiple title belts, it seems, almost before he turns pro . . . People don't realize how hard it was years ago to become a top contender, much less win a title when there were eight weight classes and eight world champions. They have no idea what an accomplishment that was against the type of competition they had to face."[4]

A LOST ART

The creation of a Golden Age in any time period, in any field of endeavor, requires the availability of highly gifted individuals developing their skills in an environment that fosters their growth and enables them to flourish to their full potential. Whether we are talking about the Golden Age of Greek philosophy that spawned the likes of Socrates, Plato, and Aristotle, or the Golden Age of Boxing that gave us Dempsey, Louis, and Sugar Ray Robinson, the basic ingredients to create "gold" must be present. These ingredients were in abundance during boxing's heyday, but are sadly lacking today. That is why the art of boxing has deteriorated to an alarming degree, especially since the mid-1990s. A dearth of qualified teacher-trainers is a major contributing factor, but also adding to the problem is a lack of experience. Most of today's boxers have only three or four fights a year and ascend to a title with less than 25 bouts and a meager 150 to 200 rounds of boxing, if that. Their counterparts who were active from the early 1900s to the 1950s averaged at least three or four times the number of bouts and rounds.

Tune into a televised fight today and you will rarely see correct punching technique, fluid movement, adequate defense, mobile footwork, skillful feinting, proper timing, and accurate judgment of distance. Also missing is consistent and effective body punching (a staple of the old school) and drawing a lead to set up a counterpunch. What is especially disturbing is the almost total lack of defensive moves that involve slipping, blocking, parrying, ducking, or rolling away from punches. The left jab, boxing's most basic and important punch, is rarely taught or used the way it was intended. Undefeated records, multiple title belts, high knockout percentages, and the ubiquitous "punch stats" are today's measure of quality. Television encourages crude slugfests devoid of defense because that type of contest appeals to a much broader and less knowledgeable audience than one featuring intelligent strategy, artful use of a left jab, and clever offensive and defensive maneuvers.

Many of today's boxers put forth a tremendous effort but rarely display the finer points of ring generalship. The all-important *seasoning* that comes with dozens of competitive bouts against quality opposition, combined with expert instruction, has resulted in a dumbed-down version of professional boxing. Today's champions and contenders have not had the type of bout-to-bout education that empowered the great fighters of the past.

As far as boxing safety is concerned, it is this writer's opinion that a majority of today's boxers are taking more head punches and suffering more brain damage in fewer fights than their Golden Age predecessors because they are not taught how to avoid punishment. Toughness and aggression coupled with impressive "punch stats" are the most desired qualities, especially when trying to impress a large TV audience.

"I DON'T BLAME THE FIGHTERS"

Michael Capriano Jr. saw his first professional boxing match in 1940. He is a former licensed manager and trainer. During the 1950s he trained more service champions than any other Marine Corps boxing coach. He laments what is missing from today's practitioners. "There are no super-skilled boxers like Tippy Larkin, Billy Graham, or Maxie Shapiro," says Capriano. "I don't see them around. Years ago there were many different types of fighters, and you'd see many different styles, and that's probably what made them better fighters. I don't see anyone with that type of skill today—in any weight division. Some of today's fighters look good, and they seem to have the natural instincts and maybe somebody is teaching them, but I still don't see the moves. They need more seasoning."[5]

Capriano adds another reason for their inconsistency. "Fighters are weaker today," he observes. "The old-timers had a psychological resiliency. When they got knocked down it was like they were insulted. They would get up and try to take you apart. They had that extra dimension. Among the modern-day fighters, Arturo Gatti had that quality, but not the rest of the equipment.

"The Golden Age contenders and champions were battle-tested. They survived the killers of their eras as they came up through the ranks. How many killers are there today to fight on the way up? Years ago you had to fight who they told you to fight. You could not pick and choose your opponents. They fought other good fighters who at any given time could put forth a great fight and beat them. The competition from the 1920s to the 1950s was brutal. You cannot compare it to today."[6]

Former middleweight contender Wilbert "Skeeter" McClure knows a thing or two about brutal competition. In the early 1960s he fought the likes of Rubin "Hurricane" Carter, Jose Torres, and Luis Rodriguez. Before turning pro in 1961, McClure had 148 amateur fights and won 7 national and international titles, including an Olympic gold medal. A college graduate with degrees in literature and philosophy, McClure also earned a PhD in psychology and was the first African-American chairman of the Massachusetts Boxing Commission.

"Boxing, in my opinion, is the only sport in which the participants haven't gotten better since the 1930s, '40s, and '50s," says McClure. "Football players today are better than the ones who were playing in the '50s. It's the same with basketball and baseball. The fighters today couldn't even hold a candle to the fighters of the 1960s and '70s. They just couldn't do it. They were too tough, and too strong and too savvy and too skilled. Part of the reason is owing to the fact that they fought more frequently. You have champions today who fight once a year or twice a year. Anybody who applies his craft to any trade or profession and performs it only twice a year can't be good. You just cannot develop that way."[7]

Bill Goodman, who saw his first boxing match in 1947, agrees. "I never see a sharp varied attack that includes slipping, blocking, sidestepping, moving on good legs with good balance, and using an active left hand properly. They throw a jab and they stop. It's a big deal if they throw two in a row.

"Years ago you had 50, 70 fights before you fought for a title. You knew how to handle all situations—or you should have known. You had to handle opponents who were awkward, fast, slow, sluggers, boxers, clever guys, and southpaws. You had experience with those types of styles. . . . A seasoned pro can adapt his style to avoid punishment. You used to see fighters adapting fast to avoid punishment. Today it's all the same, minute after minute, round after round. If you see one round you saw the whole fight. You can go home. One round is the same as the other round. They don't have variance in it. They all fight the same way. You saw the guy fight once, even if he's fighting the same opponent he fought previously, he's going to fight the same way."[8]

In a later interview Bill Goodman told me: "I don't blame the fighters. It's not their fault. They are not being taught properly. Occasionally a trainer can be heard telling a fighter during the one-minute rest between rounds to 'throw more jabs.' That is good advice, but by itself is not adequate. A good trainer understands that there are many ways to jab. A jab can be aimed at the body or head, used as a feint, doubled or tripled, it can keep an opponent off balance, or set up combinations, or draw a lead.

"In the old days a fighter was capable of switching from the head to the body without any loss of effectiveness. They were constantly pressing forward, or were taught to, anyway, with a blinding attack that was interesting to watch. The guys were throwing sharp damaging punches with either hand. The speed and relentless pace was very effective. It gave their opponents no rest. And that's how they won their fights. You put two guys together like that and you have something to watch. But you don't have that anymore. And that doesn't necessarily relate to whether a fighter was Irish, Italian, or Jewish . . . they all fought that way, but like everything else, some boys were better than others—and that was what made the difference."[9]

Teddy Atlas, aside from being one of the sport's top trainers, is also an astute boxing historian with a deep appreciation for the past practitioners of the sweet science. He adds his thoughts on the subject: "I still see fighters from the 1930s and 1940s. I have been privileged to see the films. Those old-timers are doing things that I still do not see today's guys doing. Whether it's judging distance better, or jabbing an opponent's shoulder to distract or unbalance him, or letting an opponent think he's safe when he's not safe, or doing a feint for more than just motion but actually to make something happen. So many subtleties are missing. I'd just love to hear the trainers talk about the old-timers. They'd say things like, 'He'd feint you and make you bend down and tie your shoelaces.' "[10]

What these genuine boxing experts have to say about the current state of the art is based on years of experience and thoughtful analysis. While it is true that many of today's fighters are superb athletes, their potential will never be fully realized because they do not get the experience, training, and competition necessary to round out their education.

NOBLE ATHLETES IN AN IGNOBLE SPORT

Whoever coined the phrase "The Noble Art of Boxing" understood that the only redeeming elements of this ancient and eternal sport reside in the courage, pride, dignity, and skill of its athletes. It was no different when the ancient Greek boxers, hands encased in the leather *caestus* fought for the coveted laurel wreath on Mount Olympus. Boxing's ongoing problems are not the fault of the dedicated athletes who enter the sport, but with the depleted and corrupt environment in which they ply their trade.

Professional boxing will probably always be plagued by a certain level of corruption and exploitation. It is the nature of the beast. But the decades-long lunacy of the absurd sanctioning organizations in combination with rapacious promoters who care nothing for the future of the sport is unprecedented. Over the past three decades they have managed to turn a once-glamorous and exciting sport into a sodden and boorish spectacle unworthy of our attention or respect. It makes one appreciate even more the treasured memories of the great Golden Age of boxing talent and activity that came and went all too quickly.

REMEMBERING A GOLDEN AGE

On my fifth birthday my father presented me with a pair of junior-size boxing gloves. In the 1950s, boxing, thanks to television, was still very much a staple of American popular culture, so it was not unusual for a five-year-old to receive such a gift. Junior gloves notwithstanding, my passion for the sport of boxing did not begin to develop for another nine years. By that time the careers of legendary fighters such as Sugar Ray Robinson, Archie Moore, and Willie Pep were almost over. Fortunately, thanks to the nationally televised Wednesday and Friday night *Fight of the Week* programs, I was privileged to watch other great boxers who continued to fuel my interest in the sport. I can still remember the catchy jingle that signaled the beginning of Friday night's much-anticipated *Gillette Cavalcade of Sports Fight of the Week*.

Adding to my enjoyment was the opportunity for me and my brother to watch the fights with our father. Today they call it "bonding." All across America from the late 1940s to the early 1960s, other baby-boomer sons were also bonding with their fathers over the Friday-night televised-fight ritual. My dad's story is not unlike so many other newly minted Americans who came to this country as penniless immigrants and through much hard work and sacrifice built successful lives in the golden land.

Growing up on the Lower East Side of New York during the 1920s meant that my father also grew up with boxing. He even boxed a bit as an amateur at the Educational Alliance, the famous settlement house on East Broadway, located just a few blocks from where he lived. Considering the milieu, it would have been more unusual had my father not laced up the gloves. There was no escaping it. In those days boxing was everywhere—and just about every kid wanted to box.

As we watched the action unfold on the small screen of our Dumont television set, my father might speak of former ring greats such as Jack Dempsey (his favorite), Gene Tunney, Harry Greb, and Mickey Walker. It was from my father that I first heard of the famous "long count" controversy surrounding the second Jack Dempsey vs. Gene Tunney heavyweight championship. I also vividly remember him talking with pride about some of the great Jewish fighters of that era, men like Sid Terris, Barney Ross, and, of course, Benny Leonard.

These stories conjured up a fascinating era of American immigrant history. Yet most people today, especially third- and fourth-generation American Jews, cannot name even one of the 34 Jewish boxing world champions. When told about it for the first time, a common response is either incredulous laughter or puzzlement, as if the topic doesn't quite register. The entire concept of Jewish boxers is so foreign and atypical to most people, it is not surprising that the first reaction would be laughter. In a way, this is understandable. As Jewish people prospered in America, the memories of their poverty-ridden immigrant past were left behind. There was no need to revisit the old neighborhood. The promise of America did not have to come with a broken nose or cauliflower ear.

But even after presenting the impressive statistics and explaining the whys and wherefores, I still sense a bit of resistance, if not discomfort, in accepting the fact that their poor immigrant forebears actually became very good at hitting people for a living. Part of this resistance, I believe, is because boxing has been stigmatized as a violent, corrupt, and physically damaging activity, and not a sport for bright people to get involved with. But years ago that attitude was not nearly as strong or pervasive when boxing was on a higher pedestal and professional boxers were viewed as masculine heroes and accorded far greater respect and admiration. Let us not forget that boxing was important enough to give every ethnic minority their first American heroes. That is why it is necessary to view this sport in its historical context in order to fully appreciate and celebrate the accomplishments of the Golden Age greats.

Recent books that deal with the history of the Jewish athlete and include some mention of boxers, either as an individual topic or as part of a broader, all-encompassing treatise, often state their major contribution was in challenging the stereotype that Jews did not possess the athletic ability and toughness to succeed in boxing. But the reality is, those stereotypes hardly existed when Jewish boxers were inundating the sport. Most of these books were written within the past 30 years, long after Jewish boxers had left the scene. The authors, all of whom entered adulthood in an era of unprecedented prosperity and opportunity for Jews in America, had no personal connection to the Golden Age of boxing and the poor immigrant neighborhoods that gave rise to it. Perhaps this is a case of projecting contemporary attitudes back retrospectively on another generation, whose experience was quite different from our own.

The scene in the 1980 movie comedy *Airplane*, where a passenger asks the stewardess for "something light to read" and she returns with a single page titled "Famous Jewish Sports Legends," always gets a laugh, but it encourages a stereotype that has no basis in fact. Twenty-five years after *Airplane*, a real book titled *Famous Jewish Sports Legends* was published by the International Jewish Sports Hall of Fame. Contained within its 300 pages are the biographies of hundreds of world-class Jewish athletes, including 345 Olympic medalists. Boxing has 29 entries, more than any other sport; basketball comes in second, with 23.

Novelist Philip Roth caught the tail end of the Golden Age of Jewish boxers, growing up in Newark, New Jersey, in the 1940s. In his autobiography, *The Facts*, Roth recalls he was a fan of the sport during his adolescence, and even briefly subscribed to *The Ring* magazine. He first heard of the prowess of Benny Leonard, Barney Ross, Max Baer, and "Slapsie Maxie" Rosenbloom from his father, an insurance salesman, who sometimes took him and his brother to the local boxing arena. Even so, Roth viewed boxing as a strange deviation from the Jewish norm.

Roth loved sports, especially baseball, but he considered boxing an anomaly for Jews because it seemed incompatible with the values of his middle-class Jewish upbringing: "In the world whose values first formed me unrestrained physical violence was considered contemptible everywhere else," he writes. "I could no more smash a nose with a fist than fire a pistol into someone's heart. And what imposed this restraint, if not on Slapsie Maxie Rosenbloom, then on me, was my being Jewish. In my scheme of things, Slapsie Maxie was a more miraculous Jewish phenomenon by far than Dr. Albert Einstein."[11]

Great Jewish boxers may have been a phenomenon to Philip Roth, but not to the millions of Americans who followed the sport in the 1910s, '20s, and '30s. By the time Slapsie Maxie Rosenbloom won the light heavyweight title in 1930, 22 other Jewish world-champion boxers had already preceded him, not to mention scores of top-ranked contenders. No one was talking or writing about "stereotypes being challenged," because that was not how American Jews were perceived at that time. In the long run the real benefit of boxing to the Jewish people was the role it played in the Americanization process and the stepping-stone it provided into the socioeconomic mainstream.

When I began to write this book, I had to ask myself: Why do a book about Jewish boxers? Would it be more than just an exercise in nostalgia? I believed then, as I do now, that it is indeed much more than that. As the last Jewish boxers of the Golden Age die off, it becomes even more important to document their accomplishments so that future generations can acknowledge and appreciate how a people with no athletic tradition, and with so many doors closed to them, used their intelligence and drive to open another door to opportunity, and eventually dominate, both as athletes and entrepreneurs, what was for several decades the most popular sport in America.

In researching the boxing careers and lives of the champions and contenders in this book, I constantly found myself moved by the heart and character displayed by these men as they struggled to master their unusual craft and succeed in such an unforgiving sport. They not only excelled as professional athletes, but also as role models and as men.

Greatness, in any age, deserves to be carefully examined and understood. Too often in our fast-paced, instant-messaging, tweeting, iPhone culture, the youth of today tend to ignore the past or dismiss it as irrelevant. That is a mistake, for there are lessons to be learned and standards to consider that remain timeless and relevant, as exemplified in the heyday of the great Jewish champions and contenders who made their indelible mark in the Golden Age of boxing.

APPENDIX

I. AUTHOR'S CHOICE OF THE TOP 25 JEWISH BOXERS OF ALL TIME

(In order of greatness)

Benny Leonard	Jackie Fields	Abe Goldstein
Abe Attell	Battling Levinsky	Al Singer
Barney Ross	Sid Terris	Georgie Abrams
Maxie Rosenbloom	Joe Choynski	Allie Stolz
Ted "Kid" Lewis	Charley White	Newsboy Brown
Lew Tendler	Jack Bernstein	Ray Miller
Louis "Kid" Kaplan	Harry Lewis	Solly Seeman
Benny Bass	Benny Valgar	
Jackie "Kid" Berg	Charley Phil Rosenberg	

II. JEWISH WORLD CHAMPIONS 1901–2014

Name	Title Reign	Weight Division
Harry Harris	1901	Bantamweight
Abe Attell	1904–12	Featherweight
Harry Lewis	1908–11	Welterweight
Monte Attell	1909–10	Bantamweight
Sid Smith	1912	Flyweight
Matt Wells	1914–15	Welterweight
Al McCoy	1914–17	Middleweight
Ted "Kid" Lewis	1915–16 / 1917–19	Welterweight
Battling Levinsky	1916–20	Light Heavyweight
Benny Leonard	1917–25	Lightweight
Dave Rosenberg	1922	Middleweight
Jack Bernstein	1923	Junior Lightweight
Abe Goldstein	1924	Bantamweight
Louis "Kid" Kaplan	1925–27	Featherweight
Charley Phil Rosenberg	1925–27	Bantamweight
Mushy Callahan	1926–30	Junior Welterweight
Pinky Silverberg	1927	Bantamweight
Benny Bass	1927–28	Featherweight
Corporal Izzy Schwartz	1927–29	Flyweight
Newsboy Brown	1928	Flyweight
Jackie Fields	1929–30, 1932–33	Welterweight
Al Singer	1930	Lightweight
Maxie Rosenbloom	1930–34	Light Heavyweight
Jackie "Kid" Berg	1930–31	Junior Welterweight
Young Perez	1931–32	Flyweight
Ben Jeby	1933	Middleweight
Barney Ross	1933	Lightweight
Barney Ross	1933–35	Junior Welterweight
Barney Ross	1934, 1935–38	Welterweight
Bob Olin	1934–35	Light Heavyweight
Solly Krieger	1938–39	Middleweight
Robert Cohen	1954	Bantamweight
Alfonse Halimi	1959	Bantamweight
Mike Rossman	1978–79	Light Heavyweight
Saoul Mamby	1980–82	Junior Welterweight
Yuri Foreman	2009–10	Junior Middleweight

III. TOP 10 JEWISH BOXERS BY WEIGHT CLASS

Heavyweight Light	Heavyweight	Middleweight	Welterweight
Maxie Rosenbloom	Maxie Rosenbloom	Georgie Abrams	Barney Ross
King Levinsky	Battling Levinsky	Solly Krieger	Ted "Kid" Lewis
Art Lasky	Joe Choynski	Ben Jeby	Jackie Fields
Abe Simon	Bob Olin	Augie Ratner	Harry Lewis
Roy Lazer	Yale Okun	KO Phil Kaplan	Matt Wells
Natie Brown	Abie Bain	Harold Green	Soldier Bartfield
Jack Gross	Armand Emanuel	Al McCoy	Phil Bloom
Abe Feldman	Herbie Katz	Dave Rosenberg	Al "Bummy" Davis
Bill Weinberg	Jack Bloomfield	Erich Seelig	Sammy Luftspring
Erv Sarlin	Mike Rossman	Artie Levine	Mike Kaplan

Junior Welterweight	Lightweight	Junior Lightweight
Barney Ross	Benny Leonard	Louis "Kid" Kaplan
Jackie "Kid" Berg	Barney Ross	Benny Bass
Davey Day	Sid Terris	Benny Valgar
Jack Portney	Charley White	Ray Miller
Joe Glick	Jack Bernstein	Leach Cross
Maxie Berger	Al Singer	Maxie Shapiro
Harry "Kid" Brown	Allie Stolz	Al Foreman
Mushy Callahan	Solly Seeman	Eddie "Kid" Wagner
Joey Goodman	Willie Jackson	Lew Feldman
Ruby Goldstein	Sammy Dorfman	Abe "Kid" Goodman

Featherweight	Bantamweight	Flyweight
Abe Attell	Charley Phil Rosenberg	Newsboy Brown
Louis "Kid" Kaplan	Abe Goldstein	Corporal Izzy Schwartz
Benny Bass	Newsboy Brown	Young Perez
Charlie Beecher	Joe Burman	Marty Gold
Red Chapman	Jackie "Kid" Wolfe	Phil Tobias
Danny Kramer	Kid Frances	Johnny Rosner
Harry Blitman	Archie Bell	Pinky Silverberg
Joey Sangor	Robert Cohen	Sid Smith
Joe Bernstein	Alphonse Halimi	Dave Adelman
Al Reid	Benny Goldberg	Harry Goldstein

IV. TOP 10 JEWISH BOXERS BY LOCATION
(In alphabetical order)

New York City	Philadelphia	Chicago
Jack Bernstein	Benny Bass	Milt Aron
Leach Cross	Harry Blitman	Joe Burman
Abe Goldstein	Harry "Kid" Brown	Davey Day
Benny Leonard	Sailor Friedman	Jackie Fields
Charley Phil Rosenberg	Al Gordon	Harry Harris
Maxie Rosenbloom	Danny Kramer	King Levinsky
Solly Seeman	Battling Levinsky	Joe Medill
Al Singer	Harry Lewis	Ray Miller
Sid Terris	Lew Tendler	Barney Ross
Benny Valgar	Eddie "Kid" Wagner	Charley White

Baltimore	San Francisco/Los Angeles	Montreal/Toronto
Sylvan Bass	Abe Attell	Maxie Berger
Nate Carp	Monte Attell	Solly Cantor
Benny Goldstein	Joe Benjamin	Al Foreman
Charley Gomer	Newsboy Brown	Benny Gould
Tommy Herman	Mushy Callahan	Harry Hurst
Sid Lampe	Joe Choynski	Sammy Luftspring
Jack Portney	Oakland Jimmy Duffy	Bert Schneider
Frankie Rice	Armand Emanuel	Solly Smith
Benny Schwartz	Georgie Levine	Curley Wilshur
Herman Weiner	Georgie Marks	Baby Yack

Brooklyn	Boston	England
Soldier Bartfield	Nat Bor	Jackie "Kid" Berg
Archie Bell	Red Chapman	Benny Caplan
Frankie Callahan	Johnny Clinton	Ted "Kid" Lewis
Al "Bummy" Davis	Eddie "Newsboy" Curley	Harry Mason
Lew Feldman	Abe Denner	Harry Mizler
Bernie Friedkin	Harry Devine	Al Phillips
Harold Green	Abe Friedman	Benny Sharkey
Solly Krieger	Abe "Kid" Goodman	Harry Silver
Herbie Kronowitz	Mike Kaplan	Sid Smith
Artie Levine	Jake Zeramby	Matt Wells

Pittsburgh	Cleveland	Newark
Max Elling	Matt Brock	Nat Arno
Young Eppie (Epstein)	Phil Brock	Abie Bain
Young Goldie (Gold)	Jackie Davis	Sollie Castellane
Phil Goldstein	Dick Evans*	Maxie Fisher
Marty Gornick	Danny Frush	Lou Halper
Nat Litfin	Benny Gershe	KO Phil Kaplan
Johnny Ray	Joey Goodman	Dave Kurtz
Erv Sarlin	Maxie Holub	Roy Lazer
	Jackie "Kid Wolfe	Benny Levine
		Allie Stolz
		Young Perez

*Youngstown, Ohio

Buffalo/Rochester/Syracuse	France	Detroit
Joey Goldberg	Sauveur Benamou	Frankie Abrams
Johnny Helstein	Felix Brami	Leonard Bennett
Gustave Humery	Gilbert Cohen	Benny Goldberg
Joey Kushner	Nessim Max Cohen	Allie Gronik
Meyer Lichtenstein	Robert Cohen	Clarence Rosen
Benny Ross	Gilles Elbilia	Morrie Sherman
Jake Schiffer	Kid Francis	
Sammy Weinrib	Alphonse Halimi	
Dick Wipperman		

V. JEWISH BOXERS IN WORLD CHAMPIONSHIP CONTESTS, 1901–2014

Of the following 242 title bouts, 213 took place between 1901 and 1939. In a no-decision bout ("ND"), a champion automatically retains his title if a bout goes the scheduled distance, meaning his name stays in the win column. Jewish boxers faced each other for a world title 14 times. (Jewish boxers appear in bold type.)

FLYWEIGHT TITLE

Date	Won	Lost	Result	City
April 11, 1913*	**Sid Smith**	Eugène Criqui	Decision 20	Paris
June 2, 1913*	Bill Ladbury	**Sid Smith**	TKO 11	London
April 24, 1916	Jimmy Wilde	**Johnny Rosner**	KO 11	Liverpool
October 13, 1923	Pancho Villa	**Benny Schwartz**	Decision 15	Baltimore
October 22, 1927	**Pinky Silverberg**	Ruby Bradley	DQ 7	Bridgeport
December 16, 1927	**Corp. Izzy Schwartz**	**Newsboy Brown**	Decision 15	New York
January 3, 1928	**Newsboy Brown**	Johnny McCoy	Decision 15	New York
April 9, 1928	**Corp. Izzy Schwartz**	Routien Parra	Decision 15	New York
July 20, 1928	**Corp. Izzy Schwartz**	Frisco Grande	WF 4	Rockaway
August 3, 1928	**Corp. Izzy Schwartz**	Little Jeff Smith	KO 4	Rockaway
August 29, 1929	Johnny Hill	**Newsboy Brown**	Decision 15	London
March 12, 1929	**Corp. Izzy Schwartz**	Frenchy Belanger	Decision12	Toronto
August 22, 1929	Willie LaMorte	**Corp. Izzy Schwartz**	Decision 15	Newark
October 26, 1931	**Victor Young Perez**	Frankie Genaro	KO 2	Paris
February 19, 1934	Jackie Brown	**Victor Young Perez**	KO 13	Manchester

*Recognized by EBU (European Boxing Union)

BANTAMWEIGHT TITLE

Date	Won	Lost	Result	City
March 18, 1901	**Harry Harris**	Pedlar Palmer	Decision 15	London
June 19, 1909	**Monte Attell**	Frankie Neil	KO 18	Colma
December 7, 1909	**Monte Attell**	Danny Webster	Draw 20	San Francisco
February 22, 1910	Frankie Conley	**Monte Attell**	KO 42	Vernon
April 25, 1911	Johnny Coulon	**Eddie O'Keefe**	Draw 10	Kansas
November 24, 1922	Joe Lynch	**Benny Schwartz**	KO 5	Springfield
October 19, 1923	**Abe Goldstein**	**Joe Burman**	Decision 12	New York
March 21, 1924	**Abe Goldstein**	Joe Lynch	Decision 15	New York
May 5, 1924	**Abe Goldstein**	**Clarence Rosen**	ND 10	Detroit
July 16, 1924	**Abe Goldstein**	Charles Ledoux	Decision 15	Bronx
September 8, 1924	**Abe Goldstein**	Tommy Ryan	Decision 15	New York
December 19, 1924	Eddie "Cannonball" Martin	**Abe Goldstein**	Decision 15	New York
March 20, 1925	**Charley Phil Rosenberg**	Eddie "Cannonball" Martin	Decision 15	New York
May 5, 1927*	Teddy Baldock	**Archie Bell**	Decision 15	London
July 23, 1935	**Charley Phil Rosenberg**	Eddie Shea	KO 4	New York City
February 4, 1927	**Charley Phil Rosenberg**	Bushy Graham	Decision 15	New York
February 25, 1928	Bushy Graham	**Corp. Izzy Schwartz**	Decision 15	Brooklyn
June 12, 1929**	Bushy Graham	**Archie Bell**	Decision 10	Wilkes-Barre
May 20, 1931***	Pete Sanstol	**Archie Bell**	Decision 10	Montreal
February 19, 1934	Panama Al Brown	**Young Perez**	Decision 15	Paris
November 23, 1943	Manuel Ortiz	**Benny Goldberg**	Decision 15	Los Angeles
September 19, 1954	**Robert Cohen**	Chamroen Songkitrat	Decision 15	Bangkok
September 3, 1955	**Robert Cohen**	Willie Toweel	Draw 15	Johannesburg
June 29, 1956	Mario D'Agata	**Robert Cohen**	TKO 7	Paris
April 1, 1957	**Alphonse Halimi**	Mario D'Agata	Decision 15	Paris
November 6, 1957	**Alphonse Halimi**	Raul Macias	Decision 15	Los Angeles
July 8, 1959	Jose Becerra	**Alphonse Halimi**	KO 8	Los Angeles
February 4, 1960	Jose Becerra	**Alphonse Halimi**	KO 9	Los Angeles
October 25, 1960	**Alphonse Halimi**	Freddie Gilroy	Decision 15	London

*British version of title; **Pennsylvania Boxing Commission; ***Canadian Boxing Federation

FEATHERWEIGHT TITLE

Date	Won	Lost	Result	City
June 2, 1899	George Dixon	**Joe Bernstein**	Decision 25	New York City
November 2, 1900	Terry McGovern	**Joe Bernstein**	KO 7	Louisville
October 16, 1902	Young Corbett	**Joe Bernstein**	TKO 7	Baltimore
September 3, 1903	**Abe Attell**	Johnny Reagan	Decision 20	St. Louis
January 4, 1904	**Abe Attell**	Harry Forbes	Draw 10	Indianapolis
February 1, 1904	**Abe Attell**	Harry Forbes	KO 5	St. Louis
March 9, 1904	**Abe Attell**	Patsy Haley	KO 5	Hot Springs
June 23, 1904	**Abe Attell**	Johnny Reagan	Decision 15	St. Louis
February 22, 1906	**Abe Attell**	Jimmy Walsh	Decision 15	Chelsea
July 4, 1906	**Abe Attell**	Frankie Neil	Decision 20	Los Angeles
October 30, 1906	**Abe Attell**	Harry Baker	Decision 20	Los Angeles
November 16, 1906	**Abe Attell**	Billy DeCoursey	Decision 15	San Diego
December 7, 1906	**Abe Attell**	Jimmy Walsh	TKO 9	Los Angeles
November 18, 1907	**Abe Attell**	Harry Baker	KO 8	Los Angeles
May 24, 1907	**Abe Attell**	**Benny "Kid" Solomon**	Decision 20	Los Angeles
September 12, 1907	**Abe Attell**	Jimmy Walsh	Decision 10	Indianapolis
October 29, 1907	**Abe Attell**	Freddie Weeks	TKO 4	Los Angeles
January 1, 1908	**Abe Attell**	Owen Moran	Draw 25	Colma
January 31, 1908	**Abe Attell**	Frankie Neil	TKO13	San Francisco
February 28, 1908	**Abe Attell**	Eddie Kelly	TKO 7	San Francisco
September 7, 1908	**Abe Attell**	Owen Moran	Draw 23	San Francisco
December 29, 1908	**Abe Attell**	Buzz Mackey	KO 8	New Orleans
January 14, 1909	**Abe Attell**	Freddie Weeks	KO 10	Goldfield
February 14, 1909	**Abe Attell**	Eddie Kelly	TKO 7	New Orleans
November 22, 1909	**Abe Attell**	Johnny Moran	Decision 8	Memphis
October 24, 1910	**Abe Attell**	Johnny Kilbane	Decision 10	Kansas
February 1, 1912	Johnny Kilbane	**Abe Attell**	Decision 20	Vernon
February 25, 1920	Johnny Kilbane	**Benny Valgar**	ND 8**	Newark
August 15, 1922	Johnny Dundee	**Danny Frush**	KO 9	Brooklyn
January 2, 1925	**Louis "Kid" Kaplan**	**Danny Kramer**	TKO 9	New York
August 27, 1925	**Louis "Kid" Kaplan**	Babe Herman	Decision 15	Waterbury
December 18, 1925	**Louis "Kid" Kaplan**	Babe Herman	Decision 15	New York
June 28, 1926	**Louis "Kid" Kaplan**	Bobby Garcia	TKO 10	Hartford
September 12, 1928	**Benny Bass**	**Red Chapman**	Decision 10	Philadelphia
February 13, 1933	Kid Chocolate	**Benny Bass**	Decision 15	New York

**Valgar won most newspaper verdicts, but "ND" mandated he could only win title by KO.

FEATHERWEIGHT TITLE (CONTINUED)

Date	Won	Lost	Result	City
October 18, 1932*	Baby Arizmendi	**Newsboy Brown**	W10	Los Angeles
December 2, 1932*	Baby Arizmendi	**Archie Bell**	Decision 10	Los Angeles
January 6, 1933*	Baby Arizmendi	**Archie Bell**	Decision 10	San Francisco
July 11, 1933	Freddie Miller	**Abie Israel**	KO 4	Seattle
December 29, 1938	Leo Rodak	**Leone Efrati**	Decision 10	Chicago

*Recognized by California Boxing Commission as world title bout.

JUNIOR LIGHTWEIGHT TITLE

Date	Won	Lost	Result	City
May 30, 1923	**Jack Bernstein**	Johnny Dundee	Decision 15	New York
June 25, 1923	**Jack Bernstein**	**Freddie Jacks**	KO 5	Philadelphia
December 17, 1923	Johnny Dundee	**Joe Bernstein**	Decision 15	New York
September 30, 1926	Tod Morgan	**Joe Glick**	Decision 15	New York
December 16, 1927	Tod Morgan	**Joe Glick**	DQ 14	New York
January 1, 1929	Tod Morgan	**Joey Sangor**	ND 10	Milwaukee
December 12, 1929	**Benny Bass**	Tod Morgan	KO 2	NYC
February 3, 1930	**Benny Bass**	Davey Abad	TKO 4	St. Louis
March 28, 1930	**Benny Bass**	Eddie Shea	ND 10	St. Louis
January 5, 1931	**Benny Bass**	Lew Massey	Decision 10	Philadelphia
July 15, 1931	Kid Chocolate	**Benny Bass**	TKO 7	Philadelphia
October 13, 1932	Kid Chocolate	**Lew Feldman**	TKO 12	NYC

LIGHTWEIGHT TITLE

Date	Won	Lost	Result	City
January 1, 1907	Joe Gans	**Kid Herman**	KO 8	Tonopah
March 31, 1916	Freddie Welsh	**Benny Leonard**	ND 10	New York
September 14, 1916	Freddie Welsh	**Charley White**	Decision 20	Colorado Springs
May 28, 1917	**Benny Leonard**	Freddie Welsh	TKO 9	New York
September 21, 1917	**Benny Leonard**	Leo Johnson	TKO 1	New York
November 26, 1920	**Benny Leonard**	Joe Welling	TKO 4	New York
January 14, 1921	**Benny Leonard**	Ritchie Mitchell	TKO 6	New York
February 10, 1922	**Benny Leonard**	Rocky Kansas	Decision 15	New York
July 4, 1922	**Benny Leonard**	Rocky Kansas	TKO 8	Michigan City
July 27, 1922	**Benny Leonard**	**Lew Tendler**	ND 12	Jersey City
July 24, 1923	**Benny Leonard**	**Lew Tendler**	Decision 15	New York
July 17, 1930	**Al Singer**	Sammy Mandell	KO 1	New York
November 14, 1930	Tony Canzoneri	**Al Singer**	KO 1	New York
April 24, 1931	Tony Canzoneri	**Jackie "Kid" Berg**	KO 3	Chicago
September 10, 1931	Tony Canzoneri	**Jackie "Kid" Berg**	Decision 15	New York
June 23, 1933*	**Barney Ross**	Tony Canzoneri	Decision 10	Chicago
September 12, 1933*	**Barney Ross**	Tony Canzoneri	Decision 15	New York
October 4, 1935	Tony Canzoneri	**Al Roth**	Decision 15	New York
May 3, 1940	Sammy Angott	**Davey Day**	Decision 15	Louisville
May 14, 1942	Sammy Angott	**Allie Stolz**	Decision 15	New York
June 28, 1946	Bob Montgomery	**Allie Stolz**	KO 13	New York

*Ross won the Lightweight and Junior Welterweight titles.

JUNIOR WELTERWEIGHT TITLE (AKA, LIGHT WELTERWEIGHT)

Date	Won	Lost	Result	City
July 9, 1923	Pinkey Mitchell	**Nat Goldman**	ND 10	Philadelphia
September 21, 1926	**Mushy Callahan**	Pinky Mitchell	Decision 10	Vernon
March 14, 1927	**Mushy Callahan**	Andy DiVodi	KO 2	New York
May 31, 1927	**Mushy Callahan**	Spug Myers	Decision 10	Chicago
May 28, 1929	**Mushy Callahan**	Fred Mahon	KO 3	Los Angeles
February 18, 1930	**Jackie "Kid" Berg**	**Mushy Callahan**	TKO 10	London
April 4, 1930	**Jackie "Kid" Berg**	**Joe Glick**	Decision 10	New York
May 29, 1930	**Jackie "Kid" Berg**	Al Delmont	TKO 4	Newark
September 30, 1930	**Jackie "Kid" Berg**	Buster Brown	Decision 10	Newark
January 23, 1931	**Jackie "Kid" Berg**	Goldie Hess	Decision 10	Chicago
January 30, 1931	**Jackie "Kid" Berg**	Herman Perlick	Decision 10	New York
April 10, 1931	**Jackie "Kid" Berg**	Billy Wallace	Decision 10	Detroit
April 24, 1931	Tony Canzoneri	**Jackie "Kid" Berg**	KO 3	Chicago
September 10, 1931	Tony Canzoneri	**Jackie "Kid" Berg**	Decision 15	New York
June 23, 1933	**Barney Ross***	Tony Canzoneri	Decision 10	Chicago
July 26, 1933	**Barney Ross**	Johnny Farr	TKO 6	Kansas City
September 12, 1933*	**Barney Ross**	Tony Canzoneri	Decision 15	New York
November 17, 1933	**Barney Ross**	Sammy Fuller	Decision 10	Chicago
February 7, 1934	**Barney Ross**	Pete Nebo	Decision 12	New Orleans
March 5, 1934	**Barney Ross**	Frankie Klick	Draw 10	San Francisco
March 14, 1934	**Barney Ross**	Kid Moro	Decision 10	Oakland
March 27, 1934	**Barney Ross**	Bobby Pacho	Decision 10	Los Angeles
December 10, 1934	**Barney Ross**	Bobby Pacho	Decision 12	Cleveland
January 28, 1935	**Barney Ross**	Frankie Klick	Decision 12	Miami
April 9, 1938	**Barney Ross**	Harry Woods	Decision 12	Seattle
February 23, 1980	**Saoul Mamby**	Sang-Hyun Kim	TKO 14	Seoul
July 7, 1980	**Saoul Mamby**	Esteban De Jesus	TKO 13	Bloomington
October 2, 1980	**Saoul Mamby**	Maurice Watkins	Decision 15	Las Vegas
June 12, 1981	**Saoul Mamby**	Joe Kimpuani	Decision 15	Detroit
August 29, 1981	**Saoul Mamby**	Thomas Americo	Decision 15	Jakarta
December 19, 1981	**Saoul Mamby**	Obisia Nwankpa	Decision 15	Lagos
June 26, 1982	Leroy Haley	**Saoul Mamby**	Decision 15	Highland Heights
February 13, 1983	Leroy Haley	**Saoul Mamby**	Decision 12	Cleveland
November 3, 1984	Billy Costello	**Saoul Mamby**	Decision 12	Kingston
December 5, 2009	Amir Khan	**Dmitriy Salita**	TKO 1	Newcastle

*Ross won the Lightweight and Junior Welterweight titles.

WELTERWEIGHT TITLE

Date	Won	Lost	Result	City
November 27, 1907	Mike "Twin" Sullivan	**Kid Farmer**	KO13	Los Angeles
June 27, 1910	**Harry Lewis**	**Young Joseph**	KO 7	London
March 21, 1914	**Matt Wells**	Tom McCormick	Decision 20	Sydney
June 1, 1915	Mike Glover	**Matt Wells**	Decision	Boston
August 31, 1915	**Ted "Kid" Lewis**	Jack Britton	Decision 12	Boston
September 28, 1915	**Ted "Kid" Lewis**	Jack Britton	Decision 12	Boston
October 26, 1915	**Ted "Kid" Lewis**	Joe Mandot	Decision 12	Boston
December 28, 1915	**Ted "Kid" Lewis**	Willie Ritchie	Decision 10	New York
January 17, 1916	**Ted "Kid" Lewis**	Kid Graves	Decision 10	Milwaukee
February 15, 1916	**Ted "Kid" Lewis**	Jack Britton	ND 10	Brooklyn
February 21, 1916	**Ted "Kid" Lewis**	Lockport Jimmy Duffy	ND 10	Buffalo
March 1, 1916	**Ted "Kid" Lewis**	**Harry Stone**	Decision 20	Dayton, Ohio
April 24, 1916	Jack Britton	**Ted "Kid" Lewis**	Decision 20	New Orleans
November 21, 1916	Jack Britton	**Charley White**	Decision 12	Boston
June 25, 1917	**Ted "Kid" Lewis**	Jack Britton	Decision 20	Dayton
December 17, 1917	**Ted "Kid" Lewis**	Bryan Downey	Decision 12	Columbus
March 6, 1918	**Ted "Kid" Lewis**	Jack Britton	ND 10	Atlanta
May 2, 1918	**Ted "Kid" Lewis**	Jack Britton	ND10	Scranton
September 23, 1918	**Ted "Kid" Lewis**	**Benny Leonard**	ND 8	Newark
March 17, 1919	Jack Britton	**Ted "Kid" Lewis**	KO 9	Canton
August 4, 1919	Jack Britton	**Ted "Kid" Lewis**	ND 8	Jersey City
February 7, 1921	Jack Britton	**Ted "Kid" Lewis**	Decision 15	New York
June 26, 1922	Jack Britton	**Benny Leonard**	DQ 13	Bronx
November 25, 1925	Mickey Walker	**Sailor Friedman**	ND 12	Newark
June 24, 1925	Mickey Walker	**Lew Tendler**	Decision 10	Philadelphia
July 9, 1926	Pete Latzo	**Georgie Levine**	DQ 4	New York
March 25, 1929	**Jackie Fields**	Young Jack Thompson	Decision 10	Chicago
July 25, 1929	**Jackie Fields**	Joe Dundee	DQ 2	Detroit
May 19, 1930	Young Jack Thompson	**Jackie Fields**	Decision 10	Detroit
January 28, 1932	**Jackie Fields**	Lou Brouillard	Decision 10	Chicago
February 22, 1933	Young Corbett III	**Jackie Fields**	Decision 10	San Francisco
September 17, 1934	Jimmy McLarnin	**Barney Ross**	Decision 15	Long Island City
May 28, 1935	**Barney Ross**	Jimmy McLarnin	Decision 15	New York
November 27, 1936	**Barney Ross**	Izzy Jannazzo	Decision 15	New York
September 23, 1937	**Barney Ross**	Ceferino Garcia	Decision 15	New York

WELTERWEIGHT TITLE (CONTINUED)

Date	Won	Lost	Result	City
May 31, 1938	Henry Armstrong	**Barney Ross**	Decision 15	Long Island City
March 16, 1939	Henry Armstrong	Lew Feldman	KO 1	St. Louis
March 31, 1939	Henry Armstrong	**Davey Day**	TKO 12	New York City
April 15, 1984	Milton McCrory	**Gilles Elbilia**	TKO 6	Detroit

SUPER WELTERWEIGHT TITLE (AKA JUNIOR MIDDLEWEIGHT) (ESTABLISHED 1962)

Date	Won	Lost	Result	City
November 14, 2009	**Yuri Foreman**	Daniel Santos	Decision 12	Las Vegas
June 5, 2010	Miguel Cotto	**Yuri Foreman**	TKO 9	Bronx

MIDDLEWEIGHT TITLE

Date	Won	Lost	Result	City
April 7, 1914	**Al McCoy**	George Chip	KO 1	Brooklyn
April 6, 1915	**Al McCoy**	George Chip	ND 10	Brooklyn
May 4, 1915	**Al McCoy**	Jimmy Clabby	ND 10	Brooklyn
May 31, 1915	**Al McCoy**	Silent Martin	ND 10	Brooklyn
September 9, 1915	**Al McCoy**	Young Ahearn	ND 10	Brooklyn
October 14, 1917	Mike O'Dowd	**Al McCoy**	KO 6	Brooklyn
September 19, 1919	Mike O'Dowd	**Soldier Bartfield**	ND 10	St. Paul
July 1, 1920	Johnny Wilson	**Soldier Bartfield**	ND 12	Newark
August 14, 1922	**Dave Rosenberg**	Phil Krug	W 15	Bronx
November 30, 1922	Mike O'Dowd	**Dave Rosenberg**	DQ 8	Brooklyn
January 13, 1933	**Ben Jeby**	Frank Battaglia	TKO 12	New York
March 17, 1933	**Ben Jeby**	Vince Dundee	Draw 15	New York
July 10, 1933	**Ben Jeby**	Young Terry	Decision 15	Newark
August 9, 1933	Lou Brouillard	**Ben Jeby**	KO 7	New York
November 1, 1938	**Solly Krieger**	Al Hostak	Decision 15	Seattle
June 27, 1939	Al Hostak	**Solly Krieger**	KO 4	Seattle
December 11, 1939	Al Hostak	**Erich Seelig**	KO 1	Cleveland
November 28, 1941	Tony Zale	**Georgie Abrams**	Decision15	New York
March 28, 1976	Rodrigo Valdez	**Nessim Cohen**	TKO 4	Paris

LIGHT HEAVYWEIGHT TITLE

Date	Won	Lost	Result	City
April 25, 1916	Jack Dillon	**Battling Levinsky**	Decision 15	Kansas City
September 12, 1916	Jack Dillon	**Battling Levinsky**	ND 8	Memphis
October 24, 1916	**Battling Levinsky**	Jack Dillon	Decision 12	Boston
March 23, 1917	**Battling Levinsky**	Tommy Gibbons	ND 10	St. Paul
May 9, 1917	**Battling Levinsky**	Bob McAllister	ND 10	Bronx
June 20, 1917	**Battling Levinsky**	Johnny Howard	Decision 12	Marieville
February 17, 1919	**Battling Levinsky**	Harry Greb	ND 10	New York
July 3, 1919	**Battling Levinsky**	Billy Miske	ND 12	Rossford
September 3, 1919	**Battling Levinsky**	Harry Greb	ND 10	Wheeling
November 24, 1919	**Battling Levinsky**	Clay Turner	ND 10	Detroit
October 12, 1920	George Carpentier	**Battling Levinsky**	KO 4	Jersey City
May 11, 1922	Georges Carpentier	**Ted "Kid" Lewis**	KO 1	London
August 30, 1927	Jimmy Slattery	**Maxie Rosenbloom**	Decision 10	Hartford
June 25, 1930	**Maxie Rosenbloom**	Jimmy Slattery	Decision 15	Buffalo
October 22, 1930	**Maxie Rosenbloom**	**Abie Bain**	TKO 11	New York
August 5, 1931	**Maxie Rosenbloom**	Jimmy Slattery	Decision 10	Brooklyn
July 14, 1932	**Maxie Rosenbloom**	Lou Scozza	Decision 15	Boston
March 10, 1933	**Maxie Rosenbloom**	Adolf Heuser	Decision 15	New York
March 24, 1933	**Maxie Rosenbloom**	Bob Godwin	TKO 4	New York
November 3, 1933	**Maxie Rosenbloom**	Mickey Walker	Decision 15	New York
February 5, 1934	**Maxie Rosenbloom**	Joe Knight	Draw 15	Miami
November 1, 1934	**Bob Olin**	**Maxie Rosenbloom**	Decision 15	New York
October 31, 1935	John Henry Lewis	**Bob Olin**	Decision 15	St. Louis
June 3, 1937	John Henry Lewis	**Bob Olin**	TKO 8	St. Louis
September 15, 1978	**Mike Rossman**	Victor Galindez	TKO 13	New Orleans
December 5, 1978	**Mike Rossman**	Aldo Traversaro	TKO 6	Philadelphia
April 14, 1979	Victor Galindez	**Mike Rossman**	TKO 10	New Orleans

HEAVYWEIGHT TITLE

Date	Won	Lost	Result	City
April 18, 1908	Tommy Burns	**Jewey Smith**	KO 5	Paris
March 21, 1941	Joe Louis	**Abe Simon**	KO 13	Detroit
March 27, 1942	Joe Louis	**Abe Simon**	KO 6	New York

VI. MADISON SQUARE GARDEN MAIN EVENTS FEATURING JEWISH BOXERS: 1920–2014

Prior to 1920, boxing activity in New York State was dependent on the sport's legal status. It was either feast or famine depending on how the state's political winds were blowing. As a result, only 89 fight cards were staged at Madison Square Garden between 1900 and 1919. With the passage of the Walker Law in 1920, all legal roadblocks were removed and boxing thrived as never before. New York's Madison Square Garden (both old and new versions) became the sport's premier arena for the next 60 years.

In the 1920s Madison Square Garden staged 288 boxing cards. Jewish boxers appeared in 122 (42 percent) of the main events. From 1930 to 1950, the number was 119 of 529 (22 percent) main events. Over the next 63 years, only two Garden main events have featured a Jewish boxer.

Names of Jewish boxers appear in bold type. In a draw decision the Jewish boxer is listed first.

1920

Date	Won	Lost	Result
September 28, 1920	**Abe Goldstein**	Patsy Wallace	Decision 10
October 22, 1920	Lou Bogash	**Marty Cross**	Decision 10
October 29, 1920	**Willie Jackson**	Eddie Fitzsimmons	TKO 10
November 5, 1920	Joe Lynch	**Abe Goldstein**	KO 11
November 26, 1920	**Benny Leonard**	Joe Welling	TKO 14

1921

Date	Won	Lost	Result
January 7, 1921	**Willie Jackson**	Pinky Mitchell	Draw 15
January 14, 1921	**Benny Leonard**	Ritchie Mitchell	TKO 6
January 17, 1921	Andy Chaney	**Charlie Beecher**	Decision 15
January 26, 1921	Memphis Pal Moore	**Young Montreal**	Decision 15
February 7, 1921	Jack Britton	**Ted "Kid" Lewis**	Decision 15
February 15, 1921	**Abe Goldstein**	Frankie Daly	Decision 10
February 22, 1921	**Soldier Bartfield**	Lou Bogash	Draw 15
February 25, 1921	**Willie Jackson**	Johnny Dundee	Decision 15
March 2, 1921	**Charlie Beecher**	Dick Loadman	Decision 12
March 10 1921	**Battling Levinsky**	Homer Smith	Decision 12
March 21, 1921	Rocky Kansas	**Willie Jackson**	Decision 12
September 30, 1921	**Willie Jackson**	Pete Hartley	Draw 15
October 7, 1921	**Joe Burman**	Midget Smith	Decision 10

1921 (CONTINUED)

Date	Won	Lost	Result
October 21, 1921	Rocky Kansas	**Lew Tendler**	Decision 15
October 28, 1921	**Sailor Friedman**	Ernie Rice	TKO 7
November 29, 1921	**Joe Benjamin**	Pete Hartley	Decision 10
December 16, 1921	**Lew Tendler**	**Sailor Friedman**	Decision 15
December 30, 1921	**Willie Jackson**	Johnny Dundee	Draw 15

1922

Date	Won	Lost	Result
January 6, 1922	**Abe Goldstein**	Andy "Kid" Davis	TKO 6
January 13, 1922	Gene Tunney	**Battling Levinsky**	Decision 12
February 3, 1922	Johnny Dundee	**Joe Benjamin**	Decision 15
February 10, 1922	**Benny Leonard**	Rocky Kansas	Decision 15
February 20, 1922	**Willie Jackson**	Charley White	Decision 15
February 24, 1922	**Lew Tendler**	**Oakland Jimmy Duffy**	TKO 8
March 17, 1922	Johnny Dundee	**Charley White**	Decision 15
March 20, 1922	**Joe Burman**	Midget Smith	Decision 10
May 5, 1922	**Lew Tendler**	Johnny Dundee	Decision 15
May 16, 1922	**Augie Ratner**	Jock Malone	Draw 15
May 19, 1922	**Benny Leonard**	**Soldier Bartfield**	Decision 4*
September 21, 1922	**Jackie "Kid" Wolfe**	Joe Lynch	Decision 15
October 20, 1922	**Charley White**	**Sid Marks**	KO 2
November 24, 1922	**Louis "Kid" Kaplan**	Steve "Kid" Sullivan	Decision 12
December 11, 1922	**Jack Bernstein**	**Eddie "Kid" Wagner**	Decision 10
November 1, 1922	**Sailor Friedman**	Eddie Fitzsimmons	KO 8
November 16, 1922	**Abe Goldstein**	Pancho Villa	Decision 15
December 11, 1922	**Charlie Beecher**	Frankie Garcia	Decision 12
December 15, 1922	**Charley White**	Ritchie Mitchell	TKO 10

*Program of 10 four-round bouts to raise money for National Sports Alliance

1923

Date	Won	Lost	Result
January 5, 1923	**Jack Bernstein**	Pepper Martin	Decision 12
January 17, 1923	**Eddie "Kid" Wagner**	Henry Mick	Decision 10
January 19, 1923	**Lew Tendler**	Pal Moran	Decision 15
February 9, 1923	Rocky Kansas	**Charley White**	Decision 15
February 16, 1923	**Danny Lee**	**Sonny Smith**	TKO 10
September 21, 1923	**Joey Sangor**	Spencer Gardner	Decision 12
September 28, 1923	**Louis "Kid" Kaplan**	Jimmy Goodrich	Decision 10
October 5, 1923	Pal Moran	**Charley White**	Decision 10
October 12, 1923	**Jack Bernstein**	Rocky Kansas	Decision 15
October 19, 1923	**Abe Goldstein**	**Joe Burman**	Decision 12
December 17, 1923	Johnny Dundee	**Jack Bernstein**	Decision 15
December 28, 1923	**Sailor Friedman**	Johnny Clinton	Decision 10

1924

Date	Won	Lost	Result
January 4, 1924	**Sid Terris**	**Eddie "Kid" Wagner**	KO 6
January 11, 1924	**Jack Bernstein**	Sammy Mandell	Draw 15
February 8, 1924	Pancho Villa	**Georgie Marks**	Decision 15
March 21, 1924	**Abe Goldstein**	Joe Lynch	Decision 15
April 29, 1924	**Charley Phil Rosenberg**	Eddie Martin	Draw 10
October 10, 1924	**Louis "Kid" Kaplan**	Angel Diaz	Decision 10
November 7, 1924	Sammy Mandell	**Jack Bernstein**	Decision 12
November 21, 1924	**Louis "Kid" Kaplan**	Bobby Garcia	Decision 10
November 26, 1924	**Sid Terris**	Luis Vicentini	Decision 10
December 12, 1924	**Louis "Kid" Kaplan**	Jose Lombardo	KO 4
December 19, 1924	Eddie Martin	**Abe Goldstein**	Decision 15

1925

Date	Won	Lost	Result
January 2, 1925	**Louis "Kid" Kaplan**	**Danny Kramer**	TKO 9
January 9, 1925	**Jack Bernstein**	Tommy O'Brien	Decision 10
February 6, 1925	Sammy Mandell	**Sid Terris**	Decision 12
February 20, 1925	**Danny Kramer**	Leo "Kid" Roy	TKO 8
March 20, 1925	**Charley Phil Rosenberg**	Eddie Martin	Decision 15

1925 (CONTINUED)

Date	Won	Lost	Result
May 5, 1925*	**Sid Terris**	Johnny Dundee	Decision 12
December 12, 1925	**Jack Bernstein**	Rocky Kansas	Decision 15
December 18, 1925	**Louis "Kid" Kaplan**	Babe Herman	Decision 15

*Last bout at old Madison Square Garden on 24th Street and Madison Square

1926

Date	Won	Lost	Result
January 8, 1926	**Sid Terris**	Lucien Vinez	Decision 10
January 29, 1926	**Joe Glick**	Johnny Dundee	Decision 10
February 19, 1926	**Sammy Vogel**	Billy Petrolle	Decision 10
May 17, 1926	**Willie Harmon**	Jack Zivic	Draw 10
May 27, 1926	**Eddie "Kid" Wagner**	Phil McGraw	Decision 10
July 29, 1926	**Benny Bass**	Johnny Farr	Decision 10
September 30, 1926	Tod Morgan	**Joe Glick**	Decision 15
October 15, 1926	**Lew Tendler**	Farmer Joe Cooper	Decision 10
December 13, 1926	**Maxie Rosenbloom**	**KO Phil Kaplan**	Decision 10

1927

Date	Won	Lost	Result
January 1, 1927	**Benny Bass**	**Red Chapman**	WF 1
February 4, 1927	**Charley Phil Rosenberg**	Bushy Graham	Decision 15
March 14, 1927	**Mushy Callahan**	Andy DiVodi	KO 1
March 18, 1927	**Sid Terris**	Billy Wallace	Decision 10
May 13, 1927	**Sid Terris**	Stanislaus Loayza	Decision 10
September 15, 1927	**Joe Glick**	Doc Snell	Decision 10
December 16, 1927	Tod Morgan	**Joe Glick**	WF 4
December 23, 1927	**Sid Terris**	Phil McGraw	Decision 10

1928

Date	Won	Lost	Result
January 20, 1928	Ace Hudkins	**Lew Tendler**	Decision 10
February 10, 1928	Tony Canzoneri	**Benny Bass**	Decision 15

1928 (CONTINUED)

Date	Won	Lost	Result
February 24, 1928	Jimmy McLarnin	**Sid Terris**	KO 1
May 4, 1928	**Joe Glick**	Lope Tenorio	Decision 10
May 31, 1928	Manuel Quintero	**Louis "Kid" Kaplan**	Decision 10
June 28, 1928	Tommy Loughran	**Armand Emmanuel**	Decision 10
September 13, 1928	Panama Al Brown	**Kid Francis**	Decision 12
October 5, 1928	**Joe Glick**	Tommy Grogan	Decision 10
October 11, 1928	Rene DeVos	**KO Phil Kaplan**	Decision 10
November 16, 1928	**Joe Glick**	Baby Joe Gans	Decision 10
November 23, 1928	Harry Ebbets	**KO Phil Kaplan**	W DQ 4
December 14, 1928	Tony Canzoneri	**Al Singer**	KO 1

1929

Date	Won	Lost	Result
January 11, 1929	Jimmy McLarnin	**Joe Glick**	Decision 10
February 8, 1929	**Al Singer**	Bud Taylor	WF 4
February 15, 1929	**Jackie Fields**	Baby Joe Gans	Decision 10
March 1, 1929	Jimmy McLarnin	**Joe Glick**	KO 2
March 11, 1929	**Maxie Rosenbloom**	Osk Till	Decision 10
March 15, 1929	**Al Singer**	Bud Taylor	Decision 10
March 22, 1929	Jimmy McLarnin	**Ray Miller**	Decision 10
April 26, 1929	Tony Canzoneri	**Sammy Dorfman**	Decision 10
May 10 1929	Billy Wallace	**Louis "Kid" Kaplan**	Decision 10
May 17, 1929	Ignacio Fernandez	**Al Singer**	KO 3
May 23, 1929	**Jackie "Kid Berg"**	Bruce Flowers	Decision 10
October 3, 1929	Stanislaus Loayza	**Sid Terris**	Decision 10
October 11, 1929	**Al Singer**	Young Zazzarino	KO 6
October 21, 1929	**Al Singer**	Davey Abad	Decision 10
November 4, 1929	Eugene Huat	**Izzy Schwartz**	Decision 10
November 15, 1929	**Maxie Rosenbloom**	Jimmy Braddock	Decision 10
November 29, 1929	**Al Singer**	Pete Nebo	TKO 4
December 9, 1929	**Maxie Rosenbloom**	**Yale Okun**	Decision 10
December 13, 1929	Jimmy McLarnin	**Ruby Goldstein**	KO 2
December 20, 1929	**Benny Bass**	Tod Morgan	KO 2

1930

Date	Won	Lost	Result
January 3, 1930	**Maxie Rosenbloom**	Leo Lomski	Decision 10
January 17 1930	**Jackie "Kid" Berg**	Tony Canzoneri	Decision 10
January 31, 1930	**Al Singer**	Stanislaus Loayza	Decision 10
February 14, 1930	**Maxie Rosenbloom**	Ace Hudkins	Decision 10
February 28, 1930	**Ted Sandwina**	Riccardo Bertazzolo	Decision 10
March 10, 193	**Maxie Rosenbloom**	Larry Johnson	WF 6
April 4 1930	**Jackie "Kid" Berg**	**Joe Glick**	Decision 10
April 30, 1930	**Maxie Rosenbloom**	Larry Johnson	Decision 10
May 23, 1930	**Al Singer**	Ignacio Fernandez	Decision 10
October 3, 1930	Justo Suarez	**Ray Miller**	Decision 10
October 10, 1930	**Jackie "Kid" Berg**	Billy Petrolle	Decision 10

1931

Date	Won	Lost	Result
January 30, 1931	**Jackie "Kid" Berg**	Herman Perlick	Decision 10
February 20, 1931	**Kid Francis**	Eddie Shea	Decision 10
March 20, 1931	**Ben Jeby**	Len Harvey	Decision 10
March 27, 1931	Fidel La Barba	**Kid Francis**	Decision 10
May 8, 1931	**Jackie "Kid" Berg**	Tony Herrera	Decision 10
June 4, 1931	Vince Dundee	**Ben Jeby**	Decision 10
June 18, 1931	**Al Singer**	Lew Massey	Decision 10
August 13, 1932	Phil Rafferty	**Eddie Shapiro**	Decision 10
September 3, 1931	Joey Costa	**Lew Feldman**	Decision 8
September 17, 1931	Young Terry	**Jackie Fields**	Decision 10
October 2, 1931	Dave Shade	**Ben Jeby**	Decision 10
October 16, 1931	Vince Dundee	**Solly Krieger**	TKO 8
December 11, 1931	Bat Battalino	**Al Singer**	TKO 2
December 18, 1931	**King Levinsky**	Tommy Loughran	Decision 10

1932

Date	Won	Lost	Result
January 29, 1932	Max Baer	**King Levinsky**	Decision 10
February 19, 1932	**Eddie Wolfe**	Baby Joe Gans	Draw 10
February 26, 1932	Sammy Fuller	**Ray Miller**	Decision 10
March 18, 1932	**Morrie Sherman**	Franta Nekolny	Draw 10

1932 (CONTINUED)

Date	Won	Lost	Result
April 1, 1932	Sammy Fuller	**Jackie "Kid" Berg**	Decision 10
May 13, 1932	King Tut	**Morrie Sherman**	Decision 10
May 20, 1932	Sammy Fuller	**Jackie "Kid" Berg**	Decision 10
October 7, 1932	Jimmy McLarnin	**Benny Leonard**	TKO 6
October 13, 1932	Kid Chocolate	**Lew Feldman**	Decision 10

1933

Date	Won	Lost	Result
January 13, 1933	**Ben Jeby**	Frank Battaglia	TKO 12
February 24, 1933	Johnny Risko	**King Levinsky**	Decision 10
March 10, 1933	**Maxie Rosenbloom**	Adolph Heuser	Decision 15
March 17, 1933	**Ben Jeby**	Vince Dundee	Draw 15
March 24, 1933	**Maxie Rosenbloom**	Bob Godwin	TKO 4
November 3, 1933	**Maxie Rosenbloom**	Mickey Walker	Decision 15

1934

Date	Won	Lost	Result
January 12, 1934	Cleo Locatelli	**Jackie "Kid" Berg**	Decision 10
January 19, 1934	Lou Brouillard	**Bob Olin**	Decision 10
February 9, 1934	**King Levinsky**	Charley Massera	Decision 10
March 9, 1934	Walter Neusel	**King Levinsky**	Decision 10
May 11, 1934	Baby Arizmendi	**Al Roth**	Decision 10
October 5, 1934	Steve Hamas	**Art Lasky**	Decision 10
November 2, 1934	**Al Roth**	Eddie Cool	Decision 10
November 16, 1934	**Bob Olin**	**Maxie Rosenbloom**	Decision 15
November 23, 1934	John Henry Lewis	**Yale Okun**	TKO 3

1935

Date	Won	Lost	Result
March 22, 1935	Jimmy Braddock	**Art Lasky**	Decision 15
October 4, 1935	Tony Canzoneri	**Al Roth**	Decision 15
November 22, 1935	Frankie Klick	**Al Roth**	Decision 10

1936

Date	Won	Lost	Result
November 27, 1936	**Barney Ross**	Izzy Jannazzo	Decision 15

1937

Date	Won	Lost	Result
August 12, 1937	**Solly Krieger**	Walter Woods	KO 8
September 9, 1937	**Al Roth**	Paul Junior	Draw 10

1938

Date	Won	Lost	Result
May 20, 1938	Glen Lee	**Solly Krieger**	Decision 10
May 31, 1938*	Henry Armstrong	**Barney Ross**	Decision 15
July 21, 1938	**Al "Bummy" Davis**	**Bernie Friedkin**	TKO 4

*Madison Square Garden Bowl

1939

Date	Won	Lost	Result
March 17, 1939	**Al "Bummy" Davis**	**Mickey Farber**	Decision 10
March 31, 1938	Henry Armstrong	**Davey Day**	TKO 12
May 12, 1938	Billy Conn	**Solly Krieger**	Decision 10
May 23, 1938	**Davey Day**	Pedro Montanez	TKO 8
June 8, 1938	**Al "Bummy" Davis**	Eddie Brink	Decision 10
November 1, 1938	**Al "Bummy" Davis**	Tony Canzoneri	TKO 3
December 1, 1938	Petey Scalzo	**Allie Stolz**	KO 4
December 15, 1938	**Al "Bummy" Davis**	Tippy Larkin	KO 5

1940

Date	Won	Lost	Result
January 10, 1940	Billy Conn	**Henry Cooper**	Decision 10
February 23, 1940	Lou Ambers	**Al "Bummy" Davis**	Decision 10
September 20, 1940	**Al "Bummy" Davis**	Tony Marteliano	Decision 10
November 15, 1940	Fritzie Zivic	**Al "Bummy" Davis**	DQ 2

1941

Date	Won	Lost	Result
July 30, 1941	**Georgie Abrams**	Billy Soose	Decision 10
September 19, 1941	Sugar Ray Robinson	**Maxie Shapiro**	TKO 3
November 28, 1941	Tony Zale	**Georgie Abrams**	Decision 15

1942

Date	Won	Lost	Result
February 20, 1942	Sugar Ray Robinson	**Maxie Berger**	TKO 2
February 27, 1942	**Allie Stolz**	Bobby Ruffin	Decision 12
March 27, 1942	Joe Louis	**Abe Simon**	TKO 6
May 15, 1942	Sammy Angott	**Allie Stolz**	Decision 15
August 6, 1942	**Allie Stolz**	Chalkey Wright	Decision 15
August 28, 1942	Cleo Shans	**Maxie Shapiro**	Decision 10
November 13, 1941	Beau Jack	**Allie Stolz**	TKO 7

1943

Date	Won	Lost	Result
January 29, 1943	Willie Pep	**Allie Stolz**	Decision 10

1944

Date	Won	Lost	Result
February 18, 1944	**Al "Bummy" Davis**	Bob Montgomery	KO 1
March 17, 1944	Beau Jack	**Al "Bummy" Davis**	Decision 10
March 23, 1944	Tippy Larkin	**Allie Stolz**	TKO 3
June 15, 1944	Henry Armstrong	**Al "Bummy" Davis**	TKO 2
July 20, 1944	Ike Williams	**Julie Kogon**	Decision 10
November 3, 1944	**Harold Green**	Rocky Graziano	Decision 10
December 22, 1944	**Harold Green**	Rocky Graziano	Decision 10
December 29, 1944	**Danny Bartfield**	Morris Reif	Decision 10

1945

Date	Won	Lost	Result
February 9, 1945	**Harold Green**	**Morris Reif**	Decision 10
February 16, 1945	**Danny Bartfield**	Humberto Zavala	Decision 10

1945 (CONTINUED)

Date	Won	Lost	Result
May 25, 1945	Rocky Graziano	**Al "Bummy" Davis**	TKO 4
June 22, 1945	**Harold Green**	Fritzie Zivic	Decision 10
August 31, 1945	**Artie Levine**	Sonny Horne	TKO 5
September 14, 1945	Willie Joyce	**Danny Bartfield**	TKO 6
September 28, 1945	Rocky Graziano	**Harold Green**	KO 3
November 12, 1945	**Allie Stolz**	Willie Joyce	Decision 10
December 7, 1945	Sonny Horne	Artie Levine	Decision 10

1946

Date	Won	Lost	Result
January 4, 1946	Beau Jack	**Morris Reif**	KO 4
February 15, 1946	**Allie Stolz**	Willie Joyce	Decision 10
March 15, 1946	Willie Joyce	**Danny Kapilow**	Draw 10
June 28, 1946	Bob Montgomery	**Allie Stolz**	KO 13
August 2, 1946	**Danny Kapilow**	**Willie Joyce**	Draw 10
August 9, 1946	Tony Pellone	**Ruby Kessler**	Decision 10
August 23, 1946	**Georgie Abrams**	Steve Belloise	Decision 10
December 6, 1946	Marcel Cerdan	**Georgie Abrams**	Decision 10

1947

Date	Won	Lost	Result
January 17, 1947	Billy Graham	**Ruby Kessler**	Decision 10
January 31, 1947	**Harold Green**	Pete Mead	Decision 10
March 7, 1947	**Artie Levine**	**Herbie Kronowitz**	Decision 10
March 28, 1947	Marcel Cerdan	**Harold Green**	TKO 2
May 16, 1947	Sugar Ray Robinson	**Georgie Abrams**	Decision 10
June 27, 1947	Billy Fox	**Artie Levine**	TKO 3
July 11, 1947	Steve Belloise	**Georgie Abrams**	TKO 5
September 5, 1947	Pete Mead	**Herbie Kronowitz**	Decision 10

(Note: In 1948, 1949, and 1951, no main events featured a Jewish boxer. From 1951 to 2014, only two Jewish boxers appeared in a main event.)

1950

Date	Won	Lost	Result
May 26, 1950	Kid Gavilan	**Georgie Small**	Decision 10

1975

Date	Won	Lost	Result
September 30, 1975	Mike Quarry	**Mike Rossman**	Decision 10

1977

Date	Won	Lost	Result
May 11, 1977	**Mike Rossman**	Mike Quarry	TKO 6

VII. JEWISH BOXERS WHO WON AN OLYMPIC MEDAL

1904 St. Louis
Sam Berger (USA) Gold Medal—Heavyweight

No Boxing at 1912 Games

1920 Antwerp
Sam Mosberg (USA) Gold Medal—Lightweight
Albert Schneider (Canada) Gold Medal—Middleweight
Montgomery "Moe" Herscovitch (Canada) Bronze Medal—Middleweight

1924 Paris
Jacob "Jackie" Fields (USA) Gold Medal—Featherweight

1928 Amsterdam
Harold Devine (USA) Bronze Medal—Featherweight
Harry Isaacs (South Africa) Bronze Medal—Bantamweight
Jacob Michaelson (Denmark) Bronze Medal—Heavyweight

1932 Los Angeles
Nat Bor (USA) Bronze Medal—Lightweight

1960 Rome
Gyula Torok (Hungary) Gold Medal—Flyweight

1972 Munich
Gyorgy Gedo (Hungary) Gold Medal—Light Flyweight

1976 Montreal
Victor Zilberman (Romania) Bronze Medal—Welterweight

1980 Moscow
Shamil Sabyrov (USSR) Gold Medal—Light Flyweight

VIII. JEWISH BOXERS WHO WON A NEW YORK GOLDEN GLOVES CHAMPIONSHIP

The *Daily News*–sponsored New York Golden Gloves amateur boxing tournament began in 1927. For the next 60 years it was the most prestigious citywide amateur tournament in the United States. Although the Golden Gloves no longer attracts the same amount of attention or participation as in boxing's heyday, the tournament is still popular. Since its inception more than 80,000 amateurs have climbed through the ropes to trade punches with other young hopefuls, but only 1,500 have actually won the coveted trophy—a small diamond-studded gold replica of a pair of boxing gloves. I have met former Golden Gloves champions in their eighties who still proudly wear those precious gloves on a chain around their necks. Bob Olin was the first New York Golden Gloves champions to win a professional championship.

(*Note*: The New York tournament has two categories: "Sub-Novice" for amateurs with less than 11 bouts, and an "Open Division" for boxers with more extensive amateur experience.)

YEAR	TITLE	WINNER
1927	112 lb. Open	Terry Roth
1927	126 lb. Sub-Novice	Nat Collenstein
1928	175 lb. Open	Robert Olin
1928	160 lb. Sub-Novice	Daniel Auerbach (Solly Krieger)
1928	175 lb. Sub-Novice	Yale Rubin
1929	160 lb. Sub-Novice	Milton Hunter
1930	Hvwt. Sub-Novice	Max Glickman
1931	118 lb. Open	Al Roth
1931	126 lb. Sub-Novice	Lew Mendelsohn
1931	175 lb. Sub-Novice	Sam Portney
1932	147 lb. Sub-Novice	Sam Kanterwitz
1932	160 lb. Sub-Novice	Oscar Waxman
1933	118 lb. Open	Julie Katz
1935	135 lb. Open	Marty Pomerantz
1935	112 lb. Sub-Novice	Frank Levine
1935	126 lb. Sub-Novice	Aaron Seltzer
1935	135 lb. Sub-Novice	Isidore Eisenberg
1936	135 lb. Open	Murray Kravitz
1936	135 lb. Sub-Novice	Marcus Cohn
1936	160 lb. Sub-Novice	Phil Pollack
1939	Hvwt. Sub-Novice	Nat Wolcoff
1940	112 lb. Sub-Novice	Gus Levine

YEAR	TITLE	WINNER
1941	147 lb. Sub-Novice	Joseph Kantor
1942	175 lb. Sub Novice	Sam Springer
1943	Hvwt. Open	Eddie Irwin (Edward Gersh)
1944	118 lb. Open	Sam Chernoff
1944	160 lb. Open	Hy Bronstein
1948	175 lb. Open	Alfred Kohn
1958	147 lb. Sub-Novice	Leonard Weiner
2001	139 lb. Open	Dmitriy Salita
2001	156 lb. Open	Yuri Foreman

IX. JEWISH BOXERS WITH MORE THAN 200 CAREER BOUTS

Of the tens of thousands of professional boxers active from the 1890s to 2014, only 120 have fought more than 200 documented bouts. Among these superathletes are 11 Jewish boxers. The list includes Harry Stone and Benny Valgar, the only two boxers with more than 200 bouts to have never been knocked out or stopped.*

Ted "Kid" Lewis—302
Maxie Rosenbloom—298
Battling Levinsky—293
Harry Stone—274
Joe Glick—245
Benny Bass—241
Benny Valgar—239
Soldier Bartfield—227
Harry Mason 215
Benny Leonard—212
Phil Bloom—202

---

* Jewish boxer Abe "the Newsboy" Hollandersky, who fought from 1906 to the mid-1920s, claimed to have had over 1,000 bouts. But included in that figure are many sparring matches and exhibitions while serving with the navy. The 150-pound boxer fought several contenders but only 98 professional contests have actually been verified.

X. THE 10 BEST JEWISH BOXER NICKNAMES

If there was an award for the sport with the most colorful nicknames, boxing would win hands down. The best boxers' nicknames have staying power and are accurately descriptive, which is why a powder-puff puncher or defensive specialist is never called "Tiger" or "Hurricane." Many times the nickname combines the fighter's persona with his hometown, as in "The Manassa Mauler," "The Brockton Blockbuster," or "The Bronx Bull." Listed below is the author's choice of the 10 best Jewish boxer nicknames:

"The Little Hebrew"	Abe Attell
"The Pride of the Bowery"	Joe Bernstein
"The Whitechapel Windmill"	Jackie "Kid" Berg
"The Fighting Dentist"	Leach Cross
"The Boxing Barrister"	Armand Emmanuel
"The Jewel of the Ghetto"	Ruby Goldstein
"Special Delivery Hirsch"	Samuel Hirsch
"The Aldgate Iron Man"	Freddie Jacks
"Slapsie Maxie"	Maxie Rosenbloom
"The Ghetto Ghost"	Sid Terris

XI. PROMINENT JEWISH BOXERS WHO FOUGHT USING IRISH NAMES

Except for Goldie Ahearn, Mushy Callahan, and Newsboy Curley, all of these boxers turned pro before 1920. (Their real names are in parentheses.)

Goldie Ahearn (Isadore Goldstein)	Al McCoy (Albert Rudolph)
Frankie Bradley (Frank Bloch)	Young McGowan (Sam Goldberg)
Frankie Callahan (Sam Holtzman)	Johnny Murray (Herman Sloves)
Mushy Callahan (Morris Scheer)	Tommy Murray (Harry Greenberg)
Johnny Clinton (Morris Elstein)	Denver Jack O'Keefe (Jacob Buxbaum)
Ty Cobb (Sam Kolb)	Eddie O'Keefe (Morris Paley)
Eddie "Newsboy" Curley (Isaac Morochnik)	Artie O'Leary (Arthur Lieberman)
Dandy Danny Dillon (Moishe Josofsky)	Young O'Leary (Nat Lieberman)
Oakland Jimmy Duffy (Hyman Gold)	Bobby Reynolds (Israel Goldstein)
Kid Farmer (Benny Feinberg)	Frankie Rice (Benjamin Lipsitz)
Barney Ford (Bernard Paley)	Archie Walker (Irving Wolkow)
Willie Jackson (Oscar Tobin)	Eddie Wallace (Abe Kwalick)
Blink McCloskey (Louis Silverman)	Maxie Williamson (Max Krupnick)

XII. TOP BARE-KNUCKLE-ERA PRIZEFIGHTERS

The following list was compiled by Tony Gee, world's foremost authority on the English bare-knuckle era and author of *Up to Scratch: Bareknuckle Fighting and Heroes of the Prize-ring*. According to Tony's extensive research, although it has been said that there were a significant number of English-born Jewish combatants active in the bare-knuckle arena (despite comparatively infrequent involvement until the late 18th century), there were surprisingly few who could claim to have been of the first rank; this lack of in-depth quality is clearly reflected in Tony's limiting his choices to six prominent boxers.

(In chronological order)
Daniel Mendoza
Dutch Sam (Samuel Elias)
Barney Aaron
Young Barney Aaron
Aby Belasco
Izzy Lazarus

XIII. JEWS IN BOXING'S HALLS OF FAME

It should not be surprising to those who follow the poorly regulated sport that boxing has more than one Hall of Fame. The first HOF was started by *The Ring* magazine founder and publisher Nat Fleischer in 1954. It was discontinued after the 1987 inductions. The World Boxing Hall of Fame was established in 1980. It is currently housed in the Los Angeles Athletic Club. The International Boxing Hall of Fame opened in 1991 and is located in Canastota, New York. The most recent addition (2013) is The Boxing Hall of Fame Las Vegas, Nevada. There are also various state boxing Halls of Fame.

Jewish boxers inducted into the three international Halls of Fame are all deserving of the honor, but many other greats are still waiting to be honored even as less talented and undeserving individuals make the cut. It is for this reason that I do not favor labeling a boxer with the words "Hall of Fame fighter." It would be a mistake to elevate a boxer's rating based solely on whether or not his name appears in a Hall of Fame. There are other, more accurate ways to measure a boxer's worth, most obviously his record against quality opponents. Although *The Ring*'s Hall of Fame focused primarily on honoring the boxers, those of more recent vintage include non-boxer categories, such as promoters, trainers, journalists, announcers, and referees.

International Boxing Hall of Fame (Canastota, New York)

BOXERS

Barney Aaron
Young Barney Aaron
Abe Attell
Benny Bass
Jackie "Kid" Berg
Newsboy Brown
Joe Choynski
Jackie Fields
Louis "Kid" Kaplan

Benny Leonard
Battling Levinsky
Harry Lewis
Ted "Kid" Lewis
Daniel Mendoza
"Slapsie Maxie" Rosenbloom
Barney Ross
Dutch Sam
Lew Tendler

NONPARTICIPANT AND OBSERVER CATEGORY

Ray Arcel—Trainer
Bob Arum—Promoter
Al Bernstein—Broadcaster
Whitey Bimstein—Trainer
Teddy Brenner—Matchmaker
Lester Bromberg—Journalist
William Cayton—Manager
Irving Cohen—Manager
Howard Cosell—Broadcaster
Mickey Duff—Promoter
Shelly Finkel—Promoter
Jack Fiske—Journalist
Nat Fleischer—Publisher/Historian
Charley Goldman—Trainer
Ruby Goldstein—Referee
Bob Goodman—Publicist
Murray Goodman—Publicist

Abe J. Green—Commissioner
Jimmy Jacobs—Manager
Mike Jacobs—Promoter
Hank Kaplan—Historian
Michael Katz—Journalist
A. J. Liebling—Journalist
Harry Markson—Promoter
Larry Merchant—Broadcaster
Barney Nagler—Journalist
J. Russell Peltz—Promoter
Irving Rudd—Publicist
Sam Silverman—Promoter
Jack Solomons—Promoter
Sam Taub—Broadcaster
Herman Taylor—Promoter
Al Weill—Manager
Stanley Weston—Publisher/Journalist

International Jewish Sports Hall of Fame (Israel)

Abe Attell

Max Baer*

Jackie "Kid" Berg

Jack Bernstein

Whitey Bimstein—Trainer

Joe Choynski

Robert Cohen

Howard Cosell—Broadcaster

Jackie Fields

Charley Goldman—Trainer

Ruby Goldstein—Referee

Alphonse Halimi

Harry Harris

Ben Jeby

Louis "Kid" Kaplan

Solly Krieger

Benny Leonard

Battling Levinsky

Harry Lewis

Ted "Kid" Lewis

Al McCoy

Daniel Mendoza

Sam Mosberg

Bob Olin

Victor "Young" Perez

"Slapsie Maxie" Rosenbloom

Barney Ross

Dutch Sam (Samuel Elias)

Corporal Izzy Schwartz

Al Singer

Jack Solomons—Promoter

Lew Tendler

*According to a spokesperson, Max Baer's wearing of the Star of David on his trunks, and his paternal grandfather's Jewish background, were enough to qualify him for inclusion.

The Ring Magazine Hall of Fame (discontinued after 1987 inductions)

BOXERS

Abe Attell

Jackie "Kid" Berg

Joe Choynski

Jackie Fields

Benny Leonard

Battling Levinsky

Ted "Kid" Lewis

Daniel Mendoza

"Slapsie Maxie" Rosenbloom

Barney Ross

Lew Tendler

MERITORIOUS SERVICE

Ray Arcel—Trainer

Nat Fleischer—Publisher/Journalist

Mike Jacobs—Promoter

Sam Taub—Broadcaster

World Boxing Hall of Fame (Los Angeles, California)

BOXERS

Georgie Abrams

Abe Attell

Jackie "Kid" Berg

Mushy Callahan

Jackie Fields

Benny Goldberg

Benny Leonard

Maxie Rosenbloom

Barney Ross

Lew Tendler

EXPANDED CATEGORY

Steve Albert—Broadcaster

Ray Arcel—Trainer

Bob Arum—Promoter

Al Bernstein—Broadcaster

Whitey Bimstein—Trainer

Teddy Brenner—Matchmaker

Jack Fiske—Journalist

Nat Fleischer—Magazine Publisher

Charley Goldman—Trainer

Ruby Goldstein—Referee

Jimmy Jacobs—Manager

Mike Jacobs—Promoter

Harry Kabakoff—Manager

Hank Kaplan—Historian/Journalist

Mike Katz—Journalist

Harold Lederman—Judge

A. J. Liebling—Journalist

Max Novich, MD—Physician

J. Russel Peltz—Promoter

Marc Ratner—Commissioner

Jack Solomons—Promoter

Howie Steindler—Manager

Boxing Hall of Fame Las Vegas, Nevada (begun in 2013)

Benny Leonard

Barney Ross

ENDNOTES

INTRODUCTION
1. Al Lurie in the *Philadelphia Jewish Exponent*, April 25, 1947. Cited in Peter Levine, *Ellis Island to Ebbets Field: Sport and the American Jewish Experience* (New York: Oxford University Press, 1992), p. 153.
2. Baseball-Almanac.com, "Jewish baseball players."
3. Steven A. Riess, *City Games: The Evolution of American Urban Society and the Rise of Sports* (Urbana: University of Illinois Press, 1989), p. 116.
4. Goldman, Herbert (ed.), *The Ring Record Book and Boxing Encyclopedia* 1985 Edition (New York: The Ring Bookshop).
5. JewsInSports.com, "Boxing."
6. Arne K. Lange, *Prizefighting: An American History* (Jefferson, NC: McFarland, 2008), p. 77.
7. Interview with the author, June 23, 2014.
8. Ron Ross, "Morris Reif Passes Away," *International Boxing Research Journal*, Issue 120, December 2013, p. 30.

CHAPTER 1: BARE-KNUCKLE BRUISERS
1. Elliot Gorn, *The Manly Art: Bare-Knuckle Prize Fighting in America* (Ithaca and London: Cornell University Press, 1986), p. 205.

CHAPTER 2: THE MELTING POT SPORT
1. Arthur Hertzberg, *The Jews in America: Four Centuries of an Uneasy Encounter: A History* (New York, London: Simon & Schuster, 1989), p. 13.
2. Michael B. Katz and Mark J. Stern, *Poverty in Twentieth-Century America, Working Paper No. 7*, November 2007, p. 6.
3. Ibid., p. 7.
4. Adam J. Pollack, *In the Ring with James J. Corbett* (Iowa City: WIN BY KO Publications, 2012), p. 16.
5. David Margolick, *Beyond Glory: Joe Louis vs. Max Schmeling and a World on the Brink* (New York: Alfred A. Knopf, 2005), p. 205.
6. Ibid., p. 38.
7. Ibid.
8. *Chicago Jewish News*, Online Edition, April 2005.
9. Cited in Hertzberg, *The Jews in America*, p. 203.
10. Levine, *Ellis Island to Ebbets Field*, p. 152.
11. Quoted by Pete Hamill in the documentary, *Boxing in America*, ESPN, 2004.
12. Kasia Body, *Boxing: A Cultural History* (London: Reaktion Books Ltd., 2008), p. 282.
13. Don Cogswell, "Boxing's Good Book," *Journal of the International Boxing Research Organization*, Issue 91, September 27, 2006, p. 33.

14. Ibid.
15. Murray Rose, "Farewell to Stillman's," *Boxing Illustrated* (February 1962), p. 19.
16. Dara Kahn, "Yiddish: The Mamloshen Lives," *B'nai B'rith Magazine* (Spring 2013), p. 23.
17. Allen Bodner, *When Boxing Was a Jewish Sport* (Westport, CT: Praeger, 1997), p. 17.

CHAPTER 3: PIONEERS OF PUGILISM: THE EARLY QUEENSBERRY ERA, 1892–1919

1. Quoted in Pat Putnam, "Benny Leonard: Fabulous Ghetto Wizard," TheSweetScience.com (September 1, 2005).
2. Documentary: *The Gentleman Prizefighter*, Fastnet Films, 2013.
3. Mike Silver, *The Arc of Boxing: The Rise and Decline of the Sweet Science* (Jefferson, NC: McFarland, 2008), p. 19.
4. Riess, *City Games*, p. 116.
5. Ibid.
6. Nat Fleischer, *The Ring Record Book and Boxing Encyclopedia*, 1960 Edition (New York: The Ring Bookshop).
7. J. J. Johnston and Don Cogswell, *Uncrowned Champions*, (Los Angeles: Blurb Publications, 2011), p. 102.
8. Ibid.
9. Jeffrey T. Sammons, *Beyond the Ring: The Role of Boxing in American Society* (Urbana and Chicago: University of Illinois Press, 1990), pp. 48–49.
10. Hertzberg, *The Jews in America*, p. 140.
11. Riess, *Sports and the American Jew*, p. 18.
12. Steven A. Riess (ed.), *Sports and the American Jew* (New York: Syracuse University Press, 1998), p. 62.
13. Christopher Rivers (ed., translator), *Jack Johnson: My Life and Battles* (Washington, DC: Potomac Books, 2009), p. 32.
14. William Schutte, *The Fighting Dentist: The Boxing Career of Dr. Leach Cross* (Fullerton, CA: Self-published, 1977), p. 19.
15. Ibid., p. 36.
16. Colleen Aycock and Mark Scott, *Tex Rickard: Boxing's Greatest Promoter* (Jefferson, NC: McFarland, 2012), p. 67.
17. Ibid., p. 66.
18. Ibid., p. 169.
19. Mike Casey, "Benny Leonard: Golden Talent of a Golden Age," East Side Boxing, www.boxing247.com/weblog/archives/122454, (January 16, 2009).
20. Pat Putnam, "Benny Leonard: Fabulous Ghetto Wizard," TheSweetScience.com (September 1, 2005).
21. Franklin Foer and Mark Tracy (eds.), *Jewish Jocks: An Unorthodox Hall of Fame* (New York & Boston: Twelve, 2012), p. 24.
22. Silver, *The Arc of Boxing*, p. 11.
23. Levine, *Ellis Island to Ebbets Field*, p. 159.
24. Author's interview with Philadelphia boxing historian Chuck Hasson, January 26, 2012.

25. John D. McCallum, *Encyclopedia of World Boxing Champions* (Radnor, PA: Chilton Book Co., 1975), p. 87.

26. Stanley Weston and Steven Farhood, *The Ring: Boxing in the Twentieth Century* (New York: BDD Illustrated Books, 1993), p. 31.

27. Herbert G. Goldman, *Boxing: A Worldwide Record of Bouts and Boxers*, Vol. 4 (Jefferson, NC: McFarland, 2012), pp. 1482–83.

28. Levine, *Ellis Island to Ebbets Field*, p. 167.

CHAPTER 4: GOLDEN AGE GLADIATORS: 1920–1940

1. Bob Considine and Bill Slocum, *Dempsey by the Man Himself* (New York: Simon & Schuster, 1960), p. 11.

2. Figures provided by Boxrec.com and the American Association of Boxing Commissions.

3. Riess, *Sports and the American Jew*, p. 84.

4. Howard M. Sachar, *A History of the Jews in America* (New York: Vintage, 1993), p. 353.

5. Margolick, *Beyond Glory*, 2005), p. 38.

6. David Margolick, "Max Schmeling, German Boxer, Is Dead at 99," *New York Times*, February 4, 2005.

7. Randy Roberts, *Joe Louis: Hard Times Man* (New Haven and London: Yale University Press, 2010), p. 164.

8. "Jews and Sports in Poland before the Second World War," by Diethelm Blecking, in *Jews and the Sporting Life: Studies in Contemporary Jewry XXIII*, ed. Ezra Mendelsohn (USA: Oxford University Press, 2009), pp. 21–22.

9. Ibid., p. 21.

10. Ibid., p. 27.

11. Michael Berkowitz and Ruti Ungar, eds., *Fighting Back: Jewish and Black Boxers in Britain* (London: Jewish Museum, 2004), p. 6.

12. Gerald R. Gems, *Boxing: A Concise History of the Sweet Science* (Lanham, MD: Rowman & Littlefield, 2014), p. 93.

13. Tony Collins, "Jews, Anti-Semitism, and Sports in Britain, 1900–1939" in *Emancipation through Muscles: Jews and Sport in Europe*, eds. Michael Brenner and Gideon Reuveni (Lincoln: University of Nebraska Press, 2004), p. 149.

14. Figures compiled by British boxing historian Miles Templeton (www.boxinghistory.org.uk).

15. Silver, *The Arc of Boxing*, pp. 51–54.

16. Ibid., p. 56.

17. Ibid., p. 57.

18. Ibid.

19. Warren Grover, *Nazis in Newark* (New Brunswick, NJ: Transaction Publishers, 2003), pp. 48–52.

20. John Harding with Jack Kid Berg, *Jack Kid Berg: The Whitechapel Windmill* (London: Robson Books, 1987), p. 103.

21. John Jarrett, *Champ in the Corner: The Ray Arcel Story* (Gloucestershire: Stadia), p. 42.

22. Harding, *Jack Kid Berg*, p. 105.

23. www.Jewishfilm.org, website for The National Center for Jewish Film.

24. Marv Moss, "Maxie Berger: Fighter and Referee," *Montreal Gazette*, February 23, 1972, p. 19.

25. Ken Blady, *The Jewish Boxers' Hall of Fame* (New York: Shapolsky, 1988), p. 133.

26. Robert Trumbull, "AMA, Citing Danger, Asks [for] Abolition of Boxing," *New York Times*, December 6, 1984.

27. "Feldman Conquers Lewis in 10 Rounds," *New York Times*, July 25, 1935.

28. "Forgotten Men of Boxing," *Boxing & Wrestling* (November 1957), p. 60.

29. Ibid., p. 63.

30. Ibid. p. 64.

31. Pollack, *In the Ring with James J. Corbett*, p. 332.

32. Harvey Marc Zucker and Lawrence J. Babich, *Sports Films: A Complete Reference* (Jefferson, NC: McFarland, 1987), pp. 53–144.

33. Ruby Goldstein, as told to Frank Graham, *Third Man in the Ring* (New York: Funk & Wagnalls, 1959), pp. 47–48.

34. Ibid., pp. 60–61.

35. Dave Anderson, "Izzy's Posters," *New York Times*, September 26, 1976, Sports Section, p. S5.

36. Blady, *The Jewish Boxers' Hall of Fame*, p. 182.

37. "Kaplan Is Victor at the Queensboro," *New York Times*, July 18, 1928, p. 17.

38. McCallum, *Encyclopedia of World Boxing Champions*, p. 160.

39. Joseph C. Nichols, "Battering Attack Enables Braddock to Triumph over Lasky at Garden Bout," *New York Times*, March 23, 1935, p. 19.

40. Michael Silver, "Ray Arcel: Trainer of Champions," *The Ring*, September 1980, p. 76.

41. Robert Ecksell, "Ray Arcel: Dean of Them All," Boxing.com website, January 8, 2013.

42. Ibid.

43. Gilbert Odd, *The Woman in the Corner: Her Influence on Boxing* (London: Pelham Books, 1978), p. 33.

44. Ibid., p. 35.

45. Sammy Luftspring, *Call Me Sammy* (Scarborough, Ontario: Prentice Hall of Canada, Ltd., 1975), p. 180.

46. David Wallechinsky and Jaime Loucky, *The Complete Book of the Olympics: The 2012 Edition* (London: Aurum Press, 2012).

47. Weston and Farhood, *The Ring: Boxing in the Twentieth Century*, p. 61.

48. Yossi Katz, *A Voice Called: Stories of Jewish Heroism* (Jerusalem and New York: Gefen Publishing House, 2010), p. 77.

49. Ibid.

50. Ibid., p. 78.

51. Joseph Siegman, *Jewish Sports Legends*, Fourth Edition (Washington, DC: Potomac Books, 2005), p. 291.

52. Harry Cleavelin, "Augie Ratner: Champ without a Crown!," *Boxing Illustrated* (February 1967), pp. 39–40.

53. Peter Heller, *In This Corner . . . ! Forty World Champions Tell Their Stories* (New York: Simon & Schuster, 1973), p. 86.

54. Ibid., p. 93.

55. Lester Bromberg, *World's Champs* (USA: Retail Distributors, Inc., 1958), p. 72.

56. Ibid.

57. Robert E. Tomasson, "Maxie Rosenbloom Dead; Boxer and Actor was 71," *New York Times*, March 8, 1976, p. 27.

58. Douglas Century, *Barney Ross* (New York: Nextbooks/Schocken, 2006), pp. 66–67.

59. Ibid., p. 59.

60. Martin Abramson, *No Man Stands Alone: The True Story of Barney Ross* (Philadelphia and New York: J. B. Lippincott, 1957), p. 167.

61. Century, *Barney Ross*, p. 119.

62. Ibid., p. 122.

63. Century, *Barney Ross*, p. 146.

64. *New York Times*, "Abe Simon, Who Lost to Louis For Championship Twice, Dies," October 25, 1969, p. 33.

CHAPTER 5: WAR AND PEACE: 1941–1963

1. Bill Goodman, interview by author, July 17, 2007.

2. Kevin Baker, "The Case for the Draft," *American Heritage*, Vol. 54, Issue 3 (June/July 2003), p. 16.

3. Riess, *City Games*, p. 116.

4. John R. Tunis, "Sad State of the Boxing Business, *New York Times*, Sunday Magazine section, November 6, 1949, p. 26.

5. Bill Goodman, interview by author, in Silver, *The Arc of Boxing*, p. 40.

6. Sammons, *Beyond the Ring*, p. 149.

7. Ibid., pp. 139–40, 149–52.

8. McCallum, *Encyclopedia of World Champions*, p. xix.

9. Arthur Daley, "Is Boxing on the Ropes?" *New York Times*, Sunday Magazine section, January 31, 1954, p. 25.

10. Nat Fleischer, *Fifty Years at Ringside* (New York: Fleet Publishing, 1958), p. 274.

11. Alter F. Landesman, *Brownsville: The Birth, Development, and Passing of a Jewish Community in New York* (New York: Bloch Publishing Co., 1969), p. 96.

12. Yossi Katz, *A Voice Called: Stories of Jewish Heroism* (Jerusalem and New York: Gefen Publishing, 2010), p. 106.

13. Ibid., p. 107.

14. Seymour "Sy" Brody, *Jewish Heroes in America* (Delray Beach, FL: RSB Publishers, 1995), pp. 139–40.

15. *Manchester Guardian*, May 23, 1936, cited in A. J. Sherman, *Island Refuge: Britain and the Refugees from the Third Reich 1933–1939* (London: Elek Books, 1973), p. 112.

16. Anthony Hughes, *Sport and Jewish Identity in the Shanghai Jewish Community 1938–1949*, International Sports Studies, vol. 21, no. 1 (Sydney, Australia: University of New South Wales, 2001), p. 49.

17. Ibid., p. 48.

18. Yaacov Lieberman, *My China: Jewish Life in the Orient 1900–1950* (Jerusalem: Gefen Publishing House, 1998), p. 140.

19. Ibid., p. 137.

20. "Vic Herman," www.HeraldScotland.com.

21. Gabriel N. Finder, "Boxing for Everyone: Jewish DPs, Sports, and Boxing," in *Jews and the Sporting Life: Studies in Contemporary Jewry*: vol. XXIII, ed. Ezra Mendelsohn (USA: Oxford University Press, 2008), pp. 36–37, 45.

22. See www.spielbergfilmarchive.org.il.

23. Phillip Grammes, "Sports in the DP Camps, 1945–1948" in E*mancipation Through Muscles: Jews and Sports in Europe*, eds. Michael Brenner and Gideon Reuveni (Lincoln: University of Nebraska Press, 2006), p. 187. Reprinted in Ezra Mendelsohn (ed.) *Jews and the Sporting Life: Studies in Contemporary Judaism* Vol. XXIII, p. 49.

24. Bodner, *When Boxing Was a Jewish Sport*, p. 172.

25. Sugar Ray Robinson with Dave Anderson, *Sugar Ray* (New York: Viking Press, 1969), pp. 139–40.

26. Alan Scott Haft, *Harry Haft: Survivor of Auschwitz, Challenger of Rocky Marciano* (Syracuse, NY: Syracuse University Press, 2006).

27. Anat Helman, "Sports in the Young State of Israel," in *Jews and the Sporting Life: Studies in Contemporary Judaism*, Vol. XXIII, ed. Ezra Mendelsohn (USA: Oxford University Press, 2008), p. 104.

28. "Israel's Boxing Association Unites Arab and Jewish Youths," AP Online, July 5, 2012.

29. James P. Dawson, "Beau Jack Halts Reif in 4th Round," *New York Times*, Sports Section, January 6, 1946, p. 8.

30. Transcript of Mogen David kosher wine commercial.

31. Eric Lax, *Woody Allen* (New York: Alfred A. Knopf, 1991), p. 47.

32. YouTube Broadcast of Jackie Mason (www.youtube.com/watch?v=jgE2AXkanR8).

33. Hank Bordowitz, *Billy Joel: The Life and Hard Times of an Angry Young Man Revisited* (New York: Billboard Books, 2006), p. 39.

34. Fred Schruers, *Billy Joel* (New York: Crown Archetype, 2014), p. 30.

CHAPTER 6: NOT YOUR GRANDFATHER'S SPORT: BOXING FROM THE 1960S TO THE PRESENT

1. Silver, *The Arc of Boxing*, pp. 51–52.

2. Jack Newfield, "The Shame of Boxing," *The Nation* (November 12, 2001), p. 14.

3. Jim Brady, *Boxing Confidential: Power, Corruption, and the Biggest Prize in Sport* (Lytham Lancashire, UK: Milo Books Ltd., 2002), p. 165.

4. Tony Arnold, interview by author, in Silver, *The Arc of Boxing*, p. 207.

5. Michael Capriano Jr., interview by author, in Silver, *The Arc of Boxing*, p. 119.

6. Ibid., p. 100.

7. Wilbert "Skeeter" McClure, interview by author, in Silver, *The Arc of Boxing*, p. 64.

8. Bill Goodman, interview by author, in Silver, *The Arc of Boxing*, pp. 100, 120.

9. Bill Goodman, unpublished interview by author, November 2, 2013.

10. Teddy Atlas, interview by author, in Silver, *The Arc of Boxing*, p. 120.

11. Philip Roth, *The Facts: A Novelist's Autobiography* (New York: Farrar, Straus and Giroux, 1988), p. 28.

BIBLIOGRAPHY

BOOKS

Abramson, Martin. *No Man Stands Alone: The True Story of Barney Ross*. Philadelphia and New York: J. B. Lippincott, 1957.

Anderson, Dave. *In the Corner: Great Boxing Trainers Talk about Their Art*. New York: William Morrow, 1991.

Andrews, Thomas S. *World's Sporting Annual Record Book 1915*. Milwaukee, WI: T. S. Andrews, 1915.

Aycock, Colleen, and Mark Scott. *Tex Rickard: Boxing's Greatest Promoter*. Jefferson, NC: McFarland, 2012.

Berkowitz, Michael, and Ruti Ungar (eds.). *Fighting Back: Jewish and Black Boxers in Britain*. London: UCL Hebrew & Jewish Studies in Association with The Jewish Museum, London, 2004.

Blady, Ken. *The Jewish Boxers' Hall of Fame*. New York: Shapolsky, 1988.

Bodner, Allen. *When Boxing Was a Jewish Sport*. Westport, CT: Praeger, 1997.

Body, Kasia. *Boxing: A Cultural History*. London: Reaktion Books Ltd., 2008.

Brady, Jim. *Boxing Confidential: Power, Corruption, and the Biggest Prize in Sport*. Lytham Lancashire, UK: Milo Books Ltd., 2002.

Brenner, Michael, and Gideon Reuveni (eds.). *Emancipation through Muscles: Jews and Sport in Europe*. Lincoln: University of Nebraska Press, 2004.

Bromberg, Lester. *Boxing's Unforgettable Fights*. New York: The Ronald Press Co., 1962.

———. *World's Champs*. USA: Retail Distributors, Inc., 1958.

Callis, Tracy, and Chuck Johnston. *Boxing in the Los Angeles Area: 1880–2005*. USA: Trafford Publishing, 2009.

Callis, Tracy, Chuck Hasson, and Mike DeLisa. *Philadelphia's Boxing Heritage: 1876–1976*. Charleston, SC: Arcadia, 2002.

Cavanaugh, Jack. *Tunney: Boxing's Brainiest Champ and His Upset of the Great Jack Dempsey*. New York: Random House, 2006.

Century, Douglas. *Barney Ross*. New York: Nextbooks/Schocken, 2006.

Considine, Bob, and Bill Slocum. *Dempsey by the Man Himself*. New York: Simon & Schuster, 1960.

Dewey, Donald. *Ray Arcel: A Boxing Biography*. Jefferson, NC: McFarland, 2012.

Farrell, Bill. *Cradle of Champions: 80 Years of* New York Daily News *Golden Gloves*. Champaign, IL: Sports Publishing, 2006.

Fleischer, Nat. *Fifty Years at Ringside*. New York: Fleet Publishing, 1958.

——— (ed.). *The Ring Record Book and Boxing Encyclopedia, 1960*. New York: The Ring Publishing Corp., 1960.

———. *Leonard the Magnificent*. New York: The Ring Bookshop, 1947.

Foer, Franklin, and Mark Tracy (eds.). *Jewish Jocks: An Unorthodox Hall of Fame*. New York and Boston: 12, 2012.

Fried, Ronald K. *Corner Men: Great Boxing Trainers*. New York: Four Walls Eight Windows, 1991.

Gee, Tony. *Up to Scratch: Bareknuckle Fighting and the Champions of the Prize-ring*. Herts, England: Queen Anne Press, 1998.

Gems, Gerald R. *Boxing: A Concise History of the Sweet Science*. Lanham, MD: Rowman & Littlefield, 2014.

Goldman, Herbert G. *Boxing: A Worldwide Record of Bouts and Boxers, Vol. 4*. Jefferson, NC: McFarland, 2012.

Goldstein, Ruby, and Frank Graham. *Third Man in the Ring*. New York: Funk & Wagnalls, 1959.

Gorn, Elliot. *The Manly Art: Bare-Knuckle Prize Fighting in America*. Ithaca and London: Cornell University Press, 1986.

Grombach, John V. *The Saga of the Fist: The 9,000-Year Story of Boxing*. New York: A. S. Barnes, 1977.

Grover, Warren. *Nazis in Newark*. New Brunswick, NJ: Transaction Publishers, 2003.

Gurock, Jeffrey S. *Jews in Gotham: New York Jews in a Changing City 1920–2010*. New York and London: New York University Press, 2012.

Haft, Alan Scott. *Harry Haft: Survivor of Auschwitz, Challenger of Rocky Marciano*. New York: Syracuse University Press, 2006.

Harding, John, with Jack "Kid" Berg. *Jack Kid Berg: The Whitechapel Windmill*. London: Robson Books, 1987.

Heller, Peter. *In This Corner . . . ! Forty World Champions Tell Their Stories*. New York: Simon & Schuster, 1973.

Hertzberg, Arthur. *The Jews in America: Four Centuries of An Uneasy Encounter: A History*. New York and London: Simon & Schuster, 1989.

Hugman, Barry J. (ed.). *The British Boxing Board of Control Yearbook 1996*. Essex, England: Robson Books, 1996.

Isenberg, Michael T. *John L. Sullivan and His America*. Urbana and Chicago: University of Illinois Press, 1988.

Jarrett, John. *Champ in the Corner: The Ray Arcel Story*. Gloucestershire: Stadia, 2007.

Johnston, J. J., and Sean Curtin. *Chicago Boxing*. Charleston, SC: Arcadia Publishing, 2005.

Johnston, J. J., and Don Cogswell. *Uncrowned Champions*. Blurb Publications, 2011.

Katz, Yossi. *A Voice Called: Stories of Jewish Heroism*. Jerusalem and New York: Gefen Publishing, 2010.

La Force, Christopher J. *The Choynski Chronicles: A Biography of Hall of Fame Boxer Jewish Joe Choynski*. Iowa City: WIN BY KO Publishing, 2013.

Landesman, Alter F. *Brownsville: The Birth, Development, and Passing of a Jewish Community in New York*. New York: Bloch Publishing Co., 1969.

Lange, Arne K. *Prizefighting: An American History*. Jefferson, NC: McFarland, 2008.

Levine, Peter. *Ellis Island to Ebbets Field: Sport and the American Jewish Experience*. New York: Oxford University Press, 1992.

Lewis, Morton. *Ted Kid Lewis: His Life and Times*. London: Robson Books Ltd., 1992.

Luftspring, Sammy. *Call Me Sammy*. Scarborough, Ontario: Prentice Hall of Canada, Ltd., 1975.

Margolick, David. *Beyond Glory: Joe Louis vs. Max Schmeling and a World on the Brink*. New York: Alfred A. Knopf, 2005.

McCallum, John D. *Encyclopedia of World Boxing Champions*. Radnor, PA: Chilton Book Co., 1975.

Mendelsohn, Ezra (ed.). *Jews and the Sporting Life: Studies in Contemporary Jewry: Vol. XXIII*. USA: Oxford University Press, 2009.

Newfield, Jack. *Only in America: The Life and Crimes of Don King*. New York: William Morrow, 1995.

Odd, Gilbert. *The Woman in the Corner: Her Influence on Boxing*. London: Pelham Books, 1978.

Pollack, Adam J. *In the Ring with James J. Corbett*. Iowa City: WIN BY KO Publishing, 2007.

Riess, Steven A. *City Games: The Evolution of American Urban Society and the Rise of Sports*. Urbana: University of Illinois Press, 1989.

———— (ed.). *Sports and the American Jew*. New York: Syracuse University Press, 1998.

Ripley, Robert (ed.). *Everlast Boxing Record 1925*. New York: Everlast Sport Publishing Co., 1925.

Rivers, Christopher (ed., translator). *Jack Johnson: My Life and Battles* (Washington, DC: Potomac Books, 2009.

Roberts, James B., and Alexander G. Skutt. *The Boxing Register: International Boxing Hall of Fame Official Record Book, 4th Edition*. Ithaca, New York: McBooks Press, Inc., 2006.

Roberts, Randy. *Jack Dempsey: The Manassa Mauler*. New York: Grove Press, Inc., 1979.

————. *Joe Louis: Hard Times Man*. New Haven and London: Yale University Press, 2010.

Robinson, Sugar Ray, with Dave Anderson. *Sugar Ray*. New York: Viking Press, 1969.

Romano, Frederick V. *The Boxing Filmography: American Features, 1920–2003*. Jefferson, NC: McFarland, 2004.

Ross, Ron. *Bummy Davis vs. Murder, Inc.: The Rise and Fall of the Jewish Mafia and an Ill-Fated Prizefighter*. New York: St. Martin's Press, 2003.

Roth, Philip. *The Facts: A Novelist's Autobiography*. New York: Farrar, Straus and Giroux, 1988.

Sachar, Howard M. *A History of the Jews in America*. New York: Vintage, 1993.

Sammons, Jeffrey T. *Beyond the Ring: The Role of Boxing in American Society*. Urbana and Chicago: University of Illinois Press, 1990.

Scharf, Thomas. *Baltimore's Boxing Legacy 1893–2003*. Charleston, SC: Arcadia, 2005.

Schechter, Ronald. *Mendoza the Jew: Boxing, Manliness, and Nationalism, A Graphic History*. New York and Oxford: Oxford University Press, 2013.

Schulberg, Budd. *Ringside: A Treasury of Boxing Reportage*. Chicago: Ivan R. Dee, 2006.

Schutte, William. *The Fighting Dentist: The Boxing Career of Dr. Leach Cross*. Fullerton, CA: Self-published, 1977.

Seigman, Joseph. *The International Jewish Sports Hall of Fame: Jewish Sports Legends* (Fourth Edition). Washington, DC: Potomac Books, 2005.

Silver, Mike. *The Arc of Boxing: The Rise and Decline of the Sweet Science*. Jefferson, NC: McFarland, 2008.

Smith, Kevin R. *The Sundowners: The History of the Black Prizefighter 1870–1930*. USA: CCK Publishing, 2006.

———. *Boston's Boxing Heritage: Prizefighting From 1882–1955*. Charleston, SC: Arcadia, 2002.

Somrack, Daniel F. *Boxing in San Francisco*. Charleston, SC: Arcadia, 2005.

Sugar, Bert Randolph. *Boxing's Greatest Fighters*. Guilford, CT: Lyons Press, 2006.

Toledo, Springs. *The Gods of War: Boxing Essays*. Tora Book Publishing, 2014.

Vitale, Rolando. *The Real Rocky: A History of the Golden Age of Italian Americans in Boxing 1900–1955*. London: RV Publishing, 2014.

Wallechinsky, David, and Jaime Loucky. *The Complete Book of the Olympics: The 2012 Edition*. London: Aurum Press, 2012.

Weston, Stanley (ed.). *The Best of* The Ring: *The Bible of Boxing*. Chicago: Bonus Books Inc., 1992.

Weston, Stanley, and Steven Farhood. The Ring: *Boxing in the Twentieth Century*. New York: BDD Illustrated Books, 1993.

Winn, George (ed.). *Boxing News Record Illustrated, 1938 Edition*. New York: The Boxing News, Inc., 1938.

———. *Boxing News Record Illustrated, 1939 Edition*. New York: The Boxing News Inc., 1939.

Zucker, Harvey Marc, and Lawrence J. Babich. *Sports Films: A Complete Reference*. Jefferson, NC: McFarland, 1987.

ARTICLES

Anderson, Dave. "Izzy's Posters," *New York Times*, September 26, 1976.

Baker, Kevin. "The Case for the Draft," *American Heritage*, Vol. 54, Issue 3, June/July 2003.

Cleavelin, Harry. "Augie Ratner: Champ without a Crown!," *Boxing Illustrated*, February 1967.

Cogswell, Don. "Boxing's Good Book," *Journal of the International Boxing Research Organization* (Issue 91), September 27, 2006.

Daley, Arthur. "Is Boxing on the Ropes?," *New York Times*, Sunday Magazine section, January 31, 1954.

Dawson, James P. "Beau Jack Halts Reif in 4th Round," *New York Times*, Sports Section, January 6, 1946.

"Feldman Conquers Lewis in 10 Rounds," *New York Times*, July 25, 1935.

"Forgotten Men of Boxing," *Boxing & Wrestling*, November 1957.

Kahn, Dara. "Yiddish, The Mamloshen Lives," *B'nai B'rith Magazine*, Spring 2013.

"Kaplan Is Victor at the Queensboro," *New York Times*, July 18, 1928.

Katz, Michael B., and Mark J. Stern. *Poverty in Twentieth-Century America, Working Paper No. 7*, November 2007.

Margolick, David. "Max Schmeling, German Boxer, Is Dead at 99," *New York Times*, February 4, 2005.

Moss, Marv. "Maxie Berger: Fighter and Referee," *Montreal Gazette*, February 23, 1972.

Newfield, Jack. "The Shame of Boxing," The Nation, November 12, 2001.

Nichols, Joseph C. "Battering Attack Enables Braddock to Triumph over Lasky at Garden Bout," *New York Times*, March 23, 1935.

Rose, Murray. "Farewell to Stillman's," *Boxing Illustrated*, February 1962.

Ross, Ron. "Morris Reif Passes Away," *International Boxing Research Journal*, Issue 120, December 2013.

Tomasson, Robert E. "Maxie Rosenbloom Dead; Boxer and Actor was 71," *New York Times*, March 8, 1976.

Tunis, John R. "Sad State of the Boxing Business, New York Times, Sunday Magazine section, November 6, 1949.

FILMS

Boxing in America (documentary), ESPN, 2004.
The Gentleman Prizefighter (documentary) Fastnet Films, 2013.

ARCHIVES

Boxing scrapbooks (author's collection)
Chicago History Museum
Hank Kaplan Boxing Archive at Brooklyn College Library
Library of Congress
Los Angeles Public Library
Museum of the City of New York
Newark Public Library
New York Public Library
The Ring magazine, various issues, 1922–1961
University of Texas at Austin's H. J. Lutcher Stark Center for Physical Culture and Sport
YIVO Institute for Jewish Research

INTERNET SOURCES

Baseball-Almanac.com
Boxing.com
boxinghistory.org.uk
boxing247.com
BoxRec.com
Chicagojewishnews.com
HeraldScotland.com
Ibroresearch.com
Jewishvirtualibrary.com
JewsInSports.com
Nytimes.com
Phillyboxinghistory.com
TheSweetScience.com

INDEX